ex   libris

DEREK SHORTHOUSE

heluonis   librorum

STAFFORD CRIPPS

Also by Chris Bryant

Possible Dreams

STAFFORD CRIPPS

The First Modern Chancellor

Chris Bryant

Hodder & Stoughton
LONDON SYDNEY AUCKLAND

Copyright © 1997 by Chris Bryant

The right of Chris Bryant to be identified as the Author of
the Work has been asserted by him in accordance with the
Copyright, Designs and Patents Act 1988.

First published in Great Britain in 1997
by Hodder and Stoughton Ltd.
A division of Hodder Headline PLC

1 3 5 7 9 10 8 6 4 2

A CIP catalogue record for this title is available
from the British Library

ISBN 0 340 67892 5

Typeset by Avon Dataset Ltd, Bidford-on-Avon, Warks

Printed and bound in Great Britain by
Mackays of Chatham PLC, Chatham, Kent

Hodder and Stoughton
A division of Hodder Headline PLC
338 Euston Road
London NW1 3BH

Contents

1

Mothers and Aunts

It was a dangerous business, giving birth, even in a large Chelsea townhouse with a fleet of servants to carry boiling water up the four flights of stairs to the master bedroom. It was a dangerous business, even when it was not the first child, though in this case the mother's first pregnancy had nearly killed her. Yet it was a necessary part of life, certainly to Theresa's way of thinking. The pain itself was part of the business of living because sacrifice strengthened the soul, and the practicalities of giving birth, with all the ritual of lying in, of absent husbands, of children banished to the nursery, of the parson's visitation, and of the subsequent christening and churching, all this was part and parcel of being the wife of a successful – extremely successful – lawyer.

So, on 24 April 1889, Theresa Cripps gave birth to her fifth child. Each of her births had been difficult, through from Seddon, Frederick, Leonard and Ruth to this, her latest, and last, Richard Stafford. But then her health had never been good. During puberty she suffered from bulimia and had to be removed from boarding school after a single term due to an undiagnosed debilitating illness. In her later teens there was also much talk of selling the family home because of its effect on her health and each of her sisters worried in turn about her frailty in a way that betokens more than the fashionable Victorian belief in the beauty of frail women. It was a sense of weakness that persisted with her into adulthood and married life. Her sister Beatrice said that 'weariness, possibly physical weariness, was one of the notes of Theresa's married life'[1] and noted at one of her first visits to her married home in the country, in November 1884, that she was 'fascinating as ever, slightly depressed with poor health, but sweetly happy in her marriage'.[2] Another sister, Kate, wrote that though she was as tall as their sisters Georgina and Blanche she had 'lost her looks a great deal lately' and though she was buoyant, yet this was 'despite much illness'.[3]

Elm Park Gardens off the Fulham Road in Chelsea had been her London home since her marriage in October 1881, although her husband had taken over Parmoor, his father's country house outside Frieth in South Buckinghamshire in 1884, and Parmoor rapidly became the real family home as Theresa stayed there for much of the year and was joined by her husband every weekend during the Parliamentary season, and for the whole of the recess.

Theresa had learnt how to mother from her own mother, Lawrencina Potter, the daughter of Lawrence Heyworth, the radical MP for Derby. A clever, scholarly woman born into an all male household she subsequently brought up nine daughters, losing her only son Richard at the age of two and a half. Lawrencina was a poor and moralistic novelist (*Laura Gray*), but a good linguist who could keep the philosopher Herbert Spencer engaged in earnest debate well past her husband's bedtime. By all accounts, though, she was not a very willing mother. Her husband's work regularly carried him away and abroad, often for protracted periods and sometimes with two or three of his older daughters (Theresa travelled with him to Canada and America in 1872, 1874 and 1878), so Lawrencina was frequently left alone with the girls: Lawrencina ('Lallie', b.1845), Catherine ('Kate', b. 1847), Mary (b. 1848), Georgina ('Georgie' b. 1850), Blanche (b.1851), Theresa (b. 1852), Margaret ('Maggie' b. 1854), Beatrice ('Bo'

b. 1858) and Rosalind ('Rosie' b. 1865). As Barbara Caine has rather triumphantly put it 'Lawrencina is one of the few mid-Victorian women who can be shown to have refused to surrender to maternity and family duties with a good grace'[4] and her daughters clearly lived in fear of her. Beatrice described her as 'a remote personage discussing business with my father or poring over books in her boudoir; a source of arbitrary authority whose rare interventions in my life I silently resented. I regarded her as an obstacle to be turned, as a person from whom one withheld facts and whose temper one watched and humoured so that she should not interfere with one's own little plans.'[5] And Theresa, so her husband later recorded, though enjoying something of a favourite daughter status after Maggie had left home, temporarily felt that she 'sometimes forfeited their sympathy through showing too little tolerance for their natures'.[6] Her grandson, Stephen Hobhouse, put it rather more strongly, 'It is difficult . . . not to feel that she was led by her mental and spiritual interests and her delicacy of health to a certain neglect of most of her children and to leaving them too much to the care of nurses and governesses, of whose character and competence she did not always take sufficient cognisance.'[7] In her own journal she recorded her rigorous supervision of the children's progress, 'I should weekly or at least fortnightly examine all their copy and exercise books and if they do not make further progress change their teachers. For childhood is a precious time which profitlessly wasted can never be afterwards redeemed.'[8]

The sisters, in the emotional absence or unpredictability of their mother, came to develop powerful emotional attachments to one another and to act as one another's mother. Naturally enough, when Lawrencina died in 1882, each of the daughters took it in turns to act as housekeeper and even before then the age difference between them meant that some of the maternal nurturing of the younger children was the responsibility of the eldest daughters. Indeed by the time Rosie was born Lallie was already twenty and had come out as a débutante the previous year. For all the daughters, except Kate, who unequivocally rejected the life of Society, the London Season was a central part of their growing up and Theresa, despite her oft-commented frailty, took an active part in the household amateur dramatics. In a revealing letter to her younger sister Theresa wrote, 'Maggie and I were at a ball the other night at the Dobrees: they are immensely wealthy and seem to have a very nice position, not among swells but in our own class, substantial but not fashionable.'[9]

Substantial they certainly were. There was the Chelsea townhouse; Standish House near Gloucester which Richard Potter had bought from Lord Sherborne; Argoed, a Jacobean farmhouse in Monmouthshire; and from the late 1870s Rusland Hall, near Windermere, from which several of the daughters' weddings were held and which was useful for their father's business interests in the North West. Each of the daughters had £250 a year settled on them and £5,000 to come six months after their father's death. As for 'not fashionable', it is clear that none of the daughters was ever close to royalty or aristocracy or High Society. Their father had made his own money as Chairman of the Great Western Railway and President of the Grand Truck Railway of Canada, and made many enemies among his fellow directors who saw him as violent in manner and language. Along with countless others he was part of the newly landed gentry, not the old families, and no amount of money could cloak his middle class origins and aspirations.

With so many daughters, weddings were an important matter, both emotionally and financially. Indeed when Blanche, one of the sisters with whom Theresa was particularly close, met and married a young surgeon Willie Cripps, her father, egged on by Lallie, was particularly offensive to her suitor because of his inferior social standing. Beatrice described him as 'at first sight repellent, almost unclean looking, with the manners and conversation of a clever cad,'[10] yet it seems more likely that the real reason for the Potter dislike for Cripps was his profession. Despite the fact that he would later be an extremely successful surgeon at St Bartholomew's Hospital, there was considerable disdain in Society for surgeons, who were thought of as no more than saw-bones. Indeed in the 1870s most of London's gentlemen's clubs still refused to admit surgeons. The antipathy from the Potter household was so marked that when it came to the next marriage, that of Theresa to Willie's younger brother Alfred, Georgie was writing to Beatrice that the whole Cripps family had to be 're-embraced . . . They are wealthy people, quite as good as we are.'[11] Even so the imperious Lallie tried to alter the marriage settlement right up to the last minute.

In fact Blanche's marriage, like that of several of her sisters, proved to be extremely unhappy. Willie was a nasty and brutish man with an aggressive manner who took advantage of Blanche's artistic talents to draw and copy textbooks for him, and his arrogant and bullying manner made Blanche prone to dramatic nervous breakdowns. Twenty years after the wedding, Willie took an Italian opera singer by the name of Giulia Ravogli as a mistress and was cruel enough to invite her regularly to the family house. Blanche confronted Giulia with the affair and after five years of constant denials and recriminations, Blanche hanged herself over the bath – this at a time when suicides were still considered so immoral that their offending hand was severed from their bodies which were buried in unconsecrated plots.

The next to marry after Blanche, though, was Theresa, who had met Willie's younger brother Alfred. In October 1881, after boring Mary almost to death 'with never ceasing accounts of his perfections – according to her he is the best, the cleverest, the most perfect man that ever lived'[12] – they married. This marriage was a success, or so it seems. Certainly both Beatrice and Kate wrote that the couple were happy, but in each of their accounts there is a sense of a melancholy left unstated. For Beatrice they were 'absolutely happy – except that Alfred's companionship, able and warm-hearted man that he be, left unsatisfied the "spiritual" needs of Theresa's nature'[13] and 'she seemed like a bird with its wings clipped – somewhat weary of the routine and longing to escape upwards'.[14] For Kate it was more a sense that Theresa always made the best of a bad lot: 'Theresa . . . has lost her looks a great deal lately' but she was 'still sentimental and full of interest and . . . of skill at embroidering "the charming art of touching up the truth" with gold what she's interested in; her geese still swans and her spirit, despite much illness, buoyant; very happy in her husband Alfred.'[15]

Whatever the strength of their marriage, what is certain is that Theresa was a very different kind of mother from Lawrencina. Though a governess was taken on in 1888, we know from Alfred's later memoir of Theresa that he wrote for his children that she was much keener on keeping her children close by than her mother had been and that she would have preferred 'to keep her boys at home, providing for them a good tutor, or sending them to a good day school',[16] but had agreed, under some pressure from her Wykehamist husband, that they should go away to school. In this she was entirely typical of her class and her age. This was the era when the middle classes invented childhood. No longer were children expected to be silent until spoken to. Meals were no longer endured in silence and children were no longer confined to the nursery or the dormitory because childhood was now seen to be a time of discovery and individualism. What was more unusual in Theresa was the fact that her powerful nurturing instinct could express itself equally in the care of children or of others. Beatrice called it her 'tenderness' and recalled a holiday with her in Rome when she had been ill for nearly six weeks and Theresa, reliving an ambition to be a nurse, had forgone all her sightseeing to prepare her poultices with 'the same gracious, loving cheering smile, absolutely forgetful of herself'.[17] As Beatrice put it 'The burden of her life was love given to, and taken from, husband and children, friendship yielded to all unfortunates and all whom the world misunderstood.'[18]

Theresa had a history of caring for 'unfortunates'. She was brought into it by Kate who in 1875 had turned her back on the London Season and had gone to live on her own at 7 Great College Street, in the shadow of Westminster Abbey. There she met and worked with the vicar of St Jude's Whitechapel, the Rev. (later Canon) Samuel Barnett, collecting rents in the poorest slums in the East End of London. In 1878 Kate travelled to Egypt during the winter and Theresa took over her job, thereby fulfilling, albeit briefly, another early dream of establishing a celibate sisterhood which would nurse the poor and engage in other charitable works.[19] One of the few memories Freddie Cripps later had of his mother was very much in keeping with this Lady Bountiful picture of her, as he recalled her 'driving off from Parmoor in a victoria filled with flowers she had cut in the garden. These she was taking to her friends in the East End of London, many of whose children came to Parmoor in the Summer to enjoy a day in the sunshine in gracious surroundings.'[20] Even back at Parmoor she helped set up a scheme for the technical education of young women and girls.[21]

Theresa's work with Sam Barnett may have introduced her to the liberal theology of the day, but her own predilection had been since childhood for spiritualism, which was fashionable in the 1860s and 1870s. Her statements of Christian faith seem entirely orthodox, even conventional, yet they also betray a mind that had thought hard about religion and could express it in the language of modern theology: 'I look upon Christ's words and the record of his life as we have it in the Four Gospels, and the spirit of his faith as St Paul preached it, as the great hope and light to guide mankind to the entrance of a vast spiritual existence,'[22] she wrote. Such a neat distinction between the Gospels and St Paul would have been equally the staple diet of the congregation at St Jude's in Whitechapel and of the tiny church of St John the Evangelist at Frieth, where the Cripps family were extremely loyal parishioners, and it is interesting that it was this intellectual or spiritual questioning that Canon Barnett's wife Henrietta picked up on later in a letter of condolence describing Theresa as 'so beautiful in her stately body, and still more beautiful in her enquiring soul, daring in her quest for truth to assault heaven in face of hell'.[23]

One final aspect of Theresa is worth commenting on, for whilst it was a relatively common occupation for a woman of the late Victorian period, Theresa clearly had some skill as a painter in water colours. Her son Freddie certainly recalled her as an 'expert aquarellist',[24] and according to Beatrice, she 'was a born artist. That is, of course, apparent in her wonderful gift of expression, her power of seizing the really significant facts about a person or an event – a power which I imagine to be the essence of the artist's faculty. But it was also apparent in the intense pleasure that great works of art gave her.'[25]

All these elements, the religious belief, the care for 'unfortunates' and the love of art, were features that were to appear in the young child, but if Theresa was sickly, the young baby Stafford was almost invalid, and for the first two years of his life both parents worried that he would not survive. This was not uncommon, of course. That catch-all disease puerperal fever took nearly one in five of all infants in their first year and ironically, although there were great advances in other medical spheres, the fact that many wealthier families decided to eschew the services of midwives in favour of surgeons, who brought with them all the infectious diseases of their hospitals, meant that infant mortality remained high right the way through to the end of the century. Moreover Stafford's being born in the city brought further risks, with pollution and poor public hygiene taking its toll on children just as surely among the middle classes right up until the age of five. So these early years were fraught and the youngest child, by far the least healthy of the brood, became the most watched and cosseted of all the family.

It was not only the young child that was a cause for concern, however. Childbirth had not been easy for Theresa and as for many women of her time it was the most touch and go period of her life. Her much-vaunted frailty might have been attractive as a sign of her femininity, but to survive the rigours of giving birth without succumbing to any of the various forms of puerperal fever long before the invention of Prontosil was a feat in itself. The concerns expressed by her sisters soon proved more than justified, for when the child was still only four, just five months after her own father's death, Theresa died following a brief throat infection. The death was sudden and the shock struck Alfred with a full force:

> On a Sunday morning, we were walking together in the woods and gardens at Parmoor, on Sunday midday we were having luncheon together with the children, on Sunday afternoon we were told that there was no reason for the slightest anxiety, on Monday morning, the 22nd May, 1893, just before ten o'clock the end came and my wife rested from illness and pain.[26]

Beatrice was immediately summoned from the Co-operative Congress at Bristol to attend the funeral the next day. Lallie, Georgie and Mary also attended, but Kate was in France with her husband Leonard, and Maggie was ill and only just recovering from the loss of her own baby daughter Esther. Two immediate sensations hit the sisters: a deep sense of loss, breaking the bond of the 'sisterhood', and a concern for Alfred and the children. Georgie, in a rather cloying poem, clearly felt that this death might bring the sisters closer than ever:

So close the ranks, my sisters dear,
When lives are passing, God is near.[27]

Kate, by contrast, was more straightforwardly upset at the 'most tragic death [of] a sweet, gracious woman to look at, most loving and sympathetic [person] in all one's sorrows and joys, a believer and a liver in the spiritual world, and yet with a human zest for this world . . . all gone in a few hours out of this life!'[28] and Beatrice wrote in her diary in remarkably similar words,

> Our dear sweet sister – the artist, now the 'spiritualist' (used in its true sense) of the family – gifted with an ardent imagination, extraordinary vivid sympathy with all forms of life. Perhaps the best loved of the sisters, for she was open-minded, more ready to believe, without reserve, in the good intentions and high ideals of others than the rest of the hard-hearted, matter-of-fact family.[29]

Beatrice felt Theresa's death so strongly because she alone had striven to understand her own marriage to the *outré* Sidney Webb, but at a gathering of all the sisters at Georgie's house in Hampstead a month later she felt that Georgie was the saddest of them all with her belief that the sisters would pull together: 'I doubt it. I doubt whether there can ever be companionship without a common faith. And so we go on in life – eight sisters – bound together yet not combining.'[30] A fortnight after the funeral Maggie wrote to Georgie of her concern for the family, 'I cannot tell you how I pity Alfred. We shall all have to lighten his trouble.'[31] But like many benevolent bereavement well-wishers, she was too late off the mark as Mary had spent most of the fortnight with Alfred at Parmoor and had already drawn up plans for the children to come to live with her and her husband at Longfords near Cirencester.

Theresa's legacy was not just the concern and attention of

her sisters, however. She had long had intimations of her own mortality and had drawn up explicit advice not only on what should be done with her own body, but with the children's future education. In keeping with her spiritualist ideas she encouraged Alfred that 'it makes no difference to me, my own husband, where you bury my body because I will always be there with you when you are near it or far away from it, in my own living spirit, if God will allow me, and surely he cannot separate such love as ours'. She was also keen that he should not grieve too much 'and if you can find another companionship where there can be the truest help and love between you, it is better you should marry; whom you can love, I shall love too'.[32] As for the children,

> I should like [them] brought up as much as possible in the country, and to be educated much in the same style as their father was. I should like their living to be of the simplest, without reference to show or other follies. I should like them trained to be undogmatic and unsectarian Christians, charitable to all churches and sects studying the precepts and actions of Christ as their example, taking their religious inspiration directly from the teachings of the New Testament . . . No quarrelling in money matters; I trust my children's sense of what is fair and right. I implore my children to stand by one another through thick and thin, in joy, sorrow, success or failure, or even disgrace, and to choose Christ as their sole Hero and Master.[33]

2

'Dad'

Theresa's death made a dramatic difference to young Stafford's life. His own uncertain start and precarious hold on life had endeared him to her and like many a family benjamin he had been cosseted by nannies, by housemaids, by his brothers and sister, and most of all, by his mother. There are photographs of him with her adoringly watching on, photos which were not taken with the other children. She also detected incipient greatness in him, according to her husband, even when worrying about his health soon after his first birthday in June 1890 'Baby does not sleep well, but his mother thinks he has too great a brain-development, and looks to him as the rising genius among her boys.'[1] In fact so strong was the association that Alfred had in his mind's eye of Theresa with Stafford, alone of all the children, that he after her death commissioned a Miss Grant to paint a keepsake portrait of Stafford sitting on Theresa's lap. As he wrote to Stafford, 'It is such a treat for him [Stafford] to be in Mother's picture – Pater remembers how often he saw you sitting in Mother's lap, just as you will be sitting in the portrait.'[2] To us it may seem cloying, and to some of Theresa's sisters it seemed as if Alfred was refusing to accept the fact of his wife's death. 'I hear from Mary', wrote Maggie two months after her death, 'that the poor fellow [Alfred Cripps] is nursing an idea that Theresa still is always by his side and that he is in constant communion with her. Such, alas, cannot be, and must in the end be an undesirable delusion for a man to cling to.'[3] Maggie's son Stephen later attributed this to a form of spiritualism supposedly inherited from Theresa, but the truth is that Alfred's robust Christian faith would have readily allowed for a sense of an abiding spirit. Alfred believed his wife still lived, and encouraged Stafford to think the same, whether as a consoling fiction or as an item of Christian faith in life after death, 'I am writing to you in the evening just when I think you are saying your prayers and thinking of dear Mother. You will never forget her if you ask her spirit to help you and to come quite near to you whenever you want love and help.'[4] Alfred wanted his children, and especially those who were too young to have their own memory of her, to remember Theresa. So he wrote a memoir of her for the children, and even when Stafford was ten he would remind him that 'Father's love and Mother's spirit are always quite near to you.'[5] This was not spiritualism, but the grief of a dedicated husband.

Christianity was a central part of that close-knit family group. Alfred's memory of his own parents was that they got up at six o'clock every morning to spend at least an hour reading and praying before breakfast. His father had made his money as an ecclesiastical lawyer and he and his wife saw 'religious duties . . . as a natural Christian obligation, and as a part of the daily life and common task' though they 'were not concerned with theological criticism, and never encouraged it'.[6] So Alfred had grown up with daily morning and evening prayers and with strict Sunday observance, and the same model was passed on to his children. Miriam Cripps, later Leonard's wife, recalled that her father-in-law was himself 'much addicted to family prayers. One morning when we were all kneeling in the smoking-room before breakfast, facing inwards to our chairs, a gardener, one Barlow by name, passed by the window and the expression on his face, at which I took a surreptitious peep, as he gazed on the fourteen assorted behinds, I shall never forget!'[7]

For all the apparent respectability of the new Cripps house-hold, there were tensions within the family. For convention would have it that a widower with five children under the age of eleven would either find an alternative home for them or would take in a sister or cousin to act as a chaperone and to take the lead in supervising the children's education. Alfred, however, was having none of this. Stafford's sister Ruth main-tained that her father was 'a radical in this matter' as he had no intention of allowing the aunts to overrun Parmoor. He decided instead to take a keen interest in the education of the children himself. In fact Alfred was no typical absentee Victorian father even before Theresa's death, and his relation-ship with his children was already strong enough for him to take over the nurturing role in the family, supervising the education of the children and becoming, in Barbara Caine's words, 'the pivot of a close-knit family group'.[8] In this he was helped by the fact that by the time of Theresa's death the older boys Seddon and Freddie were already away at school and a governess had been taken for Ruth, but whether out of a desire to be alone with his grief or because he held his own views about their education Alfred himself took a very close hand in their upbringing, almost spurning the help of his sisters-in-law. During term time, though he was often up in London while Stafford was in Parmoor, he wrote regularly and at length, and during the holidays, when Seddon and Freddie would return from school, although there was an hour of lessons every day with a Mr Elwell, for the most part at Parmoor 'the children lived a life all their own'[9] as Ruth put it. 'My father did not believe in intensive education. He himself believed that he was overworked at school. He wanted his children to take responsibility.'[10]

It is interesting that it is the words trust and responsibility that most frequently recur in Alfred's letters to his children. Just as Theresa had 'trusted' her children to make wise decisions, so 'trust' was clearly part of Alfred's educational system and it was to this that Ruth attributed Stafford's developing confidence, 'Stafford in those days was very independent and sure of himself. This may be ascribed to my father's tendency to treat children as adults. As a result Stafford never shirks taking responsibilities.'[11] As part of this emphasis on individuality, the children were unusually each given their own bedroom and encouraged, not dissuaded, when they talked at mealtimes or challenged their father's views. This was radical behaviour for the time and it almost certainly was the reason why Stafford became such an individualist. Miriam, though, drew a different lesson from the children's almost enforced independence, 'The children were taught that they must hold together above all things, all through life. This produced a most devoted family wherein no criticism of each other was allowed or even considered a possibility.'[12]

For all his independence, Alfred did not manage running both a townhouse and a country estate as well as the education of four children on his own. Indeed in the August after Theresa's death the children went for their first summer to their aunt and uncle's house at Longfords. Even before Theresa's death Mary Playne had become something of a friend and ally to Alfred. Mary had been the first of the sisters to welcome him as a possible brother-in-law, approving of his legal profession because 'we want an Attorney General or even a Lord Chancellor in the family and Theresa won't make a bad Law Peeress'.[13] Furthermore, soon after the 1892 General Election at which the Stroud seat where she lived had been narrowly won by a Liberal with a majority of 203, Mary had secured him both an invitation to a Unionist selection meeting at Badbrook Hall in February 1893, and the nomination. Despite the fact that most of her ancestors on her father's side had been convinced Radicals, Mary was one of the founding members of the Mid-Gloucester Women's Unionist Association and, in stout defiance of her sister Kate, a staunch supporter of the Boer War. Mary subsequently went on to sit on the Gloucester County Council Education Committee and was President of the Stroud and Nailsworth District Nursing Association and a Christian Scientist, but at the time of Theresa's death she had got to know Alfred well, had encouraged him to seek the Unionist nomination, and had subsequently joined him, Theresa and, although she was a Liberal, Kate, on the hustings.

So not only was there a strong personal connection between Alfred and Mary, but having the children stay at Longfords, at least for part of the Summer, was quite useful for the new candidate nursing his constituency in the run-up to the 1895 election. Several summers ended up being spent at Longfords, and Stafford grew to know it as a second home. Indeed he maintained, inaccurately, that 'Mrs Playne played a tremendous part in my life. She more or less adopted me directly my mother died. She was a most brilliant woman and most like my mother in character.'[14] Kate would have disagreed with Stafford. She saw Mary, like Theresa, as 'one of the family beauties with her long dark eyes, rich brown and red complexion and dark brown hair' but unlike the rather frail languid Theresa, Mary was a constant source of energy, 'always straining her utmost strength over some scheme . . . a gigantic flower-show . . . a golf club . . . cooking and technical schools for all Gloucestershire'.[15]

Stafford did however spend much of his early childhood with the Playnes. He was page at their son William's wedding and spent nearly every summer at Longfords where large parties brought together the whole of the Potter clan. Mary was not the only Potter sister to form part of the Cripps family during this early period after the bereavement, though. Freddie, who was already away at school when Theresa died, felt that he came 'to know Aunt Bo [Beatrice] better than any of my other aunts, since, after my mother's death, she was constantly with my father'.[16] Indeed Beatrice, now married to

Sidney Webb, regularly spent Christmas or New Year at Parmoor. Stafford's account of her visits suggests that he was not so keen on his aunt Bo and he confessed that 'although she was my godmother, I never came close to her as a child – she was rather a terrifying person, so obviously interested in the intellectual development of the grown boys of the family that she did not attract young children'.[17] Beatrice's accounts are again rather different. Writing after spending Christmas 1894 at Parmoor, she felt that

> Alfred's home is strangely attractive, with a dash of sadness in it, especially to Theresa's sisters. A charming house, designed largely by Theresa, the soft luxurious colouring, the quaintness of the furniture, the walls covered with her portraits, all bring back to me the memory of her gracious personality, so full of sympathy, wit and vivid imagination. And yet the home seems complete without her – the children revel in high spirits and health, the servants are contented. Alfred has regained all the light-heartedness of his charming disposition.[18]

As the children grew up she became more appreciative of their individual natures and more critical of their lifestyle, writing, again at Christmas, in 1909,

> Seddon, who has taste, is allowed to lavish money on each separate room [at Parmoor] to bring it up to a high standard of ease and elegance. Both Seddon and Stafford look pasty and slack, overfed and under exercised in body and mind; but they are agreeable lads and dutiful to their father. Stafford has distinct talent, if not a touch of genius, and would naturally be strenuously ambitious. But the indefinite ease of the life, and the very slight demands made on him, are loosening his moral and intellectual fibre. It is odd that exactly the 'school' that thinks the

most terrible struggle against fearful odds is good for the poor, takes steps to prevent young persons of their own class from having some kind of struggle – even for the pleasures of life! It is strange that these excellent persons should not see that their self-contradictory philosophy of life strikes the ordinary Labour man as hypocritical.[19]

In the meantime the young Stafford had developed in his own precocious way. The very word precocious implies at least half a criticism, and the several accounts of how Stafford acquired his family nickname, 'Dad', suggest ambivalent sibling attitudes to the baby of the family. For Freddie at different times it was because 'he was fond of giving advice to the elder members of the family'[20] or it was out of respect 'for his superior knowledge on most subjects' or it was because he was downright bossy. For Leonard, who could recall 'aunts and uncles who were vastly amused at our small Solomon, and who agreed that he would at least finish up as Lord Chancellor', it was his 'wisecracks and judgement in his very childhood . . . achieved with great care and solemnity'.[21] But Stafford's precocity was not limited to wisecracks. As Leonard put it, he 'was the darling of the gods – that is, of our nurse and governesses. Others of us may have felt neglected while our little infant brother absorbed the spotlight and began to create a sort of controlling interest in our nursery.'[22] Some of his earliest letters to his father are dated and addressed in French which was spoken throughout meals at Parmoor at least two or three times a week, and his reading at the age of eight included *Short History of the English People*, which he considered 'much nicer than that dry tripe of Sir Henry Havelock. Sir H.H. is all the names of the musses and Pa's tutors etc. – and their addresses why he was at one school and not at another and how he liked them, oh gracious all rot and bunkum you might call it.'[23] By this time he had also adopted a rather precocious charitable instinct and was sending ten shillings a year – a not inconsiderable sum for an eight-year-old in 1897 – to a home for the destitute. Indeed so unusual was his generosity that the home presumed that he was a Mrs rather than Master Cripps.

Both Leonard and Freddie record that around this age he also started a tea shop in one of the rooms next to the bathroom on Saturdays and Sundays, where his father's guests could purchase their tea instead of enjoying it in the drawing room for free. He also seems to have organised and run the children's allotment about a mile from the house, from which they sold vegetables to the house, as well as a summertime service whereby all the rakings and gleanings were gathered in a cart, for a fee. As the youngest child the entrepreneurial Stafford invariably rode the cart. Leonard was convinced that 'the truth of the matter was that Stafford's moral education was so strong in him that he could never tolerate doing nothing',[24] though Freddie's comment that Stafford also managed to collect all their money off the others by being bank at vingt-et-un suggests a rather looser understanding of that moral education. Either way, Stafford, though younger than his oldest brother by seven years, was clearly the leading light. 'I can see him now,' wrote Freddie, 'sitting up in bed, propped up with pillows, in fullest command of the situation.'[25]

Most children learn by example, and Stafford was no exception. From his mother he had already acquired a concern for 'unfortunates', from his father a deep religious conviction and from his aunt Mary a belief in hard work. The final person who played a vital role in establishing the moral parameters of Stafford's childhood was Mary Marshall. Mary arrived at Parmoor in 1888, soon after Leonard's birth, originally as governess to Ruth, but with Theresa's death she played an increasing role in the mothering of Stafford and took charge of the nursery. Mary was fifty when she came to Parmoor, had been brought up in Plymouth, but had subsequently spent a large part of her life, throughout the Franco-Prussian War, in Alsace. 'A tiny lady of the highest possible principles and great culture'[26] was how Miriam Cripps later described her and she certainly was short, a little over five feet tall. Staying on at Parmoor long after the children had grown up and married, and later acting as governess to Stafford's own children, 'Mazelle' came to play an enormously influential part in the lives of all the children. Freddie confessed 'she was a great influence on our lives, not least on that of my brother Stafford, with whom she drove about the estate seated regally in a pony cart. She had the very best type of intelligence, with a love of nature in all her moods, which included a knowledge of the names of the flowers.'[27] She was also a determined, if conventionally simplistic Christian who regularly brought Christian messages into her nursery teaching and her letters to the boys,

> I love to think that when you are far from those you love best, there is One near you and loves you even better than we *can love*. If you think He your *Father* in Heaven, is always watching over you, my darling, that He will always *help* you, in your work and in your play, you will be able to get over all difficulties, and will be always glad to feel that He is near – and that He sees you, and helps you. And you will come to understand how very, very much 'Our Father' loves you and that will be indeed a strength and joy to you dear, dearest Dad.[28]

Theresa's death, then, not only pushed the infant Stafford closer to his father and his aunt, but it brought this third, rather pious French-speaking woman into his life and it is likely that it was her influence that gave the young Stafford the air of intense moral earnestness which attended him. Even at the age of eight he castigated himself in a letter to his father for not coming top of the class and then when he did come top by fifty marks, worrying that he only got fifteen out of twenty for neatness.

Two other prominent features of Stafford's make-up established themselves early on, for there was a regular pattern of illness and a great aptitude with his hands. Though Stafford later laughed it off as 'a death bed scene but no death', during his first year at his first school, St David's in Reigate, he contracted both measles and pneumonia. He was doing well at school (indeed so well that 'as there was some danger of his surpassing Leonard in his lessons'[29] he was moved to a new school at Rottingdean) and he was an active footballer and rider both at school and at Parmoor, but throughout his childhood both Mazelle and Alfred were permanently worried that he would not survive.

As for Stafford being 'good with his hands', there was no end to his projects. With his brother Leonard and a friend he shared a small carpenter's shop at Parmoor, he built a boat ('a good one too, one that will hold you sitting down and in ordinary clothes not change'[30]), he helped construct the concrete water tank at the bottom of the garden, and he made fretwork brackets. As Freddie put it, Stafford was 'constructive by nature' and spent 'much of his childhood at Parmoor building underground houses, bridging the pond, and generally using his hands',[31] although his practical nature did not stretch as far as rescuing the two alligators which Freddie bought through a newspaper advertisement. 'They were placed into a tank filled with water for fire prevention, situated at the bottom of the garden. When in the winter they were put into the grape-house they sat on the hot pipes and died.'[32]

By the age of twelve, then, much that his mother had hoped for had been achieved. Stafford had been brought up largely in the country, either at Parmoor or Longfords, and had a strong training in the Christian faith. And just as Theresa had said that she trusted her children, Alfred trusted them, giving them great leeway, treating them as adults and encouraging a sense of their own individuality and responsibility. Yet through all the accounts of Stafford's childhood there is a sense of a young man preternaturally old. Like the young Paul in *Dombey and Son* it was the furrowed brow and the wheezing chest that were the emblems of his first twelve years and it is not too fanciful to see in Dickens's description something of the young Richard Stafford:

> He was childish and sportive enough at times, and not of a sullen disposition; but he had a strange, old-fashioned, thoughtful way, at other times, of sitting brooding in his miniature arm-chair, when he looked (and talked) like one of those terrible little Beings in Fairy tales, who, at a hundred and fifty or two hundred years of age, fantastically represent the children for whom they have been substituted.[33]

3

Winchester Notions

The myth of the English public schools is very potent. Wealth, pubescent masculinity, power, tradition, cloistered erudition, eccentricity, violence and sadism, homosexuality, religion – a heady mix that reeks of popular fiction. As Cyril Connolly put it, 'The experiences undergone by boys at the great public schools, their glories and disappointments, are so intense as to dominate their lives and to arrest their development. From these it results that the greater part of the ruling class remains adolescent, school-minded, self-conscious, cowardly, sentimental and in the last analysis homosexual.'[1] A potent myth.

Yet elements of the myth are true, especially for schools so encrusted with the accretions of centuries of historical allusion as Winchester College. Founded by William of Wykeham in 1382 alongside the Cathedral of which he was Bishop, by the time Stafford Cripps passed through its portals it had acquired five centuries of oral tradition jealously guarded by five centuries of old Wykehamists. It was a world of its own, where corporal punishment in the shape of the ground-ash was still meted out by prefects, where social behaviour was totally governed by a set of rules known as the 'Winchester Notions' and where hierarchies were strictly enforced. It was a rough and almost entirely male environment where most of the staff were bachelors well over fifty, and the older boys had every opportunity to tyrannise their younger colleagues. One seventeen-year-old boy wrote home two years before Stafford's arrival,

> Today I am glad to say that I have had an opportunity of putting into practice my principles with regard to juniors and the ground-ash. One of Smith's most prejudiced enemies, a famous licking prefect, took the opportunity of a formal and totally inadequate excuse for telling him to come and be licked this evening with another junior. Of course everyone in College almost was savagely delighted and the way they talked about it was sickening . . . Smith appealed to the Bear [the Headmaster, Dr Fearon] who . . . put his veto on the matter.[2]

Life at Winchester was largely spent in one of the boarding houses and Stafford, like his brothers Seddon and Freddie, went to Chernocke, where he went through the same initiation ceremonies as his brothers, having to learn the new language and take up his allotted duties. The College historian wrote in 1982 that 'the Public Schools of the last century were in many respects tribal societies: they were self-contained and largely self-governing, with a complex set of regulations and conventions whose enforcement was necessary to mark the gradations of power in the hierarchy'[3] – and, he might have added, so as to mark the entry to a social caste.

Complex is hardly the word. In fact before any formal learning could take place at Winchester there was a phenomenally convoluted set of 'notions' to absorb, a new language to master and a whole rigmarole of how things were done and how they definitely were not done. A new 'man' in 1896 told the tale of one tiny part of this, 'Everything here is so different, they have such extraordinary ideas about things, one thing is that you have your coat buttoned up all your first half (half is the word for term) and you are allowed to unbutton one button every half you have been here . . . it is awful rot.'[4] This was, of course, the initiation process not only to a school, but to a whole social caste, and it is interesting that Stafford's older brother Seddon was one of three 'Beetleites' to edit and publish a full list of the 'Winchester Notions' only months before he arrived. New arrivals at the school were 'in sweat' for two years, apart from their first two weeks and the initiation ceremonies could go to extraordinary lengths: 'I remember one [old boy] saying that in his time the new men were stood up in a narrow cupboard and pelted with soap. "A mere trifle" retorted his clerical companion; "why, in our house we were knocked over the head with iron bars".'[5] Not only were there 'good notions', there were effective prohibitions as well, which reinforced the hierarchies even more securely. Thus it was a 'bad notion' for a 'man' who had been in the school less than four years to sport a speckled straw hat, and for one who had been less than two years to use the verb 'to think' because 'in College a man may not "think" until he has twenty men junior to him'.[6] It was complicated enough knowing what to call one's own House as Chernocke men were referred to as 'Beetleites' after the first Housemaster of Chernocke, the Rev. H. J. Wickham, who had laboured under the nickname of 'The Beetle', but the House was normally referred to as Furley's after the present Housemaster.

For Stafford, though, much of this initiation would have been plain sailing. He already knew that sports were 'athla', that his face was his 'duck', that he needed 'dibs' rather than money for his excursions to the Green Man public house, that teachers were 'dons' and a 'baulk' was a rumour. He might even have picked up that an 'Ebenezer' was what happened when a ball hit the wooden bar in a Fives Court and flew straight up. His eldest brothers had already been through the mill and Freddie was still in his last year. His father and grandfather were both Wykehamists, and the new Warden was a friend of his father's. So Stafford could be confident that he belonged. Nonetheless he had to fag for Duggie Udal, a task which not only included looking after his clothes, running his bath and preparing food for him, but also removing his football clothes after games and washing him down.

Stafford was twelve when he arrived at Chernocke. That same year the Rev. Hubert Murray Burge was appointed the College Warden or head teacher. Over the years the college had had a series of impressive Wardens with progressive views. George Moberley, Warden from 1835 to 1866, was later an outspoken Tractarian Bishop of Salisbury. George Ridding (1860-84), described as 'the second founder of Winchester', had extended the school buildings, modernised the curriculum and established a School Mission at Landport and appointed the ritualist Christian Socialist Father Dolling as its controversial, and ultimately sacked, Missioner before becoming the first Bishop of Southwell. And Dr Fearon, Burge's immediate predecessor, also held 'what were then considered to be advanced views on social and political issues'.[7]

So the fact that Burge arrived with what was already a fairly pronounced predilection for social liberalism was less a shock than the fact that for the first time ever, the Warden was not himself a Wykehamist, and therefore could not possibly understand the 'Winchester Notions'. More significantly he also arrived, after only a term as Headmaster at Repton, with a determination to bring changes to the school. For a start the curriculum was modified. D.N. Pritt, who was just two years ahead of Stafford at Winchester, complained that '95 per cent of [his] work consisted of translating Latin and Greek into English, and English into those languages, in prose and in verse'[8] but when Burge arrived all this changed. Science was given a new emphasis, art, music and carpentry were introduced and compulsory Greek was abolished. Burge even challenged some of the 'Notions', allowing boys to befriend boys from other houses and upholding appeals against 'tunding' (beating). A major building project, with two new boarding houses, a science block and a music school was started, reflecting his principle that 'it was necessary to adapt a boy's education to his character and ability'[9] rather than force him into a classical mould.

Burge also maintained the steady transformation of the school religion which had begun under Moberley. As with nearly all the major public schools of England, the College was deeply immersed in the life of the Church of England. It had been founded by a Bishop who had also founded New College at Oxford, it had always chosen an ordained priest for its Headmaster and boys were required to attend worship daily either in the Chapel or the Chantry. Under Moberly confirmation had been made the central moment in a boy's spiritual life at the school, and preparation for confirmation was provided by the Headmaster with the help of his Housemasters. Indeed as a High Church Tractarian, Moberly believed that the very aim of education was to 'make the boys religious, not sentimentally, not argumentatively, not captiously, not inventively; but catechize them faithfully and painfully, prepare them faithfully for Confirmation . . . Carry all this out . . . and you need not fear for the general growth of that Christian high-mindedness and sense of responsibility in which the system of fagging is to find its security and efficacy.'[10] Fearon kept Moberly's Advent Confirmation service and the main structure of Sunday with its compulsory services at 8.00 a.m., 10.30 a.m. and 5.00 p.m., although he changed the 10.30 service from attendance at the Cathedral for the Litany to a Church History lesson in Chapel. When Burge arrived further changes came. The eight o'clock was made an optional communion service and the morning service was shortened while the evening service remained Evensong with a sermon.

Public School religion, with its air of sultry compulsion, has always been something of a hybrid. 'Staid orthodoxy sung heartily' might sum it up. When the College history was being written in 1936 the kind of worship that the boys were subjected to was described as 'full and stately services, rather formal perhaps, and unemotional' and it is likely that little had changed in the preceding fifty years. But the author, one of the College dons, went on in words that expressed the quintessence of the young gentlemen's view of religion, 'Still, a certain austerity is better than gush; and it certainly teaches one great qualification for any service to God or man – discipline.'[11] Religion, Anglican and understated, was at the very heart of the education of the young gentleman at Winchester.

It has often been maintained that Burge was a major influence on Stafford Cripps during these early years, but it seems unlikely. The only truly pivotal influence in any man's life at Winchester was their Housemaster or a particular don who took an interest in their studies and Stafford would have seen far more of his Housemaster Furley, who maintained that Stafford 'was lovable and disarmed hostility' and was 'liked and respected by all the boys', than of Burge. In fact Stafford maintained a friendship with Furley into later life and when Furley retired he lived as an almost next-door neighbour in Gloucestershire.

Nonetheless Stafford did come into some direct contact with Burge. Burge helped prepare him for confirmation and for his scholarship exams for New College in 1906. He admitted to liking Stafford in a letter to his father, and said of his prospects in the forthcoming exams,

I have an encouraging report about your boy's work . . . he seems to me to be shaping up into a really stronger . . . candidate for a scholarship [than the previous winner]. The point is that the boy is developing well and has an intelligent and independent interest in his subject . . . He has been doing some English reading and writing for me, chiefly on Bagehot's *Physics and Politics* – I find he is quite good in getting the main point of what he reads, but needs a great deal more practice in setting out his point, leading up to it and seeing what follows from it. I shall give him a great deal more practice in this presently. He is a thoroughly good fellow. Ever yours sincerely, H.M. Burge.[12]

Yet the direct contact was minimal. Far more significant was Burge's indirect effect on Stafford through the ethical environment he created at the school, the contours of which were clear: social leadership, self-discipline and Anglican non-conformity.

Burge inculcated in all the prefects of the school a sense that leadership was a tough calling and that they must make up their minds to the hardship of their position. He believed that 'a man needs the stimulus of ambition, and if he hasn't got it he must school himself very strictly'[13] and while at this stage he was far from being a Socialist, he did have a profound belief in the need for Christianity to find its expression as much in the world of politics as in theology. As Lord Charnwood put it, he was 'decidedly a political animal . . . because he steadily looked on life as a whole, and upon all its concerns as the interests of God's family' and 'he kept his mind alive to all the movements of his time'.[14] Though he was anything but a revolutionary 'the thought of something profoundly amiss in our social system, requiring leadership with large vision to seek a remedy, sunk deep into him'.[15] This underlying sense that society was changing rapidly and that the Church had to respond to the challenges of a new generation imbued many of Burge's sermons. He was convinced that privilege entailed responsibility and that moral and social leadership was the duty of every Christian. It was a rigorous gospel of self-discipline that Burge espoused. 'Our part is the discipline of ourselves', he preached in 1922, 'the discipline of motive, in spirituality flowing out into holiness of life, not surface goodness but the deepening sense of trusting God and being with Him. It means searching questions: Is my motive merely to win commendation, to escape censure? Or is it devotion to

Christ?'[16] In his biographical note on Burge Lord Charnwood wrote that 'there was a strong sense of personal austerity in him',[17] and three of Cripps's previous biographers have taken this at face value, but the truth is that Burge's doctrine of self-discipline was little more than Victorian and Edwardian convention and such austerity as Burge did embrace was really due to the fact that, unlike most other Winchester Wardens and Bishops of the time, he was not a wealthy man and had no family connections or expectations to rely on.

Social leadership, impregnated with self-discipline, then, was at the heart of the Christian message, but it did not mean subjugating the individuality of the person. Christianity was about 'society and fellowship – yet the intense individuality of each member of it. Individuality emphasised, enriched by society, not lost in it.'[18] In this individuality was the seed of a powerful sense of Anglican non-conformity, not necessarily going with the stream, but branching out, exercising leadership. Even when he addressed politics this sense of the need for the Christian to discover his personal destiny is clear, 'they will leave behind nothing but bitterness or dismay or the exultations of party triumph or blind opportunism or the dreary doctrine of the swing of the pendulum . . . unless there be one inspiring motive – the secret of constructive statesmanship'.[19]

This would later form the basis of something very close to a Crippsian creed, but when Stafford was at Winchester he was less than interested either in socialism or in religion, except in so far as it affected his own life and family and the earnestness that had characterised his childhood had worn off. Thus he wrote to his father before the 1906 election wishing him luck in Stretford where he was standing for the Unionists, but otherwise his interests seem to have lain in riding, racquets and practical jokes. Indeed he spent more time at the local pub, where his father allowed him to entertain at his expense, than in earnest debate, although one of his contemporaries,

Horace Woodhouse, later Lord Terrington, maintained that Stafford thought him a dangerous radical because his father was a Liberal MP. Freddie, who shared a year with him at Winchester insisted that he was 'a beefy young chap in those days, and a great player of the Winchester game of football',[20] and in later years the novelist and Independent MP A. P. Herbert used to tease him as his old football team captain, recalling photographs of them both sporting Chernocke's dark green, light blue, dark green stripes.

The major difference Burge did make to Stafford's early life did not really happen until he was sixteen, however. For with the new science block recently opened and science now placed on a par with the classical subjects in the school curriculum, Stafford decided to pursue an unusual course by specialising in chemistry. He was already the youngest member of the top form in the school, so it could reasonably be expected that he could take his pick of subjects, but though he studied Latin and Greek through to fifteen, and his scholarship exams at New College Oxford included classics papers, what really enthralled him was science, something that would not have been possible without Burge's curriculum changes.

This first unorthodox decision in turn led to another, for when Stafford sat the chemistry scholarship examination for New College in 1907 (the first year that such exams were held) and when he won the scholarship at his father's and his brothers' old college, he turned it down. His chemistry papers had so impressed the examiners that they had sent them to the distinguished chemist Sir William Ramsay at University College London who decided to poach Stafford for his own team. So Stafford was offered, and accepted, a place at the only recently inaugurated UCL. Inevitably his science don, W. B. Croft, was immensely proud and wrote to Stafford's father

[he] has been working in the right way; his eyes fixed not

always on the prize but usually a little beyond that, entering into the love and enthusiasm for the subject which belongs to it. Without this feeling school exercises are often an injury to the mind ... The examiners spoke with enthusiasm about your son's work. I should like also to commend his habits of readiness and punctuality which quietly add to the power of good abilities.[21]

Burge capped the congratulations with his own praise of the young scientist, 'I can only say that I told the Warden of New College he is a fellow of quite first rate ability. But better than all that, he is a fellow of real high purpose and genuine appreciation – I respect and like him very much.'[22]

Winchester gave Stafford far more than just a place at UCL and a scientific training, though. Richard Crossman, a Wykehamist some years after Stafford, reckoned that a boy's experience of mastering 'a complex structure of rules, a rigid hierarchy of values, and a system of taboos, privileges and obligations utterly remote as from his home life or from the world outside' made more of a mark on him than the classical education tradition itself. How a man responded to this peculiar world placed him in one of three camps: the 'permanent Wykehamists who remain all their lives spiritually at school'; the sceptics who 'alternate the reverent amen with a snigger'; or the few who,

their minds sharpened by six years of mental struggle with the tradition but in lifelong reaction against it – remain grateful to Winchester for teaching them that all institutions, laws and persons in authority may well turn out to be as bizarre a mixture of the good and the fraudulent as their old Headmaster. They are the radical throw-outs of the Public school system; and some of them even become 'traitors to their class'.[23]

Crossman, of course, identified with this last group, but for Stafford the Winchester experience was different. Though plenty, including some of his friends and family, would later call him a traitor to his class he always retained an affection for Winchester and he sent his son John there in the 1920s.

Winchester did mark him. It schooled his intelligence. It made him value independence of thought. It ushered him into the realms of the upper class. It gave him a respect for poetry, for religion, for team sports. It instilled in him, as it did in Crossman, 'that blend of intellectual arrogance and conventional good manners which is so much resented by those who do not qualify for the old school tie'. What it did not do was determine either what he thought or how he should vote. Indeed Winchester, of all the ancient British public schools, was perhaps the least effective ministerial machine of them all. For despite a few near misses (Disraeli failed to follow his brothers to Winchester because of illness and Gaitskell died as Leader of the Opposition) it has still only produced one Prime Minister, Lord Addington, and the 1936 College history waspishly pointed out that 'when we are called . . . a training ground of respectable conventionality, it is of interest to reflect that perhaps the two most vigorous and strongly contrasting aspirants to popular leadership are both Wykehamists, Sir Oswald Mosley and Sir Stafford Cripps'.[24]

For all the toughness of schoolboy life at Winchester and despite his febrile childhood, Stafford thrived there, and though he did not enter a scholar, he certainly left flying his academic colours high. Winchester retained his loyalty throughout his adult life, and as a young lawyer he offered a prize for the best essay on nineteenth-century international arbitration, a prize that was won by the young Hugh Gaitskell. When the prize was given to him, in the back of a taxi, Stafford told him that the world's ills could only be remedied by the union of the churches, effectively repeating his old Warden's belief.

But Stafford's education did not end with Winchester. The least direct, but most immediately significant effect Burge had on Stafford was to make it possible for him to study chemistry, and in 1907 Stafford started at UCL under the tutelage of Sir William Ramsay, one of the most famous scientists of the age. In fact at the time Ramsay was absorbed with the discovery of the inert gases, and such was Stafford's evident ability that he was invited to assist with the experiments in the Gower Street laboratories, eventually leading to his co-authorship of a paper which was read to the Royal Society on 'The critical constants and orthoberic densities of xenon'. Stafford was a good scientist. He had both the precision of mind and the inventiveness of imagination to be able to capture complex issues rapidly and he had an excellent ability to visualise spacial concepts, but his training at UCL also provided him with an education in forensic skills, dissecting, analysing, distilling, spotting patterns, that would later be invaluable to him both as a patent lawyer and as technocrat in the Ministry of Aircraft Production. It was a training that ran with the grain of his personality, slightly fastidious and controlling but always accurate and meticulous.

If early childhood had been rather earnest, however, Stafford's youth was largely free from solemnity. At Winchester he had a reputation as an excellent host at the Green Man, and at UCL he was elected President of the Union, less for his political views than for his prowess at organising social events. He was still good with his hands and in 1910 spent many hours building a glider which rather ignominiously collapsed on its first flight. He was a regular ice skater at Olympia when in London, and a rider when at Parmoor, and although he was never quite as ebullient as his elder brother Freddie, who got the draghounds to come all the way from Oxford to Parmoor every Christmas, yet all the pictures of the teenage Stafford present an elegant and extremely well- and expensively-dressed, if rather myopic, young man. As for politics, as he told Eric Estorick, 'I was almost entirely politically unconscious.'[25]

4

The Little Jewel of an Advocate

Though Stafford's early childhood was almost entirely dominated by women, with a governess and eight aunts to replace
his mother, his elder brothers away at school and the only
other companion in the nursery for large chunks of the year
his sister Ruth, by the time he had finished with Winchester it
was his father who provided the model for his adult life. While
Stafford was still at Winchester Beatrice Webb wrote in her
diary,

> Dear Old Father used to call [Alfred] 'the little jewel of an
> advocate' – a term which just fits him. There is something
> jewelled in his nature, intellectual skilfulness raised to the
> highest degree, a perfect deftness in execution, a loving
> disposition, unruffled temper, a cheery optimism – all these
> bright qualities set in a solid determination that all things
> shall fit in with his view of what is desirable for himself and
> others. He is a delightful father – the children obeying
> him implicitly with no consciousness of being ruled or
> regulated, a charming host, seeming to place his whole
> establishment at the service of his guests, a most indulgent
> master and landlord. And yet, for all that, he gets his own
> way in life, and takes a very large share of the good things
> of the world, both material and spiritual. With this dis-
> position he could hardly be a reformer.[1]

Charles Alfred (the family had a custom of using the second Christian name) was born at home near West Ilsley, in Berkshire on 3 October 1852, the third son and sixth child out of a family of eleven. The family was in every sense professional, for his great-grandfather Joseph Cripps had been MP for Cirencester for ten successive parliaments and had died only five years before Alfred's birth. His grandfather Henry had been a parson, and successively vicar of Stonehouse and rector of Preston in Gloucestershire. His father, William Henry, became a lawyer, was called to the Bar in 1840 and devoted himself almost exclusively to parliamentary committee and ecclesiastical work and by way of completing the list of professions, his mother was the niece of Sir William Lawrence who was twice President of the Royal College of Surgeons and taught and practised as a surgeon for thirty years at St Bartholomew's Hospital.

All of this placed Alfred, like his father, very firmly in the ranks of the rising upper middle class, for the second half of the nineteenth century saw the drastic collapse of the nobility as the backbone of the professions. Where the younger scions of the landed families might once have expected a comfortable living in the church or the law, now a growing professionalism meant that there was fierce competition and it was the academically qualified rather than the connected who made good money. Barristers, judges, even Lord Chancellors now came to be drawn from the ranks of the aspiring classes and those families, such as the Crippses, which had a long respectable middle class pedigree, became the breeding ground of the new professionals.

Henry was a perfect example of this transition. Coming from old Cirencester stock (Richard Cripps was buried there in 1575), but with few family pretensions to fame or fortune, he had three strings to his bow: the law, the Church and, although he eschewed a parliamentary career, politics. Called to the Bar in 1840, he specialised in parliamentary committee work and was eventually made a Queen's Counsel in 1886, by which time he had already amassed enough of a fortune to buy the then rather small country house of Parmoor with its 200 acres where he could enjoy hunting with a pack of harriers and he could be more conveniently placed for the journey into London. Here he took a keen interest in the local church at Frieth and at the request of Bishop Mackarness, he became Chancellor of the Diocese of Oxford before writing what was to become one of the classic texts of Ecclesiastical Law, *The Law Relating to Church and Clergy*. As one of the leading squires in the county he was Chairman of the Buckingham Quarter Sessions through until 1889 when he was unanimously elected Chairman of the Buckinghamshire County Council, a post he held till his death ten years later.

This made him part of that class which was both respectable and new in Society at a time when the seismic shift in the British class system was taking place, and it is certain that Alfred acquired from his father not only the respectable religious accoutrements of the last generation of squirearchs, but the professional determination to make money by hard work and to prove himself equal to the family's new social standing. Alfred's later concern, when writing his autobiography, was to explain how he ended up a Socialist, ascribing it in part to his father's leniency as a magistrate and magnanimity as a landlord:

> It was characteristic of his generous outlook that he was an advocate of lighter sentences in criminal cases, and thought as a rule that the punishments inflicted, especially for minor offences, or in the case of first convictions, were too harsh, tending rather to promote criminality than to encourage reform . . . No doubt early associations and the constant care of my Father, who showed a continuous interest in the social welfare of his farm labourers, by

providing better cottage accommodation, and by bringing within their reach new opportunities for education, turned my thoughts in the direction of an economic change, now generally designated as a Socialist System.[2]

Such special pleading is in fact far from the mark. Cripps senior was at best a paternalist and claimed to be a Conservative who believed that his son was always a Liberal. What was more significant about Alfred's heritage was that when he had finished his education at Winchester and New College Oxford, he followed his father into the law, living in London with his brother Willie and practising in the Middle Temple where, like his father, he largely limited himself to parliamentary committee work and ecclesiastical law. He later maintained that at this point, in 1875, he was a member of the Reform Club and 'classed as a left-wing Liberal' but the truth is that his main interest was in making money out of what was now, for an accomplished advocate, a very lucrative profession. Such political ideals as he did hold were purely allied to his professional advancement and financial interests. Even his free trade principles and his belief 'on the one hand that production should be primarily for the benefit of the consumer, not for the profit of the capitalist or money-lender, and on the other that private interests should be carefully subordinated to public requirements'[3] would have allied him more with the aspiring middle class than with radical opinion and he was openly dismissive of the view that there are 'quasi-mechanical rules which could generally be relied upon to regulate demand and supply'.[4]

Ten years later Beatrice Webb noted that Alfred was so successful at the Bar that he had already been able to buy Parmoor from his father and had taken up farming as a recreation. She also reckoned that his political views, such as they were, relied more on religious perceptions than any scientific approach:

He is not a leader of men; his opinions do not represent the desires of the masses; they are the result of an attempt to deduce laws of government from certain first principles of morality. His theory as to the present state of political life is that the tendency is to ignore principle and follow instinct; that this is based on the fallacious belief that what the people wish is right. He believes in principle, and not in the possibility of reducing politics to a science.[5]

Another decade later, when Stafford was five, Beatrice reckoned that his views had been swayed by his new affluence:

He has become of late years more and more a Conservative opportunist, bent on keeping the soft places of the world for his own class, but ready to compromise and 'deal' whenever his class would lose more by fighting. He has almost a constitutional dislike of economic or social principle. With his skill and charm he will succeed in politics as he has succeeded at the Bar.[6]

Alfred's first excursion into party politics, in the 1895 election, coincided with this period of 'Conservative opportunism' and it was as a Conservative and Unionist that he was elected. Beatrice felt that this was simply an aspect of his own desire to protect his considerable lifestyle. After all he claimed to be earning £1,000 a week during parliamentary sessions, at a time when £300 a year was considered a very decent income for a middle class family. Alfred interpreted his own Party allegiance more generously, believing that 'as a Churchman I feared an attack on the established Church; [and] secondly, I was in agreement with Leonard Courtney ... at that time a strong Unionist, in relation to the settlement in Ireland'.[7] In other words, although Alfred Cripps MP was a Conservative and Unionist, he was really a member of the 'Fourth Party' in

British politics. His parliamentary career was something of a switchback. After his election for Stroud in 1895 he lost to the Liberals in 1900 and was immediately selected to fight the Lancashire seat of Stretford, which he won in February 1901 with Arthur Balfour as his next-door colleague. In January 1906, when Balfour had gone to the country as Prime Minister, both of them lost to Liberals and though Balfour managed to come back in March that year as MP for the City of London, it was not until 1910 that Alfred was to find another seat, this time his home seat of South Buckinghamshire, where his son Seddon had stood unsuccessfully in 1906.

This 'Fourth Party' aspect of Alfred's politics came across most potently in the election campaign of January 1910 when it was clear that he was on the moderate wing of those opposed to Lloyd George's 1909 budget which had been rejected in the House of Lords, thereby precipitating the constitutional battle over the primacy of the House of Commons. He regularly avowed that he had no intention of making a 'party speech' and claimed that if 'a settlement can be arrived at on the constitutional questions which have been raised, it would be a great national gain.'[8] In fact he subsequently chaired the Unionist meeting in July 1911 at which Balfour and Lans-downe argued that they (the Unionists) should no longer fight the Liberals over the new Parliamentary Bill which would prevent the House of Lords from blocking Finance Bills of the House of Commons. Though many of the Unionists still wanted to fight the corner, Alfred backed Balfour not only because it was clear that the King had consented to make enough Peers to carry the Bill anyway, but also because he supported an elected second chamber. Yet again he voted with the aspirational middle classes against the nobility.

Alfred's role in delivering the Unionists' support for the Parliamentary Bill had another benefit in that the Liberal Lord Chancellor, Lord Haldane, now informally offered him a place on the Judicial Committee of the Privy Council and when Asquith made the offer formal he tagged on a Peerage. Alfred contended in his autobiography that although the Privy Council job meant a cut in his earning capacity, he accepted it because he and Asquith had been contemporaries at Oxford, and both Haldane and Asquith had been called to the Bar and taken silk in the same year. This was disingenuous in the extreme, and it seems more likely that the Conservative and Unionist MP Alfred Cripps became the hereditary Baron Parmoor of Frieth less out of old-school-tie-ism and more out of gratitude for a vote delivered.

This, the first (or second if you accept his own version of his early radicalism) of Alfred's political migrations, involved little ideological movement on his part. It was less that a new idea broke in upon a fully formed political mind, more that his ideas formed and re-formed in the light of political events and, just as significantly, personal influences. Theresa's cousin Mary Macaulay and her husband Charles Booth, the author of the illuminating *Life and Labour of the People in London,* were early influences from the radical pre-Labour Party left, but the people who made by far the most significant impression on him were his brothers-in-law, Leonard Courtney, Henry Hobhouse and Sidney Webb.

Beatrice painted a fascinating portrait of Sidney, Leonard and Alfred just before Alfred's first election,

Alfred looks on Sidney as a traitor to the brainworking and propertied class, Sidney looks on Alfred as a 'kept' advocate of the *status quo,* Leonard looks on Alfred as a somewhat selfish, thoughtless and superficial conservative, on Sidney as a shallow-minded self-complacent half-educated democrat, whilst both Sidney and Alfred have much the same opinion of Leonard – an upright but wrong-headed man dominated by a worn-out economic creed and shackled by lack of sympathy and quick intelligence.[9]

Despite the fact that Alfred thought Leonard Courtney was 'wrong-headed' he exercised an enormous influence on him. Courtney was twenty years older than Alfred, having been born in Penzance in 1832, and the whole framework of his political life stemmed from a conception of the role of politics fundamentally different from that held by Alfred, for whom Parliament was a natural part of his social progress. His working life before his election to parliament in 1876 was speckled and far from lucrative, starting as a mathematics fellow at St John's College Cambridge. He had a brief period as a lawyer at Lincoln's Inn, but from about 1860 he was a hack working on *The Times*. Courtney's politics were primarily Gladstonian and it was Gladstone who offered him in 1880 the post of Secretary to the Board of Trade, a post he turned down because of his discomfort over the Government's Boer War record. Gladstone made him a further offer, Under Secretary at the Home Office, with the right to abstain over Boer War issues, and he joined the Cabinet as Secretary to the Treasury in 1882 where he remained until 1884 when he resigned over one of the issues that dominated his career, proportional representation. An early supporter of women's suffrage in 1878, he was Secretary to the Treasury when he was rather unconventionally (he was fifty-one, she thirty-six) married by Canon Barnett to Kate Potter not from the family home but in Whitechapel. For six years he was Deputy Speaker in the House of Commons, but in 1892 he resisted Liberal pressure for him to become Speaker. His reputation was of 'a strong, sturdy, self-contained individuality, standing four-square to all the winds that blow',[10] an individuality that equally rejoiced in holding a minority view as in dressing with a self-conscious delight in loud colour combinations.

The first issue over which Courtney and Alfred agreed was Gladstone's Home Rule for Ireland Bill of 1886, described by Courtney as 'an injustice before God and man'[11] and which pushed him into the Liberal Unionist camp. In Boer matters,

Courtney opposed the annexation of the Transvaal in 1877, he contested Cecil Rhodes's remaining on the Privy Council after the Jameson Raid in 1896 and attacked the 'war party' in the Boer War in 1899, becoming President of the South African Conciliation Committee, a political line which got him deselected in the 1900 election. Courtney did stand again, in West Edinburgh in 1905, but his return to Parliament was in 1906 as a Lord, where he steadily grew more and more disgruntled with the Asquith Liberals.

For much of his career, especially where it touched on that of Alfred, they were in violent opposition. Courtney was always a passionate anti-Imperialist, whereas Alfred announced to the burghers of Wycombe in the 1910 election that not only would he 'have no truck or part in the dis-Union of the United Kingdom', but that he 'stood for the union and co-operation of all classes, for the union of the Empire and Kingdom; and let them all be Patriots and Imperialists'.[12] On the Jameson Raid Courtney was virulently critical of Rhodes, whereas Alfred sat through the whole of the 1897 Jameson Raid Select Committee in silence. Even on religion Courtney and Alfred disagreed. Though they were both active Church-men, Courtney's *The Diary of a Churchgoer*, originally published anonymously in 1904, took a dramatically liberal theological line which would have shocked his thoroughly theologically conventional Anglican brother-in-law.

Alfred's second brother-in-law to enter Parliament was another Liberal, Henry Hobhouse, who married Maggie Potter. Hobhouse knew Kate Courtney through the Charity Organisation Society for which she worked and of which he was the Honorary Secretary, and it was only natural that Courtney should take him under his wing when he entered Parliament in 1885 as the Liberal MP for Somerset, so much so that when Gladstone pushed Home Rule the following April, he joined Courtney as a Liberal Unionist. Hobhouse wrote of Courtney that 'his sisters-in-law held him in some awe, as he could snub them ruthlessly'[13] but it is equally possible that Courtney himself felt rather swamped by the Potter sisters. After all Georgie wrote to him when he was engaged to Kate, 'You will find some crotchety old Tories among your new relations, whom you must influence towards the right way of thinking. You must be prepared to be taken possession of by our large family. Any new member is drawn into it with wonderful rapidity.'[14]

Either way Hobhouse was very attached to Courtney and felt 'a great grief . . . when our political paths fell apart because of his "pro-Boer" views'.[15] In fact Hobhouse was elected unopposed in 1900 when Courtney lost his seat, and it was not until 1904 that he fell out with his local Liberals, when he stood down from Parliament and took an active part in local politics as Chairman of Somerset County Council.

These three parliamentarians who married into the Potter family, then, were at some stage members of the 'Fourth Party' in British turn-of-the-century politics, falling out with their original Party. So if Stafford intuited anything of his father's politics by the time he left Winchester it was that Party politics was a risky and inadequate way of running the country and that it was underlying principles rather than Party allegiance that mattered. This Party fluidity meant that there were few 'safe seats' and making politics a profession was therefore folly. For Alfred there were defining issues, the role of the Church of England, the maintenance of the Union and the Empire, free trade, but these did not push him irrevocably into one camp. In this Alfred was no more unusual than any other free trade Unionist. Nor, for that matter, was Alfred's growing democratic concern (he was an advocate of proportional representation) unusual for a Churchman. The Christian Social Union had been formed in 1889, the year of Stafford's birth, explicitly 'to study in common how to apply the moral truths and principles of Christianity to the social and economic difficulties of the present time'.[16] This group, headed by

Bishops Charles Gore and Fosse Brooke Westcott and Canon Henry Scott Holland, had pretty much seized control of the Anglican ramparts by the turn of the century and Alfred would have worked with them in campaigning for the rights of the Church of England through the many battles with the Liberals over education from the 1870s to the 1890s.

For all that Alfred was a child of his times, however, there was something peculiarly Crippsian about the way he saw politics. His faith, and his allegiance to the Church of England, was heartfelt and by the time of his elevation to the House of Lords he was passionately convinced that an independent mind was the best tool for government. There was still a thoroughly middle class desire to please, an element of deference and a belief in free trade and the untrammelled market, but what really motivated Alfred was a peculiar belief that the laws of God could be the laws of the land.

5

Marriage and Munitions

If, when he started at UCL, Stafford thought that he was going to be an industrial chemist with a future in business he was mistaken, for though he clearly had a sufficiently forensic mind, the plain and simple truth was that there was not enough money to be made in that direction. As the youngest son he was never going to be able to survive on parental expectations, so, like his father, the third son, and his grandfather, the fourth son, he would make his own way which meant a career that paid. Seddon had already opted for the law, had been called to the Bar and was working in his father's chambers in Essex Court, and in 1910 Stafford decided to hedge his bets by starting training for the Bar as well as continuing his studies at UCL.

It was a brief involvement in his father's political career that decided the issue, however. For, now in the middle of his third year at UCL, he spent most of the downright vituperative 1910 election campaign on the hustings with his father. The Liberal candidate was the sitting MP, Arnold Herbert, who enjoyed the support of a large number of the local businesses in High Wycombe, the main town in the constituency. As usual the main focus of the campaign was a series of public endorsement meetings, at which Seddon and Stafford were present. The Liberal attack on Alfred was simple – he was in favour of taxes on food, he would abolish pensions and he

47

was opposed to democracy – and they put it about that 'Tory roughs' had thrown mud at Liberal ladies attending a meeting at Tylers Green. The *South Bucks Free Press*, the newspaper in competition with Alfred's own *South Bucks Standard*, announced its position,

> To men of Business. We have to vote today. Free from party cries and lying posters, there are two great national issues at stake. First – shall we keep our old, well-tried servant, 'Free Trade', or shall we dismiss him for a mere experiment and believe that 'to tax food will make it cheaper'? Second – shall we support our own 'House of Commons', elected by ourselves, against the hereditary 'House of Lords' elected by nobody?[1]

Alfred's reply was to rebut the lies the Liberals were telling and to condemn a 'weakened Navy, Home Rule for Ireland, single Chamber Government, and a Socialistic Budget'.[2]

Though Stafford would still have classed himself as apolitical at this stage he was naturally supportive of his father and even worked for some time as Director of the *South Bucks Standard* which was known as the 'Cripps Chronicle' as it was the main source of party propaganda. There was considerable excitement at the result in the town. Several other local seats had already announced their results by the time South Bucks declared, so few expected the result, a clear majority for Alfred of 2,556. Though it was January both election day (Friday 21) and the following day when the result was announced to a crowd of 10,000 at the Guildhall, were sunny and warm. 'The number surpassed any election gathering in the past and never before in a vast assembly of this description, have so many favours been worn and the colours displayed by both parties in the brilliant sunshine prevailing contributed not a little to the animation of the scene.'[3]

Stafford, who was present at the count, had also been

present a week earlier at the meeting in the Bowyer Room in Denham when a Commander Swithinbank had chaired the meeting and his younger daughter Isobel had been helping with preparing election material. Stafford noticed her – a young blonde woman, slightly untidy, wealthy, robust in stature – and contrived to end up in the same pub for lunch that day, although he did not manage to engineer an introduction. That came a few weeks later when his sister Ruth invited Isobel over to Parmoor for a house party which included a small brigade of Leonard's fellow officers in the Fourth Hussars. On the way to Henley that day Stafford and Isobel spoke for the first time, and two weeks later, when Stafford and Ruth were up in London staying at the Queens Gate Gardens house, Ruth again invited Isobel to stay and plans were laid for a skiing holiday after Christmas in Klosters.

For the rest of the summer the couple were apart – Isobel with her parents in Scotland and Stafford on a trip to Munich and Nuremberg – but by the beginning of Stafford's autumn term the plans for the Klosters trip were well advanced and his UCL friend Alfred Egerton and Ethel Slocock, a family friend who was to act as chaperone, had agreed to join Ruth, Leonard, Stafford and Isobel.

The trip did not last long for within a couple of days Stafford had proposed to Isobel, she had accepted and the young couple, accompanied by the indefatigable chaperone, trundled back to England to explain all to their families. It was clear that there was some explaining to do. For a start Stafford had no real expectations, either of career or of inheritance at this stage, and Isobel's family was not just well-off, she was a minor heiress, standing to inherit the whole of the Eno's Fruit Salts fortune which had been amassed by her maternal grandfather and was still raking in money. Such disparity was a problem. So was the fact that Stafford was still young. None of his elder brothers had yet married and he had not even completed his studies. A marriage in this situation was almost unthinkable, especially if Stafford were to stick with chemistry. Just as Alfred and his brother Willie had been faced with opposition when they married into the Potter clan, so there were complex negotiations now and Isobel's father wrote to Alfred in January outlining what he saw as the alternatives:

a. That your son should take advantage of the scientific training he has had and a natural aptitude he possesses for the application of science to practical purposes, to engage in business life with a view not only to eventually becoming a successful business man, but of being able the sooner to make a comfortable home for his future wife.

b. That he should, following his father's footsteps, adopt a career at the bar, for which he is already entered, with a view to turning his scientific training and knowledge to account in that profession, and eventually entering political life.[4]

Isobel already had some Eno's income of her own and with an annuity from Alfred the couple were able to satisfy the Commander's desire to see his daughter properly settled, so on Saturday 12 July 1911 Stafford and Isobel were married at Denham church before going on a short honeymoon. By now Stafford had made his career decision and he spent the next year preparing for the Bar exams whilst still trying to keep up his scientific studies. Inevitably this was a tall order and though he was credited as the inventor of the Pycnometer he never managed to complete his chemistry degree. In fact, only weeks before the Bar exams in the summer of 1912 Isobel bore their first child, John, on 10 May. Despite the interruption to the exam preparations, Stafford passed easily and like Seddon had little difficulty in getting a tutelage. In the autumn of 1912 he started in his father's chambers in the Middle Temple.

By now Stafford was far and away the most staid of the young Cripps family. Freddie had already gained a reputation as an habitué of the Oxford Music Hall and had taken up with the mildly aristocratic group that included Winston Churchill, Neil Primrose, the son of the Earl of Rosebery, and Jimmy de Rothschild. Like many an Edwardian gentleman he was a member of a host of clubs (White's, the Turf, the Marlborough, Pratt's, Wells and the Thieves' Kitchen) and he had taken a job with the Russian and English Bank and was now working in St Petersburg. Leonard's lifestyle had been equally grand. After a three-year spell in South Africa with the Fourth Hussars he had taken a well-paid job in the city in 1911, though his greatest interest remained hunting. In the middle of 1911 he also met a young lady, this time the even younger débutante Miriam Joyce, the daughter of a Chancery Judge, and the following spring they were engaged on her nineteenth birthday, with a party for 300 at the Hyde Park Hotel to the accompaniment of Cassano's band. Married in April 1913 they had their first child, Tony (later a Tory MP), less than eight months later. Meanwhile Ruth had married Stafford's UCL friend 'Jack' Egerton.

The first years of any legal career are tedious and repetitive, and it was no different for the young Stafford, who in September 1913 became father to a second child, Diana. He set about producing the latest edition of his grandfather's work on ecclesiastical law, he revised his father's tome on compensation, and he was made a Bucks JP in 1913, but in the main his work through to the start of the war was pedestrian and if he was absorbed in anything it was his family life. His father's elevation to the House of Lords and his appointment to the Judicial Committee of the Privy Council had little effect on him and, not being a socialite like his two elder brothers, it was Isobel, John and Diana that engaged his attentions.

On Sunday 28 June 1914 the Archduke Franz Ferdinand, heir to the Austro-Hungarian throne, was shot, along with his wife, on their wedding anniversary, as they drove through the streets of Sarajevo and the tinderbox of European diplomacy was set alight. By 5 August all the major European powers were officially at war. That same day Parmoor wrote in his diary, 'Fred has gone to his yeomanry at Wycombe, Leonard to the Fourth Hussars at the Curragh'[5] and so, just as for every family in the land, began the most debilitating and worrying period of the twentieth century. All three of the older brothers immediately signed up for active service, although Seddon, who joined the Lincolnshire Yeomanry, served throughout the war as a Court Martial officer. Freddie, who had returned from Russia earlier in the year, took up a commission in the Royal Buckinghamshire Hussars with whom he spent the first year of the war in training on the East Coast before leaving for Cairo on 5 April 1915 and taking part at Gallipoli in August. Shot through the chest and right knee, he was rescued by a Westminster Dragoon and brought back to England for a brief convalescence, before going out to Libya with his friend Primrose who resigned his post as Under Secretary for the Colonies to fight in the Palestinian campaign. Within weeks of arriving in Libya he was appointed to command the regiment and on 17 November 1917 he led his troops into battle at El Mughar, when both his No. 2 Evelyn de Rothschild and Primrose were killed. Again he returned to Britain for training in machine-guns, whereupon he was given the DSO and bar for his Palestinian service before a final bout in France, first at Étaples and then at Arras, and a final decoration, the Croix de Guerre.

Leonard, who rejoined the Hussars the day war was declared, was immediately sent to the Curragh. In August there was news that his whole Brigade had been wiped out in the retreat from Mons but Miriam eventually learnt he had survived, and in October he was badly wounded when a shell came though a window in Hazebrouk. After his recuperation in Ballieul, Boulogne and Chatham, Lloyd George appointed him Controller of Stores at the Ministry of Munitions, where he stayed for the rest of the war, being awarded the CBE in 1917 at the suggestion of Churchill. As for Ruth, she had by now married Jack Egerton and was in London where Jack was also working for the Ministry of Munitions.

The options that were open to Leonard and Freddie were not available to Stafford for the very simple reason that his health was still not strong and intermittent bouts of illness continued to plague him. Though he presented for military service he was refused on medical grounds and it was not until October that he was accepted for any service at all, when he joined the Red Cross and was sent to France where he drove a lorry which Isobel's grandfather had presented. Based in Boulogne in part of the back-up to the Western Front he spent the autumn and winter ferrying troops and coal to and from the trenches where the first battle of Ypres was being waged. On 14 November the Ypres salient was reinforced and the battle ended, but when winter turned to spring the German commander, Archduke Albrecht, agreed to use gas in the next bid to seize Ypres and at five o'clock in the afternoon on 22 April chlorine was released for the first time, temporarily pushing back the choking and spluttering Algerian and French troops. As the army commanders had no idea of how to deal with this new German weapon, Stafford was recruited as a chemist to help find a better solution than simply fighting with wet handkerchiefs tied round their mouths, but while he was still awaiting specific orders news came from his brother Leonard at the Ministry of Munitions that there was an urgent need for chemists back in Britain.

So in May 1915 Stafford journeyed back to London and was reunited with Isobel and the family, having accepted a post at the new Queen's Ferry explosives factory which was being built outside Chester. Although Stafford's chemical training was more than sufficient for the job, he was not trained in the industrial manufacture of any of the products of the new factory, so he was sent for a brief spell to the long-established explosives factory at Waltham Abbey and with Isobel and the two children took a small house in Cheshunt. His training over, the family moved north to Chester and he took up his post as Assistant Superintendent at Queen's Ferry.

The Queen's Ferry munitions factory was the largest in Britain and was one of the very few to be specially commissioned for the war. Built on lands vacated by Messrs Willans and Robinson some seven miles outside Chester near the village of Sandycroft and only a mile to the North West of Hawarden Castle, it had been designed and built as a village apart, with its own accommodation for staff and managers, a church and a whole bevy of cafeterias and restaurants. At the heart of the vast complex was the manufacturing plant, originally conceived of as a Guncotton plant, but by the time of Stafford's arrival devoted to churning out enormous quantities of Nitro-Cellulose, Mono-Nitro-Toluene, Di-Nitro-Toluene and Tri-Nitro-Toluene. Not only was it a massive building with a vast army of chemists and workers, some 7,325 in all, but it was a security problem, a transport problem, an accommodation problem, and a chemical problem. Stafford's job as Assistant Superintendent was vast, with at least ten senior managers reporting directly to him, with full responsibility for the works, the staffing, health and safety and security.

Here, for the first time, Stafford was in a management position with significant responsibility, and though this was not a commercial venture yet the complexities of the operation and the necessity to meet tight production targets within strict financial and time parameters made for a very sharp learning curve. Intriguingly, too, the accident of health that meant Stafford saw no active service, meant that of all Labour's latter day economic leaders Cripps was the lone industrialist. Furthermore the fact that Queen's Ferry was not an established firm meant that it was not encrusted with the 'gifted amateur' ethos of management that so hampered the main body of British industry well into the 1980s. With, as yet, no ideological bent, he learnt a style of management and of administrative leadership that was less hierarchical, less obsessed with status and more focused on production targets and scientific efficiency and competence – a style and an ethos that he would later carry into Whitehall, but which soon bore fruits in the rapid development to full capacity of the Queen's Ferry factory. In all some 37,000 tons of MNT were produced for the TNT plant which in turn produced 50,000 tons. The factory did not last long and almost the moment the war was over it was closed down, but it was one of the supreme examples of what logistical planning and assertive organisation could achieve and Stafford threw himself into the work.

The achievements of Queen's Ferry also instilled in Stafford a perception of capitalism that was later reinforced and underpinned much of his later objection to the untrammelled market. When, at the start of the Second World War, there was a parliamentary debate on profiteering, Stafford explained what he had learned:

> Among other units in this factory at Queen's Ferry were the two finest sulphuric-acid plants in the world at the time, and part of my job was to deal with the cost accounts of the factory. In order to deal with them efficiently I had access to the cost accounts of every other sulphuric-acid manufacturing plant in England France, Italy, Canada and the United Sates of America, to compare the standard which we were manufacturing and to see what economies could be made. We had to start with an entirely unskilled staff. Not a single person either of the management or the operatives had ever worked in a chemical or explosive factory before that factory was started in wartime. It was started up on war prices. We had to pay very heavy prices for our sulphur . . . owing to war insurance and freight and for other war materials as well. Our cost figures were lower than those of any pre-war sulphuric-acid manu-

facturers in this country. In fact they were so much lower that a year or two after we had started up a deputation of the sulphuric acid manufacturers of England came to see the Minister of Munitions and said, 'We ask you to give an undertaking that you will destroy this factory at the end of the war, as otherwise every sulphuric acid manufacturer goes out of business.'[6]

In other words although as yet Stafford considered himself entirely apolitical, yet there was a nagging doubt about whether a system that relied on heavy profits could deliver the social and economic benefits it aspired to.

Almost certainly Stafford overworked during his time at Queen's Ferry, and only months after his arrival he fell ill, eventually succumbing in June of 1916. Whether it was exhaustion or the effects of chemical fumes or a recurrence of a stomach problem that had afflicted him while he was in France, he was extremely ill, having to be hospitalised in Chester for more than a month. Even when he was eventually allowed to leave hospital he was forced to give up his arduous post and the family moved back south to a small flat in Half Moon Street opposite Green Park. A simpler job was found at a desk in the Ministry of Agriculture, but again Stafford suffered a relapse and spent the rest of the war as an invalid.

The First World War, then, almost passed the young lawyer by, and for the rest of his life he felt an element of guilt about his relative inactivity. While millions had lost their lives, he had spent most of the time in his bed. While even his brothers had shown great gallantry and heroism, he had been confined to the home front. While others had lost brothers, parents, friends, he scarcely lost a single friend or relative. In later years, when he was embroiled in the politics of the Second World War, this sense of guilt played a real part in determining the direction he would take. His enthusiasm for the task of aircraft production was fired equally by his hatred for Hitler and his desire to expiate a sense of his own inadequacy in the first war.

Just as importantly, however, ill health forced on Stafford an earnestness of purpose that stuck with him for the rest of his life. He had nearly three years of almost total invalidity during which the sole focus of his daily round was his family and regaining his health. Almost inevitably this sharpened the introspective nature of his mind, and it drew Isobel and Stafford closer. It also threw Stafford on to his own personal resources and in later years when he worked ludicrous hours as Chancellor of the Exchequer it was evident that this long bout of ill health had made him believe that while he had breath he must make the fullest possible use of it. The very fact that he had survived death bed scenes in infancy, in childhood and at the start of his professional career meant that there must be some purpose to his life. Already he was a convinced Churchman and illness, rather than questioning that faith, sharpened his belief in his own vocation. In this he was entirely typical of his generation and his class. Christian teaching still held, in St Paul's words, that 'suffering produces endurance, and endurance produces character and character produces hope' (Rom. 5:3-4, RSV) and Stafford saw forbearance and the battle against physical inadequacy as an elemental part of his own spiritual journey to be borne with fortitude. The weaker the flesh, the more willing must be the spirit. Gratitude to God for his survival, a belief in public service as a Christian calling, these meant that by the time Stafford came back to work in 1919 it was hard work, service, forbearance, fortitude that were the ultimate Christian virtues – laziness and not making the best of your abilities the ultimate vices. For one whose health would always remain in question this was, of course, a gruelling creed to live by, but it was something he would have shared with the vast majority of ordinary Anglicans of his time, and it was in part at least this evident resilience that later made him such a popular politician.

There was one other effect of Stafford's three years of illness that lasted through into his ministerial career. For the young couple and their two children spent a remarkable amount of time together. Though Stafford might have been a rather absent father to the children born after the war, to John and Diana he was an extraordinarily present father, as much involved in their early nurture as their mother. Ever since their brief stay in Waltham Abbey the eminently undomesticated Isobel had taken on staff, and so for the first eight years of their married life, apart from Stafford's brief stay in France, they were together far more than any other young couple of their time. From the outset this meant that their marriage developed as an equal partnership rather than the more conventional Georgian pattern where the wife followed where the husband led. Isobel in fact never ran her own home and throughout Stafford's political career she answered his mail, she shared in his campaigns, she sat in the Strangers' Gallery and she supplemented his work with ventures of her own. It was the closest of political alliances, and even if Beatrice Webb thought Isobel 'attractive but workaday' and later complained that she 'follows Stafford in opinion, works hard, associates with Labour women, dresses simply'[7] and like Barbara Castle thought that she simply toed the Stafford line, it was as a thoroughly independent woman that Isobel was honoured with a CBE in her own right in 1946 and all those who knew her well were clear that she played much more than the usual role of a politician's wife.

6

Essex Court and Goodfellows

In 1919, at first tentatively and then more resolutely, Stafford returned to work at his father's old chambers in the Middle Temple. If Winchester College had been a bastion of old England, the Inns of Court at the start of the 1920s were every bit as conservative an institution, founded in 1609 on lands bequeathed by the Knights Templar and styled on the Oxford and Winchester model of staircases and quadrangles, formal halls and chapel.

Yet the legal profession had changed dramatically over the previous fifty years, and like every other part of the apparatus of State, had been rudely opened up to professionalism and competition, with the introduction of Bar exams in 1877, following the inauguration of the Honours School of Jurisprudence at Oxford and the Law Tripos at Cambridge. In 1893 this professionalism was made official by the setting up of the Bar Council. All of this accompanied the rise to prominence, and to judicial preferment, of successful non-aristocratic lawyers who began to supplant their noble colleagues. In this new tradition stood both Stafford's grandfather and father and it was as a professional lawyer rather than a scion of the nobility that Stafford expected to make his way.

Unfortunately, while courtrooms make for good television and movie scripts, legal careers are often dull in the execution and even duller in the repetition. Stafford's is no exception.

Even though between the resumption of his practice in 1919 and his retirement on the declaration of the Second World War he fought some of the major cases in his field of speciality, he was a lawyer's lawyer and the story can be briefly told.

The fact that the new head of chambers was now a patent lawyer, Sir Arthur Colefax, was to play an important part in shaping Stafford's career, for whereas Henry and Alfred Cripps had both devoted themselves almost exclusively to those aspects of law that still bound the Establishment together – the Parliamentary bar and ecclesiastical law – Stafford almost immediately started to make his mark in the far more commercial environment of patent and compensation work, with only occasional forays into Parliamentary committee work. It was work for which he was well qualified. His scientific training meant he could get to the nub of a patent dispute very swiftly and he could explain complex scientific issues in laymen's terms. It was also the kind of work that appealed to his expository mind. He cared little for bombast or courtroom dramatics and preferred to win a case by resolutely structured and patient explanation of the facts. What this required was immense amounts of preparation, and if there was one element of Stafford's legal career that characterised his work it was this attention to detail. Stafford researched thoroughly; he had a swift and retentive mind and when he was perplexed by a scientific problem he would spend hours making a working model of the patent in issue. Patent cases also meant that Stafford, like all barristers essentially a freelancer, was nearly always working in an entirely commercial environment. At first his lot was the normal junior's hotch-potch of provincial circuit work – in his case mostly for the Oxford Circuit and the London County Court – but he soon had some substantial cases behind him and he began to acquire significant clients: Farbenindustrie *versus* ICI, Mullard Radio Company Limited *versus* Philco Radio Company Limited, Courtaulds *versus* British Celanese, the Great Western Railway, the Lightning Fastener Company, Crompton Parkinson, Shredded Wheat and Carlton.

So by the mid-1920s (and his mid-thirties) Stafford had built up a large and lucrative practice and though he was barely known to the public, his reputation amongst lawyers was high. He had represented the Duff Development Company and got the Colonial Office to fork out £387,000, and following his work for the Great Western he had been taken on by the London County Council when four main railway companies were to be amalgamated, to represent them over the charges for workmen's fares and season tickets. This brought Stafford into contact with the young Labour political organiser Herbert Morrison who was later to invite Stafford to join the Labour Party – although for the moment Stafford was content to remain broadly apolitical. As he told Eric Estorick, 'Brought up in a traditionally Conservative middle-class family, seldom meeting anyone other than Conservatives, I accepted that environment quite naturally, and from time to time partici-pated in some election or political activity in the same way that I engaged in any other sort of social event. I was neither aware of democracy nor of politics in any real sense of the word.'[1]

So sound was Stafford's practice by the mid-1920s that he began to consider taking silk, the process whereby a bar-rister became a King's Counsel. Thus at the end of 1924 Parmoor told him that his father had made him delay the process for too long because he 'did not much like the risks and chances [inherent in renouncing the lucrative junior work] if they could be avoided', and advised in favour of applying for silk as soon as possible. As Stafford was still extremely young for this step he did wait a year, but in July 1926 he made his formal application to the Lord Chancellor's office and the following April he was made a King's Counsel at the same time as another Wykehamist who was two years older than he, D.N. Pritt. Stafford was now the youngest KC in the land, with a reputation that was guaranteeing him a good income and over the next few years he took the lead in a series of high-profile cases that drew him to the attention not just of Herbert Morrison but of the public as well, although it was not until the 1930s when he represented the miners against the mine owners in the Gresford colliery disaster inquiry that his mastery of courtroom intricacies became well known.

In the meantime, back in 1921, Stafford and Isobel, with a new daughter Theresa and another, Peggy, on the way, decided to move out of London. Both of them had been brought up in the country, and remained country people all their life, so they resolved that they wanted their children to be brought up in the country as well. The old Cripps family connections were always with Cirencester and Stafford loved the area. He even wrote one of his appallingly clumsy, sentimental and derivative poems about the Cotswolds:

> O Brave Cotswolds
> Rolling hill on hill,
> Grey in sober strength,
> Flecked with sun-kissed hamlets,
> Nestling in deep-furrowed valleys,
> Pasturing the free-browsing flocks
> Whose golden fleeces once
> Brought uncounted wealth
> And gave your craftsmen power to build
> Slender-spired churches and grey grouped homes
> Whose beauty yet bedecks your loveliness.[2]

Yet, mindful of the fact that Stafford would be spending the weeks up in London and travelling home every weekend, they began to look on the edge of the 'high wild hills and rough uneven ways' of the Cotswolds and settled on the small village of Filkins which lies on the border of Oxfordshire and

Gloucestershire. Though not actually in the Cotswolds, it still has the air of Cotswold life about it and the architect Lawrence Weaver's words could easily have been written about Filkins: 'There is an air of artless simplicity about Cotswold manor houses and cottages that might tempt the casual observer to the belief that there is little to learn about their making. Two or three gables and a bay, plain square chimneys, a stone panel or two, and simple, perchless doors – these are the ingredients.'[3]

Just such a house was the one Isobel and Stafford landed on. When the family moved in Goodfellows was a relatively simple small manor house, built in golden sandstone from the village, but as Peggy put it

as I grew, so did the house. My father was always adding new bits, and he and my mother expanded the much-loved garden. There was a stream running through whose light clayey bottom provided clay for modelling. There was a moat on three sides of the perpetually green lawn, which had deep black mud out of which the springs gurgled and which smelt strong when the weeds were dragged from it in summer. The water was icy but it supported a number of small fish like minnows and sticklebacks. The water supply for drinking came from springs across the fields, known as the Pills, and whose water was pure and good to drink and which at one time had been known for medicinal qualities – hence the name. The springs were shaded by willow trees and fenced to prevent pollution. To this day I can remember the feeling of mystery about them.[4]

Beatrice Webb was fascinated some years later by the difference between the country homes of two cousins, Arthur Hobhouse and Stafford. 'Hadspen, the 160 year old family seat with lovely gardens broadening out into avenues and parkland, fields; and Goodfellows, a much smaller Cotswold manor house, the country place of the successful barrister and Front Bench politician, laid out with classical taste – waterways, terraces, yew hedges and brilliant herbaceous borders.'[5]

If there was a model for the style and decoration of Goodfellows it came from Lawrence Weaver, whom Stafford had met during his brief sojourn at the Ministry of Agriculture, and who was a distinguished architect and commentator on modern architecture. His speciality lay in rather craftsy constructions and together with Gertrude Jekyll, the landscape gardener, he effectively brought the country life motif into British architecture in the twenties and brought the work of Edwin Lutyens into vogue. Classic English looks, with more than a deferential nod to the Arts and Crafts movement and an embodiment of William Morris's maxim to have 'nothing in your houses that you do not know to be useful or believe to be beautiful' – this was the ethos Weaver advocated and Stafford and Isobel maintained.

Lawrence was twelve years older than Stafford, but his wife, the harpist Kathleen Purcell, despite a reputation for being tyrannical, got on well with Isobel and the Weaver children were roughly the same age as the two older Cripps children, so the Weavers became firm friends, often staying at Goodfellows, and Weaver's influence can be seen in the fine parquet floors with simple but expensive runners, the gabled windows and the sympathetic additions to the old house which slowly gained an extra wing and a new limed oak panelled library. Lawrence and Stafford became not only close friends but associates so that when Stafford became the Chairman of Eno's Fruit Salts he recruited Weaver as a director and the two of them set up a small pottery in Ashtead in Surrey which employed army veterans. Like Stafford, Lawrence was a sixteen hours a day man and Clough Williams-Ellis, his successor as President of the Design and Industries Association, drew an amusing portrait of the two men when they both briefly took up bookbinding: 'the pair submitt[ed] themselves in their increasingly scanty leisure to regular tuition by a professional teacher as though their livelihoods depended upon their becoming proficient craftsmen'.[6] Weaver shared Stafford's interest in religion, although he expressed it less conventionally as a Deacon of the Catholic Apostolic (Irvingite) Church of Sunday which was based in Gordon Square in London, and many of the personal characteristics that Williams-Ellis noted about him were mirrored in Stafford, 'his cheerful vitality and businesslike directness, the slightly pedantic violence of his phrasing, and his air of slyly conspiratorial confidence . . . his obvious erudition and the "debunking" tendency of his humour'.[7] So strong was the family friendship that when Kathleen died while staying at Goodfellows in 1927 Isobel effectively became mother to their two boys Toby and Purcell and when Lawrence himself died (after a brief second marriage) in January 1930 the boys were formally adopted by the Cripps family.

Goodfellows was expensive but simple, tasteful and elegant rather than brash or ostentatious and was thus in total keeping with the Cripps household, which, even before Toby and Purcell became permanent additions, was not inconsiderable, including a parlourmaid, two housemaids, a nursery maid, a cook, a kitchenmaid, Mr Holmes who looked after the Ryeland Sheep and George Swinford the foreman. There was a whole menagerie of animals: a Sealyham called Jester who was knocked down by a motorcycle; a veritable pack of Dandie Dinmonts called Dougal, Angus, Andy and Geordie; a miniature schnauzer called Usseuf; some ponies and a goat called Betsie Maria. After a couple of years Stafford even decided to take up farming in a minor way, as his father had once done at Parmoor, and he bought some Ryeland Sheep which he began to show. So it was a thoroughly country childhood, especially for the two youngest children. Under the guidance of their nanny Elsie Lawrence – or 'Noo' – who started at Goodfellows in 1924, Theresa and Peggy joined the British Wild Flower Society. They went mushrooming and crab appling and each of the children had their own patch of the garden to cultivate.

Life was not limited to Goodfellows, however, and in the winter the family stayed at Isobel's mother's house in Sussex Square near Hyde Park and in the summer they used Commander Swithinbank's large yacht, the *Venetia,* for their holidays off the south coast. As the children grew up they also began to go off to boarding school, first John to Lambourne and Winchester, then Diana and finally Theresa and Peggy to Queen's College in Harley Street and Maltman's Green at Gerrard's Cross.

Nevertheless it was Goodfellows that was the family home and it was at Goodfellows that Isobel and Stafford began to entertain as soon as they had built enough rooms for people to stay in. Herbert Morrison, who was a regular visitor in the thirties said of a stay at Goodfellows that

> there was . . . that rigid attitude to living by a man with a mind that completely controlled emotions. A fellow guest described our host as a 'cold fish'. The mixture of charm and coldness could spoil what was otherwise a delightful visit. Rules for living were strict. Bedtime was 10 p.m. precisely and we were all bundled upstairs as the clock struck the hour whether we wanted to or not.[8]

The truth is, though, that what Morrison may have thought of as strictness was still the result of Stafford's ill health, for though Stafford kept up a full calendar of work throughout the 1920s, he was often ill and Parmoor had to write to him at the end of 1923 to get him to slow down:

> the law is a great strain even for the robust and there is no room for much outside work – above all things, avoid

evening meetings and night journeys after hard work at the courts. I know more than one of my friends who tried this, and had to suffer from the evil effects. It is more than the average strength of man can do, and it should not be attempted. I know this may mean disappointment but this must be faced. A time will come to you when the call for religious and public work will be stronger and then possibly the conditions of your professional life may be such, that you could do such work either as a judge or in some other sphere. There is no need to be cast down about the future.[9]

It was not, however, just the law that was absorbing Stafford's time and energy, for slowly and surely throughout this period he got more and more inextricably involved in the life of the Church of England and in politics.

7

A Public Life

It was not until 1931, when Stafford was already forty-one, that he was to become a Labour MP, but the tracks that eventually led him into the Labour camp were laid by his father back in the First World War, and just like his father it was religion, not politics, that he looked to for the answers to the challenges that war presented. In this both men were typical of their age, for the effect of this 'Great' war, with its unparalleled devastation and its unimagined loss of life, was to make a whole generation question the project of modern-ism. The Victorian dream of perpetual progress lay hanging on the barbed wire of no-man's-land whilst thousands looked to Christianity in all her hues for a spiritual strength that might transcend the horrors of war or a new social vision that would make war obsolete.

At the same time the official repository of the nation's faith, the Church of England, was changing rapidly, no longer recruiting its clergy from the nobility but from the professional middle classes and frequently taking up the cudgels on behalf of the labouring poor. In its liturgy, its politics and its constitu-tion it was transforming itself and throughout Alfred was as close to the helm as a layman could be. He had represented the diocese of Oxford in the House of Laymen in the Province of Canterbury since 1890. He was Vicar General successively for each of the English Provinces and was a friend of both

Frederick Temple and Randall Davidson. He presided at the episcopal confirmation of the Christian Socialist Charles Gore and in 1911 he was elected Chairman of the House of Laymen. In 1913 he moved the setting up of the Church and State Committee which eventually led to the 1919 'Enabling Act' and the inauguration of the National Assembly of the Church of England, in which he was elected the first chairman of the House of Laity the following year. From at least 1911 to 1923 he was the leading lay Anglican in the country and it was almost inevitable that Stafford, the first of the Cripps household to marry but always the most attached to his father, should retain his father's quietly passionate faith.

As for Alfred, when the war came it was not Party politics that absorbed him, but the spiritual state of the nation. In October 1914 he wrote in his diary, 'Each day the weakening influence of Christianity becomes more clear. Its real failure is that national animosities have been aroused, and that religious communities, instead of preaching Christ's Gospel of world Peace and Goodwill, too often encourage a war spirit as popular in the country to which they belong.'[1] As a Christian, then, he declared that he was 'wholly opposed' to the Liberal Cabinet's declaration of war, and from here on in classed himself as an independent Peer, aligned more with the pacifist Anglican clerics and Quakers than with any of his erstwhile political colleagues.

This rejection of the war brought him ever closer to Labour, since though Labour officially supported the war effort (as did his brother-in-law Sidney) several ILP members came out as pacifists, including Ramsay MacDonald who resigned as Chairman of the Parliamentary Party and George Lansbury who backed calls for an early cessation to violence and a sympathetic hearing for the Conscientious Objectors. In this he was joined by several of Parmoor's own family, including both his sisters-in-law Kate and Maggie. Kate indeed spent most of the war commuting from the Courtney house in

Cheyne Walk to the offices of the Emergency Committee for Germans, Austrians and Hungarians which was based in Hoxton in the East End, where she worked with Maggie's Quaker son Stephen and his wife Rosa. In late 1916 both Stephen and Rosa were arrested as Conscientious Objectors and Stephen was sentenced to imprisonment with hard labour. The following August Maggie Hobhouse then published *I Appeal Unto Caesar* outlining their harsh and immoral treatment and Parmoor, along with Lord Cecil and the Earl of Selborne, wrote a public letter of support, while Gilbert Murray wrote an introduction to the book. Parmoor had been worried for some time about the 'many complaints [that arose] in the treatment of Conscientious Objectors and persons who, in the ordinary way, do nothing more than make a fair comment on public questions',[2] but it was this personal connection that finally brought him into the fray and he now moved a resolution in the Lords which would have made non-combatant service 'of national value, and not merely of a penal character'.

Stephen Hobhouse was not the only Quaker who was involved in the process of drawing Parmoor to the pacifist left, for several of his parliamentary friends had, from the beginning of the war, been involved in the national Quaker call for peace and for an International Christian Conference as a means of preventing war. In particular the charismatic MP, Joseph Allen Baker, whom Parmoor got to know on a trip to Canada and who died just before the end of the war, set up a British Council in response to a call by the Swedish Bishop Soderblom for a world alliance of Christians to defeat violence and when the Society of Friends passed a resolution at their annual meeting in 1918 saying that there was a higher law than that of the State it was the daughter of another Quaker MP, John Ellis, who had sat on the Jameson Raid hearings with Parmoor, that published *A Challenge to Militarism* and started handing it out at Labour Party meetings. Under the 1917 Defence of the Realm Act this was a criminal activity and three people were seized and imprisoned, including Edith Ellis.

Since 1915 Parmoor had backed calls for a League of Nations, he had founded, with Lord Courtney, the League of Nations Society and had presided at the initial meeting of the League of Free Nations Associations at Central Hall in Westminster in May 1917. So when Edith's twin sister Marion was looking for new supporters for the idea of the International Christian Conference it was natural that Kate Courtney encouraged her to see Parmoor, who was so taken with the idea, and with Marion, that he agreed instantly to be the Chairman of the new Council for an International Christian Conference. It was an interesting gathering, consisting in the main of the more radical clergy: Burge, now the Bishop of Southwark and fresh from trying to resolve the London dock strike; Bishop Fred Woods of Peterborough; William Temple, the Archbishop's son and a vicar in London; Dean Inge of St Paul's; Scott Lidgett; and the ubiquitous Kate Courtney. Though the organisation was wound up before the close of the war its membership came together after the war as Fight the Famine and it was out of its Albert Hall meeting on 19 May 1919 that the Save the Children Fund was founded by two young women, Miss Jebb and Mrs Buxton.

Meanwhile Marion had also been involved since its inception in the more ecumenical British Council of the World Alliance for Promoting International Friendship through the Churches and she soon managed to get Parmoor to agree to be a Vice-President of the World Alliance in addition to his Fight the Famine responsibilities. This now brought them together on at least two Executive Committees and a few days after the May meeting of Fight the Famine Alfred and Marion became engaged before being married at Southwark Cathedral on 14 July by another Executive groupie, their friend Burge. Stafford and all the family were delighted.

Marion was not only a persuasive Quaker but a beautiful woman and Beatrice Webb wrote, 'Alfred has excellent taste in women. He chose the most charming of the Potter sisters . . . and he has now won an exceptionally attractive woman, good as gold, able and most pleasant to look at. All his children and their mates were there beaming goodwill. The two were reverently ecstatic.'[3]

The wedding put the seal on Alfred's political idealism and Beatrice reckoned that he was now 'something very like an international socialist. So does evil company corrupt good manners!' On the face of it none of the organisations Alfred and Marion participated in had any Socialist intent and were purely internationalist, but the tenor of so much of the discussion of social issues in their magazines put them wholeheartedly in the Labour camp. Thus in the early editions of *Goodwill*, the World Alliance's journal, the Christian Socialist priest and leader of the 1905 Leicester hunger march Lewis Donaldson who had coined the phrase that 'Christianity is the religion of which socialism is the practice',[4] argued that the Churches had to develop closer links with labour and W. Blackshaw commented that 'this feeling of dissatisfaction with the competitive basis of modern commerce is widespread among clergy and ministers'.[5] A March 1918 manifesto in support of the League of Nations was signed not just by Henderson and Lansbury but by Parmoor, Burge and a raft of Bishops including Randall Davidson, revealing a remarkable preparedness of even the Archbishop to align himself with Labour.

Clearly there was a large body of Anglican and non-conformist opinion that wanted to wake Christianity from its quietist slumbers and to take up the issues that affected society at large – and there were protagonists, both clerical and political, who took a direct route from the cloister garth to the corridors of Westminster and were closely involved in the plethora of internationalist and pacifist organisations that dominated the Churches at the start of the twenties. Many started the First World War as Liberals, but by the time of the 1923 election nearly all were active Labour supporters. The Union of Democratic Control (founded 1914), the League of Nations Society (1915), the World Alliance (1916), The Life and Liberty Movement (1917), the 'Fifth Report' of the National Mission (1918), Fight the Famine (1918), and the Conference on Politics Economics and Christianity (1924) all depended on the same Christian Socialist coterie, many of whom had been members of either the Christian Social Union or the Church Socialist League, and became an effective recruiting ground for the Independent Labour Party. Entering and marrying into this group made Parmoor's eventual passage into the Labour Cabinet in 1924 inevitable.

As for Stafford, he indicated that his conversion to politics, and to Socialism, was a case of follow-my-father, for Alfred's 'sense of the interference with liberty of conscience and of the injustice wrought upon the common people had convinced him that some new outlook was necessary if civilisation were to be saved from destruction'. Still his own political beliefs were only sketchy and constituted more of an emotional and spiritual abhorrence of war than any ideology or concerted programme. Still by nature a conservative, in a conservative profession, confessing a conservative theology, he nevertheless felt that his political conscience had been born as 'by the time the war was over I had become aware – indeed very aware – of the appalling and useless tragedy that the world had brought upon itself'.[6]

Partly out of this sense of the tragedy of the war and partly thanks to the good influence of people like Marion and Alfred, almost as soon as he was back on his feet and he was working at full tilt, he joined the British Council of the World Alliance and joining the Parmoors on the Executive, became its Treasurer. The following year both he and Isobel went as British delegates to the international meeting of the Alliance in Copenhagen. By now Burge had succeeded Gore as Bishop of Oxford and though he was involved in similar ecumenical and internationalist ventures he had fought shy of the World Alliance out of a fear that it would prove just another talking-shop, but when Davidson, who was the nominal President of the International Council, asked him to attend the conference on his behalf he was thrown together with his old pupil. Stafford had taken to the World Alliance with relish. As Treasurer he had launched a big appeal for funds, he was intent on reorganising the British Council and more importantly he was increasingly clear about the task ahead: 'Two paths now lie before the world,' he declared, 'the one the way of the politician, leading by intrigue and diplomacy to misunder-standings, envies, hatreds and fresh wars; the other the way of Christ, leading by love and self-sacrifice to mutual under-standing, goodwill, brotherhood and peace.'[7] When Stafford put all this, tinged with youthful enthusiasm, to Burge, sitting in his hotel room in Copenhagen, he was convinced of the Treasurer's vision for the World Alliance and agreed to become its new British President, taking over from the equally radical but more aristocratic Edward Talbot, the Bishop of Winchester. Immediately on their return to England a meeting was held at Burge's Palace at Cuddesdon where the new shape of the British Council was hammered out and a large confer-ence was planned at Church House for the following June, when the Archbishop would speak on 'The Wrong and Right Way to Obtain National Security'.

So began a period of some four years when Stafford, in close partnership with Burge, devoted much of his time to the cause of international ecumenical peace, speaking in churches and village halls across Britain, meeting with foreign ministers and desperately trying to persuade the churches of the role he and Burge believed only religion could play in ensuring there was never another war like the Great War. Burge's secretary, the young Gwen Hill, who had worked for his predecessor

Gore, became the Alliance's part-time secretary. Marion continued an influential member of the Executive, as did Alfred, who was appointed to the League of Nations in 1924. George Bell (from 1924 Dean of Canterbury) and William Temple (now Bishop of Manchester) soon set up the Conference on Politics, Economics and Citizenship which drew on the same body of radical Christians and came to fruition in 1924, and so was forged an ecumenical coterie out of which would eventually spring the British Council of Churches, just as the World Council of Churches grew out of the World Alliance.

In the meantime Stafford had also been elected to the National Assembly in 1923, its third year, and by the end of the same year Parmoor had completed his transmigration to Labour. For in the General Election on 6 December MacDonald, now reappointed leader of the Labour Party, managed to secure 191 seats against the Conservatives' 258, thereby depriving them of a majority. Because of the balance of power complications (the Liberals had 158 seats) there was some uncertainty as to who would form a Government after Christmas, but MacDonald wrote to Parmoor on Christmas Day saying that if he were to form a Government he would like to offer him a post. Parmoor had not met MacDonald very often before the election, but it was clear that if Labour was to govern it would need to garner in the support of left-leaning independents like Parmoor as well as sympathetic Peers to make up the Cabinet numbers. Parmoor, who was about to set off for France, consulted Burge, who urged him to accept the offer, saying 'I have taken into account the possible difficulties in which you might find yourself, as for instance if, to appease the extremists, Government measures were introduced which seemed rather recklessly to interfere with fundamental rights of property'[8] – and thus betraying that neither Parmoor nor Burge really understood the new Labour Party and the exigencies of minority government.

MacDonald had also been courting Sidney Webb, now MP for Seaham, and the two brothers-in-law were appointed to the first Labour Cabinet as Lord President of the Council deputising for MacDonald on Foreign Affairs in the Lords, and as President of the Board of Trade. Alfred explained to Beatrice that he had accepted his new post because 'he had faith in J.R.M[acDonald] and had worked with him through the war and since'[9] rather than out of any ideological or political affinity.

Even now that his father and uncle were Labour ministers of the Crown Stafford manifested no signs of any Socialist allegiance, not least because it was the Church rather than the world that he hoped to change. His personal relationship with God, so he believed, had sustained him in his prolonged illness, and faith would provide the answer to the world's problems, if only the Church could be rejuvenated. He was still deeply sceptical about politics and felt that a renewed unsectarian Christianity had to precede a better social order for, as Burge put it,

> a system of morality that is regarded as a substitute for personal holiness ultimately breaks down, because in the last resort it is found to rest upon no higher sanction or authority than the motive of expediency. Politics, when set in a compartment separated from the principles of human welfare which Christ taught, break down, because then politicians and financiers have no higher ideal of national life than that of a mercantile concern.[10]

In his 1957 biography Colin Cooke reckoned that 'by 1925 [Stafford's] mind had moved towards the Labour Party,'[11] but there is little evidence of this. There were personal connections with Labour and many of the people with whom he consorted in the World Alliance were no longer in the thrall of the divided Liberals, but up until Burge's sudden death in 1925 he showed no sign of getting directly involved in Party politics. His life was purely focused on earning a living as a lawyer and providing for his family, while his spare time, such as it was, was devoted to his various hobbies (bookbinding, farming, carpentry) and the Church of England.

When Burge died, a new diocesan Bishop was appointed, and Parmoor entered the Cabinet and resigned from the World Alliance; everything changed, although at first only imperceptibly. For now Stafford was not following his father or his old teacher, he was acting in his own behalf. Steadily he began to feel frustrated. The Church was too mealy-mouthed. She refused to engage with the world or to act decisively and she remained divided. Over major issues like the General Strike and the Geneva Protocol she seemed ineffectual and irrelevant and on the international level she seemed incapable of concerted action. All of this began to point the way to Parliamentary politics.

At the same time Stafford took on a series of cases on behalf of local authorities in London and began to see a rather different world from that of Filkins and the Strand,

My professional work in connection with the acquisition of land for housing schemes and for new municipal enterprises of all kinds, especially in and around London, took me to slum areas, of the meaning of which I had before been completely unconscious, though I had lived and worked in London all my life! I discovered that in this country of ours, the conditions of the workers were appallingly bad. I had long been familiar with disease-ridden hovels which in many country areas passed for houses, and the tragically low wage levels of the agricultural workers. But for the first time I began to appreciate what the urban slums really signified in terms of suffering, starvation and ill health.[12]

More important than all this was the plain and simple fact that Stafford had by now resolved that he wanted what he called 'a public life'. He later wrote to Hugh Macmillan, the Lord Advocate in the 1924 Government and the son of a former Moderator of the General Assembly of the Free Church, that it was listening to his reasons for taking up MacDonald's offer that made him feel that 'I must really make up my mind to do my share of work besides earn money'[13] and that it was out of a sense of duty that his whole political career sprang. Today's cynicism would decry such piety as so much hogwash, but in the 1920s, especially among the wealthy professional classes such concepts as duty and service were the loadstones of political *mores* and Stafford would not have been unusual in his assertion that it was no vainglory but a desire to serve which motivated his entry into politics. Even on a personal level, although he always respected ambition in others, it was this powerful belief that he had a duty to perform which drove him to take on more work than his frail health could ever really cope with, and his perception of politics as a vocation that he must fulfil was what drove him by the end of 1928 to the belief that he should become a politician.

All that was left was to choose the Party – a decision that he delayed until 1929, when MacDonald formed his second minority Government and again asked Sidney Webb, now Lord Passfield, and Parmoor, to sit in the Cabinet. What finally decided Stafford in favour of Labour is unknown. What we do know is that Stafford's belief in politics as service meant that he was not going to be interested in a Party that was never likely to form a Government. If there had been any doubts before, the election result showed that Labour could do just that. Whether he supported the broad thrust of Labour's policies, however, is far less certain, as up until now he had only made his views known on ecclesiastical and international issues.

The fact is, though, that in the end he simply succumbed to

the persistent pleas of Herbert Morrison, the new Minister of Transport. Morrison had already made several inconclusive attempts but immediately prior to the start of the May election campaign he wrote to Parmoor that it was one of his ambitions to see Stafford in the Labour Party and asked for his advice on how to approach his son.[14] When Parmoor suggested that Morrison should get in touch with Stafford directly he immediately winged off a letter saying:

> you will remember that some time ago I sounded you on the possibility of you joining the Party. I was aware of the professional considerations which arise but I am personally very anxious to see you in the Party. Please let me know if and when you would like to join the ranks of the Party and I shall be very happy to make the necessary arrangements, but of course I greatly respect your own scrupulousness in not intending to join the Labour Party until you are quite clear in your own mind that you accept our principles and our policy.[15]

Stafford's original response to Morrison in the winter of 1928-9 had been that he did not want to enter politics because 'I am more interested in the Church',[16] but this time Morrison got a 'yes' and Stafford joined the Labour Party. Even at this stage, though, Stafford was joining Labour not as an ordinary member but as a prospective candidate and immediately Morrison set about finding him the seat he had promised

The first that crossed Morrison's path was that of West Woolwich, where the Labour vote had grown steadily, but where Labour had just been defeated. In an attempt to persuade Stafford to take on such a difficult seat, where the sitting member was the Tory Kingsley Wood, Morrison wrote, 'I am sure you will not mind me reminding you that you are young; that if you do not win a constituency in the first fight you have gained valuable experience and other chances will arise later.

I do feel, however, that there is a real substantial chance to win West Woolwich at the next election and that you would be an excellent candidate of the next place.'[17] Both Parmoor and the Webbs urged Stafford to accept Morrison's offer, so he spoke to the local party on Stafford's behalf and the new Labour Party member was selected and spent much of 1930 canvassing and addressing meetings in West Woolwich.

Meanwhile Stafford was also proving useful to the Party in his legal capacity, successfully defending the newly elected Labour MP, J. J. Moses, against a Parliamentary Election Petition, the first the Labour Party had ever had to face, for free and it may well have been this that so endeared him to MacDonald and the Party hierarchy that when the Solicitor-General retired in October Stafford was approached by the Prime Minister and offered the job and the knighthood that went with it. As there was no likelihood of there being an immediate by-election in Woolwich, nor a General Election, the Party then set about finding him a seat and when the MP for Bristol East, W. T. Baker, died, the Party machine swung into operation in a resolute attempt to get him selected despite the fact that the National Union of Teachers had fixed the selection in favour of one of their members, Leah Manning. As soon as the election was called Arthur Henderson tried to persuade Manning that the seat was needed for Stafford, but Manning continued to dismiss him as 'some lawyer'[18] and in the end Hugh Dalton had to come down to Bristol to beg with the constituency and to tell Manning, 'Uncle Arthur [Henderson] asks me to tell you that he will make this a test of your loyalty to the Party.'[19] So Leah stood to one side and on 16 January 1931 Stafford Cripps was the Labour candidate.

It was a straightforward campaign. Herbert Rogers, who was to be Stafford's agent for every election through to 1950, was an able campaigner, and though Sir Thomas Inskip, the previous Tory Solicitor-General, was drowned out by the singing of 'Tell me the Old, Old Story', few of the election meetings were rowdy. The twenty-three-year-old Conservative candidate P. J. F. Chapman-Walker attacked the eighteen-month old Labour Government's record on unemployment and argued for tariff protection to prevent the dumping of surplus goods from other countries. Stafford responded that he belonged to the Labour Party because

> I know that that party stands for the increased happiness and health of the workers of the country. Our policy is to keep before us this ultimate object. We are not prepared to allow a false policy of economy to curtail our work. We want to hasten forward the time when every one in the land will have an equal opportunity of obtaining the good things of life and that the pleasures of life are not limited to the rich alone.[20]

Polling day saw a large swing to Labour and Stafford, already a minor celebrity for his work at the Bar, polled 19,261 votes against the Conservative's 7,937 and the Liberal's 4,010. Four days later the new Solicitor-General was presented in the Commons between the Attorney-General and the Chief Whip and another four days later he presented his maiden speech in the debate on the Solicitors' (Clients Accounts) Bill. Beatrice Webb commented:

> And now Stafford Cripps enters the political arena as Solicitor-General and the winner, by a huge majority, of the Bristol seat. Stafford is a convinced Christian of the Sankey [the Lord Chancellor] brand: tall, good-looking, pleasant voice, an essentially modest and well-mannered man; but a first rate advocate, in receipt of a large income. He is the only one of the 155 nephews and nieces who might become a big figure in public life. His one handicap is poor health.[21]

One question that has never been satisfactorily answered is quite how Stafford Cripps was selected for Solicitor-General. After all he was a newcomer to the party and he was not an MP. Doubtless his help in defeating the challenge to Moses's election helped, as did his strong legal reputation and family connections, but it is difficult to believe that there were not others with more secure political credentials who could have taken the post. D. N. Pritt, a possible alternative, certainly harboured resentment over the matter, for in 1930 William Jowitt, the Attorney-General, had asked him whether he would be interested in standing in a by-election and becoming Solicitor-General. Pritt maintained in his autobiography that he told Jowitt that since Stafford had both an uncle and a father in the Cabinet and was a man of considerable ability, the post would go to him should it become vacant. Jowitt replied, 'You can take it from me that that will not happen. There will certainly be pressure for Cripps, but I shall resist it. The decision is, in fact, in my hands, and you can rely on it that I shall appoint you.' Jowitt's remarks were soon to haunt him, however, as when Stafford had been appointed there were rumours that he had tried to oppose MacDonald's choice, and the following year he was telling Pritt 'Don't be afraid of not being appointed [as a law officer]. The appointment is in fact in my hands, and if I say you will be appointed, you will be. It was *I* who appointed Cripps; don't believe any of the stories told about any fights over his appointment. I insisted on Cripps, and I appointed him; and just as I appointed him I shall appoint you.'[22]

Pritt's bitterness was the inevitable result of having put his trust in princes, but it is interesting that the Jowitt that was later to stick with MacDonald in the National Government should be more keen on the infinitely more ideologically left-wing Pritt than on Cripps. It was only to be expected that the snobbish MacDonald would have preferred to take on board the son of a hereditary Peer who had already changed Parties twice, especially if, as Beatrice Webb suggested, he was already thinking of forming a coalition Government, in which, presumably, he would hope that any new appointee might be prepared to serve, and the support of Henderson was almost guaranteed because of his friendship with the Webbs and his League of Nations work with Parmoor, but the backing of Dalton is less expected, except in so far as Stafford was evidently an able and effective lawyer. Yet it has to be remembered that legal officers were not expected to be political animals but rather to give the government the best legal advice available. So unconcerned about the political purity of his legal officers was MacDonald that Jowitt was even appointed Attorney-General when he was still a Liberal MP and resigned his seat so as to enter the House as a Labour member.

Either way, Stafford's spell as Solicitor-General was not to last long and though he had a brief opportunity to make his mark when he took over the presentation of the Labour case in the Land Values Bill when the Chancellor of the Exchequer Philip Snowden was ill, there was little in the Parliamentary session that was contentious and his brief did not extend far into the realms of politics. The Cabinet intrigues which eventually led to the collapse of the Government largely passed him by and he was entirely absorbed in apolitical matters.

In the summer of 1931 the Labour Government imploded over proposed cuts in the unemployment insurance payments. MacDonald faced his Cabinet down, got them to tender their resignations, walked round to the Palace, told the King he was forming a new National Administration and then notified his old Labour colleagues that they were being replaced by Conservatives and Liberals.

When the crunch came in August, Stafford and Isobel were abroad on their annual holiday. The year before it had been Oberammergau, but this year, so that Stafford could take the waters, they were in Baden Baden, where Stafford contracted an infection that left him with an occasionally embarrassingly ruddy nose. It was here that he was contacted by MacDonald who expressed in the briefest of telegrams that he wanted Stafford to continue as Solicitor-General. Stafford immediately hurried back to England and met with both Jowitt and Sankey before finally making up his mind and writing his formal letter to MacDonald:

> It is with very great personal regret that I find myself unable to accept your kind offer. May I be allowed – without being considered impertinent – to say that I admire immensely the courage and conviction which have led you and other Labour Ministers associated with you to take the action you have taken. My own personal hope is that the rift in the party may be quickly healed and I shall do all I can to attain that end. I should like also to take this opportunity of thanking you most sincerely for your personal kindnesses to me during the past year ... I disagree with the policy of the Labour Party taking any part in a National Government having the programme of the present Government.[23]

Why did MacDonald ask Stafford to stay in post especially when Parmoor had already joined the Opposition benches? It cannot have been for lack of legally qualified MPs. There was a whole shoal of Conservative lawyers in the House. More likely is that MacDonald felt that Stafford would acquiesce in his policies for dealing with the economic crisis out of a straightforward patriotism. However others judged his actions MacDonald's own interpretation of the Labour split was that he and Snowden were the only responsible Labour leaders who were prepared to govern in the National rather than Party interest and he expected that his legal officers, who were appointed primarily for their expertise not their political allegiance, might stick with him. Indeed both Sankey and Jowitt remained in post and although Jowitt eventually returned to the Labour fold he fought (and lost) his seat as a National Labour candidate in the 1931 election. As for Stafford's decision, it had already been made in 1929 when he accepted Morrison's invitation. Though his political views were yet hazy he had already resolved that, in Beatrice Webb's words, he was on the side of the 'under dog' and this meant he, like his father, would remain in the Labour Party.

So Stafford had entered political life as a lawyer and the Labour Party as a Christian. Unlike the vast majority of his colleagues on the Labour benches he had not sought election out of a burning desire to change the world, but out of a desire to serve his nation. If he had an ambition it was to be Lord Chancellor, not Chancellor of the Exchequer, and if any Socialism coursed through his veins it was Christian Socialism, undogmatic in tone, ethical in purpose, internationalist in intent and above all rational and responsible. This could easily have swung him over into the National Labour camp as it was the same creed as that of Snowden and Sankey, but when the new front benches gathered to face each other in the autumn of 1931, Henderson against MacDonald, Stafford had made up his mind that he was now a Labour man.

In this his father, to whom he had always been reverentially attached, was important. Though very different in personal style Stafford and Alfred held remarkably similar political beliefs and for neither of them was the concept of Party very important. In the thirties this would hamper Stafford as he flailed in the stormy waters of his new-found Party with neither an ideological nor class star to guide him. In the forties, both during the Second World War and as Chancellor of the Exchequer, this manifest disregard of Party was to prove one of his greatest strengths.

8

A Slap-up Socialistic Policy

On 7 October MacDonald called the snap election that he had promised he would not hold and within the month the Parliamentary Labour Party had been laid waste. The National Government sailed into battle with all her guns blazing and Snowden and MacDonald mounted a hectic campaign of disinformation. MacDonald attended press conferences with bundles of devalued twenties German bank notes to show what would happen to inflation under Labour, while Snowden not only attacked the Labour programme as 'Bolshevism run mad' but even suggested that Labour would confiscate people's Post Office savings. What with an under-prepared and demoralised Party and a successful bid by MacDonald and Snowden to present themselves as the responsible patriots who looked beyond Party gain to the best interests of the nation, it was inevitable that Labour should lose. Polling day on 27 October delivered a massive vote of confidence in the new Government, gaining 554 seats to the Opposition's paltry 61. The Conservatives, of course, were the main beneficiaries, reaping a hefty 470 seats and more than 50 per cent of the total vote. Labour, who in 1929 had mustered 8,370,417 votes across the country, even if you combined the votes of the new National Labour members and the Labour Party itself, slipped back to less than seven million votes, and the Party that Arthur Henderson led into the election retained only forty-six MPs, although they could still rely occasionally on the three increasingly independent ILP members and three unendorsed Labour candidates.

Just as significantly, the election meant that many of Labour's strongest parliamentary figures lost their seats. Henderson himself was out. Clynes, Greenwood, Dalton, Morrison were all out. Those who were left felt a complete change of atmosphere in Parliament. As Alfred Salter, the ILP member for Bermondsey put it,

I am surrounded by a jostling crowd of wealthy, class-conscious Tories who regard the little group of Labour representatives as some noxious species of wild beasts that ought to be exterminated by decent people. This Parliament is a Rich Man's House. There are more titled members, more sprigs of the aristocracy and more pluto-crats that in any House of Commons within living memory. The dining rooms are crowded in the evening, expensive dinner parties are in full swing every night, ladies in dazzling attire are to be seen filling the . . . private dining rooms. St Stephen's is recovering its title to be the most fashionable club in Europe.[1]

And it was a shock. Beatrice Webb had only expected Labour to lose about 100 seats and on the day of the election the *Manchester Guardian* confidently expected Labour to retain 215 seats out of its 287. Stafford himself had felt that if the election could have been a few months later Labour might actually have won. The shock was all the more palpable because Labour had grown extraordinarily swiftly from its origins in the Labour Representation Committee. Many of its founding members were still active and in little more than one generation it had climbed from forming a campaign committee to forming a minority Government. Before the MacDonald split it could quite legitimately have expected to make further gains and form a majority Government in the not too distant future. MacDonald, Snowden, Thomas and Sankey's 'betrayal' was enough of a blow, but with the election defeat as well the prospect of having to start at the very beginning, returning to the 1906 Parliamentary strength of the Party, but with the flow of the political tide heavily against them, must have rendered even the strongest heart weak.

By a quirk of political fate Stafford retained his seat in Bristol with a majority of 429 and almost by default, with next to no Parliamentary or constituency apprenticeship, he was propelled into a key role on Labour's front bench at a time when major decisions had to be made and a Parliamentary Opposition had to be mounted.

The first task, though, was more straightforward. With Henderson out of Parliament there was a need to elect a new Chairman of the Parliamentary Party. This was the easiest decision of all. Attlee maintained, rather disingenuously, that when he went to the first Party meeting after the election he was informed by Henderson, who was to remain Leader of the Party, that George Lansbury would be proposed for Chairman and himself as Deputy, nominations that went through without opposition in the parliamentary meeting. In practice there was remarkably little choice. Of the Labour Cabinet the only remaining Ministers, apart from Peers, were Lansbury and Attlee. The next most senior person with ministerial experience was Stafford who could hardly be considered as a possibility for the Party leadership as he had only been in Parliament for a matter of months and, as Attlee put it, he lacked 'practical acquaintance with the Movement'.[2]

Others, however, did start to think of him as a possible Leader for the future, not least because in the few weeks between the formation of the National Government and the election he had started to make his mark in the House of Commons and he clearly felt that he had something to contribute. He wrote to Herbert Rogers, his election agent in Bristol, that 'there is a tremendous lot to be done by the Opposition, and I am most anxious to do anything I can to guide them into a constructive Socialist policy' and in equally arrogant tone he accosted William Graham, who had been Financial Secretary to the Treasury under Snowden, saying,

> The attitude of the rank and file of the Party seems to me to be extremely dangerous at the moment. There is a strong tendency to disregard the realities of the situation and to do that which our Party has shown such an inclination to do in the past, that is use a number of half-digested slogans in place of arguments and to try to avoid the responsibility of putting forward concrete proposals for putting into force the ideas which lie behind the policy of the Party in the circumstances in which we find ourselves to-day.[3]

So throughout the summer recess he tried to muscle in on the re-invention of the Party, arguing that 'it seems absolutely necessary to throw off once and for all the attitude of compromise which was impressed upon us by reason of the minority position in which the Labour Government found itself, and to come out boldly with a slap-up Socialistic policy for dealing with the whole industrial and financial situation'.[4] All of this showed a Stafford eager to work, eager to please and eager to be noticed, but as far as the movement outside Parliament was concerned he was still very much an unproven quantity and in the Union-dominated Parliamentary Party he was still regarded with suspicion as a wealthy barrister with a clipped accent and a Savile Row suit.

So Lansbury, already seventy-two years old, became chairman and *de facto*, if not *de jure*, leader. A pacifist of immense popularity and radical repute, Lansbury had strong roots in the Christian, suffragette and working-class beginnings of the Labour Movement. He was renowned for his open door policy at his home in Bow in the East End of London, he had campaigned for years against the barbarism of the Poor Law legislation and he could legitimately claim to be one of the founder members of the Party. He was not, however, the picture of moderation. Indeed his sense of political courage could take him down extreme paths. In 1912 he resigned his seat in order to fight a single issue by-election on women's suffrage, a battle he rather humiliatingly lost. He had been imprisoned for refusing to set a legal rate as a Poplar Councillor, and he had caused the Leadership of the Party considerable embarrassment during the General Strike, so much so that MacDonald had excluded him from his first Labour Cabinet in 1924 and only allowed him the relatively insignificant job of Minister of Works in his second. Attlee, whilst recognising his 'wise tolerance', described him as 'by nature an evangelist rather than a Parliamentary tactician'[5] and it is certain that the overwhelming personal affection which he enjoyed was the result of his air of uncompromising and disarming honesty.

Lansbury led the tiny Parliamentary righteous remnant, which was even weaker than its numbers might suggest, with a concern to unite rather than antagonise. Several of those who had survived were elderly members who held safe seats in mining areas and 'were not accustomed to speak frequently in the House and could not contribute much beyond their votes'.[6] Inevitably this placed a heavy burden on those who could master a brief swiftly and were able to command the attention of the House even when the numbers were stacked so overwhelmingly against Labour. So Attlee and Cripps, the most bourgeois of all the Labour MPs, soon took the lead in nearly every debate.

The other thing that Lansbury had in his favour was that his relationship with the two younger men was one of profound loyalty and affection, and they rapidly formed a close team, all based in the Leader of the Opposition's room behind the

Speaker's Chair. They had a lot in common. Both Lansbury and Attlee had their political base in the East End of London – Lansbury in Poplar, Attlee in Stepney – and Attlee had gone to stay at Toynbee Hall after University, where he came into regular contact with Stafford's aunt, Kate Courtney. Attlee's wife Vi reckoned that Isobel and Stafford were the only people in the Labour Party that she knew well and Isobel used to pass on her daughters' outworn clothes to the Attlees when they visited Goodfellows. Lansbury too was a regular visitor to Goodfellows, frequently engaging Stafford in lengthy discussions about the nature of faith and politics and when Lansbury fractured his thigh and was laid up in the Manor House hospital for several months from December 1933 the Cripps family was the most solicitous of all correspondents, with John, Isobel and Alfred all wishing him better whilst Stafford and Clem took over his work. It was inevitable that with Stafford still working at the Bar and Lansbury often out of action, Attlee took the lion's share of the Parliamentary work and Stafford arranged that he would subsidise Attlee's salary as Deputy Leader while he took all the expensive trips round the constituency Parties. So there developed an intimate and interdependent team, who inspired close loyalty in each other, a loyalty which stood Stafford in better stead than many properly understood in later years when, as Leader, Attlee had to deal with a recalcitrant and extremist Stafford.

In his autobiography Attlee wrote of Stafford that 'many great lawyers have failed to adapt themselves to the House of Commons, but from the start Cripps showed that he was the exception. He brought to our ranks wide knowledge, fine debating powers and a first-class mind,'[7] and if there was anything that began to endear Stafford to his Parliamentary colleagues it was his ability to rattle the Government. Even his second speech as an MP, when he was Solicitor-General, had impressed the Labour front bench with his determined and rebarbative support for the controversial Trade Disputes and

Trade Unions (Amendment) Bill in which he tried to dif-
ferentiate between legitimate and revolutionary or political
strikes and had to fend off full-blooded braying from the
Tories. He was also quite happy to pull off the occasional party
stunt and was not above filching a ministerial brief that had
been carelessly left on a desk and answering every one of a
lengthy run of amendments to a Government bill by reading
out the Government's own prepared reply before the Minister
could respond. Far from the haughty barrister that some might
have expected, Stafford was proving to be a valuable, imaginative and reliable member of the team and Michael Foot
reckoned that this triumvirate

> was probably the happiest collaboration that Labour had
> ever known at the top [because] George Lansbury proved
> a more successful Mark Antony than anyone could have
> expected, Cripps was the perfect Octavius, cold, remorse-
> less in the pursuit of his enemies and never deflected
> from his argument, while Lepidus, in the guise of Major
> Clement Attlee, performed his errands with such peremp-
> tory despatch that he soon seemed to make himself
> indispensable.[8]

It was not quite as simple as all that. From the outside this
team came increasingly to seem like either an alternative
power base to the National Executive or else a narrow clique.
With not a little bitterness, Dalton commented a year after the
election, 'The Parliamentary Party is a poor little affair,
isolated from the N[ational] E[xecutive] whose only MP is
Lansbury. Attlee is Deputy Leader of the Parliamentary Party
– a "purely accidental position" as someone puts it – and he
and Cripps, who are in close touch with [George] Cole, sit in
Lansbury's room at the House all day and all night and
continually influence the old man.'[9] Beatrice Webb, writing at
the same time, saw it a little more dispassionately, perceiving

'serious friction between the Parliamentary Party led by George Lansbury, guided by Stafford and forming a very united brotherhood in its own part, and the National Executive'.[10]

Much of this growing split in the Party between its Parliamentary and Executive wings was inevitable. Henderson had always been an advocate of a gradual, electorally attractive political agenda, while Lansbury was an archetypal radical, no more left-wing than Henderson but indubitably less worried about electoral niceties. After such a massive defeat it would have been extraordinary if Labour had not engaged in a major rethink of its fundamental values, but the split between the National Executive and the Parliamentary Party set up personal differences that took many years and a world war to overcome. It also had the effect of isolating Stafford, who had neither the political roots within the wider movement nor the close personal ties with other figures, to justify the high profile he unexpectedly had to take within the Party. Morrison he knew well and respected and Dalton had found the Bristol seat for him. Indeed Dalton went down with his wife Ruth to stay at Goodfellows for the weekend of 5-6 September 1931 and reported that he had followed hard on the footsteps of Morrison. But other than these two Stafford knew few of the National Executive and none of the Party activists or Trade Union leaders as yet. His closest colleagues had been Jowitt and Sankey – both now National Labour ministers – and apart from his father and Sidney Webb, both now older than Lansbury, his connections were limited. The Webbs both made strenuous efforts to get Stafford and Henderson together but soon felt that he was in danger of 'ignor[ing] the advice of wiser men like Henderson and prefer[ring] the acquiescence of inferior intelligences like George Lansbury'.[11] Parmoor, who had shared platforms with both men in support of the League of Nations, also made attempts at binding Stafford to Henderson, but in the personal struggle between the two Party leaders it was the High Anglican Lansbury, who wore his faith rather more passionately, that won Stafford's affection rather than the Methodist Henderson. This affection for Lansbury, whose influence over the ensuing political debate in the Party grew weaker as every year went by, meant that Stafford acquired a peculiarly independent role within the Party, effective but not influential, important but not senior, admired from afar rather than respected, 'substantial but not fashionable'. And the fact that he had entered politics at the age of forty-one, having effectively missed the General Strike and the economic crisis of 1929, meant that he had little grounding in the Labour movement or idea of how to ride the waves of political opinion as they ebbed and flowed within the Party.

In fact Stafford was not entirely sure that his having survived in the election was all that good a thing. For when he became Solicitor-General it was by no means certain that he intended to be anything other than a legal officer. He had intimated that he wanted to stand for Parliament, but the thought of playing a time-consuming part in the reconstruction of the Labour Party was far from his mind. Though John was now away at Oxford, the rest of his family was still young, he had a lucrative and demanding practice at the Bar and commitments to the Church – all of which left little time for such an overwhelming absorption in Parliamentary politics. When his old house-master, Furley, wrote to him after the election, he replied, 'I agree with you that from a purely personal point of view it would have been more comfortable to have been out of the House at present'[12] a point that Beatrice Webb recognised later in the year,

I am afraid you must be feeling rather lonely on that Opposition bench, though Lansbury seems to be doing well in his own way and creating a certain impression of directness and honesty as well as good humour. I am also afraid that you will find it rather difficult to combine a busy professional career with leadership in the House of Commons and that even solicitors may be frightened off by some aspects of your public work. However, that is the penalty of taking up the cause of the bottom dog – the upper dog will not love you.[13]

Certainly Stafford was still very busy in court with a string of major legal cases. Yet the very fact that he had survived the Parliamentary cull where others had not instilled in him a conviction that it was his duty to devote all his energy to politics. Moreover he caught Lansbury's infectious idealism, enthusiasm and sense of Christian vocation. 'I believe the world, and our people especially, need a purely religious message', Lansbury wrote to him after a stay at Goodfellows in 1932,

Yet there come days when my want of faith both in our actions and our courage and discretion worries me to distraction. I laugh and keep as stout a heart to the hills of difficulty as is possible, but often my heart fails and my soul seems to cry out within me whether I am spending my old age in the way that is best. At the start I felt God had given me a task to do, it may be he has, my doubt is whether I am good enough to do it or whether the way is right. You must not imagine there is self-righteousness in what I say now, but it is true my mind does not allow me to see more than a very few who see the impersonal side of life as I know I do, yet if we cannot within the framework of our party get together a body of men and women especially young ones who will see the cause of Socialism as a religion to be served as St Francis and Tolstoi [sic] served their faiths, all our work is hopeless.[14]

If Stafford's election success gave him a redoubled sense of duty, the Labour Party's defeat was greeted with great ambivalence by many within its higher councils. Indeed some on the left of the Party believed that out of the defeat would rise the phoenix of the renewed socialist Labour Party. George Cole, an active and thoughtful Oxford don on the left of the party argued, 'We have been beaten, no doubt, thoroughly, devastatingly, overwhelmingly beaten . . . But all the same the predominant feeling in my mind, and in the minds of most of those whom I meet, is not depression, but rather elation and escape'[15] and Beatrice Webb did not even want the Party to be in Government for another five years as she felt it needed more time to think.[16] Even allowing for the degree of denial that was apparent in many Labour politicians of the time, akin to a form of bereavement, there was a rampant belief that it had lost its way through the gradualist era of MacDonald and Snowden and that what was now required was precisely what Stafford had called a 'slap-up Socialistic policy'. The Christian Socialist historian R. H. Tawney put the case against MacDonald and Snowden most acutely: 'They threw themselves into the role of the Obsequious Apprentice, or Prudence Rewarded, as though bent on proving that, so far from being different from other governments, His Majesty's Labour Government could rival the most respectable of them in cautious conventionality.'[17] It was not just two years of Labour Government that had been judged in the election, but ten years of Labour politics, and a political coroner sitting on the corpse of the late Cabinet would probably give the verdict of 'neither murder nor misadventure, but pernicious anaemia producing general futility'.[18]

So the task ahead was to deliver a full-blooded, red-blooded, incarnadine Socialist programme upon which Labour could campaign and win a majority government. In Tawney's words Labour needed a 'creed . . . neither a system of transcendental doctrines nor a code of rigid formulae' but 'a common conception of the ends of political action' and it had to declare itself unequivocally for Socialism, for 'in 1918 the Labour Party finally declared itself to be a Socialist Party. It supposed, and supposes, that it thereby became one. It is mistaken. It recorded a wish, that is all; the wish has not been fulfilled. If it now disciplines itself for a decade, it may become a Socialist Party.'[19]

9

Loyal Grousers

Froom Tyler, writing over enthusiastically in 1942, maintained that 'within eighteen months of his entering Parliament Cripps was a fully fledged stormy petrel'[1] as if to suggest that his period of political extremism developed steadily in the run-up to the formation of the Socialist League in the autumn of 1932. Eric Estorick, however, reckoned that even by the time of the 1931 election Stafford was 'notorious for his revolutionary speeches'.[2] Both are wrong. For although as early as January 1932 Dalton was worried by what he saw as Stafford's 'rather wild'[3] views on money and foreign investments and he later maintained that in 1931 Stafford had 'an adolescent Marxist miasma',[4] he also acknowledged that at first he was only astonished 'that so intelligent a man could talk such nonsense' and that it was only over time that he believed that 'he seemed to have no political wits and to leave his first-class brains inside his brief-case. Gradually... my astonishment changed to vexation and impatience.'[5] Dalton's biographer Ben Pimlott also places Stafford from 1931 onwards making 'speeches of Jacobin fervour that delighted constituency activists and infuriated leaders less fortunate than himself who had lost their seats and wished to regain them'[6] – but neither Dalton nor Pimlott are entirely to be trusted.

For although Beatrice Webb guessed that Stafford was not allowed by the National Executive to speak at the Leicester

Labour Party Conference in 1932 because he was already out
of favour, he was at this stage only really articulating arguments that were common currency across a wide spectrum of
the Party. As he wrote to his father in September 1931,'there
has been a strong swing to the Left in the Party and a general
feeling of relief that we have shed a number of members who
were on the extreme Right.'[7] His 1931 Labour Party Conference speech was uncompromisingly anti-gradualist, but no
more so than many others.

> he argued these measures, necessary as they are in a
> period of transition, are mere hospital work and we are
> not here to do hospital work for the Juggernaut of Capital-
> ism. We are here to stop that Juggernaut from his progress
> through the world. The recent crisis has . . . brought home
> to all of us that the time has come when we can no longer
> try with one hand to patch up the old building of Capital-
> ism and with the other to build Socialism.[8]

This may have seemed heretical to Dalton, but to Lansbury
and Attlee it was common sense and if anything Stafford was
now presenting his mainstream Labour credentials. Beatrice
Webb even wrote to Parmoor a few days after the conference,
'On the whole I rejoice in the crisis [of the election] as I think
it will clear the issue and purify the Party. Sidney and I were
so glad at Stafford's attitude towards things and to see the ease
with which he gets on with the other leaders and with the rank
and file of the Labour Party.'[9]

Nonetheless, by May 1933 Stafford was certainly a liability
and was in open conflict with Walter Citrine of the TUC. So
when and how did he come to throw his lot in with the militant
left?

There had been an organised left wing of the Labour Party
long before the formation of the Socialist League. Originally
the ILP had been the individual members' section of the

Labour Party, in federation with the Trade Unions and the Socialist Societies like the Fabians and Co-operatives. When Henderson revised the structure of the Party in 1918 so as to allow individual membership and local constituency parties, the ILP automatically had to redefine itself and began to find a *raison d'être* as the activists' wing of the Party. In taking a more pacifist line in the First World War than the Labour Party it came into close contact with leading radical Liberals like Sir Charles Trevelyan and through the twenties this 'activism' acquired an increasingly radical edge to it, advocating a less diluted potion of Socialism and seeking through its continuing affiliation to the Labour Party to Superglue the Party to its newly adopted Socialist pretensions. With a large left-wing Scottish influx in the 1922 election and the publication of *Socialism in our Time* in 1926 the ILP stepped sharply to the left, in the process losing many of its founding members, and through people like Fenner Brockway, Nye Bevan and the Scots John Wheatley and Jimmy Maxton it set itself up in open critique of the Labour Government of 1929.

At the same time Oswald Mosley, who had entered Parliament in 1918 as a Conservative but had performed a series of political cartwheels to land himself in the Labour Party by 1924 and in the Labour Cabinet as Chancellor of the Duchy of Lancaster in 1929, had pursued a similarly anti-gradualist line. Thus in 1925 he published *Revolution by Reason* along with Allen Young and John Strachey, the nephew of the Labour MP and writer Lytton. This put the case for a much more dramatic State intervention in the fight against unemployment. In 1930 Mosley resigned from the Cabinet because a memorandum he produced which called for the public control of imports and banking and an increase in pensions as a means of boosting purchasing power was rather summarily rejected. By the end of 1931 he had founded the New Party, still accompanied by Strachey, although when Strachey, like Harold Nicolson, realised that the Fascist undertones in Mosley's beliefs were actually overtones he left and rejoined the Labour Party. The core of his message was simple and owed much to ILP thought and the 'under-consumptionist' theories of J. A. Hobson who had supported a living wage to be set at twice present average working-class incomes and the nationalisation of all basic industries. As Mosley put it later, 'If, by socialist planning, we can ensure a greater supply of goods corresponding to a greater supply of money, inflation and price rise cannot follow.'[10] Along with much of the ILP his central concern was to prevent unemployment by boosting consumption through increasing the purchasing power of the poor with a series of allowances, and he had a genuine hope at first that people as varied as Harold Macmillan, Robert Boothby, Oliver Stanley, Lloyd George, Max Beaverbrook and J. M. Keynes would join him, though in fact the only MPs that joined the New Party were Strachey, Bevan, and Oliver Baldwin, the Labour son of the Tory Prime Minister. By 1932, though, intervention and dictatorship were indistinguishable in Mosley's thought.

Meanwhile the ILP, still affiliated to the Labour Party, had kept a safe distance from Mosley, whom many mistrusted as a wealthy dilettante. Yet by 1930 many of the Labour Party leaders had resigned from the ILP which now had a heavy preponderance of Clydesiders and was led by Jimmy Maxton, and when Mosley resigned from the cabinet in May they backed his vote of censure. They now thought, acted and sat as a separate Parliamentary group, nicknamed 'The Mountain' after the extreme revolutionary groups in the French Revolution assemblies. At the Parliamentary Labour Party meeting after the formation of the National Government in 1931, when Henderson was elected the new Labour leader, the ILP very self-consciously refused to express their support for him and it was as a truculent band highly critical of the Labour leadership that they went into the 1931 election. The feeling being entirely mutual, Labour's National Executive refused to endorse nineteen of their candidates and they came out of the election with only five MPs.

The hard left was, then, fairly well defined by the time of the 1931 election. The soft left of the Party was in much less confident mood and elements of it succumbed immediately to the general anti-gradualist *cri de coeur*. There were, however, already steps afoot to build a more coherent and electorally sustainable Labour programme in the ranks of the soft left of the Party, and it was out of these that some of the most interesting ideas were to stem. Thus a series of informal meetings had been held throughout the 1920s at Easton Lodge, the delightful country home of the eccentric Countess of Warwick. She had been converted to Socialism as the result of a satirical piece in Robert Blatchford's *Clarion* which had criticised the sumptuousness of one of her Society parties, and had placed the house at the disposal of the Labour movement, thereby playing host to a gallimaufry of Christian Socialist, Labour Party, Trade Union and Co-operative meetings, conferences and conventions.

In 1930 and early 1931 these meetings gathered pace under George Cole's direction. Cole had been a fervent Guild Socialist and a founder of the National Guilds League earlier in the century and many of his Guild Socialist concerns remained with him. Community, democracy, fellowship and self-government in industry, these were the loadstones of Guild Socialism, and while by nature Cole was a constant pacifier always able to see the alternatives and full of internal tensions, he recognised that what Labour needed of his philosopher's politics was a practicable programme. So in 1930 Cole founded the Society for Socialist Inquiry and Propaganda (SSIP) and managed to persuade Ernest Bevin, the bullish creator and General Secretary of the Transport and General Workers' Union, to be its Chairman. Cole and his wife Margaret dragged into the SSIP nearly everyone they knew who might possibly be interested, including a large number of old Guild Socialist colleagues like Frank Horrabin and William Mellor. Inevitably the new Labour recruit joined up as well and managed to get a seat on the Executive.

When the 1931 election was over Cole's determination to provide a more solid intellectual basis for Labour's Socialism was given a far more urgent impetus and in April 1932 there was a further meeting at Easton Lodge with Lansbury, Cripps, Attlee, Dalton and Emmanuel ('Manny') Shinwell, and subsequent meetings were held right through to the autumn. Dalton, a more or less enthusiastic supporter of both the SSIP and the New Fabian Research Bureau (NFRB), soon spotted the dangers, however, 'A group got together by Cole meets at intervals to discuss policy', he recorded in October,

> It ends by producing a 'programme of Action' which it presents to the Executive. I refuse to sign this and have a difficult job in steering between non co-operation with Cole's group (which includes Lansbury, Cripps, Attlee, [Christopher] Addison, Shinwell, [William] Mellor, [Harold] Laski and a number of others) and the charge within the Executive Committee of indulging in 'parallel discussions' on policy.[11]

By this time the perpetual sniping between Labour and the ILP had broken out into open warfare. Before the election Henderson had initiated discussions with the ILP to put a stop to what he saw as the antics of a 'party within a party' and to bring the affiliated ILP MPs into line by enforcing new standing orders for the Parliamentary Party. After the election the remaining ILP-ers were split between those who believed that there was no choice but to sign the pledge so as to remain within the mainstream Party and those who were determined to disaffiliate from Labour. Even Bevan and Jennie Lee, later husband and wife, were split on the issue, with Bevan finally agreeing to accept the new standing orders and accusing

Jennie of being a 'pedant, bigot Salvation Army lassie'.[12] Maxton, however, who had played such a determining role in the twenties in asserting the left-wing independence of the ILP, took it one step further at its meeting in Bradford in July 1932, when he successfully urged it to disaffiliate and it agreed by 241 votes to 142.

The large minority of the ILP who opposed disaffiliation now set about either finding or creating a new home where they might enjoy both the independence of the old ILP and the political effectiveness of the Labour Party. The leader of this 'affiliationist' group was Frank Wise who became the first Chairman of the National ILP Affiliation Committee and attacked the naïveté of those who had forced the disaffiliation as people who 'honestly believe that they can encourage Socialism . . . more effectively if untrammelled by associations with anybody who has ever held responsible office'. He was equally adamant, though, that 'there will still remain the need within the Labour Party of an organised body of Socialist Opinion whose purpose is to frame and propagand the principles and practical application of Socialism, a body which would continue to the work for which the ILP was founded'[13] and it was in the search for such a body that he had already initiated discussions with Cole and the SSIP before the formation of the Affiliation Committee – discussions which bore fruit immediately prior to the Leicester Labour Party conference in 1932 with the formation of the Socialist League.

It was the mixed provenance of the Socialist League that gave it its greatest and eventually insuperable problems. For the SSIP, or 'Zip' as it was known, had an unwritten but almost explicit commitment not to set up an alternative organisation or policy platform to that of the Labour Party. It was solely there to provide research and ideas and Bevin as its Chairman would not have supported it if things had been any other way. 'We are not out to establish a new Party', he told one of the early meetings. The idea was to be a set of 'loyal grousers' critical more of the Government than of Labour and putting forward policy ideas in a constructive and well argued way. Originally the SSIP hoped that on the disaffiliation of the ILP they might inherit all the affiliationists as members of their own organisation, and Cole replied to Wise's overtures in this vein. But Wise decided that the tiny SSIP was not going to provide enough of a future for the much larger number of ex-ILP members and formed the National ILP Affiliation Committee. At this point the SSIP suddenly realised that far from being the natural new home for the affiliationists, the SSIP actually had a direct competitor. The almost inevitable result was the amalgamation of the two bodies.

At the time Cole, who had just been diagnosed for diabetes and was not in fine health, wrote to several of those involved in SSIP, including Attlee and Cripps, explaining the agreement that had been reached and adding in a postscript to Stafford, in acknowledgment of his expressed worries, 'So far I am sending you an exact replica of a letter which I am sending to several other people, but I know you have been specially concerned about the possibility of Wise and his friends wanting to make the Socialist League the nucleus for a political party with the possible danger of a row with the Labour Party at a later stage.'[14]

If Cripps was worried, Bevin was furious, as he was not elected to chair the new organisation, a fact that Cole deeply regretted, not only because Bevin's involvement might have ensured the Socialist League's continuing in the mainstream, but also because there was a real danger that without Trade Union support it would become the toy of the middle class Labour intelligentsia. Bevin as the premier Trade Union leader of the day would have guaranteed a working class ballast, so Cole, for whom the involvement of Bevin in the SSIP and Attlee in the NFRB had been a *sine qua non*, actually voted against the merger. His attempts to get Bevin to sit on the Executive were equally unsuccessful as Bevin took umbrage and maintained that 'I do not believe the Socialist League will change very much from the old ILP attitude, whoever is in the Executive'.[15] In fact Bevin's assistant at the TGWU, Harold Clay, did take part in the Executive, but the predominant mood of the League was very much that of the professional middle classes. As Ben Pimlott has pointed out, out of the twenty-three people who served on its National Council there were two Etonians, two Wykehamists and a Harrovian, nine had been to Oxford or Cambridge and four to London University. Only two left formal education at elementary school level. The class differences were apparent, especially to Bevin, who, when Sir Charles Trevelyan, a landed ex-Liberal baronet and Lord Lieutenant for Northumberland, suggested that British workers should strike as a means of checking the Government, retorted: 'You want a strike? OK, I am to call out 600,000 dockers; will you call out the Lord Lieutenants?'[16]

Though the SSIP felt they had not got a good deal out of the merger, in fact they gained a disproportionately large number of seats on the National Council at the first, lively, meeting in Leicester on 2 October. Mellor, Horrabin, G. R. Mitchison, Cole and Arthur Pugh joined Cripps in transferring from the SSIP Executive to the Socialist League's National Council, while the affiliationists took only Wise, Noel Brailsford, Wynne Davies and David Kirkwood with them. In addition three agreed names were added, Dr Alfred Salter, the Christian Socialist ILP Bermondsey doctor, Frederick William Pethick-Lawrence, a member of the NFRB and long-time pacifist and suffragist, and Trevelyan.

If the intention was to avoid the factionalism and opposi-tionalism of the ILP – and many of the National Council regularly averred that it was – the fact was that it did not take long for the old ghosts of ILP dissent to take hold of the League. Frank Horrabin said at the outset that the League should be 'a centre of socialist research and missionary activity, but activity in and through the Labour Party and with nothing whatsoever of the separate political machine about it'[17] yet only two years later the League was arguing that 'We have passed out of the realm of programme making into the realm of action.'[18]

So Bevin was right. The whole drive behind the ILP element of the Socialist League was to maintain a lacuna of independence within the Labour Party – and steadily independence became dissent. Indeed one suspects that the original avowals of the Socialist League leaders that this was not to be another Party within a Party were motivated more by a sense that the Labour Party was now going their way. To their mind the election had proved conclusively that gradualism was a dead philosophy. Labour would now steam ahead towards a clear Socialist programme, putting crimson water between her and the National Government. Indeed the first conference went their way when the National Executive's opposition to the nationalisation of the joint stock banks as well as the Bank of England was overturned and Harold Laski wrote to Cole, 'I think you in particular, and SSIP in general, deserve warm congratulations for Leicester. Clearly for the first time you have got socialism moving in the country.'[19]

Nonetheless, the aims of the League were ambiguous from the very beginning, and though its proclaimed intention was to provide research, education and informed propaganda yet it also expressed a desire for 'the achievement of the Socialist Commonwealth in this country, within a worldwide system of Socialism', believing that 'this Socialist Commonwealth can only be established by a working-class that is Socialist'. This might have seemed uncontentious to Cripps but it was a red rag to Transport House and even on the National Council there were those who felt that the nice distinction between trying to improve the Party's official programme (which was acceptable) and putting up an alternative programme (which was not) was no longer tenable. Cole was already feeling uncomfortable by the end of 1932, stating that 'a number of us had become convinced that [the League] was heading for a disaster very like that which had befallen the ILP, by putting forward a programme of its own in opposition to that of the Labour Party, instead of trying to work for improving the official Labour programme.'[20]

Part of the difficulty lay in the fact that the whole political premise of the League was that Labour needed a comprehensive and comprehensively Socialist programme if it were to win. That meant that the task of the League was not just to delineate the contours of that comprehensive programme, but to write it and then seek to get it adopted by Labour. That required two elements, each of which looked remarkably like setting up a Party within a Party. First was a network of people, 'who can trust one another, and are trusted by the rank and file, people who have made it their business to see what a socialist government would require of their district, and to find out how it could be done. This is what the Socialist League is setting out to do – to create advance guards of the revolution, and to create them *now*. For when the revolution comes it will be too late.'[21] And second it had to bring home to the Labour Movement 'the necessity for a strong and determined drive towards a definite and clearly understood programme of real Socialism and to help in the formulation of such a programme'.[22]

By the end of 1933 the Socialist League had already set foot on its primrose path to ruin. But it started the year well with a well-publicised series of lectures, published under a title which betrayed the troubled nature of the whole enterprise, *Problems of a Socialist Government*. All the issues that had concerned the left since the twenties were covered. Wise wrote on 'The Control of Finance and the Financiers'; Horrabin on 'The Break with Imperialism'; Mellor on 'The Claim of the Unemployed'; Trevelyan on 'The Challenge to Capitalism'; and Attlee on 'Local Government and Socialism'.

The pithiest of the lectures, though, was Stafford's: 'Can Socialism come by constitutional methods?' And it is in this lecture that the full glory of his relatively new-found slap-up Socialism is to be seen. The argument is extremely bald.

Unless during the first 5 years [of a majority Labour Government] so great a degree of change has been accomplished as to deprive Capitalism of its power, it is unlikely that a Socialist Party will be able to maintain its position of control without adopting some exceptional means such as the prolongation of the life of Parliament for a further term without an election.[23]

He drew a series of nightmare scenarios: a Capitalist Government refusing to give up power on the election of a majority socialist government, leading to an Emergency Powers Bill; the refusal to co-operate by the House of Lords leading to the creation of a raft of Socialist Peers; and finally the non co-operation of the Crown, leading to the resignation of the Socialist Government and a subsequent 'uprising'. He even expected that the Crown might seize power with the backing of the armed forces. 'If the Socialist Government came to the conclusion that there was any real danger of such a step being taken, it would probably be better and more conducive to the general peace and welfare of the country for the Socialist Government to make itself temporarily into a dictatorship until the matter could again be put to the test at the polls.'[24] Though the later parts of the lecture are more technical, dealing with the need for procedural changes in the Commons, much of the lecture was grandiloquent, dangerous nonsense and though he stated that 'it is, I believe, possible to make the change by constitutional means',[25] the Conservative press had a field day with him for preaching revolutionary dictatorship.

It was not the only occasion on which he argued this constitutional case. Again and again, in meetings the length and breadth of the country he stated baldly and unequivocally that a Labour Government with a Socialist programme would have enormous problems in implementing its policies without drastic constitutional action. He was adamant that Labour 'must not accept office as a Minority Party' for 'When the capitalists realised that the very gradual move towards Socialism was carrying the country within measurable distance of legislation which might bring fundamental changes, they rapidly and decisively brought the Labour Government to an end.'[26] Nor was he alone. Wise wrote an equally intemperate piece for the *New Clarion* issue of 13 May stating that 'Free Speech, a so-called Free Press, are no more part of the eternal verities than is Free Trade', thereby inciting both Bevin, who was Chairman of the *New Clarion* Board, and the General Secretary of the TUC, Walter Citrine, who sent off a stinging letter accusing the League of preaching dictatorship. Stafford replied in robust terms, effectively telling him that it was not up to the General Secretary of the TUC to determine Labour Party policy – that was for Party Conference. Citrine retorted that much of what the League was advocating, especially its constitutional plans, would prove 'a weapon in the hands of Labour's enemies which they are only too willing to use'[27] – a point that was borne out when Inskip, now the National Government's Attorney-General, attacked Stafford for arguing that 'the day of evolutionary Socialism was past and . . . the day of revolution, according to the manner of the Russian revolution, [is] now the political creed of the party which with one or two others he led'.[28] It is little wonder that many Tories believed that every time Stafford opened his mouth he won them 100,000 votes, nor that 'his speeches [were] thought by many to be curiously "irresponsible"'[29] and that he was banned from assisting at the Cambridge by-election in 1934 despite being elected to the National Executive at Whitsun.

The row with Citrine stiffened the League's Socialist sinews and summoned up its blood just as it went into its Whitsun

1933 Conference. Already its membership had changed. Many of its original SSIP members had resigned and several of its branches closed. Wise had died and Cripps taken his place as Chair while Bevan, who had originally been suspicious of the League, joined, in his biographer's words, because Cripps was 'in his estimate a cleaner and more wholesome influence in the Labour leadership than any of his competitors who had so readily accepted MacDonaldism'.[30] Though it had not started as such it was becoming a Cripps movement, with hefty dollops of Cripps money keeping it afloat. All this went to Stafford's head, and at the conference he called for major changes in the way the League worked. From now on its task would not just be research. It explicitly resolved to put together its own programme with a list of political demands: abolition of the House of Lords, an Emergency Powers Act, nationalisation of the Bank of England and the joint stock banks. One member, J. T. Murphy, who had only just joined the League from the Communist Party, felt that the conference 'succeeded in making clear to itself and others that the Socialist League is not merely the rump of the old ILP carrying on, but the organisation of revolutionary socialists who are an integral part of the Labour movement for the purpose of winning it completely for revolutionary socialism'.[31] As Laski put, 'No compromise! The day for half-measures has passed.'[32]

So, by mid-1933 Stafford was well on the way to revolutionary status, fronting up an organisation that was in increasing danger of becoming a Party. The moment that stood out in many of Stafford's opponents' eyes as the apotheosis of his political folly, though, came the following January when in mentioning Buckingham Palace directly in a speech on 6 January he tickled the not-so-funny bone of the body politick. 'When the Labour Party comes into power' he declared,

they must act rapidly and it will be necessary to deal with

the House of Lords and the influence of the City of London. There is no doubt that we shall have to overcome opposition from Buckingham Palace and other places as well. It is absolutely essential that it should be made perfectly clear to the people exactly what it is we ask for the power to do. There must not be time to allow the forces outside to gather and to exercise their influence upon the legislature before the key points of Capitalism have been transferred to the control of the State. I look upon these two points myself as being land and finance. If other people become revolutionary then the Socialist Government, like any other Government, must take steps to stamp out the Revolution. The Socialist Government must not be mealy-mouthed about saying what they mean.[33]

The speech attracted enormous attention. The newspapers pounced on Stafford and he was forced to make a sort of retraction, arguing that he had not been referring to the King himself, but to those around him, a suggestion which did not make it any better. Anthony Eden was at Sandringham to receive his seals of office as Lord Privy Seal from George V when the news of Stafford's attack broke. 'The King was not unnaturally indignant, deeming that [his] excuse only made it worse. I was summoned for an audience on Sunday after church: "What does he mean by saying that Buckingham Palace is not me? Who else is there I should like to know? Does he mean the footmen?"'[34]

Within the Party there was a fierce reaction too and whilst Lansbury was ill in hospital Stafford was summoned to the National Executive a fortnight later to explain himself. Dalton lost his temper and demanded that 'this stream of oratorical ineptitudes should now cease, or some of us who are very reluctant to enter on public controversy with other members of the Party, will come to the limits of our tolerance' and got the backing of George Dallas, Lees-Smith and Walter Citrine.

Laski and Attlee still backed Cripps, though, and Walkden, Cripps's next-door MP in Bristol, vacillated. Stafford's excuses, at least as reported by Dalton, do sound feeble.

> Cripps seems quite unable to see the argument that he is damaging the Party electorally. It is all "misreporting" or picking sentences out of their context. He has become very vain and seems to think that only he and his cronies know what socialism is, or how it should be preached . . . It is the number of these gaffes which is so appalling. Our candidates are being stabbed in the back and pushed on to the defensive . . . Many of the speeches are simply incompetent presentation of a good case. But remarks on general Strike are most improper for a member of the professional classes . . . Attlee says I am like a pedagogue addressing a pupil. I wish the pupil were a bit brighter.[35]

Stafford did not accept that he was harming Labour in the run-up to the election. His thesis was that if Labour remained as weak-hearted as it had proved itself in Government then it would neither win power nor deserve to win power. Stating the case for Socialism at its most full-blooded would attract support for Labour, not alienate it. As for Dalton's throwaway comment that his speeches were the 'incompetent presentation of a good case', this goes some way to explaining why Attlee and others were still prepared to excuse Cripps. The fact is, however, that from every perspective Stafford's case was flawed. Tactically he was wrong: a General Strike, even if one could be delivered, would not have dented the National Government. Politically he was wrong: suggesting that a period of dictatorship would be necessary to achieve Socialism was hardly a way to win an election. And strategically he was wrong: insinuating that a Labour Government would be opposed by both the City and the Crown was never going to encourage popular confidence.

On all these grounds Stafford was wrong, but either out of pigheadedness or vanity he could not see it. Dalton, with the kind of inverse snobbery that only the son of a Canon of Windsor could muster, attacked him for being a 'member of the professional classes'. Michael Foot's complaint was more subtle, alleging that 'he knew little of the Labour movement, less of its history and amid all his other preoccupations had little time or inclination to repair the deficiency by a reading of Socialist literature. His Marxist slogans were undigested; he declared the class war without ever having studied the contours of the battlefield.'[36] It is true that Stafford maintained that he had never read Marx and several visitors to Good-fellows commented that he had remarkably few books for such an intelligent man, yet this did not explain Stafford's outlandish views. For the truth was that the period from the election defeat in 1931 to the Whitsun conference of the Socialist League in 1933 saw Stafford adopt an ideology on the hoof. He had entered Parliament as a legal officer and now, with a busy practice at the Bar and time-consuming duties in the Commons, there was little time in which to frame a more subtle and mature political programme. He was a proud man, well established in an old profession, and when he suddenly had the political limelight cast upon him it was a mixture of pride and duty that moved him to take the high road to political prominence. He was no tactician, he could not distinguish a good point from a bad one in an argument, yet he was ruthless in getting to the kernel of an issue and reiterating it, pursuing it to its logical conclusion and never giving way. As his old Wykehamist legal colleague D. N. Pritt put it, 'He was an individualist; he would think of some scheme, often a good one, would judge it to be very good indeed, and would then launch it without giving himself time to reflect, and with the very minimum of consultation with either his friends or other people or organisations.'[37]

Undoubtedly he was brilliant. That was never the issue.

Time after time his colleagues would say that he could argue them to the point where they knew their position was patently untenable. If anything, that was the problem, for as Michael Foot pointed out, his 'prodigious brain-power, energy and delight in hard work, his stamp of mastery and confidence, made him within a matter of months the most magnetic figure in the Party'.[38] By very dint of his background and evident ability he had become the focus for the 'anti-gradualist' wing of the Party and for all his logical exactitude he was forever embroiled in folly . For the right-wing press he was a dream come true. The idea of the wealthy barrister from one of Britain's best public schools – 'the Red Squire of the moated grange' – mounting the barricades and seeking to topple the very Establishment that had brought him into the world was one redolent of romantic imagery. His anti-gradualism was the accepted wisdom of the vast majority of the Party and indeed won the day at the Leicester Labour Party Conference in 1932, but when it came from his lips it somehow acquired a greater force, a more romantic penumbra. In this the Socialist League was only relevant in so far as it gave Stafford a platform and it brought him into association with other anti-gradualists.

Stafford's position had the great benefit of simplicity. George Bernard Shaw summed it up:

> he has no faith in the routine of Parliament, and foresees either a complete rupture or a period of prorogued parliaments, with the Cabinet governing as a virtual 'dictatorship of the proletariat' by means of Orders in Council, with special tribunals and commissions to supersede recalcitrant courts and departments of the Civil Service.[39]

It was only in his forensically circular mind that such a position could have been construed as an attractive electoral position. It was little wonder that, as Isobel wrote to Lansbury,

'The press come now wherever Stafford goes and sit below like vultures not caring for the substance of anything he says but waiting for any word that is spoken and can be misused, to fall into their mouths.[40]

10

Prophesying War

Discipline is an easier virtue for individuals, even those who enjoy making history happen, than for political Parties who have suffered enormous election defeats and in the run-up to the 1935 General Election the particular non-conforming heritage of British Socialism made it tough for Labour to find within its soul the strength of discipline that it required to put forward a united campaign. Intemperate and disorderly inter-necine rows dominated the left throughout these years and it is one of the ironies, or hypocrisies, of Stafford's career that though his fiscal grip on post-war Britain relied on an appeal to loyalty and discipline, it was not a philosophy he managed to live out in what can only be thought of as the pubescent years of his political life. The excuse, for Labour and for Stafford, was simple: events, dear boy.

For in January 1933 Adolf Hitler became the Chancellor of Germany. Within eighteen months he and his Italian counter-part Benito Mussolini had completely altered Europe's poli-tical map if not yet its geographical one and in Britain the spectre of European Fascism summarily swung the left's atten-tion away from the broad issue of Labour's programme to the very condensed and emotive one of how to prevent another European war, for as Sir Charles Trevelyan wrote for the Socialist League in 1933 'for the first time since the Great War there is a vivid realisation throughout the country that there may be another war before we are many years older,'[1] he was aware that the issue he was broaching was one that would tax the unity of the Labour movement.

Up until now Labour's foreign policy had been stable and straightforward. Having opposed the vengeful tone of the Versailles treaty reparations she had backed the League of Nations since its inception as the best hope of maintaining world peace. Trevelyan felt, however, that this policy of collective security under the umbrella of the League of Nations could no longer remain Labour's position. Indeed 'The condition has arisen in which all real reliance on the League of Nations as a buttress in emergency against war has ceased,'[2] and the time had come for Labour to push for closer cooperation not only with the USA, but with the USSR as well, neither of whom were members of the League (although Russia joined in 1934). It was not just Trevelyan who saw things in apocalyptic terms. In March 1933, as Hitler was taking full control of Germany, Stafford too was arguing that the League of Nations was 'rivet[ing] Capitalism upon the neck of a protesting world'[3] and demanding a plan 'by which we can prevent the war hysteria sweeping away the common-sense of the people. In my own view, this could only be achieved by a lightning general strike, well prepared and rapidly put into operation.'[4]

If there was ever an instance of a political devil and the deep blue sea, this was it. On the one hand the Socialist League stood resolutely for as vigorous an opposition to Fascism as possible. Indeed it was almost obsessive in its pursuit of Fascism, detecting it in the least likely of sources. Stafford even attacked Lloyd George for 'suggesting an Economic Communism which will take a very large part of the administrative and some part of the legislative responsibility from Parliament – a communism that has a strange and unhappy resemblance to the Corporations of Italy and the organisations of Hitler',[5] and the League fought Morrison over his 'public boards' for transport and electricity because they would be unelected and unaccountable bureaucracies reeking of the Corporate State. 'The workers', declared Stafford, 'must not be led into the acceptance of the Corporate State because it is dressed up in the vague semi-socialist phraseology of planning and reorganisation.'[6]

Most importantly, though, Stafford accused the National Government of implicit Fascist intent because of its use of the 1921 Emergency Powers Act which had effectively outlawed public sector strikes and because it pushed through an increasing amount of legislation by the back door route of ministerial instruments and regulations rather than Parliamentary legislation. 'We have not', Stafford argued, 'emerged as yet into the full flower of Fascism or anything like it, nor have we lost our democratic rights. There can, nevertheless, be no doubt that we have moved definitely along the path towards the Corporate State.'[7] Planning, if it was not Socialist, was Fascist, whilst Socialist planning would lead to the overthrow of Capitalism and an industrial democracy with workers' control. To prevent Fascism at home Britain needed a radical Socialist Government and to prevent Fascism abroad an alliance with other Socialist Governments. As Stafford contested,

It is the urgent desire for active change that is forcing the younger electors into Movements like the Fascist Movement, not because they believe in its policy but because they are caught by the cheap-jack cry for action-at-all-cost. The way to counter such movements is not to seek to restrain the allegiance of youth, but to seek to divert it into the useful channel of socialist change. This will only be accomplished if the younger generation can feel assured that the Party they were asked to support is not merely talking of some vague utopia in the far-distant future but is prepared to take action, and quick action, to accomplish that change.[8]

119

And the fight against Fascism was all the more important because there were clearly some Tories who either supported Fascism or else were quite happy to see it flourish in Europe as a defence against Communism. So on the one side stood the Scylla of European Fascism.

On the other soared the Charybdis of the 'capitalist' National Government with whom the Socialist League refused on any count to co-operate. Because the National Government could only prosecute a war in the interests of Capitalism and Imperialism and because the League of Nations was no more than a group of National Governments with similarly imperialist and anti-Communist aims, the Socialist League was determined that Labour should not give the Government its support for possible League of Nations sanctions which might lead to an anti-Soviet alliance. The only weapon that the Socialist League could countenance was the industrial weapon of a General Strike. Even if the National Government should decide to change course and back collective security, the League would remain suspicious for the very reason that it was the Capitalism of the Government rather than any declared policy that made it an impossible ally.

Inevitably this drew the League into deeper and deeper conflict with the Labour Party whose official policy was still collective security, but the first major skirmish came in 1934 when the National Executive published a statement on 'Democracy and Dictatorship' in January. At its Whitsun Conference the League overwhelmingly endorsed its own document, *Forward to Socialism,* which berated the Party for supporting the National Government's foreign policy, rejected the idea of collective security and backed calls for a General Strike. During the summer the National Executive then published its own programme, *For Socialism and Peace* and when it came before Labour Party Conference Mellor, in the name of the Socialist League and in the teeth of the National Executive, bravely and foolhardily moved seventy-five amendments, which were summarily reduced to twelve by the Standing Orders committee. One of these, with as cavalier an attitude to grammar as to politics, called for the Party to 'act with the speed called for by the situation at home and abroad in a decisive advance within five years towards a Socialist Britain'.[9] Dalton wiped the floor with it for its nonsensical generality and it was lost by 2,146,000 to 206,000, the best vote the Socialist League could muster all week.

The first major foreign policy split in Labour ranks was then not over war itself so much as the prospect of war. For the League of Nations to play any significant role it had to be able to enforce its views. This required some legitimate form of sanction – either an economic boycott or military force. The pacifists in the Labour movement had rejected sanctions of any kind when Japan invaded the Chinese province of Manchuria in September 1931 because they might lead to further Japanese aggression and eventual war. This curiously allied the left of the Party with the National Government, whose response was to try and negotiate a peace, partly because China's hold over Manchuria had been tenuous at best and partly to protect British interests in the Far East. A report to the League of Nations, prepared in 1932 and largely brokered by Britain, condemned Japanese aggression but did not actually call for sanctions, effectively calling it a moral no-score draw between the two nations. Japan left the League but within a few months China had effectively ceded Manchuria to them through the Tangku truce of May 1933. The Manchurian issue thus brought the pacifists and the Tory pragmatists together while the official Party line of collective security through the League was rather battered since the League had patently failed to stop the aggressor nation.

Stafford had his own peculiar position. It was not war that was the issue, but war waged by Imperialist Governments. If, and only if, the governments of the League countries were

Socialist, could a real war against Fascism be conjectured. He told the 1935 Whitsun Conference of the Socialist League, 'We ... declare ourselves opposed to any and every encouragement of war or arming by a capitalist government'[10] – with the emphasis heavily on the capitalist government Because a Capitalist war would be immoral 'The keynote of our policy for a Socialist Government is the necessity for such a Government to build its security upon the foundation of an economic and political alliance with the USSR and other Socialist States.'[11] So whilst the National Government remained there should be a '*mass resistance to war* by the workers of this country'[12] including refusing to build weapons and mounting a General Strike.

His view, however, was not shared by all the Socialist League. Indeed J. T. Murphy, the League's secretary, moved a resolution at the Bristol annual conference of the League to back collective security and an alliance of Britain, France and Soviet Russia; and some of Stafford's close associates backed economic but not military sanctions. Many still believed in the League of Nations and Stafford had to explain to his father in September 1935:

> I quite realise that the smaller Nations at Geneva have a great desire for protection, but it has become more and more obvious every year that the League is being run by France and England for purely imperialist reasons, and I think the people must be made to face up to this or else we shall be led under the banner of the League to another imperialist war.[13]

The League of Nations Union itself was not silent in the meantime and organised one of the most effective political campaigns Britain had ever seen, with a massive nationwide door-to-door referendum. This was launched in 1934, with the results of the answers to the five questions to be published in June 1935. The questions in many ways framed the political debate:

1. Should Britain remain in the League? 2. Should there be all-round reduction of armaments? 3. Should air warfare be abolished? 4. Should the manufacture and sale of armaments for private profit be prohibited? 5. Should an aggressor nation be stopped by a) economic and non-military measures and b) if necessary, by military measures?'

The response was remarkable, with more than 11.5 million households replying. The result gave resounding backing for the basic idea of collective security. More than 10 million answered yes to all of the first four questions, and it was only on the final question of whether military measures should be considered that there was any sizeable minority view, with 6.8 million in favour of force, 2 million abstaining and 2.4 million against.

The Socialist League campaigned against this 'Peace Ballot' just as vigorously as it opposed collective security, but when Italy threatened to invade Abyssinia soon after the announcement of the ballot results, the stakes were upped for both the Labour Party and the National Government. Baldwin, who had recently taken over as Prime Minister from MacDonald, seized the opportunity of stealing Labour's clothes in the wake of the Peace Ballot and agreed to back sanctions against Italy, deftly manoeuvring himself on to the popular ground that Labour had been occupying for several years just as the Socialist League was trying to dislodge it. The Foreign Secretary, Sir Samuel Hoare, announced Britain's support for sanctions at Geneva on 11 September and the Labour National Executive rapidly followed suit, congratulating Baldwin on finally adopting Labour's policy. In fact many of the Government's own supporters were furious with him. The service

chiefs all opposed antagonising Italy, and Churchill deliberately stayed out of the country all autumn so as to avoid
pronouncing on the issue whilst the arch-imperialist Leo
Amery actually backed the Italians.

Meanwhile Lansbury was, out of pacifist conviction, still
wholly opposed to any form of sanctions, and Stafford was
angered by the National Executive meeting at which Lansbury
was bullied by Walter Citrine into toeing the Party line at an
upcoming TUC Annual meeting, and when it passed a resolution supporting Italian sanctions by 3 million votes to 177,000,
he took the opportunity to resign from the Executive after less
than a year. He explained his decision to his father, 'I thought
the matter of resignation over very carefully and I was quite
convinced at the present moment, with so much uncertainty
and differences of view in the Party, it was wiser to get out of
the Executive in order to show people where I stood.'[14]

The final showdown over the League of Nations came a
couple of weeks later at the Party Conference in Brighton.
Conference was completely overshadowed by the spectre of
Italy's invasion of Abyssinia, which began on its second day,
3 October. Two days later the resolution calling for sanctions
against Italy and asking the Government to use 'all necessary
measures provided by the Covenant' was put, with Dalton
speaking first for the National Executive in support of the
motion.

Cripps was the next to speak and he tore into the League
of Nations describing it as no more than 'the International
Burglars' Union', 'the Haves against the Have-Nots'. He repeated his old refrain that any war entered into by a Capitalist
government must be a Capitalist war and that since Capitalism
must be diametrically opposed to Socialism Labour must
be opposed to any policy that would lead inexorably to a
Capitalist war. 'Had we a workers' Government in this
country, as they have in Russia, the whole situation would be
completely different. Then, with a Socialist Government there

would be no risk of imperialist and capitalist aims being pursued, as to-day it is certain they are being, and will be, pursued.'[15] The only sanctions he would support were working-class sanctions.

Attlee, who followed Cripps, tentatively put the case for sanctions, the only one of the three parliamentary leaders to support the National Executive line. 'We are against the use of force for imperialist and capitalist ends, but we are in favour of the proper use of force for ensuring the rule of law . . . Non resistance is not a political attitude, it is a personal attitude. I do not believe it is a possible policy for people with responsibility.'[16]

Attlee was followed by Lansbury, who was given a great ovation, whether out of genuine respect for the saintly leader or out of guilt that they were about to vote overwhelmingly against him. His speech was different from Cripps's, more personal and more directly concerned with the question of whether war was ever justifiable. It was Bevin's turn then to do the demolition job on Lansbury's position – and on Lansbury. 'I hope this conference will not be influenced by either sentiment or personal attachment' he said, before looking over directly to Lansbury and declaring, 'It is placing the Executive and the Labour Movement in an absolutely wrong position to be taking your conscience round from body to body asking to be told what to do with it.' The slaughter complete Bevin later was unrepentant. As he later said, 'Lansbury has been going around in saints' clothes for years waiting for martyrdom. I set fire to the faggots.'[17]

He did not stop at Lansbury though. Indeed he was more determined to dent Cripps who was being talked of in some quarters as a possible successor to Lansbury. 'Transport House was set on steamrolling Stafford and his group and put up Dalton to do it with the help of trade union officials' wrote Beatrice Webb.[18] 'People have been on this platform talking about the destruction of capitalism,' Bevin sniped in direct reference to Stafford, 'The middle classes are not doing too badly as a whole under capitalism and Fascism. Lawyers and members of other professions have not done too badly.'[19] He went on to deal with part of the argument but returned to Cripps, accusing him of hypocrisy in his resignation from the National Executive since he had deliberately stayed away from its meetings. 'And so vital was it to you, that Cripps never turned up. If I feel bitter, please understand it. I cannot play with my members like this.'[20] Finally Bevin accused Cripps of trying to split the Party, 'And who am I to let my personality protrude as compared with this great Movement? Who is any man on this platform? I do sincerely ask this Conference to appreciate the Trade Unionist's position. Sir Stafford Cripps said there would be no split. He has done his best.'[21]

Bevin spoke with conviction, but then he could afford to, with more than half a million votes in his pocket and the certain knowledge that while the heart strings of Conference could be played upon by the soft tunes of Lansbury and of Cripps, the political argument was definitely with the National Executive. In the event the National Executive's victory was even more overwhelming than the year before – 2,168,000 to 102,000 – and it was generally applauded in the national press. Yet the issue was not yet properly resolved. Those who supported collective security could still say that since it would work there was no need for Britain to rearm, while many of those who feared collective security would lead to war refused to support it for that very reason.

It was the most vitriolic of Party Conferences and could hardly have been the Party mangers' ideal launching pad for the campaign which was promptly started when Baldwin, spotting the Labour disarray, called the election for 14 November. Baldwin took the result, another landslide for the National Government and for the Conservatives within it, as a mandate for rearmament and set about another attempt, via Hoare and the French Prime Minister Laval, to buy off

Mussolini whereby the emperor of Abyssinia would retain his mountain kingdom while Italy took the more fertile plains. When this offer, known as the Hoare-Laval plan, became public the outcry from Bishops, Conservative politicians and the Socialist League alike was such that Baldwin had to disown his Foreign Secretary, who resigned and was replaced by Eden, while Mussolini stormed into the rest of Abyssinia and the Emperor Haile Selassie went into exile in rural England.

In some ways this simply proved Stafford right. Immediately prior to the Conference he and his son John had visited the Webbs and Beatrice commented in her diary on his air of anger and frustration:

> Stafford has grown in stature and charm as a political leader, but he is in a somewhat embittered and rebellious state of mind; thinks that the outcome of the present demoralised state of the labour movement will lead to a Fascist government in Great Britain and probably in the USA and France – in Great Britain of a well-bred type. Stafford is, in fact, more pessimistic than we are.[22]

This anger was by now the most potent element of Stafford's political armoury and he gave off a passion that erased the dry air of rationality that had once characterised his work at the bar. Moreover, when Bevin's assault on Lansbury made his position as leader untenable and he resigned, to be replaced, as a temporary measure up to the election, by Attlee, Stafford was cut off from his most reliable mooring in the Labour movement. Far from calming Stafford, this combined sense of impotence, isolation and political despair pushed him further to the passionate left whilst his belief that 'he himself is the only leader who raised enthusiasm among the rank and file and can attract crowded meetings'[23] hardened his resolve

11

Uniting the Left

The 1935 Labour Party Conference hardly dented Stafford's personal confidence. Indeed there is some evidence that the very way in which he had been dealt with by Bevin made it more likely that he would react by striding out further. For Stafford's whole education as an Edwardian gentleman had valued above all the principles of stoicism, of fortitude in adversity, of personal reticence mixed with professional confidence. The slings and arrows were part of the necessary strengthening and character building.

Nevertheless, October and November 1935 were not good months for him. For not only did the Socialist League lose at Conference, but when the election was called many of those who were by now his convinced enemies in the Party were elected back into the House and he was voted off the Parliamentary Labour Party's Executive (the then Shadow Cabinet), to be replaced by Clynes, Dalton and Morrison.

In retrospect it seems that even if the logic of Stafford's position had not determined that he would now proceed to form new alliances, the very fact that he was effectively out in the cold meant that he would personally need to seek new friends. Yet for all the accusations of aloofness that have subsequently been levelled against him, Stafford was far from friendless at this point. Indeed the next four years saw his friendships and his political alliances determine the whole agenda and future of the British left. Some of those friendships, such as with Pritt, were already long-established. Others, such as with Aneurin Bevan, would remain alliances well into the 1945 Labour Government. But two particular relationships were the specific fruit of the hothouse climate of the middle thirties. William Mellor and Harry Pollitt, sometimes together, more often in competition with each other, became potent influences upon the man who by now was the single most prominent leader of the Labour left.

Although there were other leaders of the Communist Party – Palme Dutt, Shapurji Saklatva and Willie Gallacher – it was Harry Pollitt who truly represented the soul of the British Communist Party. A proud working-class man and one-time boilermaker, he joined the ILP in 1909 and moved to the British Socialist Party two years later. An opponent of the First World War he was secretary of the Hands Off Russia Movement in 1919 and the following year joined the newly formed Communist Party. One of the leading British proponents from 1928 to 1933 of the sectarian anti-Labour 'class against class' doctrine, he became secretary of the Party in 1929, a post he held through to 1956 apart from two years when he was removed for supporting the war against Germany with whom Russia was formally in a treaty of non-aggression. John Paton, the ILP secretary said of Pollitt,

> He was conciliatory, he was deft, he was diplomatic, he knew to a hairbreadth just how far to press and when to give way ... When one of his colleagues, less far-sighted than himself, seemed likely to over-pass some point I was contesting, he'd suavely intervene with a decision – 'We'll let that go', and the insistent voice was silent. He was very definitely the man in charge of the Communist team.[1]

The *New Statesman* described him as 'one of the few men

thrown up in the last generation in England with a natural capacity for leadership. He is a man whom sincere Socialists want to follow whatever class they come from . . . Because he is inspired with a moral fervour . . . utterly alien from the opportunism and Machiavellianism of current Marxism.'[2] The similarities with Stafford's own character were striking, for all the apparent differences. Indeed Ben Pimlott avers that the social difference between them endeared Pollitt all the more to an impressionable Cripps.

Cripps, ever open to the influence of a new guru, especially a conspicuously working class one, had indeed fallen under Pollitt's spell . . . [He] had already moved further than many of his colleagues in the League towards the Communist position and Pollitt exploited this situation to the full, leading him on with great skill, careful to restrain his impetuosity.[3]

If Pollitt was conspicuously working class, William Mellor was just as conspicuously not. Barbara Betts, later Barbara Castle, who had a two-year affair with Mellor in the thirties, described the first time she met him at a meeting of the Manchester Socialist League branch.

I was impressed by him. Physically he was my kind of man: tall, black-haired, erect, with a commanding presence and strong, handsome features. It was clear from his dress that he had fastidious tastes and he stood on the platform in the dingy hall, groomed to his fingertips in his Savile Row suit, radiating authority. I could have dismissed all this, but what captivated me was his honesty: looking on the rows of rather shabby listeners, he boomed at them, 'I have just spent as much on my lunch as you earn in a week. How much longer are you going to put up with it?'[4]

Mellor's fastidiousness was not only sartorial. He abhorred any form of coarseness and would complain when a hotel provided paper rather than linen napkins. His fastidiousness had not made him a particularly thorough student, however, and though he had studied theology at Keble College Oxford because his father wanted him to be ordained, he had hated it and got a Fourth, a matter he ashamedly mentioned to Barbara.

Michael Foot, who was another friend of Barbara's at this time and a college friend of Stafford's son John, described the other side of Mellor,

Working with [him] was like living on the foothills of Vesuvius. On slight provocation the molten lava would pour forth in protest against the imbecilities of the world in general and anyone who dared to cross him in particular. All who might be suspected of betraying the Cause were in peril of being consumed by his private supply of hell-fire. A wonderful gentleness and generosity mingled with these ferocities.[5]

Mellor's major claim to fame, however, was that he had been editor of the Labour Party's *Daily Herald* until it was taken over by Odhams Press in 1931 and that he had also been an influential guild Socialist with Cole. It was Cole who persuaded him to join the Socialist League, where he met Stafford, though he rapidly rose within it so that J. T. Murphy wrote of him, 'William Mellor was the most dominating figure in the Socialist League and exercised more influence on Stafford Cripps than any other member.'[6]

Friendships often lead to alliances and that was incontrovertibly the case with Cripps, Mellor and Pollitt. Yet by the end of 1935 the potential territory for alliances had already been criss-crossed and marred by previous battles – and the hearts of both of the main bodies with which Stafford's Socialist League could form alliances were scarred by previous experiences.

In the one corner there was the rump of the continuing ILP, but this had dwindled rapidly after its disaffiliation from Labour, collapsing from a membership of 16,773 in 1932 to only 4,392 in 1935. It showed little self-confidence but had initiated discussions with others on the left, even trying to gain affiliation to the Communist International, thereby hoping to replace the Communist Party in Britain. By 1935 the group within the ILP who were particularly keen on this direction had eventually lost any real influence in the ILP and had joined the Communist Party.

In the other corner was the rather more ebullient and numerous Communist Party itself whose relationship with Labour had always been something of a switchback. Its first application for affiliation to the Labour Party had been rejected as early as 1924. In 1925 Communist Party members had been actively excluded for the first time from membership of local constituency Labour parties and in 1928 they were finally prevented from being Trade Union delegates to Labour Party Conference (under the old rules Pollitt had been a delegate to Labour Party Conference at least once). Under instructions from Moscow and the new leadership of Dutt and Pollitt the Party then moved into a period of complete opposition to Labour which lasted up until 1933 when, with some backing from the ILP, the leaders of the Communist Party approached the Labour Party about the possibility of limited joint action on unemployment. Meanwhile they had initiated a whole array of activist organisations – all of which Labour tried successfully to warn people off as no more than front organisations for the Communists.

Then in 1934 the major change of political direction in the Communist Party began to take real hold and leaders of the Communist Party and the ILP both wrote to Labour suggesting a united political front. There was even a meeting of Henderson and George Latham with Maxton and Brockway, but no steps were taken and the Labour National Executive decided in May 1934 to take a hard line on both the Communist Party itself and 'the Communist stellar system'.

With this rebuff the Communist Party then decided to give a more significant earnest of its change of heart in November 1934 when Palme Dutt offered 'big concessions in the elected Parliamentary sphere'[7] though Willie Gallacher exposed the not very hidden agenda, 'we can out of [a Labour Government] develop a situation that will produce a constitutional crisis and an open "confrontation of the classes"'.[8] Nevertheless, apart from in West Fife where Gallacher was elected, the Communist Party backed Labour in the General Election of 1935, calling on 'all working men and women to vote down this wage-cutting Government, and to return a Labour Government pledged to improve the conditions of the masses'.[9]

Finally the Communist Party applied for affiliation to the Labour Party again, in Harry Pollitt's words, 'not as a manoeuvre or for any concealed aims, but because it believes that this would unite the working class and make it better able to fight against the National Government, against Fascism and imperialist war'.[10]

So by the end of 1935 Stafford's choices were either to rebuild the Socialist League as a larger body or to form some kind of alliance with the ILP and/or the Communist Party. The option of developing the Socialist League had already been tried, without success. Following the 1934 decision to become a mass movement there had been demonstrations, meetings, camps, but numbers had not increased. Even halving the membership fee only succeeded in cutting the League's income and Stafford had been forced, with George Strauss, to subsidise it quite heavily. Even the decision after the 1935 election to be a fully fledged party in affiliation to

Labour had not affected its size. Yet Stafford and the National Council refused to give up and mass meetings were held all round Britain during early 1936, but by June these were universally acknowledged to have been a failure.

The issue of the Communist Party's affiliation was to go to the 1936 Labour Party Conference and much of the year was spent by many of the left on the affiliation campaign, trying to gain the support of individual unions, but facing the opposition of the majority and of Herbert Morrison. Nevertheless the Fabians, ASLEF, the AEU and the MFGB supported the affiliation and a close vote seemed likely. This was the ideal opportunity for Stafford and over the spring and summer months, whilst working for the Communist Party affiliation, he set about co-ordinating a 'series of long and difficult discussions'[11] in his chambers at Middle Temple aimed specifically at creating some form of unity between the three remaining left-wing groups, of which the Communist Party was 'by far the most active and confident, as well as the largest'.[12] Bevan and Mellor talked separately to the ILP and the Communist Party, but the plenary meetings Stafford chaired and led and soon gained the respect of Fenner Brockway.

> About his burning sincerity there could be no doubt; he was convinced that the official leadership of the Labour Party had not the inspiration or policy to lead the workers to socialism and (his son had obviously influenced him) that the younger generation particularly were looking to a movement resurrected through a new leadership ... I learned to respect Cripps greatly as he presided over our discussions; he had the earnestness of a crusader.[13]

From the outset they were not simple meetings. There were difficult issues to resolve such as whether to include Liberals in the planned United Front, thereby making it a Popular Front. Pollitt, in line with the Communist International's recent decision at its Seventh Congress, supported the inclusion of the Liberals, but the ILP and Mellor argued for an exclusively working-class front. There were also personal difficulties. Pollitt felt himself regularly close to anger, reporting back to his Communist Party colleagues in November 1936, 'A lot of you think I am an irritable old bastard, but I believe I gave a model so far as good temper is concerned, because I never listened to so many studied insults of the Communist Party... At the right time and the right place I shall let myself go, but I had to hold the chair etc. in order to relieve my tension a little.'[14] Brockway was also suspicious of Dutt whom he described as giving 'the impression of a Buddhist monk'[15] and he watched Pollitt assiduously woo Stafford, playing up to him in committees and staying on for chats whilst Mellor hovered in the background. There was still also an air of distrust, not least because of the first news of internecine struggles within the Republican movement in Spain. Yet Stafford took the Communist Party change of heart at face value, saying they had 'disavowed any intention, for the present, of acting in opposition to the Labour Movement in the country, and certainly their action in many constituencies during the last election gives earnest of their disavowal'.[16]

Pollitt, though, had deep reservations about the whole project of the United Front. For the whole Communist objective was to win over the Labour Party and he was consequently very 'apprehensive of doing anything that gets [the Communist Party] into the camp of the splitters'.[17] Yet Stafford's involvement in the Front meant at least that there was one Labour leader with whom the Communist Party had real influence, and besides Pollitt reckoned Cripps to be 'the only clean man in the whole of that bunch'.[18]

As for the League's formal position, in April 1933 Cole, Tawney and Wise had signed a joint letter to the Labour Movement calling for just such a united front, but the League's 1933 conference had explicitly rejected it. So Stafford really had no mandate for these meetings, though Barbara Castle maintains that the National Council of the League 'authorised' them.

Meanwhile the 1936 Labour Party Conference at Edinburgh was a fairly dismal affair, as agreed by all sides. For a start the affiliation was put paid to by the show trials in Moscow. For when Zinoviev and Kamenev went to court in the summer of 1936 the Communist paper the *Daily Worker* ran the headline, 'Shoot the Reptiles' and there was an immediate backlash against the British Communists both within the Labour Party and in the ILP. The Conference vote, better than on previous occasions, was 1,728000 to 592,000, with several Trade Unions splitting their vote.

Furthermore the start of Franco's uprising in Spain against the Republic had meant that Britain had had to decide whom to support, if anyone, in the ensuing Civil War. The National Government had resolved on a policy of non-intervention, but many in the Labour Party were determined that Britain should provide arms to the Republicans, partly because they were the democratically elected left-wing Government, and also because there was already clear evidence that Germany and Italy were supporting Franco. Philip Noel-Baker, Trevelyan and Bevan all spoke in favour of dropping the non-intervention policy, but it was carried with a similar vote of 1,836,000 to 519,000 and although, after passionate speeches from Señor de Asna and Isabel Palencia, Bevin promised to lobby the Prime Minister to make non-intervention apply to both sides, yet Jennie Lee recorded, the delegates left the conference, 'the most unhappy, guilty-looking collection of people I have ever seen'.[19] A third defeat followed, when the whole idea of joint work with the Communists in any United or Popular Front was voted down and a fourth, when the Party's long-held opposition to rearmament was ditched. It is little wonder the left came away smarting and Bevan and Jennie Lee had 'no heart for holidaying'.[20]

All of which gave extra impetus to Stafford's desire for a United Front. Not only had Labour demonstrated its timidity, but now the growing dangers in the world situation made an urgent response seem all the more important. There was also a subtle shift in Stafford's own political language. Under the influence of Pollitt, class war steadily became the focus of his Socialism and he dismissed 'the ownership of the means of production, [as] inimical, and indeed fatal, to a just and fair distribution of wealth'.[21] In November he declared boldly at Stockport that he 'did not believe it would be a bad thing for the British working class if Germany defeated us'[22] and in December he returned to his royal-bashing theme with one of his most po-faced attacks,

In all this Coronation bunting or bunkum the Government appear to have overlooked the essential nature of the struggle which is proceeding in this country. I have no objection, let me say in parenthesis, to people celebrating if they wish on any proper occasion . . . But the present circus which is being carried on and organised, for which the Government, incidentally are paying three quarters of a million out of national funds . . . is simply being run as a political stunt by the Conservative Party.[23]

Of course such a drift to the left, even a Communist left, was not unusual at the time. The Communist Party seemed to have a vigour about it and the issues that could play on the hearts of the left were Spain and the fight against Fascism. Furthermore enormously successful ventures like the Left Book Club under Victor Gollancz seemed to prove that there was a real left-wing constituency worth playing for.

Whether it was the friendship of Pollitt or the general political shift that informed Stafford's change, the end result was a growing determination to make a United Front work. Two things were needed, a body of people prepared to work together either on the cross-party lines of the European Popular Fronts in France and Spain, or the more exclusive grouping of a United Front of the working class; and an organ.

Both finally came into existence in January 1937, although a typical tactical error meant that Stafford nearly lost the vote in the Socialist League. For the first edition of *Tribune*, edited by Mellor and chaired by Cripps, boldly announced the launch of the United Front on 1 January, before the League had a chance to give its backing to the collaboration with the ILP and the Communist Party. The National Executive swiftly declared that if the United Front went ahead and Labour Party members of the Socialist League collaborated with it, the Socialist League would be disaffiliated. So when the League met in a West End tea room on 16 and 17 January, it was touch and go whether Cripps and Mellor would get the backing they needed. Indeed the vote was close, with 56 in favour, 38 against and 23 abstaining.

So the United Front was launched, with pomp, circumstance and tea, at the Free Trade Hall in Manchester on 24 January. By all accounts it was a splendiferous meeting, with Cripps, Mellor, Maxton and Pollitt all delivering their best bravura performances and several thousand people attending. People were asked to pledge their support and at the first meeting 3,763 cards were signed. A grandiose manifesto was published declaiming, 'We stand for action, for attack, for the ending of retreat, for the building of the strength, unity and power of the working class movement.' Openly class conscious, and in repudiation of the Liberals, it called for 'UNITY of all sections of the working class movement. UNITY in the struggle against Fascism, Reaction and War... UNITY in the struggle for immediate demands'[24] such as an end to the means test, paid holidays, non-contributory pensions and higher taxation of the rich in order to pay for 'social ameliorisation'. Stafford called the Manchester meeting 'the most remarkable experience of my short political career'[25] and it was clear from all the accounts of the subsequent meetings that an enormous rush of political adrenalin kept the United Front buzzing. There were visible signs of success. Invitations to speak came from all around the country, meetings were packed, thousands of pledge cards were signed and briefly the United Front was the most talked about political force in the land. Laski, then also on the National Executive, gave two reasons for joining the campaign, '(1) as a socialist I approve strongly of the measures, domestic and international, which it advocates; and (2) I believe it to be my duty to fight for all those measures alongside those who share with me the full recognition of their urgent necessity.'[26] It was clear that the Front's language of urgency, of fighting and of unity struck a chord with a swathe of opinion that was fed up with the apparent timidity of the Labour front bench.

Yet public support for the Front was not exactly over-whelming, and Stafford soon received criticism from both his father and his uncle despite the fact that both had expressed open vexation with the National Executive. Sidney Webb wrote to Stafford's father of his concern, 'We are perturbed about Stafford's recent action in getting the Socialist League to enter into alliance with the ILP and the Communist Party in flat defiance of the Labour Party ruling. We have had no opportunity of talking it over with Stafford, and I do not even know whether he had led the action or been outvoted.'[27] Webb could see little point in any electoral pact with the Communist Party unless there were a second ballot system as in France, and reckoned that the only advantage was that one could swell the attendance at a meeting by a small fraction, at the expense of alienating the rest of society. As to whether the Front was breaking new ground, about 12,000 people attended the several meetings in early 1937 – a large number. Yet the Left Book Club managed 7,000 at a single Albert Hall meeting that same year, and though 18,000 pledge cards had been signed by the end of February, 205,000 had been printed and distributed.

Meanwhile on 27 January the National Executive disaffiliated the Socialist League and there were moves, led by Arthur Greenwood, to expel Cripps without further ado. Laski reckoned the odds 'about 20:1 that Stafford will be expelled from the party, about 5:1 that I shall be too'.[28] Yet for all the high-handed independence of the League, Cripps was popular in the country, he was an effective parliamentary performer, and most importantly, he still retained the support of the Leader. Attlee's support was beginning to wane and though he was clearly still trying to save Cripps from expulsion, there is a tone of exasperation in his comments to Laski, written on 22 February,

> This is the real folly, due, I fear to a lack of understanding of the movement . . . The real difficulty will be in meeting the argument that the offenders against party discipline are prominent and for the most part middle-class people and that they should not be treated differently from rank-and-file members who offend and are dealt with by their local parties for infractions of discipline. I fight all the time against heresy hunting, but the heretics seem to seek martyrdom.[29]

In fact Stafford managed to retain his membership card thanks to his legal work, for the following day Parliament debated the long due report on the Gresford colliery disaster. Stafford had represented the miners in the original enquiry in 1934 for free and although he had not fronted any Parliamentary debate for the Party for some time, it was inevitable that the leadership should call on him for this one debate. His performance was vintage Cripps, less the prima donna of the Free Trade Hall and the National Executive, more the fastidious and meticulous 'picker up of unconsidered trifles' that could be woven into a compelling argument against the mine owners. Not only did it endear him to a key section of the Parliamentary Party, namely the miners, but it also reinforced a more measured, sane picture of him. Bevan's description of his Gresford performance is probably accurate, although it would be a mistake to regard this as his normal speaking style, 'There are rarely any highlights in his speeches. He disdains literary touches and oratorical adornments. It is difficult to pick out a phrase here and there, and he attempts no scintillating generalisations but wins the argument by detail and a lack of defensiveness.'[30]

The next day, with several of the members still baying for Stafford's blood, the National Executive met for eight hours. Morrison was still anxious to keep Cripps within the fold and actually wrote to him

> I do not believe that there has been any desire to prevent your playing a full part in the great work of the Party; I do not need to assure you that there is no such desire so far as I am concerned. But I should be less than honest if I did not say that there is, I think, a responsibility on you to make your contributions to a rapprochement, and that many of your public statements and activities have been a source of embarrassment to the Party and hardly conducive to that Labour Party unity which is so essential to the success of our work.[31]

Whether out of personal affection for the man he had recruited to the Party or out of genuine concern to avoid bad publicity at the time of the London County Council elections, Morrison argued successfully that no decision should be made until they were over. Indeed at the March meeting Morrison was still urging delay, this time until after Party conference, but the National Executive decided by a majority of 14 to 6 to declare members of the Socialist League ineligible for membership of the Labour Party as of 1 June.

This, of course, put the ball firmly in the League's court and there was a hasty series of meetings at which the plan of action was decided. Again Pollitt's influence told with Cripps, for he urged him to disband the League and to continue with the United Front as a Unity Campaign supported by individual Labour Party members. Mellor, meanwhile, was all for sticking with the League come what may despite the fact that its membership had dropped from 3,000 to 1,600 in only three months.

In the meantime the war of attrition continued between the National Executive and the League. In April there came accusations that much of the funding for the United Front was coming from Communist Russia and that *Tribune* was exclusively funded by Cripps. Attempts to rebut the insinuations were not entirely successful and by the beginning of May the tone of *Tribune* was getting more and more shrill. Cripps had been infuriated by the refusal in March of the Royal Albert Hall to allow the United Front to hold a meeting, he had inveighed against Goering coming to the coronation in February and above all he had committed himself to the cause of Republican Spain. Ironically it was this last issue, the one issue in the late thirties that seemed to be able to stir the breasts of the left with one united emotion, that actually did for the Unity campaign.

Of course the United Front had never really been very united. Three separate bodies had managed briefly to coalesce by the political will power of five or six leading men, but as Brockway commented, 'Our Unity Committee was not all unity. The preliminary negotiations nearly broke down half-a-dozen times and when the campaign was launched serious differences emerged'[32] and Cripps himself often remarked on 'the irony of unity meetings when at the door members of the two parties were selling literature bitterly attacking each other'.[33]

Yet Spain and the campaign to end the Government's policy of non-intervention, was the most effective of all rallying cries for the left. It gave a sense of urgency and idealism to the cause. Fascism was at war with Socialism. The British policy of non-intervention meant that she was refusing to support the democratically elected Socialist Government against the insurrectionist Franco forces, evidently backed by Hitler and Mussolini. The Blitzkrieging of the Basque town of Guernica, the siege of Barcelona, these became symbols for the whole Socialist endeavour, and Stafford's speeches throughout 1937 and 1938 returned again and again to the Spanish Civil War.

But in May 1937 news of splits in the Socialist command structure in Spain began to feed through to Britain and the vituperative rows and endless recriminations being played out in Barcelona were re-enacted in the ranks for the United Front. For the death of Andres Nin and the allegations of Communist abuses meant that the ILP and the Communist Party distrusted each other more than ever and as members of the two Spanish factions were killing each other so the life of the United Front ebbed away. As Brockway put it, after the Spanish revelations 'the campaign went on: Pollitt and I spoke from the same platform . . . but the inner spirit of unity was dead'.[34]

In May, with the National Executive's deadline fast approaching, the Socialist League met in Leicester and resolved to disband, though in the words of Barbara Betts's resolution, this dissolution was 'not a funeral but a conscious political tactic'.[35] Even in its death throes the League was plagued with acrimony, with Noel Brailsford determining to resign from the League before it could disband and doing so by telegram from Spain.

If the League thought that disbanding the League was a clever tactic, they were mistaken, for the National Executive rapidly acted to make sure that not only the United Front but the Unity Campaign itself would falter, telling Strauss that he would be expelled from the Party if he spoke in a meeting at Hull on the same platform as either the Communist Party or the ILP. Stafford advised him to retreat and only weeks after the Socialist League disbanded the National Unity Committee was dissolved as well. Stafford put a brave face on it, saying that 'on May 31st the Socialist League will be dissolved and the Unity Campaign will go forward even more vigorously than before'[36] but the truth was that not only had disunity proved more intransigent a left-wing attraction than working-class unity, but the National Executive was calling all the shots and could easily pick off individual Cripps associates with ease.

Still the Unity Campaign continued, with a mixture of fervour for Spain and workerist rhetoric, although none of the Labour Party members actually spoke on platforms with either ILP or Communist Party speakers. Stafford's line of attack remained the same as before, lambasting the Labour leadership in July when it lost ground in several by-elections, 'There is no fight in their opposition, no leadership to the discontented forces in the country and there is apathy not only in the electorate but in the Labour movement itself.'[37] Speaking in Oldham on the six month anniversary of the launch of the United Front he returned to the theme, 'The Labour movement is not today attracting the young men and women of the working class to its cause ... The reason is, I believe, the lack of fighting leadership, the tendency to co-operate with our class enemies,' and he excoriated the Chamberlain Government for its developing policy of appeasement, 'If the threat of war is to be used as an argument against standing up to the Fascist Dictators – then we may as well hand over the whole power to them! In fact of course it is by constantly giving in to them that the threat of war becomes greater and greater.'[38] But from June onwards Cripps was careful not to appear publicly with his ILP or Communist Party colleagues and kept his carping for purely Labour Party meetings and the pages of *Tribune* in the hope that the forth-coming Labour Party Conference at Bournemouth could be swayed towards supporting the Unity Campaign. He still refused to mince his words, however, accusing the Labour leadership of collaborating with capitalism despite having been created 'as a class Party of the workers to protect them from capitalism' and likening this betrayal to 'the poor dependant of the rich man who nursed him back to health in the hope that when he was well again he would make a will in the poor man's favour'.[39] He was furious with the National Executive for refusing in September to endorse Mellor, who had twice been a candidate in Enfield, and a week before the conference he still saw the Party as 'a lifeless machine controlled by the opinions of a few people who have got into positions of influence and importance in the Trade Unions'.[40]

In the event the debate on the Unity Campaign was fronted for the National Executive by Morrison, who dealt with the issue with some humour and there was remarkably little acrimony at the conference. Cripps complained at a meeting of the National Labour Unity Committee that same evening that 'we cannot afford to deal with [the Unity Campaign] in the spirit of an Oxford Union debate, or dispose of it by a few clever and quite irrelevant smart remarks'[41] but the truth is that not only had the National Executive won the argument and the votes, but Morrison had managed to lighten the proceedings, thereby dispelling the feeling that Cripps was being persecuted by the National Executive. The two votes, on the Socialist League (1,730,000 to 373,000) and on the United Front were both decisive (2,116,000 to 331,000) and though Cripps maintained that the decision had not changed his mind, he did resolve 'to use other methods in trying to forward [his] opinions'.[42] So both the the United Front and the Unity Campaign came to an end.

Ben Pimlott has maintained that 'as the [1937] Labour Party

conference approached, the cause of unity was killed . . . by
the effect of the Moscow Trials, which caused a deep revulsion
in the minds of the ordinary British workers',[43] but the truth is
that the Moscow show trials in which Stalin despatched a series
of senior Communist figures with fake confessions, had
already begun in July 1936 and much of the damage in terms
of public opinion had already been done before the United
Front was launched. In fact it is a miracle that with such an
unpropitious start the Front found any public favour at all.
More significantly, though, the show trials did make it difficult
for Stafford and his colleagues to wear down the Labour
Party's long-held opposition to the Communists, and set up
yet another layer of distrust within the the Front itself. In the
initial discussions Cripps may have taken Mellor's advice in
positing a United Front rather than a Popular Front but by
mid-1937 Cripps was leaning far more towards Pollitt and it
was his advice he took over the disbanding of the League. Yet
Pollitt was closely connected to Soviet Russia and for many
this meant he was inherently untrustworthy. As the Pope was
to Protestant England, so was the General Secretary of the
Russian Communist Party to 1930s Britain and this involvement undoubtedly harmed Cripps's and the Unity
Campaign's reputation, but the real problem lay in the fact
that at no stage did any of the United Front proponents take
the issues of pulling the Labour Party with them seriously
enough. The only tactic was to assert what was seen as the
urgent truth, and such impatience meant the project was
bound to be a failure, which, even by Stafford's own criteria,
it was. For it had tried 'to try and wring concessions from the
dominant party and class' and 'to build up through that
struggle the power and will to displace the government'[44] but
had succeeded in neither. If anything the Unity Campaign
only managed to weaken Labour, thereby making it less likely
that the National Government would fall. Even Stafford's
hoped for 'unity not only of existing organisations but of the

millions who are unorganised politically'[45] was no more than a pipe dream and by the end of 1937 he had achieved none of his objectives.

12

Opposing Appeasement

Barbara Castle reckons that Stafford was already 'changing tack' in 1937 and identifies 'the remarkable success of the Left Book Club, through which Gollancz had been urging the case for a popular front for some time'[1] as the inspiration for his about-turn on whether to include 'capitalist' opponents of Fascism in the campaign to unseat the National Government. The truth is, however, that Stafford's change of mind was more influenced by Pollitt and a disenchantment with Mellor than any direct relations with Gollancz. For Pollitt, in line with Communist Party policy, had always seen the inclusion of Liberals and non-aligned opponents of Fascism in the Front as a hoped-for final outcome along the lines of the French Government of Blum and the Spanish coalition under Negrin. He had tried to win Cripps over to this view in the original 1936 negotiations but it was not until the collapse of the United Front in November 1937 that he succeeded.

Mellor, though, was still arguing in January 1938 that 'No war waged, even in the name of democracy, by capitalist governments, will accomplish, at the very best, anything more than a continuance of present economic injustices and a prolongation of the reign of a method of economic life which can only fulfil its aims by robbing workers and making war on its imperialist rivals.'[2] He and his friends had not changed their position at all, but with the winding up of the United Front in

November Stafford began the slow process of readjustment to a changing political environment which rudely ruptured his friendship with Mellor in the summer of 1938.

There were other reasons for Stafford to 'change tack' at the turn of 1937/8. For a start he was relatively content with the Bournemouth Labour Party Conference. One of his primary concerns, to overturn the Labour Party's non-intervention policy, had finally borne fruit and, in one of the ironies of which only the sentimental Labour Party is capable, despite voting him down on both the League and the Front, the Conference elected him to the National Executive along with two of his United Front colleagues, Pritt and Laski.

Stafford's reappearance on the National Executive was not, however, due to his involvement in the United Front. If anything it was in spite of it. For he had also been closely involved in the campaign for greater constituency representation on the National Executive which had murmured itself discontentedly into prominence at the 1936 conference. In part this was the result of a growing imbalance between the two main sections of the Party. Since constituency Parties had been started by Henderson in 1918 there had been a steady rise in the individual membership of the Party, reaching 431,000 by the time of the 1936 Conference. Yet the National Executive still consisted of twelve Trade Unionists, five women and only five constituency members. Even these were voted on not by the constituency delegates but by the whole of conference. In effect this meant that the whole membership of the National Executive was determined by the Trade Unions. As individual membership grew and Trade Union membership declined, and as resentment of the Trade Unions' iron and 'reactionary' grip on policy grew on the left wing of the Party, the Party's constitution seemed increasingly unjust.

So at the 1936 Edinburgh Conference 200 of the 280 constituency delegates met and agreed to inaugurate a Provisional Committee of Constituency Labour Parties. Cripps was asked to chair the meeting and so successful was it that Dalton, who was Chairman-elect of the Party, announced at the final session of the conference that the Executive would 'consider the matter in the most friendly and co-operative fashion' and would speak with 'some, at any rate, of those who have proposals to put forward on this point'.[3] Over the following year he met with local representatives around the country, and by the time of the 1937 Conference, which Dalton chaired, he was in favour of direct representation of the constituency Parties. He persuaded the National Executive to back direct elections and an increase from five constituency members to seven, and after some lunchtime negotiations with Ernest Bevin and shamelessly only calling speakers in favour of the new proposals, they were carried overwhelmingly. The new rules were immediately used and the result was a very different atmosphere in the Executive with Philip Noel-Baker coming on, as well as Cripps, Laski and Pritt in the constituency section and Ellen Wilkinson, another member of the *Tribune* board, gaining one of the women's seats. Ironically, if Dalton had left the National Executive's constitution alone Stafford would never have had the platform he later used mercilessly in his campaign for a Popular Front. As *Tribune* put it in welcoming the elections, 'In the councils of the Labour Party we now have representation for our views and within those councils we must carry on the insistence and pressure that hitherto has had to be applied from outside.'[4] Which is exactly what Stafford did.

The early months of Stafford's reappearance on the National Executive were relatively calm. Dalton and Bevin made gentle but overt conciliatory gestures to the four United Front Executive members and there was a brief period during which the Party achieved a sense of common purpose. The left had done well out of the new Party constitution, even winning the battle to move Party Conference back to Whitsun so that it did not follow the TUC Conference.

Furthermore the left was not quite the monolith it had been. Charles Trevelyan, once a Socialist League stalwart who had advocated 'mass resistance to war' and flown the red flag with hammer and sickle from his Northumberland seat, was now, according to Attlee, 'rather bellicose. He contemplates war with far more equanimity than I can compass.'[5] Dalton had managed to get the Parliamentary Party to abstain rather than vote against the defence estimates during 1937, and Conference had approved a pro-rearmament line by a majority of 8 to 1, yet it was only the Christian pacifists like Lansbury that backed Bevan's condemnation that such collaboration with the Government would mean 'a voluntary totalitarian State with ourselves creating the barbed wire around'.[6]

Party unity was aided by the change of heart on Spain as Transport House began to campaign openly for an end to non-intervention. Attlee, with Noel-Baker, Ellen Wilkinson and John Dugdale even visited the Republican Prime Minister Negrin in December. Their trip, taking in Barcelona, the besieged trenches of Madrid and a narrow escape from Franco's aircraft on the return from Valencia to Barcelona, was greeted with hostility in the British press, especially when photos appeared of Attlee giving the Republican clenched fist salute to the Spanish forces. But to the left of the Party it was evidence of a real change of heart. He was welcomed back at a mass Albert Hall meeting on 19 December with warm adulation, and there were enormously successful and emotionally satisfying official Labour Party rallies for Spain through 1938. Cripps even shared a platform with Attlee, Greenwood and Dallas at Hyde Park on 10 April and with Attlee, Dalton and Wilkinson at the Albert Hall on 22 May. So Stafford clearly felt more at home in the post-Bournemouth Party than he had ever done.

British politics was changing at a breakneck speed and the National Government, for the first time since 1931, was beginning to look vulnerable. Neville Chamberlain had taken over from Baldwin as Prime Minister in May 1937 and his Government of capable but cautious administrators was still committed to appeasement. It had drawn Labour fire over its inaction against Japan in October, and when Chamberlain rejected out of hand President Roosevelt's call for an international conference at the turn of the year and seemed to bend over backwards to get Italian support against Germany, his Foreign Secretary, Anthony Eden, and his Under Secretary for Foreign Affairs, Bobbetty Cranborne, resigned. Though Eden's Commons resignation speech was poor, 'the most polite resignation of modern times',[7] Cranborne managed to stir up some support for his accusation that Chamberlain was simply succumbing to 'Italian blackmail' and Attlee backed Eden, arguing that the attempt to play off one dictator against another was bound to lead to war.

What Cripps and many on the left took from this open split in National Government ranks, with twenty-five Tories abstaining and the National Labour MP Harold Nicolson winning the applause of the House for his charge that Eden had been 'butchered to make a Roman holiday',[8] was that the way to bring an end to deals with the dictators might lie in a complete realignment of British politics. Chamberlain and his new Foreign Secretary, the extremely devout Lord Halifax, were beyond the pale. Cripps immediately lambasted Halifax for being 'pro-Hitler',[9] he condemned the Prime Minister for trying 'to harness the British people to the Rome-Berlin axis',[10] he denounced Lord Perth's meeting with Mussolini and Halifax's with von Ribbentrop and he inveighed against the 'Cliveden Baronage' of arch-appeasers like Lord Londonderry, Halifax, Oliver Stanley, Samuel Hoare and the Astors. Yet there were clearly Liberals, and possibly even some Conservatives, with whom he began to sense he could do business, and with whom several of the left had already been engaged.

Eleanor Rathbone, the Independent MP for the combined

English universities and an outspoken opponent of appeasement, as early as September 1936, had suggested that there were already two broad popular fronts:

> Both stretch from extreme right to extreme Left. Both think they are seeking peace ... Popular Front No. 1 seems to include the Rothermere press, *The Times* and several other Conservative organs, a large section of City opinion, probably a considerable proportion of the Conservative Party in Parliament, Lord Lothian, the ILP, Mr Lansbury, and all pacifists who are 'absolute' whether on Christian or on revolutionary grounds. All these want to emasculate the League by removing all its coercive provisions ... Popular Front No. 2 ... includes on the Right, Mr Winston Churchill, the Duchess of Athol, an unknown but probably large number of the more far-sighted Conservatives, probably most – certainly the best known – of the National Labour and National Liberal groups, the whole of the Labour and Liberal parties except the sections already included on the other front, the Communist Party, the opposition press, the best of the press outside London. All these ... perceive the Fascist ambitions will grow by what they feed on ... Hence all these uphold collective security through the League and oppose all its emasculations.[11]

In 1938 these two broad coalitions still existed. Lansbury, like Chamberlain, had been to see Hitler and still believed the dictators could be stopped without the threat of war, while his colleagues called this not diplomacy but appeasement. Stafford by now had moved steadily towards this second grouping, although he was still extremely diffident about Churchill, whom he had called 'a high priest of imperialist suppression'[12] in the very first edition of *Tribune*, and he had opposed an early suggestion of Lansbury's, that Lloyd George should be encouraged to join Labour. Nevertheless it is clear that by April 1938 he had begun to change his mind on what a successful alliance against the appeasers might look like.

So, in the 14 April edition of *Tribune* he declared open support for the Peace Front that had already been initiated by his one-time Socialist League colleague, J. T. Murphy. 'The call for a Peace Front is not a manoeuvre of disgruntled or disloyal people,' he maintained. 'It is a call for consolidation of forces.'[13] He explained his conversion was not a sign of his relinquishing his Socialist principles,

> I myself was bitterly opposed to any such political align-
> ment a year ago . . . [but] the real question to be decided
> is whether the chance of altering the foreign policy of this
> country and of calling a halt to Fascist aggression within
> a practicable period of time is worth the abandonment
> for the time being of the hope of real working class
> control. I say, for the time being, since such a front could
> not be considered as a permanent alignment, but only as
> a temporary co-operation, to save democracy and peace.[14]

So, two weeks later, he appeared at a meeting calling for a Peace Front that would embrace everyone to the left of Chamberlain. Held at the Queen's Hall the platform also included A.V. Alexander, Noel-Baker and Ellen Wilkinson from Labour, Harold Nicolson from National Labour, the Liberal Megan Lloyd George, Gilbert Murray, H. H. Elvin and the ubiquitous doyen of the mass meeting, Victor Gollancz. Stafford declared that his one regret was that he did not 'find among the signatories [to the call for the Peace Front] any members of the Communist Party'[15] but the meeting was an interesting mix with 1,806 delegates, 10 from religious organisations, 56 from Peace Councils, 34 Liberals, 345 Labour Party members, 461 Trade Unionists, 262 from the Left Book Club and 195 Communists. Harry Pollitt must have been delighted. It was exactly what he had always argued for, a popular front combining Liberals and the left to overthrow the Government in the pursuit of an anti-Fascist majority.

Part of the success of the event, as Barbara Castle has pointed out, was due to the work of the Left Book Club, which had been established in 1936 and had achieved remarkable results despite its rather desultory earnestness and its excessively ritualistic recitation of semi-Communist mantras. Members, of whom there were 60,000 at its height, received a monthly book chosen for them by the editorial group of Gollancz, Laski and John Strachey, who, having toyed with Mosley's New Party, had become a close associate of Palme Dutt, though never actually a member of the Communist Party. Other titles were available at a reduced price and several sold well into the hundreds of thousands. Of the Club's first twenty-seven titles, fifteen were by Communists and the proximity of the Communist Party and Left Book Club's offices made it easy for people to assume that the Club was a Communist front organisation. Yet Palme Dutt claimed that the success of the Club was 'probably the greater because it is recognised by the general public as an independent commercial enterprise on its own feet, and not the propaganda of a particular political organisation',[16] and Dalton at one point tried to infiltrate it on behalf of the Labour Party because it provided such a clear and ready market for ideas. With its 1,300 local groups and its successful monthly, *Left News*, it was commercially viable – something the left was not used to, and Gollancz spent considerable effort on widening its appeal with books like George Orwell's *The Road to Wigan Pier*, although he turned down Hemingway's *Homage to Catalonia* even before it was written lest it spark off rows over Communist involvement in Spain. Another part of Gollancz's broadening of the Club was an attempt to bring a couple of left-leaning Liberals on to the Board, just as he began to advocate a Popular Front along Spanish and French lines and sought to change the name of the Club to the Anti-Fascist Association.

There are two common misconceptions about this stage of Stafford's career. The first, that he was the inspiration of the British Popular Front, is easily dismissed, for well before Stafford was converted to the cause there had been both Popular Front advocates and an organisation. Indeed by the time Cripps and Bevan joined in there were already local Popular Front councils meeting around the country, there had been calls for a 'United Peace Alliance' and while there was considerable uncertainty as to whether the variously named groupings were actually one and the same thing, masquerading under a host of different names, yet there was a single clear objective – in the words of Michael Foot, 'to produce such a ferment of opinion, such hostility to the appeasement policy of the Government, such a pressure in Parliament that British policy could be diverted from its dangerous course before more damage was done.'[17]

In fact, much of the legwork for these early People's Fronts had been done by Stafford's ex-colleague at the Socialist League, J. T. Murphy. Murphy had resigned as the paid secretary of the Socialist League when his proposals for a Popular Front were only supported by one other member of the National Council, Louis Fenn, and they were rather brusquely squashed by Cripps. This was in 1936, when he proceeded to build a 'People's Front propaganda Committee' with Jim Delahaye, Allen Young, David Davies, Allan Sainsbury and Le Gros Clarke. This had attracted some support from the *News Chronicle* and the *Manchester Guardian*, and there was a successful Friends House meeting in London when 2,000 gathered to hear Robert Boothby and Richard Acland, respectively Tory and Liberal MPs, join Cole and Strachey in calling for a combination to defeat the appeasers. But it was not until the LBC took off, a 'Popular Front in miniature', that public pressure became strong enough to register on the Richter Scale and though Gollancz maintained that the 7 February 1937

LBC rally at the Albert Hall with Acland, Laski, Strachey, Pollitt and Pritt (which Cripps missed due to flu) was 'a sort of Popular Front that *happens to have happened*[18] and it was not until 1938 that the Co-op Movement's weekly paper *Reynold's News*, openly backed the Front. The alternatives, as Bevan articulated them in Pontypool on May Day were clear, 'If the National Government remains in office another two or three years we shall rue in blood and tears that we did not take action earlier. The country is faced with two alternatives – the establishment of a Popular Front in this country, under the leadership of the Labour Party, or drift to disaster under the National Government.'[19]

As for the second misconception, that Cripps was advocating a realignment of British politics that would unite the centre in a new Party and disrupt the two main political tribes, this too is patent nonsense.

There were thoughts of realignment, though. As long ago as just after the 1931 election Lloyd George, while hoping that any efforts at co-operation would not be confined to Labour or Radicalism, had identified 'a fruitful belt of territory that Liberal and Labour without touching the regions of divergence, could cultivate together for the benefit of the nation'.[20] That same year some of this territory was then mapped out by a group calling itself Political and Economic Planning (PEP). Based on an original article by Max Nicholson in the new periodical the *Weekend Review*, entitled 'A National Plan for Britain', this brought together a variety of industrialists and economists like Israel Sieff, Arthur Salter and Julian Huxley, together with the National Labour MP Kenneth Lindsay. Papers were produced, on housing (1934), the health and social services (1937) and the location of industry (1939), all stressing the importance of Government planning within each industry for a healthy economy – a concept that would later lie very close to Labour and Crippsian thinking.

Meanwhile, in 1934, the Next Five Years Group was formed, bringing together, in Paul Addison's words, 'the stage army of the good'.[21] Under the Chairmanship of the once Labour Clifford Allen, who had been a conscientious objector in the war, and with the active support of the young Tory MP Harold Macmillan, this attracted a wide range of support with some of the later Popular Front agitators already combining: Lionel Curtis, R. C. K. Ensor, H. A. L. Fisher, G. P. Gooch, J. A. Hobson, Oliver Lodge, Gilbert Murray, Seebohm Rowntree, Siefried Sassoon, H.G. Wells, William Temple and Eleanor Rathbone.

The political agenda for both these central groupings was progressive and indeed many of their prescriptions were actually put into effect by the wartime coalition and Labour Governments of the forties. Social and industrial planning, economic development for the depressed areas, the expansion of secondary schooling, public investment in housing – all these were issues that united both the PEP and the Next Five Years Group to the Radical Lloyd George stream in the Liberal Party and the Labour Party itself. Indeed the brief precursor of the Next Five Years Group, the Liberty and Democratic Leadership Group, enjoyed the support of Dalton, Bevin, Lansbury and Noel-Baker, and Macmillan often spoke of the possibility of a new centre Party with Morrison at the helm.

So there was a gently cultivated political centre ground and many of its occasional gardeners were now the strongest advocates for a Popular Front. But for Stafford the aims of socialism were still paramount and were only to be subjugated to the pressing need to face up to Fascist aggression and unseat the National Government – made all the more pressing by Hitler's annexation of Austria in March 1938.

So in April 1938 Stafford tabled a proposal at the National Executive for a Popular Front and called for a special Party Conference on Spain, 'to decide on measures to force a General Election'. The first half of his proposals was swiftly dealt with and a statement from the National Executive laying out the case against a Popular Front was circulated to all the constituencies. Stafford's second suggestion, however, was more reasonable. Because of moving the Party Conference from October to Whitsun there was to be no conference until May 1939, and though the rest of the Executive felt that there was no need to revisit the 1937 Conference position on Spain, nevertheless Stafford was allowed to move a resolution every month from April until his expulsion calling for a special conference and a more supportive policy for Democratic Spain.

In the weeks after the April Executive Stafford again suffered from bad colitis. He had acted as if he had been on a permanent election footing pretty much since 1931. He had four years of front bench Parliamentary responsibility, as well as chairing the Socialist League and *Tribune*. And all this while holding down a successful and lucrative practice at the Bar. He very rarely managed a full weekend at Goodfellows. In short, he was physically exhausted and his old illness returned, this time forcing him to take the longest break of his adult life, leaving for Jamaica for a full ten weeks in the summer.

Before he went, though, he decided to sort out the problems at *Tribune*. Since its first edition, due to grossly over-optimistic calculations, it had financial problems which had been resolved temporarily by an injection of £20,000 from Cripps and Strauss. But with the prospect of a deal with the Left Book Club Stafford saw the possibility of finally establishing it on a secure viable financial footing. At the same time he was keen to change the editorial stance of the paper in favour of the Peace Front. Wilkinson and Laski were already on board, but the greatest obstacle to both the LBC deal and the Peace Front was the editor and his two young journalists, Michael Foot and Barbara Castle. Mellor's intransigence was partly due to his long-held suspicion of the Communist sympathies of Gollancz, who was now to join the *Tribune* board, and Laski and Strachey. So when Stafford tried to force through a change in the editorial stance, Mellor resigned. Stafford first approached Foot to succeed Mellor but was indignantly rebuffed so, on Pollitt's advice, he appointed the fellow traveller H. J. Hartshorn as the new editor.

Barbara Castle reckons that the reason for changing *Tribune*'s policy from the United Front to the Popular Front was so as to attract some of Gollancz's readers, and it is certainly true that Stafford was eager to make the paper pay its own way. Indeed it is clear that Stafford's early days at the *South Bucks Standard* had made of him a fairly tough commercial newspaper proprietor. Yet for all Barbara Castle's bitterness about the 'saintly knight's manoeuvrings', *Tribune* had to become financially viable in order to gain its independence. Otherwise, just like the *South Bucks Standard* before it, it would always remain 'Cripps's Chronicle'.

Foot was also critical of Stafford. He agreed with Mellor over the Popular Front and he felt Mellor was treated abominably. Indeed in a letter to Stafford refusing the offer of the editorship he accused Gollancz of having demanded the sacking of Mellor as a prerequisite to his joining the *Tribune* board. Cripps replied by pointing out that it was not only Gollancz, but all three of the LBC selectors who had required a new editor. This scarcely softened the injustice of the sacking in Foot's eyes, especially as it was couched in what must count as some of Stafford's most platitudinous, pompous and pious comments:

> Certain facts must be made clear and two of them seem important. First, it was not Gollancz who alone imposed the condition as to change of Editor. It came from all three of the selectors, nor was it based on or because of any policy of the *Tribune* in the past or future. I think you may give me credit for the fact that I don't propose to pay many thousands a year to run a paper which is

not in harmony – broadly – with my views.

Second, Gollancz and the LBC will not control the policy of the *Tribune* in the future. I may be foolish politically in William's view... but I am not to be completely ignored as Chairman of the Board and broadly the paper will carry out my policy... You may be quite assured that I shall not continue putting my money and energies into running a paper for a policy I don't believe in ...

I admire your sense of loyalty to William and, as you say, the *Tribune* won't come to an end because you leave us, but it does make me sad to think that I shan't have the joy of working with you in the future as I had hoped since we first met at Oxford some years ago. You must make your own choice and you must satisfy your conscience which is certainly the most important thing in this life. If you are straight with yourself you can hold up your head and fight through difficulties that may come ... God bless you, Stafford.[22]

All that can be said in Stafford's defence is that whilst Foot and Betts felt Gollancz had staged a takeover in which Cripps willingly acquiesced, even giving way on the policy of the paper regarding the Popular Front, the truth is that the whole idea of the LBC itself had sprung from a lunchtime meeting in January 1936 when Stafford had invited Gollancz and Strachey to discuss the idea of setting up a weekly left-wing paper. Nothing came directly of the meeting, but as they left Gollancz and Strachey decided to co-operate on a different project, selecting books for a left-wing book club, whilst Stafford went on with George Strauss to form *Tribune*. So the new collaboration was a reunion rather than a takeover, and whilst later events showed that Cripps should have been more careful than to allow *Tribune* to become so directly linked to Communism, there were financial realities to be faced and

Cripps had genuinely changed his mind over the Popular Front. So, having dealt, roughly, with *Tribune*, Stafford, accompanied by Isobel and the family, set sail on a banana boat for Jamaica and Diana and Purcell's wedding.

His return coincided with the fulfilment of his own prediction that Czechoslovakia would soon be ceded to Germany. Chamberlain had been aware since the annexation of Austria in March that Czechoslovakia was next on Hitler's shopping list, but, unlike Churchill, he refused to accept that Europe was 'confronted with a programme of aggression, nicely calculated and timed, unfolding stage by stage'.[23] Furthermore he did not really see Czechoslovakia's independence as a matter for British intervention and was reported as saying that he did not care 'two hoots' for the Sudeten Germans whom Hitler wanted to include in his greater Germany. What he did care about was the Czecho-Soviet pact. France was also in alliance with Czechoslovakia, but was reluctant to call Hitler's bluff unless she had advance guarantees of British support, a position which left President Beneš of Czechoslovakia at the mercy of German aggression and British diplomacy.

On 4 September Beneš therefore agreed to most of the Sudeten Germans' demands, though nine days later they decided to revolt and when order was restored French resolve was so feeble that Chamberlain was effectively on his own in any attempt to resolve the Czech crisis. On 15 September he flew, for the first time in his sixty-nine years, to see Hitler at Berchtesgaden and offered the separation of Czechoslovakia which Hitler, not surprisingly, accepted. The French Prime Minister, Daladier, came to London on 18 September to remonstrate with Chamberlain for the high-handed way in which he had summarily rendered a strong Czechoslovakia impotent but Beneš was issued an ultimatum that unless he agreed to the 'deal' neither France nor Britain would support him, and on 21 September he caved in.

The following day Chamberlain returned to Germany, this

time meeting Hitler at Godesberg. Instead of simply confirming the arrangements, however, Hitler pushed for immediate occupation of the Sudeten lands and Chamberlain had to return to London with nothing but a commitment that Hitler would not do anything before October.

Everyone in London now expected war. The Foreign Office issued a declaration that 'if German attack is made upon Czechoslovakia ... France will be bound to come to her assistance, and Great Britain and Russia will certainly stand by France'. Trenches were dug in London parks, plans were drawn up for the evacuation of the capital's children, thirty-eight million gas masks were issued, the fleet was mobilised and the House of Commons was recalled for 28 September. Stafford predicted that war would start the following day, a view shared by many of his colleagues who sat in sullen nervous silence through the Prime Minister's tedious recital of the long series of his negotiations. Finally he got to the most recent events.

Harold Nicolson, deeply sceptical of Chamberlain, and Henry Channon, Rab Butler's PPS and a Chamberlain fan, both described the events. Nicolson: ' "Yesterday morning", began the Prime Minister, and we were again conscious that some revelation was approaching. He began to tell us of his final appeal to Hitler and Mussolini. I glanced at the clock. It was twelve minutes after four. The Prime Minister had been speaking for exactly an hour.'[24] Channon: 'I suddenly saw the FO officials in the box signalling frantically to me; I could not get to them, as it meant climbing over 20 PPS's, so Dunglass fetched a bit of paper from them which he handed to Sir John Simon, who glanced at it, and I tried to read it over his shoulder, but there was not time, as he suddenly, and excitedly, tugged at the PM's coat; Chamberlain turned from the box on which he was leaning, and there was a second's consultation – "Shall I tell them?" I heard him whisper. "Yes", Simon, Sam Hoare and David Margesson all nodded.'

Nicolson: 'He adjusted his pince-nez and read the document that had been handed to him. His whole face, his whole body, seemed to change. He raised his face so that the light from the ceiling fell full upon it. All the lines of anxiety and weariness seemed suddenly to have been smoothed out; he appeared ten years younger and triumphant. "Herr Hitler" he said, "has just agreed to postpone his mobilisation for twenty-four hours and to meet me in conference with Signor Mussolini and Monsieur Daladier at Munich."' Channon was over the moon. 'I felt sick with enthusiasm, longed to clutch [Chamberlain] – he continued for a word or two and then the House rose and in a scene of riotous delight, cheered, bellowed their approval. We stood on our benches, waved our order papers, shouted – until we were hoarse – a scene of indescribable enthusiasm – Peace must now be saved, and with it the world.'[25]

The following day Chamberlain flew to Munich where he met with Mussolini, Daladier and Hitler and in a few brief hours hammered out the division of Czechoslovakia before notifying Beneš's representatives. The next morning Chamberlain presented Hitler with an innocuous statement to the effect that Britain and Germany never wanted to go to war together, which Hitler happily signed. That night, brandishing the slip of paper aloft at the window of No. 10 he proclaimed, 'This is the second time there has come back from Germany to Downing Street peace with honour. I believe it is peace for our time.'

So Czechoslovakia became Czecho-Slovakia and Britain applauded. Only Duff Cooper resigned as a Minister. A few of the Eden/Churchill Tories sat in their glum seats and the Labour Party and Liberals objected on moral grounds, but broadly speaking Chamberlain's evasion of war was popular.

As far as Stafford was concerned, though, the whole Munich affair 'sacrificed the interests of Britain, not those of Czecho-slovakia'.[26] It was the worst of betrayals of principle and of the Czechs and he blamed Chamberlain's own ambivalence, 'It is because Chamberlain feels himself ideologically at one with Hitler and Mussolini that he persuades himself to believe their oft-broken word.'[27] Already there had been a shift in Stafford's political views, as we have seen, but if there had been any doubt that Stafford's views had been changed by the events of the previous weeks and months, the Parliamentary debate on Munich proved it as he argued in direct contradiction of his own ardently held beliefs of 1935 through to 1937, that only strong international organisations backed up by armaments and sanctions, could prevent war. He took the Government to task because it had 'failed, and purposely failed, to give that lead for strengthening these organisations of peace which might have given real effect to them as implements for securing the salvation of this country and other democratic countries'. Another new note entered his speech:

> Maybe to-day we have staved off war by the sacrifice of other people's national interests. That is a comparatively easy way of buying peace . . . You will not forever satisfy rival imperialism by handing over to them the smaller nations of the world. The time will come when the clash will be at your own door . . . Sweet reasonableness which consists in giving away the property of others and building up huge armaments to protect what is your own will never resolve the problem of peace; yet such is the policy of His Majesty's Government to-day.[28]

The final reversal of his foreign policy was completed as he argued in the *Guardian* three days later, 'I would be prepared to see the country armed. If you are going to try to get collective security especially in a world where there are gangsters, then you have got to have armed forces to keep the peace. The vital thing is that those armed forces should be under the control of the common people.'[29]

Meanwhile, unbeknown to him, as the Munich debate

continued, there were moves afoot to make a further breach in the Tory ranks. On 3 October, after Dalton's own condemnation of Chamberlain, Harold Macmillan approached him to suggest a meeting with those around Churchill – a suggestion Dalton cautiously and privately took up. The meeting took place later that night at Brendan Bracken's house in Lord North Street, where Churchill and Eden were gathered with a small band of supporters. Two issues were discussed. First, could the Labour amendment be re-worded so that Tory rebels might vote for it or at least abstain? And second, if Chamberlain, on the crest of popular support for Munich, decided to call a snap election and the rebels were deselected, was it possible to come to an electoral arrangement with Labour in key constituencies?

Dalton, more attracted to Churchill than to Eden, who had up till now been touted as the rebel leader, was clearly interested, though he remained sceptical as to whether such a deal could ever be delivered. After all, the Labour Party had declared itself against all forms of Crippsian pacts for years and even to suggest such an idea publicly would be to expose his flank to the accusations of hypocrisy from the left. So when Cripps approached Dalton on the morning of the Munich vote and suggested a meeting between Dalton, Attlee and Morrison on the Labour side, Churchill, Eden and Amery for the Tory rebels and Archibald Sinclair for the Liberals, he was both surprised and relieved. The Labour amendment, suitably toned down, did manage to attract between thirty and forty Tory Government abstentions, and Dalton got Attlee's permission to arrange further meetings along the lines Cripps had suggested. The rebels, however, when the threat of an election had subsided and their rebellion had passed without great incident or retribution from the whips, backed off and no further deal was done.

After Munich, then, Stafford resolved to use whatever means he could muster to achieve the objective of removing the appeasers and when the putative discussions with the rebels came to naught, he moved into a final and decisive stage of Popular Front advocacy. Already there was much talk of a General Election and when a couple of by-elections came up, in Oxford and in Bridgewater, Stafford decided to test his newest theory, that Labour could not win a General Election on its own, but a Popular Front could.

In the first of these, though, the waters were muddied by the fact that the selected Labour candidate was an old Unity Campaign friend, Patrick Gordon-Walker. When, immediately after the Munich debate, suggestions were made that a sole candidate should be put up against the Tory Quintin Hogg, Gordon-Walker at first refused to stand down and the National Executive initially agreed to back him if the local General Council of the Party agreed. A resolution to 'refrain from putting forward a candidate in the Oxford Parliamentary by-election' was then carried by forty-eight votes to twelve, with the support of Richard Crossman and Frank Pakenham (later the Labour PPC for Oxford City) – and Gordon-Walker stood down in favour of the Independent Master of Balliol College, A. D. Lindsay who was then supported by a Lib/Lab co-ordinating committee and fought under the title 'Independent Progressive'. Gordon-Walker was fairly bitter about the event, blaming his effective deselection on Labour Party unhappiness at his having supported Cripps's earlier Unity Campaign: 'I think this predisposed some of them to listen to the argument that the campaign was wrecked and thus to give them a conscientious reason for voting against me, even though I was now standing solidly for Labour.'[30] Whatever the reasons, Lindsay lost and Chamberlain received a fillip, despite a 3.9 per cent swing against the Government.

Some have argued that the failure in Oxford nevertheless established the precedent for sole anti-Government candidates and gave an impetus to Vernon Bartlett's campaign in Bridgewater. In fact the long-time peace campaigner and later Nobel

Peace Prize winner, Philip Noel-Baker, who had lost his Coventry seat in 1935, had fought the July 1936 Derby by-election as a Popular Front candidate in all but name since the local Liberals and Lloyd George's Council of Action had backed him. His opponent, the National Labour candidate and occasional Labour MP Albert Church who had stood against Stafford in 1935, attacked him for being supported by the Communist Willie Gallacher as well – proof positive, when Lloyd George came to speak, that this was 'a Popular Front of the one true Liberal, a Communist and an intellectual pacifist'.[31] Admittedly this particular Popular Front was cemented as much by Megan Lloyd George's secret affair with the married Noel-Baker as by any political realignment, but it is important to point out that throughout the thirties the Labour Party and the Liberals regularly declined to put up candidates in by-elections and by the time of Bridgewater a Popular Front candidate had already won. The difference about Bartlett, who had written in the second edition of *Tribune* that he was opposed to anything other than a United Front, was that he was now standing under an 'Independent Progressive' banner and openly referring to himself as a Popular Front candidate. So, without the early uncertainty that surrounded the Oxford campaign, and with Cripps's backing against the express decision of the National Executive, he had a clear run. When he won on 17 November, Stafford took the result as a vindication of his position and decided to steam ahead with plans for a re-shaped and newly invigorated Popular Front.

Stafford's roll call for the Popular Front varied enormously. At one moment 'all who are prepared to put the defence of democracy before their own personal or private interests [were] to be welcomed as allies' though the 'backbone of any anti-government bloc [would have] to be the mass movement of the workers'.[32] At another he was stating that 'At this moment [Eden] appears as an anti-Chamberlain champion as does that very mercurial politician Mr Winston Churchill, but neither of them represents anything but Imperialism and capitalism.'[33] Yet in the same breath he could state 'It would indeed be a different matter if some of the more democratically minded Conservatives were to join in with the forces of the left in this country where the power would be controlled by their democratic and progressive associates.'[34] In January 1939 he was still attacking the idea of a Churchill leadership, despite his earlier suggestions to Dalton and when Churchill's son-in-law the MP Duncan Sandys organised a meeting for young people as a thinly-veiled attempt to get a 'Churchill for PM' campaign going, Stafford argued that 'a combined opposition if ever we are to have one, must be led from the Left and not from the Right'.[35]

If Stafford was uncertain about the personnel, he was nonetheless clear about the policy and the implementation and in the closing months of 1938 he and Bevan, with the support of Pollitt, set about putting together a coherent and systematic campaign for the relaunch of the Popular Front – in secret. Stafford had learnt much from the abortive Socialist League and United Front campaigns. Reckoning that forward planning and an element of surprise were of the essence of an effective campaign, he prepared everything for 9 January when he wrote to the General Secretary of the Party demanding an urgent meeting of the Executive to discuss a lengthy memorandum he had drafted and enclosed. This was summoned the following Friday, the 13th. Even with a significant swing against the Government, Stafford argued, if both the Liberals and Labour won every seat where there was a majority of less than 3,000 the Government would still have a majority. If, however, the opposition combined behind a single candidate thirty-nine other seats could be won, which would give them a working majority. Cripps therefore advocated that Labour should lead a systematic co-operation between all the oppositional forces. There should be 'no permanent sacrifice of socialist principles' and 'the areas of co-operation sought, if any, must be wide enough to contribute an effective increase in oppositional power but not so wide as to bring in elements so discordant that combined working with them is impossible.' Furthermore, the new front should appeal to 'unpolitically minded people' including the young, and once electoral deals had been agreed a nationwide Popular Front campaign should be launched on the basis of a twelve point manifesto. This should stipulate the protection of democratic rights; peace by collective action with the USA, Russia and France; co-opera-tion with the Trade Unions on working conditions; higher standards of nutrition; removal of the family Means Test; improved pensions; raising the school leaving age; national planning of industrial development; planned assistance to agriculture; national control of transport and fair wages; controlled planning of mining; and control of finance through the Bank of England with 'the increase of direct taxation if necessary'.[36]

Inevitably the memorandum was voted down. To have accepted it would have meant that the Labour Party was announcing it could not win a future election, and many were extremely sceptical that electoral deals would ever deliver votes from one party to another. The vote, seventeen to three, with Pritt and Wilkinson supporting Cripps, and Laski away, was almost irrelevant to Stafford though, as Pritt realised when at the end of the meeting he told him 'I shall take this to the Party... I shall circulate all the Divisional and Borough Labour Parties, and other Party organisations.' Stafford then showed Pritt a letter he was proposing to send out, which he supposed to be in draft, though when Pritt suggested some amendments he admitted, 'As a matter of fact, all the docu-ments are ready. I want everyone in the local organisations to be able to consider them before the week-end is over. The documents are in envelopes ready addressed, and my people are waiting to hear from me. I shall telephone them, and they will post them at once.'[37] So saying, he left the meeting, borrowed a coin from a passing journalist and rang from the call-box opposite Transport House, thereby giving the journalist an unexpected scoop. The tactic may have been clever in stealing a march in the Party on the National Executive, but it was fatally flawed in two regards. For a start it was hardly the way to win the heartfelt backing of his closest allies on the Executive itself. As Pritt put it: 'We were at school together, at the Bar together, in Parliament together, and on the National Executive Committee together; but I never knew him well.'[38] This was not the way to win friends and influence them.

Cripps's actions also gave the National Executive a perfect excuse to punish him not for what he said but for how he had gone about saying it. When all became known a further meeting of the Executive was scheduled for four fifteen in the afternoon of 18 January so that he could attend after court but he declined to attend, maintaining that he had an urgent consultation with the Midland Bank, thereby infuriating the leadership even more. The matter was then referred to the Labour Party Organisational Sub-Committee, which recommended that Stafford must withdraw both the memorandum and his call for a special conference forthwith, or be expelled. Stafford's reply was equally forthright: 'To suggest that the objective discussion of the case for a combined opposition against the National Government is to create harmful confusion and division within the Party, is to refuse recognition of the fact that there is already a ferment of opinion in the Party upon this subject'[39] and he determined to fight on. So on 25 January, with Pritt laid up with gout and Laski still away in America, Wilkinson was the only person to vote for him, and Cripps was expelled. In fact it is probable that Pritt chose not to attend the meeting as he later confessed: 'For myself I decided that I ought to obey Party discipline and not follow Cripps into exile; he had probably assumed that I would follow him, for he was always convinced that he was in the right in whatever policy he adopted, and expected everyone to agree with him.'[40]

Stafford now let himself loose on the mass meeting circuit. At an 'Arms for Spain' meeting with Bartlett, Lindsay, and J. B. Priestley organized by Gollancz in the Queen's Hall that same night, he declared that 'the accepted shibboleths of parties and organisations may pass unchallenged in times of comparative peace and quiet but when the heart of every citizen of this country is wracked with constant fear, as it is today, the tactics and strategies of the past come under review, if not by those in authority then by the common people of the country.' He demanded

Why is it that this Government, out of touch with and antagonistic to the sentiments and wishes of the People remains in power? It was for answering that question and circulating the answer in a memorandum throughout the Labour Party that I was deprived of my membership . . . The answer . . . is because the opposition to [the National Government] is not a strong united opposition but an opposition fighting amongst itself, with all the uncertainness doubt and hesitation that such internecine struggles inevitably create.[41]

Rebel Tories might be involved in the new campaign but it must be the forces of progress that led it. In biblical cadences he argued,

The new wine of common sense, decency and justice must be put into new bottles . . . This is the moment to drive out of office the incompetent gang of betrayers who have already brought our country to ruin . . . We don't want a new unity facade for the old conservative building. We want a new progressive building into which to move at once.[42]

The message carried emotional and moral force, at least for

a while. A selection of Labour Prospective Candidates backed
him, successful meetings were held in Dundee, Arbroath,
Glasgow and Paisley and *Tribune* reported a warm reception
with 1,200 offers of help and 400 new Labour Party members.
In York 1,500 people turned up to a meeting and the Palace
Theatre in Manchester hosted 3,500. Stafford declared: 'I
could sense the oft-deferred hopes of many in the audience
struggling to break through the disillusionments and disappointments of the past.'[43] The Liberal Lady Violet Bonham
Carter, a close friend of both the Crippses and Churchill,
backed him declaring that 'his powerful appeal to all those
who think and feel alike to face realities and act together has
given the first definite hope to the forces of progress'[44] and on
the night of Stafford's expulsion Bevan announced that 'if Sir
Stafford Cripps is expelled for wanting to unite the forces of
freedom and democracy they can go on expelling others. They
can expel me. His crime is my crime.'[45] Recognising the
emotional force of his fellow Wykehamist's argument, Richard
Crossman wrote in the *New Statesman and Nation*, 'we know
that we are not living in a world which is evolving towards
socialism and in which there is time to wait. That is why many
of us, who often disagree with Sir Stafford Cripps's tactics and
opinions, feel that he is fundamentally on our side. He knows
the urgency of the situation and realises that Labour cannot
jog along in the old traditional way.'[46]

In February the campaign was given a new edge with the
launch of a 'petition' under six headings: defend democracy;
plan for plenty; secure our Britain; protect the people's interest; defend the people; and build for peace and justice.
National and Regional Petition Committees were set up under
the slogan 'Make the Petition your Protection' and *Tribune*
reported thirty-five Divisional Labour Parties, forty Leagues
of Youth and eight Trades Councils pledging support. Cripps's
own divisional party backed him, despite threats of suspension, as did the West of England Liberal Party and major

packed meetings were held in the Kelvin Hall in Glasgow, the Music Hall in Edinburgh and the Cambridge Corn Exchange.

Meanwhile Stafford kept up his Parliamentary battle as well, declaring in the motion of censure debate over Unemployment on 16 February that

> what the people are looking for is not a particularist Government, not even a Government cloaked under the camouflage of 'National' . . . They are looking for a true Government of the people that will protect them and will face all the evils of unemployment not with crocodile tears and excuses or capitalists' selected statistics, but with measures that are practicable and which can be financed if the will and the desire to carry them through are there. The true moral of this debate is that those many elements which are sick and tired of the Government should combine together and replace it at the earliest possible moment.[47]

The climax of the Petition Campaign though, came in March when a massive 7,000 filled the Empress Hall to see 'Stafford Cripps, hands in jacket pockets, alert, grave, outlined by spotlights in the darked arena'[48] and to take part in the March for Unity with miners with pit lamps, railwaymen from the St Pancras station strike and a parade of seamen.

As for the big guns, several Liberal MPs, Richard Acland, Wilfrid Roberts, Violet Bonham Carter and their Leader, Sir Archibald Sinclair, supported the Petition, and Maynard Keynes wrote that he was 'in full sympathy with what you are doing'.[49] Alfred Barnes, the Chair of the Co-op threw his weight behind it, chairing several of its meetings, and from the Parliamentary Labour Party Cecil Poole, Sam Watson and Noel Brailsford joined Bevan, Strauss, Trevelyan and Will Lawther in the rebel camp. Gollancz threw himself into the campaign, writing to another supporter, Hewlett Johnson, that he was 'up to the eyes over the whole Cripps situation' and he even persuaded Johnson to add a special postscript to his *Act Now: An appeal to the Mind and Heart of Britain* in support of the Petition – though not one of the two million copies it sold was available until well after the Cripps expulsion was done and dusted. Wilkinson, refusing to support the petition, like Pritt, resigned from the board of *Tribune* as soon as the National Executive expelled Cripps but Bernard Shaw was certain of Stafford's success,

> Sir Stafford Cripps proposed a Holy Alliance to get rid of the present Government as Napoleon was got rid of at Waterloo, by a mixed force of British, Belgians and Prussians under an Irish General. If a Labour member may not propose this he may not propose anything. But the Labour Party Executive, taking a leaf out of Herr Hitler's book, promptly expels Sir Stafford, who, whether right or wrong, will presently wipe the floor with it for being so silly.[50]

Tawney, however, along with the Webbs, Christopher Addison, Leonard Woolf and J. A. Hobson, remained ambivalent about the Petition tactics, but signed a letter to the National Executive calling for a compromise whilst seven MPs, Bevan, Strauss, S. O. Davis, John Parker, Cecil Poole, Ben Riley and Phillips Price wrote in with Crossman, Cole and Pakenham deploring Cripps's expulsion and saying that 'we regard it as in keeping with the failure of the Executive to mobilise effectively the opposition to the National Government which exists in this country among members of all parties and among those who belong to no party. There is a great danger that this failure, if continued, will reduce the Labour Party to political impotence.'[51]

Meanwhile Beatrice Webb recorded a conversation at her home at Passfield Corner with Tawney that revealed the bewilderment many on the left felt about Stafford's activities,

> He takes the same view as we do of Stafford Cripps's brilliancy and charm – but inability to take counsel with fellow workers, and instability in ends and means. 'It was only yesterday that Stafford was insisting on uniting in the Socialist League the extreme left – C.P., ILP – with the Labour Party against the other two parties, in favour of thoroughgoing socialism with no compromise. Today he argues for joining hands with Liberals and dissentient Conservatives with a moderate programme in another sort of National government, dominated by the Labour Party. It is difficult to accept a heretic into your command who is always changing his creed,' says Tawney.[52]

It was a point that Attlee took up in his first ever personal attack on Cripps:

> The swing over by a man of great ability in a few months from the advocacy of a rigid and exclusive unity of the working classes to a demand for an alliance with the capitalists, and from insistence on the need for a Government carrying out a Socialist policy to put Socialism in cold storage for the duration of the international crisis, is a remarkable phenomenon. Such instability gives me little trust in his judgement. In a few months he may ask us all to change again.[53]

The next day he wrote to his brother Tom: 'It is a great pity about Stafford, but like all the Potter family he is so absolutely convinced that the policy which he puts forward for the time being is absolutely right that he will listen to no arguments.'[54]

The March meeting of the National Executive, on a much closer vote of thirteen to eleven, made support for Cripps an offence and two PPCs, Robert Bruce and Lt-Commander

Edgar Young, as well as Bevan, Strauss, Trevelyan, Poole and Lawther, were told that they must recant within seven days. Only the last two gave in and the remainder followed Cripps into exile on 30 March. A fairly vindictive personal campaign was also waged, with accusations that Stafford's staff at Filkins were not unionised and insinuations about his wealth. As the general secretary of the National Union of Distributive and Allied Workers put it,

> Cripps as a gentleman is a very fine fellow indeed, but I do not think that he is a Socialist. He is a most peculiar type of man. For four years no one knew precisely where he was going to jump next. We have not expelled Cripps for his memorandum only, but for four years of grave indiscretions against the policy of our party.[55]

Many ordinary party members, as Attlee had foreseen, resented Stafford's easy access to a platform and his wealth just as much as they objected to his apparent undermining of the Party and in open criticism of him there often crept in a hint of envy, as in G. Ridley of the Railway Clerk's Association's line that 'by accident of birth and a privileged capacity to earn a fabulous income, a privately controlled political machine is being created that gravely menaces the authority of the Party'.[56]

At the same time international events were pulling the Labour movement in two different directions. For on 5 March General Franco marched into Madrid and despite strong rumours of mass executions, Chamberlain recognised his new Government – and on the 15th Hitler reneged on the whole Munich agreement, invading Czechoslovakia and renaming it the German Protectorate of Bohemia. On the one hand these new developments proved both the aggression of the Fascist dictators and the equal determination of the National Government to appease them. This might have strengthened the left's arm but, as Ben Pimlott has pointed out, the collapse of Barcelona and then of Madrid was crucial in finally wearing down the spirit of the petition campaign which was 'for many . . . a final throw to save Spain; when it failed there seemed little worth fighting for'.[57] Even Bevan's ebullience was stemmed: 'We have seen the ideals of our movement and the gallant workers who have fought for them harried and slaughtered all over Europe, and we have not helped them to victory or succoured them in defeat.'[58]

So began a steady run of defeats for the Petition in the run-up to the Labour Party Conference in May. First came the April Co-operative Party Conference which, despite its Chairman's support rejected the Popular Front by 2,854,000 to 1,923,000. There were still heart-warming set pieces like the Left Book Club rally at the Empress Hall on 24 April when Cripps appeared again with Acland, Pollitt, Strachey and Roberts and was joined by the Nobel Peace Prize winner Norman Angell, the singer and activist Paul Robeson and the veteran Lloyd George who had finally declared his open support for Popular Front initiatives. The meeting was the most successful yet, but the run of meetings at which Popular Front resolutions were defeated grew faster right through to May and Gollancz recorded that he already felt the cause was lost.

When the Party Conference came at the end of the month the Petition-ers tried to act as a group, although in the end it was only Cripps who was heard and Cripps became the issue. So far they had been rigorous in arguing that Labour must lead any Popular Front rather than simply be enveloped in a new Party, and they had made a particular point of using the Campaign to recruit new Labour Party members – all of which was designed to mitigate the charges of undermining the Party. So Bevan wrote an open letter in *Tribune* to Labour Party Conference saying 'We do not ourselves seek to form the Popular Front. We wish the Labour Party to lead it . . . Nothing has been further from our minds than to introduce another political party into the confusion which already exists.'[59] Clearly the aim was to argue that if their campaign to get the Labour Party to lead a Popular Front was a transgression of the rules then it must logically be impossible for anyone to seek to change Party policy on any matter. To agree the expulsions was to turn the Party into 'an intellectual concentration camp', and 'if every organized effort to change Party policy is to be described as an organized attack on the Party itself then the rigidity imposed by Party discipline will soon change into *rigor mortis*'.[60]

There were already Popular Front resolutions on the Conference agenda but the first issue to be resolved was whether Conference would back the National Executive's expulsions of the rebels. Both Bevan and Cripps were supported by their constituencies and Bevan had even managed to win over the South Wales Miners' Federation, so despite the fact that they were not able to speak themselves they did have an indirect voice. Furthermore, once the Bristol East constituency delegate had moved that the expulsions be referred back and thus effectively overturned, the suspension of standing orders was moved to allow Cripps and Bevan to speak. The vote on the suspension of standing orders was close – 1,227,000 to 1,083,000 – and Bevin, who was still determined that neither of them should be able to address Conference, managed to intervene to get Cripps to speak on his own.

Michael Foot has argued that this was fatal for the rebels, for 'if ever Cripps needed Bevan, this was the hour'. Certainly Stafford's speech seems to have been lacklustre, meticulous and over-restrained, refusing to appeal to the hearts of the delegates and presenting his argument more like a lawyer than a Labour leader, but much of the problem lay with the whole approach of the rebels at Southport. Both Bevan in his articles for *Tribune* and Stafford himself at the Conference, narrowed the issue to whether Cripps had been right to circulate his Memorandum. It was a dry argument and it was drily put. Stafford would have been better to attack the Government, expose the inadequacies of the National Executive's case, hint at what might be achieved under a Popular Front Government, recall Spain, inveigh against Fascism and excite the Conference with a call for the honour of dissent. Instead he foolishly raised some of the insinuations that had until now remained unvoiced. 'I am bound to say one thing in view of the somewhat unpleasant statements made about me by some members of the Executive, and that is that they never showed any objection to the fact that I earned a large income when I was in the party. Indeed, I was regarded, I believe, as somewhat of an asset to the party.'[61] He even appealed to the Conference for leniency on the basis of his having appeared for the miners after the Gresford disaster without pay, bringing in an element of rather overt and unattractive special pleading – all of which only really gave the impression of an aloof and self-righteous lawyer. In truth the National Executive barely had to answer his speech.

It was a young Transport Workers' Union officer, George Brown, the constituency delegate for Stafford Albans, who was to play the role of Cripps's chief executioner, just as his boss Bevin had done for Lansbury in 1935. Earlier he had attended the Transport Workers' delegation meeting and told Bevin 'that I thought he was doing a wicked thing in using the union's massive card vote against giving Cripps a hearing' and when Bevin 'thanked [him] politely for [his] advice and told [him] to keep [his] mouth shut'[62] he resolved to cast his paltry 1,000 votes against Bevin's 337,000, in favour of suspending standing orders.

When Cripps spoke, though, Brown thought he was 'disastrous'[63] and asked to speak. When he was called, on the first day of his first Labour Party Conference, he 'nearly fell off the rostrum with fright', but he knew what he wanted to say and he argued with spontaneous sentiment, clearly reflecting the feeling of the hall.

> I had been in favour of giving Cripps a hearing, but I still thought that he ought to be expelled and his speech made me angry. I set about him in no uncertain fashion and said that I didn't see any reason why he should have wanted money for representing miners after Gresford. I thought that my members in Hertfordshire were doing quite a lot for him, and some of them had less than 35s. a week to live on.[64]

Brown managed to rally his argument far more effectively than Cripps and won the day, before Dalton summed up for the National Executive, with his declaration that

> the fact is that we have wasted nine blasted months in a pre-election year just doing nothing but argue the toss about Cripps . . . I think we ought to remind Sir Stafford Cripps, Mr Bevan and my old boss, Lt-Commander Young, who probably remembers ordering me around the show-rooms in Oxford Street – we ought to remind these people that the part is not greater than the whole, and while we are members of the Party and the Executive may be a pack of idiots, once we have decided we are, we may as well go forward.[65]

All that was left was for Dalton to put the National Executive's case calmly and without rancour – which he did.

If there had ever been any doubt as to whether Conference would overturn the National Executive's decision the combination of Stafford's dry and rather haughty speech and Brown's straight speaking meant the National Executive won the vote easily and the expulsions were confirmed by an overwhelming vote of five to one. Whether Brown's intervention was truly decisive or not is a moot point. After all Crossman, who had supported the Popular Front, now felt that Cripps had bored and irritated most of the Party to distraction and it seems far more likely that Brown was simply articulating what others already felt. Nevertheless he certainly held that Cripps and Bevan blamed him personally for their expulsion. 'Neither Bevan nor Cripps ever took kindly to me after that. Bevan did relent in time, but Cripps never spoke to me again. I've even stood in a toilet with him when we were both Ministers, and he still couldn't remember my name. He was a great Christian, and certainly had faith and hope, but it never seemed to me he really got the point about charity.'[66]

The Conference proceeded two days later to despatch the Popular Front resolutions even more overwhelmingly than the expulsions. Ellen Wilkinson was left to write: 'He forgets that party government is an essential instrument of political liberty in a democracy . . . Yet by his sheer honesty and selflessness Cripps can always command loyalty. He is a bad leader but a magnificent lieutenant.'[67] So Stafford Cripps walked away from Southport an Independent MP.

13

Why?

When Stafford and Isobel walked away from the Conference at Southport there were many who were perplexed at how he had managed to cast himself into the wilderness. After all, here was a man who could speak better than any of his colleagues, could pack a meeting almost without notice, had been twice elected to the National Executive and topped the elections for the Parliamentary Labour Party for four years; a man evidently capable as an administrator and as a Parliamentary performer, especially on technical matters; a man of sharp forensic intelligence with powerful political allies and relatives in the Labour movement. Admittedly he had been catapulted into leadership in the dying moments of the 1929–31 Labour Government and so had perhaps unfairly earned the reputation of 'the man to watch', but in less than a decade this putative leader seemed systematically to have thrown away every chance of influence and every hope of advancement. His leadership of the Labour left, moreover, had finally led neither to the reinvigoration of the Labour Party, nor to a 'slap-up Socialism' but to the humiliating expulsion from the Party of most of its leading lights.

Others had their explanations. Many echoed Bevin's allegation of self-martyrdom against Lansbury, and Morrison saw in him a 'subconscious belief that he was a political Messiah'.[1] In part this fed off his deeply-felt religious beliefs. The stone that the builders rejected has now become the cornerstone. The prophet crying in the wilderness is the true voice of God. Blessed are those who thirst after righteousness. Blessed are those who are persecuted for righteousness' sake. These were the texts that Stafford could refer to in his assertion that to be considered wrong, to be out of synch with the times was no sin but a virtue, and to be expelled from the Party, by logical extension, was a manifestation not of political folly but of moral strength. This 'suffering servant' model was, of course, dangerous, for a belief in one's own destiny is equally the creed of the self-deluding madman and the excuse of the arrogant and the ambitious.

But Stafford believed in the need for a whole body of people who, in the words of Lansbury, would 'see the cause of Socialism as a religion to be served as Saint Francis, Savanarola and Tolstoy served their faiths'.[2] As Raymond Postgate, Lansbury's biographer and son-in-law and post-Cripps editor of *Tribune*, argued, the left's 'struggle was a crusade, the object was to win converts to a socialist faith'.[3] It was inevitable that the rhetoric and imagery of the Labour left was as often theological as political. At dinner with the Webbs in 1933 Tawney and Cripps had agreed that 'the Labour Party would never be effective until it was led by a compact group who would live the life' and it was this almost monastic ethic that informed Stafford's sense of his own calling. The problem was that as a political philosophy it left him very exposed and because there was no fixed point in his ever-turning world other than his faith, he had little to judge ideas or people by and he appeared 'oddly immature in intellect and unbalanced in judgement, [showing] a strange lack of discrimination and low standard of reasoning in picking up ideas'.[4] But strength of personality and independence of spirit had been the most regular of sermon themes in the Edwardian Church of England and Stafford would have drunk deep at that particular well at Winchester. In a revealing letter to his daughter Peggy, who opted out of

University to spend a year in Italy with the painter Audrey Waterfield, he preached the ethic that he himself lived by:

> The real function of education is not as many educated seem to think, to turn out a good standardised article, but to draw out the peculiar capacities of individuals. The trouble is these so often get squashed before they can even get strong enough to grow. Don't let yours get sat on by anyone ... There's an objective for you, my dear. In the meantime your aged parents stagger on in this very trying world, attempting to do something to remedy it but meeting with very little apparent success. Fortunately we both believe no good effort is ever wasted in the long run, so we go along as best we may, trying to do what we can.[5]

Just as Stafford and Isobel subscribed to the ideal of personal reticence and privacy, so they respected the pioneer, the radical individualist, even the maverick and the eccentric. For the Edwardian gentleman was not supposed to show his emotions, nor relate his religious beliefs. Personal privacy was a virtue and the guardianship of the heart, as of the body, was an absolute maxim. Even in the days of the World Alliance Stafford had rarely spoken of God and he resolutely stuck to good form by not showing his feelings. Morrison, who regularly visited Goodfellows, called him 'a man with a mind that completely controlled emotions' and another guest referred to their host as a 'cold fish', yet few denied his evident 'charm' and Morrison admitted it was 'the mixture of charm and coldness [that] could spoil what was otherwise a delightful visit'.[6]

So Stafford's course through the thirties was as much determined by his evangelical fervour and his Edwardian credal adherence to spirited independence as by the actual logic of his own position and his manifest brilliance simply made things worse as he could argue everyone into the ground. 'In private discussions he was invincible,' confessed Morrison. 'There was many an occasion when in our personal talks I took the opposite view to his. We would argue until he got me to a point where my case could no longer be argued, yet I knew in my bones that he was wrong and I was right, which subsequent events usually proved to be so.'[7] He was a prophet new inspired at the turn of every political corner, and because he grasped a part of the truth each time and could articulate it more powerfully than anyone else could express the complicated whole truth, he boxed himself into corners.

But there was another aspect of Stafford's character which acted as a powerful political motor and this was his intellectual fastidiousness. Many mentioned his punctiliousness. Both Betts and Morrison complained about being packed off to bed as the clock struck ten, and Stafford was as precise about his rising as about his retiring. Yet he was no Puritan. He dressed immaculately, in well-tailored Savile Row suits. He was well manicured and as a conventional gentleman wore a gold signet ring. He smoked almost incessantly, a habit that the real Puritans of his day decried as appalling looseness. What mattered to him was that things should be in their right place and at their right time.

As with time, so with ideas. For Cripps's mind was always most attracted to an idea, a plan or a creed if it could demonstrate a perfect internal logic. Even if the premises upon which it was based might be wrong, if it could satisfy his quest for internal consistency, it would do. Thus his support for the Unity Campaign and his whole position on the prospect of war up until 1937 was, in the oldest sense of the word, a 'nice argument'. Labour has been prevented from instituting Socialism by the bankers because its gradualism was too mealy-mouthed and lacking in courage. Success must lie in a slap-up Socialism that was class based and stout-hearted enough to seize hold of the constitution so as to prevent further defeat.

Fascism, whether that of Hitler and Mussolini, or that of the National Government, was the final flourish of capitalism, and must be defeated, but because Capitalist Governments will only wage war in the defence of capitalism, the workers' only resort is to overthrow the Capitalist Government either in an election or by means of a General Strike. The argument was tidy and pure and it allowed for no give or take. It was indeed the ideological embodiment of the words of Revelation, 'you are neither cold nor hot. Would that you were cold or hot! So, because you are lukewarm and neither cold nor hot, I will spew you out of my mouth.'[8]

In the end logical consistency is not enough, and it is difficult not to sympathise with Dalton's complaint, 'Report of another outrageous speech by Cripps, saying that if, under Locarno, there were "a capitalist war, in the ordinary sense of the term, the Labour Party would resist it and organise a General Strike if it could."!!! Every word wrong!'[9] There were gaping holes in Stafford's argument and it was based on fundamentally false premises: that it was possible to achieve a Socialist Government at least in Britain before the final con-flagration with Nazi aggression would have to be faced; that the League of Nations could only be made to work by the world-wide collaboration of the working class; and, most significantly, that the workers were themselves prepared to strike.

Yet even when the utter implausibility of his arguments was brought home to Stafford at the turn of 1937 and he began to advocate the Popular Front, it was again the logical consis-tency of his position that attracted him, even though others could and did point to the fact that he was now urging exactly the opposite of what he had supported only a few months earlier. Now, he argued, an impending confrontation with Fascism was inevitable. Deals with dictators were morally indefensible. The appeasers must therefore be removed. Labour could not win an election on its own, and a General

Election need not be held before the end of 1939, so all the 'democratic forces' who opposed Chamberlain should combine both in campaigning against the National Government *and* in electoral pacts to secure victory either in Parliament or at the polls. Never mind that the argument relied on a very optimistic reading of how voters would redistribute themselves in the event of there only being two candidates; or that it assumed that if Labour announced that it felt it could not win the election it would gain support in the polls. What mattered to Stafford was that here was an internally consistent plan of action.

One of the other factors to which Stafford's steady extravagant and erring progress was attributed at the time was his lack of experience or understanding of the Labour movement. This was put in one of two ways, either he was inexpert in Socialist philosophy, or he was not a real man of the Labour movement. Thus Pritt reckoned Stafford 'had the reputation of being a left-winger; like so many who "go left" because they grow impatient with the abuses of capitalism, but have no serious political education – he for example, boasted that he had never read a line of Marx'.[10] Morrison said that Stafford had been promoted too fast, Foot that his Marxist slogans were only half digested, and Attlee that his acquaintance with the Labour movement was too fleeting for him to understand his colleagues.

Yet none of these is entirely convincing. He had little time or energy for political nuances and he was impatient of party politics, but the real nub of complaint for many was that he was never really a 'Labour man'. Unlike Attlee or Dalton, both of whom were just as middle class as Stafford, he never sought or managed to court the Trade Union mainstream of the movement and the loyalty he inspired came almost entirely from the ranks of Labour's Liberal converts, the Christian Socialists and the principled intelligentsia.

Two other points need mentioning at this point that help

explain the Cripps of the thirties. The first is that he was not quite in the minority that he might appear. For British opinion, as the Peace Ballot showed, was not unanimous. There was a significant minority, more than one in five, who refused to back force, a fact which pacifists like Alfred Salter took as a vindication of their position. Furthermore in the Church circles which Stafford frequented, there was a strong and devoted body of opinion that leaned towards pacifism. Indeed Christians were among many of the leading pacifists and in opposing rearmament Stafford was in the company not only of the likes of Lansbury but of Bishop Barnes of Birmingham who chaired the National Peace Council and attacked the Bishop of Gloucester for his belief that, 'the Fuehrer belongs to those who fulfil the will of God and realise the life of Christ in this life to an extraordinary degree';[11] and Dick Sheppard, the rector of St Martin-in-the-Fields and one-time Dean of Canterbury who, in 1936, together with Lansbury, Salter, Cecil Wilson, Vera Brittain and A. A. Milne initiated both the 'War we say No' campaign and then the Peace Pledge Union, inviting men of military age to sign a declaration that they would never again, directly or indirectly, support or sanction a war. Again there was a large public response with half a million signatures collected within a few weeks.

Moreover, in industrial and economic politics Stafford was by no means a lone voice in the Church. George Bell, the Bishop of Chichester, Leslie Hunter, the Bishop of Sheffield, Frank Woods at Peterborough and, most notably, William Temple, the Archbishop of York, were all outspoken on political issues, and two of the Labour Government's last clerical appointments, Alfred Blunt as Bishop of Bradford and Hewlett Johnson as Dean of Canterbury, spoke in remarkably similar tones to those of Cripps. Indeed Cripps's brief advocacy of Major Douglas's crackpot economic idea was thanks to the influence of Johnson, to whom he wrote in 1935,

I can assure you that I have taken a good deal of trouble in studying the Social Credit system, and last summer Major Douglas came and had a good talk with me for about three hours. I should very much like to meet you and to discuss it . . . Social Credit, like Family Allowances and other suggestions for distribution, cannot operate except as inflationary measures under the capitalist system. Once the State has control of the monetary and credit machinery, I have always taken the view that Social Credit could be introduced, though whether it would be the best way of planning distribution is another problem.[12]

Johnson, with his peacock personal extravagance, in many ways the dialectical opposite of Cripps, shared his friendship with Gollancz and interest in Soviet Russia and was a regular contributor to *Tribune*. He was far from a unique clerical supporter of the LBC and Cripps regularly shared a platform with equally left-wing Anglicans such as G.O. Iredell, the vicar of the 'Red Church' of St Clement's Barnsbury and Stanley Evans, and when in 1934 he joined the Socialist Christian League of which Lansbury was president, he came into contact with a whole range of active Christian Socialists, the vast majority of whom were on the pacifist or radical wings of the Labour movement.

Moreover Bishop Blunt, who was not a pacifist but was a member of the Labour Party, was uncompromising in his attack on privilege and the innate conservatism of the Church of England, telling his Diocesan Conference in 1936:

A really converted Christian will want to sacrifice privilege of the sake of justice to others . . . I want a Christian Crusade to Mayfair as well as to Limehouse. But Mayfair will never be aroused to listen so long as the Church puts an embargo on any words of Christ which would condemn the iniquity by which Mayfair is allowed to remain

Mayfair while Limehouse remains Limehouse.'[13]

Even when under attack from Tory MPs he would retaliate,

> The Church of England is predominantly composed of
> Conservatives – of people who are the defenders of the
> status quo, and who therefore do not want any reform
> except reform so timid that it does not reform much; and
> so naturally they suggest that the Church of England
> should accept the status quo. They fail to observe that by
> accepting the blessing of the status quo, the Church of
> England is a partisan. It is a partisan of that particular
> party that loves the status quo.[14]

So Stafford would not have felt alone. He was part of a large
minority who saw a common cause between pure pacifism
and an ideological opposition to a Capitalist war. It was a
minority that could command public attention and knew how
to organise regular mass meetings with several thousands
lauding and cheering their courageous and independently-
minded leaders. These gave Cripps the sense of being right, of
being able to turn the wheel of politics, however slowly, and
every year there came a new moment when it genuinely
seemed possible that the miracle would happen and Britain
would shake off her yoke.

Furthermore, Stafford enjoyed the luxury of an extremely
supportive family in which it would have been difficult to feel
a loner. Michael Foot and Barbara Betts, who regularly visited
Goodfellows in the thirties, were very critical of the family:

> we [Foot and Betts] shared a streak of irreverence, so we
> were not quite what Stafford hoped for. At Filkins we
> were expected to sit round with the family listening
> respectfully to the great man as his children seemed to
> do, but we were not very good at it. We were both fond of

Isobel, Stafford's wife, a kindly, understanding woman, but she had had to learn domestic diplomacy, so we were the only people who ever challenged Stafford's arguments.[15]

Betts's account seems rather wide of the mark, though. For John Cripps had himself become by now something of a young radical, albeit with a fogey air. He had travelled with the Webbs to Russia in 1932, regularly accompanied Stafford to Party Conference, and was often reckoned by Stafford's colleagues to have been the major influence on his great concern with capturing the hearts and minds of young people in the Petition Campaign. Theresa went to Spain during the Civil War and Peggy, whose commitment to revolutionary politics was later confirmed by her marriage to Joe Appiah, was just as deeply committed to Christian Socialism as her father. As for Isobel, it is true that much of the thirties were absorbed with the business of running a large home, though her daughter Theresa maintains that she was 'never domesticated' and it was not really until the war itself that she came into her own as a political animal. Lord Parmoor was also broadly supportive of Stafford throughout the 1930s, although his increasing frailty meant that he was less and less involved in the minutiae of Labour politics, and his wife Marion was very much involved in issues that Stafford took a close interest in, most notably the India Conciliation Group and the Friends' Peace Committee.

As for Cripps's real and enduring faults, these are manifest. He refused to listen to reason. There was a great deal of vanity and arrogance in his self-righteous belief in himself. He rarely communicated with others before he went into action and regularly risked alienating his closest allies. Murphy argued that in late 1938 and early 1939 he should have presented himself as the spokesman for the 120 constituency parties that had called for a Popular Front, but instead he decided to branch out on his own, re-inventing a campaign that already existed and making himself the fulcrum. Pritt accused him of not consulting, and Foot reckoned his sacking of Mellor was decidedly cruel. Indeed he left many people questioning his intelligence or bitter at his apparent coldness.

Tactically, of course, his big mistake was not to have turned against Lansbury in 1935. There was no real reason not to. After all his politics were not pacifist. He believed in a legitimate use of force, but not towards Capitalist ends. Whether it was this or a personal adherence to Lansbury – or perhaps a false estimation that Lansbury would survive as leader – either way it meant that he was thereafter left to the side in any serious consideration of possible leaders. Attlee, who did change his view at the 1935 Conference, won the leadership on the back of his change of mind, and undoubtedly if Cripps had done the same he would have been a strong contender. But that takes us into the bounds of wild conjecture. The fact is that Cripps could no more have deserted Lansbury than he could have backed Dalton. Lansbury and later Gollancz, Bevan, Pollitt, Mellor, all belonged to a strain of British Labour that believed the task was to delineate a slap-up Socialism that individuals could actually live by. Socialism was an article of faith, not a political tactic, and it needed adherents not supporters. To have turned on Lansbury would have been to betray one of his own and to surrender all pretence of integrity.

14

Applying for Active Service

The day after the Southport expulsion Stafford, Bevan, Strauss and the rest reapplied for membership of the Party agreeing to accept the Party's decision on the Popular Front and offering to sign the usual undertakings. The National Executive, though, refused even to consider the issue before the autumn, (by which time war had been declared), and when they did they required each of the applicants to sign further statements committing them not to oppose Party policy and expressing regret for their past deeds. At first all of them refused to sign and in October Stafford wrote in high indignation to the Executive pointing out that if his advice had been followed 'we should not be in the ghastly position we are in today'. He castigated the Labour leadership for having effectively engine-ered the situation whereby they had to support the 'most reactionary Government which has not only been responsible for our present plight but which bids fair to destroy the country by its continued ineptitudes and inefficiencies'. He refused to sign any declaration that he would never oppose any Party policy, a demand which he felt 'might well form part of the credo of some totalitarian party in a dictatorship state'.[1] And finally, mustering all his self-righteousness, he was not pre-pared 'to express regret at the action taken by me, as I am now, more than ever, convinced that the action was not only fully justified, but was the only action that I could have taken consistently with my duty to my constituents, and the best interests of the workers of this country'.[2] Thus spake Stafford Cripps, but two of his co-exiles were more sanguine about the prospects of achieving anything outside the Party and after the Wales Miners' Federation had intervened on Bevan's behalf, a less draconian formula was found and Bevan and Strauss agreed to undertake 'to refrain from conducting or taking part in campaigns in opposition to the declared policy of the Party; but this declaration does not interfere with my legitimate rights within the Party Constitution'.[3] So in December 1939 Bevan and Strauss were readmitted.

The difference between Cripps and Bevan at this point is interesting, and reinforces the oft-cited belief that Cripps never had a proper grounding in the Labour movement. Of those who were expelled at Southport it was the two wealthy revolutionaries, Stafford Cripps and Charles Trevelyan, who decided to hold fast to principle rather than buckle under. For neither of them was the term 'Independent' a bogey word. Trevelyan had started out in the Liberal Party and underwent the same transmigration as Alfred, with a long wartime stretch of semi-detached independence. So there was little sense of urgency in Stafford's desire to get back into the Labour Party. Several of the Bristol constituency officers also had their membership withdrawn because they chose to support him and the Bristol East Party was suspended – and he expected that if there were a General Election he might hold the seat as an Independent.

Maurice Shock, who worked on a biography of Cripps for several years, maintains that when Stafford left Southport he resolved never again to be Party-less. The truth is, though, that he was scarcely interested by now in political Parties and if he made any resolution in Southport it was to do everything in his power by secret negotiation to bring about the end of the Chamberlain Government. In Eric Estorick's words he set about using 'every personal contact he possessed among the supporters of Chamberlain to disintegrate their support'.[4] His personal contacts in the enemy camp were not inconsiderable. Clearly the prime figures he had to gain access to if he was to succeed in fracturing the Chamberlain alliance were well enough known to him – as opponents. Many of them he had lambasted in the pages of *Tribune* and others he had mocked, cajoled and inveighed against across the floor of the House. But in order to bring about the end of the Government he either had to make new overtures to the rebel Tories or he had to split the Government itself. Stafford tried both ploys. The first moves, inevitably, were with the rebels and on 19 June he met with Chamberlain's predecessor Baldwin, who he thought was on the verge of rebellion. 'We had a long conversation' Stafford wrote, 'I gained the impression that I could not expect anything from him in the way of action, though the political sense and observation were obviously acute. However, he promised to consider all I had said and to see whether he could do anything.' This was followed three days later by a secret meeting at Churchill's flat at which Winston maintained he and Eden were still opposed to the Government's appeasement policy and would be prepared to join an all-in Government.

The second ploy was to win over the Government's own ministers. Here Stafford was no fool. He realised that the only real chance of getting rid of Chamberlain must lie with 'intrigue from within the Cabinet itself' and so set about a series of meetings with Cabinet members, although he admitted to himself that 'It remains to be seen what will eventuate from that. If nothing occurs within the next week, I shall consider launching a press campaign to try and bring the result about.'[5] So the day after his meeting with Churchill Stafford sent the Tory Secretary of State for Air, Kingsley Wood, a draft of a speech he would like to make to the German people, including a strong repudiation of Imperialism and the acceptance of international co-operation as the new basis of world development. Wood passed this on to the Foreign Secretary, Lord Halifax, who asked to meet him on 28 June at 4.30 p.m. at the House of Lords with Lord Perth. Halifax was already privately expressing some doubts about the appeasement policy and Stafford now had his most fruitful discussions as when he raised the issue of 'an all-in Government . . . Halifax agreed that it was the right policy'. That same evening he also managed to get an hour with the President of the Board of Trade, Oliver Stanley, whom he maintained in his diary he 'completely convinced . . . of the urgent need of an all-in Government. I told him who I had already seen and begged him to start doing something . . . Before I left he said he would discuss it at once with others and see what, if anything, could be done.'

Stafford was also looking for a proper job. With the collapse of the Popular Front and with no Parliamentary responsibilities other than as an independent backbencher he had time on his hands. Unless there were an 'all-in' Government in which he might be given a post, the only possibility was either a post in the gift of the National Government (which would cut him off once and for all from the Labour Party) or posting abroad which was less overtly Party related. For years his main interests had been with international relations, in the tradition of his father, and as war loomed on the horizon, he began to consider some form of diplomatic job.

International events had moved on apace. In the hope of seeing off reported German troop movements on the Polish border, Britain had formed an alliance with Poland at the end of March and given a unilateral guarantee to Romania – both of which she then asked Russia to match. In response the Soviets suggested on 17 April a triple pact of mutual assistance between France, Britain and Russia with a military convention and a guarantee of all the states from the Baltic to the Black Sea. Chamberlain was nervous of this suggestion, fearing it might tie Britain into an inevitable war between the two halves of Europe, and on 1 May, an inopportune date for turning the Russians down, he rejected their advances, simply reiterating the guarantees for Poland and Romania and seeking a pledge of Soviet assistance. By the end of May, under some pressure from the Labour Party and the Liberals, the Government made it at least half-clear to Russia that they were still interested in negotiating a pact and a second round of talk was opened although Russia had already made further moves to hedge its bets, commencing trade negotiations with the Germans. New suggestions were made at this point by Russia – to match British and French guarantees for Belgium, Greece, Romania, Poland and Turkey in return for protection of the Baltic States – but Britain held out over the issue of 'indirect aggression', fearing that Russia would use the threat of German invasion as an excuse for supposedly friendly annexation of the Baltic States without their consent. So on 8 June Halifax seemed to turn the Soviet proposal down, although a British delegation did go to Russia with the French a week later. The meetings were fraught and one of the Russian delegation wrote in *Pravda* on 29 June that 'the British and French Governments are not out for a real agreement acceptable to the USSR but only for talks about an agreement whilst facilitating the conclusion of an agreement with the aggressors' – a position that many Russia sympathisers, like Stafford, felt was painfully close to the truth. As A. J. P. Taylor put it 'No alliance has been pursued less enthusiastically.'[6]

The issue of which way Russia would turn in the event of war was one of Stafford's paramount concerns, and this mishandling of the negotiations was at the heart of his criticism of the Government. For years he and *Tribune* had been urging that Britain should go all out to form a pact with Russia, France and the USA. So, when the article appeared in *Pravda* Stafford made the first of several job applications. On 30 June 'I rang up Kingsley Wood and offered my services to go at once to Moscow to get the Russian agreement concluded, as I feel I could do this if I was given the authority.'[7] Not for the last time, his offer was turned down by Halifax a few days later, but it was clear that the matter had not been refused out of hand. When he discovered the next day, 4 July, that Britain had been minded to do a deal with Russia, but had changed its mind at the last minute, he dashed round to the House of Commons to try and get ministers to reconsider, only to find the place deserted due to the Scottish night debate.

The reasons for this, the first of Stafford's attempts to get in on the Anglo-Soviet act, were mixed. Admittedly he had campaigned over the issue of Russia's involvement in preventing further Fascist advances, but he had never even visited Russia. His son John had travelled with Sidney Webb in 1932, he had paid for Barbara Betts to go out in 1937, and he had argued for Russia at countless meetings, but he had never visited the country himself. Yet he believed that he had particularly strong credentials for dealing with the Soviets. His friendship with Pollitt would endear him to the Communist Party as would his advocacy of a British-Soviet alliance. But two points militated against his being chosen for the delegation. For a start Chamberlain and Halifax still had no real intention of doing a deal with Russia. They believed it possible to settle European problems through careful negotiations with Hitler and Mussolini, negotiations which would be directly threatened by any formal engagement of the Russians. Indeed Chamberlain was enormously sceptical about Russia, confessing in private at least that 'I have no belief in her ability to maintain an effective offensive, even if she wanted to. And I distrust her motives which seem to me to have little connection with our ideas of liberty, and to be concerned only with getting everyone else by the ears.'[8] Furthermore Halifax estimated that though Stafford might see his independent status as a bonus, the Russians would reckon that it meant he had rendered himself impotent by effectively expelling himself from the Labour Party. Nevertheless, Stafford refused to give up and even wrote to Churchill trying to persuade *him* to offer to join the delegation. His elliptical reply – 'I am sure that any such démarche on my part would be unwise and weaken me in any discussion I might have to have with the gentleman in question [Chamberlain]'[9] – was disappointing and the next day Stafford vented some of his depression on the Webbs, whom he and Isobel visited at their home at Passfield Corner, 'He despaired of the Labour Party: they were losing ground in the country: no one was interested in their worn-out programme . . . Chaos everywhere was his summing-up of life at home and abroad.' Interestingly Beatrice predicted that this life of independence would be the pattern rather than the exception for the rest of Stafford's career, 'I doubt whether he will reappear in the inner counsels of the Labour Party . . . More likely he will find himself eventually on the Front Bench of a National Govern-ment composed mainly of the old governing class, converted by the course of events, to a compromise with the new social order.'[10] By the end of July Stafford was convinced that a British pact with Russia was in the offing and even suspected that Chamberlain would go to the country on the back of successful deals with Russia and Germany and that the Labour Party would be annihilated 'as they will really stand for noth-ing in particular'.[11]

So it was in a mood of some depression that Stafford returned to Goodfellows for the summer recess at the end of July and he and the family decided to go on what Roy Jenkins described as one of their most extravagant holidays, chartering a small yacht from Cannes and sailing round the Tyrrhenian Sea for a fortnight.

Stafford had an uncanny knack of being away when some of the most dramatic political events came to pass, and August 1939 was no exception. For on 15 August Count von Schulen-burge told Molotov, the Soviet Commissar for Foreign Affairs, who was then engaged in a third, military, round of talks with Britain, that Germany wanted to sign a pact of non-aggression with Russia. The Russians, feeling that they were getting nowhere with Britain decided to go ahead and six days later they announced that Von Ribbentrop had been invited to Moscow, where, two days later, he and Molotov signed the Soviet-Nazi Pact of Non-Aggression.

The day before the signing of the pact Britain made it plain that her commitment to Poland would stand and after a swift meeting of Parliament to agree Emergency Powers on 24 August, the treaty with Poland was finally agreed and signed. Hitler, having now made his back safe, intended to move forwards by striking immediately against Poland, though he delayed invasion whilst demanding that the Poles negotiate with him. Halifax, still hoping to see war avoided, urged the Polish Government to see Hitler, which they refused and on 31 August Hitler gave the orders for the assault on Poland which began the following morning at four forty-five. By lunchtime German planes were bombing Warsaw and British Ministers were trying to find yet another way out. Ultimata were suggested but not made, in the desperate hope that a conference might be called to resolve the conflict. Chamberlain's appearance in the House of Commons on the evening of 2 September, which all sides of the House had confidently expected would include the announcement of an ultimatum to Germany, was greeted with stony silence when no such announcement was forthcoming, and when Arthur Greenwood stood up to speak in Attlee's stead, Amery shouted from the Tory benches, 'Speak for England, Arthur.' A late night Cabinet meeting followed, at which Stanley, Simon and Walter Elliott all argued for an immediate declaration and it was agreed that Germany should be told to order a withdrawal from Poland by 11 a.m. the next day or else Britain and Germany would be at war. So at 11.15 a.m. Chamberlain broadcast that he had received no such undertaking from the German Chancellor and the war began.

All this was happening just as Stafford and Isobel were

returning from France with the children. Jennie Lee and Aneurin Bevan had been in Britain throughout the summer, however, and felt a strange mixture of relief and anxiety at the final declaration of war. 'Our enemy Hitler had become the national enemy' wrote Jennie, 'the cause was just, however much it might have been tarnished by Chamberlain and the Munichites through the preceding years.'[12] Bevan's and Cripps's response to the war was published in *Tribune* the following day, 'A very heavy responsibility rests on the British Government and upon those who have allowed that Government to remain in office during the last vital months. The policy of doing nothing and hoping for the best, which many have adopted, is now seen to be one of the prime factors in our tragedy.' Yet there was a hope that 'out of the war, whatever else comes, will come an opportunity for the working class of the world to do something effective to save themselves from fresh tragedies and suffering. That opportunity they must seize and it is already time to start preparing for the moment when it comes.'[13] As for other colleagues on the left, many had been shocked by the Nazi-Soviet pact, Gollancz had set about distancing himself from the Communist Party and even Pollitt was opposed to Russia's apparent accommodation with Fascism – an opposition that earned him the sack as British Secretary General.

Three things struck Stafford as vital. First was the matter of what the Government should be doing both to win the war and to give it a sense of purpose. Just like his father in the First World War, so now he campaigned for a clear statement of peace aims. He wanted to avoid another Versailles treaty and while he was determined that there was 'no question of compromise until the world has been freed of this terrible and vicious system of force and suppression'[14] yet he was keen that the war should not be yet another attempt to grind Germany into the ground. Besides which he wanted Britons to be fighting *for* something. As he argued in the Commons, 'Today, there are in this country a large and growing number of people who are feeling that, whatever comes out of this war, it is absolutely impossible that we should go back again to the conditions that existed before the war . . . They are concerned also with what will come for them out of this war besides the slaughter, the tragedy and the suffering.'[15] So he went on to castigate the Government's own war aims as 'excellently vague in their definition, those aims, in my view, when examined, amount to nothing more than a determination to try and revert to the *status quo* before the war'.[16] A declaration of peace aims would both give moral fibre to the war effort and satisfy his own political objectives and he confessed to Beatrice Webb in June that he no longer believed 'party politics in the old sense will have any meaning in this country for a very long time to come'[17] and by September he was 'trying very tentatively to organize an all-party group of persons who are prepared to devote themselves to a new beginning at the end of the war'.

His second concern was what he should do himself in the war. Here there was one relatively easy decision to make, and that he did with remarkably little hesitation, for Stafford had carried on working at the Bar right through the thirties, but with the advent of war he finally decided to stop practising. Indeed when his friend Walter Monckton came round to his chambers 'he was clear that we must both give up practice which, he said, had become "irrelevant". The war struck me as right, and the argument as conclusive, so we both gave up the Bar forthwith.'[18]

As for what Stafford should actually do with his new freedom, this he evidently hoped would be solved by his third concern which remained the issue of how Russia could be brought into an alliance with Britain. So he wrote again to Halifax, who had the advantage of being a friend of Monckton's,

I think that the extent of the hostility that is thus deve-

203

loped towards this country in Russia is not yet finally determined and that it is possible yet for something to be done to allay the danger of our finding a new and very powerful enemy arrayed against us in company with Germany. It is not necessary to stress the extreme danger of such an eventuality. The question seems to be, can anything be done at this stage to prevent such a tragic development? . . . could not an all-party delegation fly to Moscow at once in order to try to influence Russian opinion in our direction?'[19]

In effect this was another job application and Stafford followed it up with a visit to Churchill, now First Lord of the Admiralty, and a memo suggesting practical conversations with the Soviet Ambassador Ivan Maisky. These were to moot trade negotiations as a prelude to a possible visit to Moscow by a Cabinet Minister.

Halifax's reply of 22 September made clear that Stafford was also offering to do some of the groundwork in Moscow: 'I am grateful to you for offering to go out to Moscow to sound the Soviet authorities and am quite prepared to facilitate your journey, on the understanding, of course, that you will be travelling as a private individual . . . I should like if possible to see you before you start.'[20] Meanwhile Stafford's proposals seemed to be bearing some fruit. There were meetings in October between Maisky and Halifax and Stanley, in which trade negotiations were discussed but delays turned into a final break when the Russians became convinced that the Finns were only refusing to sign a pact with Russia because of British pressure.

Hitler was not only waging a military war, of course, but had stepped up the diplomatic pressure on Britain with his so-called Peace Offensive and Stafford linked what he felt should be the British reply to Hitler with the question of war, or peace, aims.

Any definitive world settlement must envisage democracy and freedom, if that is our true aim, not only in
territories that have been conquered by the Germans, but
throughout the world. Our care for India must be as great
as our care for Poland. Our readiness to re-establish the
map of Europe must be equalled by our readiness to
reconsider the whole question of the Imperial conquests
of the past. We cannot, without laying ourselves open to
the charge of cynicism, select the territories of others for
the benefits of democracy and freedom while withhold-
ing those benefits from which we derive economic
advantage.[21]

Chamberlain replied on 10 October that he was interested
but he felt that several of Stafford's ideas were impracticable.
So Stafford saw Halifax and persuaded him that he should
telephone Supreme Court Justice Felix Frankfurter and ask
him to get the US President to suggest to Britain that if Hitler
really meant what he said about the ethnographic division of
Europe, then there did not seem any reason why a conference
should not take place. He was given the clear indication that if
such a suggestion were made by Roosevelt Britain would not
be embarrassed and would follow it up.

Stafford had not been idle through the time since his expulsion. Indeed he had undertaken one specific piece of work for
Gwilym Lloyd George and Oliver Stanley in drafting the anti-
profiteering legislation that was steered through the House.
When it came to appointing someone to oversee the implementation of the new legislation as Chairman of the Central
Price Regulation Committee, however, he was passed over
because many of the manufacturers were nervous about him.

Yet there was little sense of purpose to what he was doing,
and he must have felt like a young relative who is mildly
tolerated rather than relied upon. So it was inevitable that he

should start to seek a more exciting venture, and by the end of October he had already framed in his mind a plan that would provide just that. Two other areas of interest that had been with him since the early thirties were China and India, and he established strong friendships in particular with Krishna Menon and with Nehru. Indeed Mahatma Gandhi had visited him in 1938, and his stepmother Marion was very much involved in a group called the India Conciliation Group.

On 23 October he went to see Halifax, who, as Lord Irwin, had been Viceroy of India, and told him that his original plan to visit Russia had now changed. Instead he was to go to India, China and Russia and he had some specific proposals to make regarding India. Halifax expressed some concern lest the trip be seen in any way as official, and reiterated his fear that it would be interpreted as the move towards a Sino-Anglo-Soviet move, but as Stafford maintained that he had no desire to be seen as anything other than a private visitor, he was prepared to guarantee that the Government would take seriously what he had to say on his return. So, after a series of meetings in early November with others interested in Indian independence Stafford had enough hope that he would be taken seriously, at least in his suggestions for the future for India, for him to write, 'This is really promising progress and means that if I can get the Indians to consider my proposals, there may be a chance of acceptance by the Government of this country.'[22]

One of the interesting points of conjecture in Stafford's life is why he turned at this point to Lord Halifax, a man he had regularly condemned as being pro-Hitler. Walter Monckton maintained it was thanks to him, though he does not acknowledge these early meetings between Halifax and Cripps, but refers to the later process whereby Cripps ended up as Ambassador to Moscow,

I kept in touch with [Cripps] and was later instrumental

in bringing about his appointment as our Ambassador in Moscow. For I persuaded Lord Halifax to ask him and me to dine in Lady Halifax's rooms in the Dorchester, and while I was happily engaged in conversation with Lady Halifax, Cripps and Halifax gradually thawed to each other and Halifax began to see that I was right in respecting and trusting Stafford.[23]

While it may be true that there was a further thawing out between the two men in 1940 immediately prior to the appointment, it is obvious that Halifax was already prepared to do business with Cripps in late 1939. In part this may be to do with the one thing above any other which they had in common – their religion. For Halifax was an openly devout Anglo-Catholic. Yet the other factor that must have told in Cripps's mind was the simple fact that Halifax was a likely contender for the post of Prime Minister should Chamberlain fall. He had intimated that the Government should have a broader base and this had endeared him to the Labour Party, and even in May 1940, when the Norwegian débacle made it clear that Chamberlain's days were numbered, Dalton and others were touting him as their favoured candidate. So, having started with Chamberlain's predecessor, Cripps had moved on to the person he assumed would be his successor, in his attempt to change the Government's policy and its composition. Equally, Halifax may have chosen to give Cripps some time and space purely because he thought that he might need the support of independent left-wingers like him if there were to be a new Coalition Government. Either way, by the end of November there was at least half an understanding between the two men who would later be respectively Ambassadors to Washington and Moscow.

So on 29 November Cripps left his chambers at Essex Court for the last time and wrote a lengthy letter to his Bristol constituents saying,

I have thought very seriously over the question of whether I was justified in leaving the country at the present time and have come to the conclusion that nothing decisive is likely to occur here before the late Spring and I shall be utilising the intervening time to the best advantage by equipping myself with knowledge of the Indian and Chinese situation.'[24]

The next day he set off in the company of one of his son's College friends and another barrister from the Middle Temple, Geoffrey Wilson, who also happened to be the son of Marion's Quaker friend Alexander Wilson, by train and boat to Paris and thence to Rome, Athens, Alexandria, Lydda, Baghdad, Basra and Karachi.

15

The World Over

'Travel', wrote Francis Bacon, 'in the younger sort, is a part of education; in the elder, a part of experience.'[1] For Cripps now it was an exile dressed up as a political exploration.

He had always been a traveller. As a child he had journeyed to Germany and France with his elder brothers, he had toured Bavaria on his own in 1910, and he proposed to Isobel in Klosters. Every summer there was a main family holiday, sailing off the Isle of Wight with Michael Foot or travelling through Germany and Switzerland and staying at Lake Garda or Lake Como, or taking the waters at Baden Baden. The children had grown up to enjoy travelling and used it as a form of convalescence. When Purcell Weaver had a nervous breakdown he made for Samoa, when Diana was ill she went to Italy and it was their brief and unconsummated marriage that took the whole family on a banana boat to Jamaica for ten weeks in 1938.

So Stafford's political recuperation took the form of a lengthy journey. As on the longer family holidays, so there was a ritual to this journey. Stafford gave up smoking, to show that he was not addicted to cigarettes, and he started a diary. Unfortunately his powers of self-restraining reticence meant that it was more an anodyne narrative of events and social conditions than evidence of what was going through his mind. Stafford still felt guilty about this trip and was determined that it should be no holiday. So in putting together his itinerary he resolutely stuck to visiting countries that he could justify to himself. This was a typical pattern. Even in 1938, when the family was in Jamaica and Stafford was ill, he ended up going to see the Acting Governor and meeting with the young Norman Manley and his cousin W. A. Bustamente before speaking at the inaugural meeting of the People's National Party (which eventually won power under Manley in 1955). Guilt and the Protestant work ethic determined his itinerary.

First was India, which had been in a state of almost perpetual upheaval for the last two decades. Ever since the Amritsar Massacre in April 1919 when the British had opened fire on the crowds, killing 379 and injuring nearly 1,200, Britain had been careful, trying to balance the claims of the Hindu majority against the Muslims and negotiating on a separate basis with the main body of British India and the 560 individual princely states. So Mahatma Gandhi, who had returned from South Africa in 1914, kept up a steady pressure for full independence through a series of civil disobedience campaigns which saw him imprisoned for two years. In 1929 Irwin, as Viceroy, announced that the British Government's ultimate aim was Dominion Status for India and in 1930 the Simon Report argued that a federation including the princely states would have to be set up before any real degree of autonomy could be granted to India. This then led to the First Round Table Conference in October at which the princes said they were prepared to join a federation if there was to be a responsible Central Government. When no final agreements were arrived at, however, and there was no prospect of a timetable for independence, Gandhi organised a new nonviolent civil disobedience campaign, leading to the Second Round Table Conference.

It was at this point that Marion first took an interest. For she was involved from the outset in a small group based around the Central London Quakers called the India Conciliation

Group. This started after the collapse in October 1931 of the Second Round Table Conference which had brought Gandhi and Nehru to England following a brief respite in the campaign of civil disobedience. During a weekend break in the conference Gandhi, supported by his main adviser, an Englishman called Charlie Andrews, had gone to stay with Lindsay at Balliol where there was an unofficial meeting with Malcolm MacDonald (Ramsay's son and a National Labour MP) and Lord Lothian, the Under-Secretary for India, which came surprisingly close to an agreement. When the ideas were put to the rest of the Round Table delegates they were over-whelmingly rejected and the National Government ended up having to put forward unilateral proposals of its own, but the ICG was founded out of a belief that this brief agreement demonstrated that conciliation was possible.

The key players in the group included not only Andrews himself, but the Methodist turned Quaker LSE tutor Agatha Harrison, who was close to Nehru and his sister Vijaya Lakshmi; another Quaker educationalist and Secretary of the National Peace Council, Carl Heath; the suffragette preacher Maud Royden; Alexander Wilson the Quaker father of Stafford's companion Geoffrey; the Dean of Canterbury, Hewlett Johnson; Emmeline Pethick-Lawrence and Marion Cripps.

In the meantime 1932 saw Ramsay MacDonald draw up his 'Communal Award' which suggested the special constitutional recognition of the Untouchables, which in turn led to Gandhi going on hunger strike in opposition to the whole concept of untouchability. This was finally patched up in the Poona Pact between Gandhi and Dr Ambedkar, the leader of the Un-touchables, but in 1933 the Government White Paper on India made more allowances for religious minorities and for the princely states than Congress cared for and so in July Gandhi started a new fast and was again arrested. Meanwhile, back in England MacDonald was having difficulties with getting the legislation through the Commons and there was overt opposition to constitutional change from Lords Salisbury and Lloyd. Churchill even called the proposed Bill a 'monstrous monument of sham built by the pygmies'.[2] With the rise of the Muslim League, newly reorganised in 1934 under Mohammed Ali Jinnah, and with Hoare reckoning that 'in the present condition of politics in England it [is] quite impossible to get anything that [goes] further than the White Paper. It will only founder on the House of Commons'[3] – the India Bill was likely to be an ineffectual measure.

Indeed the Government of India Act which was passed the following year stipulated an Indian federation of British India and the princely states which never came to pass, and an indianised council and provincial self-government by legislatures elected on a newly enlarged franchise and with different electorates for each of the ethno-religious groups, which did. Elections held in February 1937 gave Congress control of seven out of the eleven provinces and the Muslim League control of the North-West Frontier province, whilst the new Viceroy, Lord Linlithgow, was still meant to be negotiating the Indian federation with the princely states.

By the time of Stafford's visit, then, there was a degree of stability in the large part of British India controlled by Congress, but many issues remained unresolved: the status of the princely states, the long-term future of the Muslim League province, and the long-held desire for full independence. The ICG had been burrowing away throughout the intervening period, having remarkably good contacts within the National Government. Andrews was himself a friend of Lord Halifax, and Clifford Allen and Samuel Hoare, both members of MacDonald's kitchen cabinet, had close links to the group. With the passing of MacDonald they lost some of their influence, but in 1936 Carl Heath, Agatha Harrison and Charlie Andrews all visited Gandhi at Wardha and in 1938 they persuaded Lord Lothian to see both Gandhi and Nehru. When

Linlithgow unilaterally declared that India was at war with Germany in September 1939, there was an enormous storm of protest, effectively posing the question afresh for Congress – what was the point of giving false legitimacy to the British system when there was still no offer of independence? Congress threatened to withdraw all co-operation with the Government whilst back in England Cripps wrote to Nehru that Attlee was 'bringing pressure to bear'[4] on Linlithgow and the Government. So on 18 October Linlithgow made an offer of eventual Dominion status for India, but refused to give a timetable for any consultation process after the war, or to consider anything other than an advisory committee during the war. Not surprisingly Congress decided to withdraw from co-operation and all its provincial ministries resigned whilst Jinnah offered the full support of the Muslims in the war effort in the hope of extracting further concessions from the British.

In the meantime the ICG had also been influential in framing the Labour Party position on India and when Nehru had spent three months in Britain in 1938 he had broadly supported a Labour plan for the transfer of power to a constituent assembly at a meeting of the ICG on 14 July.

Of course, if Stafford had taken his advice or ideas on India only from the ICG he would have made more mistakes than he did, for one of the failings of the group was its overidentification with Gandhi and the Congress Party. They only ever held one meeting with Jinnah of the Muslim League, despite the fact that he lived in London for a large part of the period, and it is clear that they thought Gandhi was the full expression of the mind of India, even brushing aside many of the other Congress leaders. Furthermore, they had remarkably little to do with the India League, another British group which was championed by Noel Brailsford and Reg Sorenson and was most closely linked to Krishna Menon.

As for Cripps himself, he had met Gandhi on several

occasions and both Gandhi and Nehru stayed at Goodfellows in 1938. He had also given Krishna Menon space in *Tribune*, and through his friend Walter Monckton had contact with one of the more influential Indian princes, the Nizam of Hyderabad who had sought his legal advice in 1932 on whether he should accede to the proposed federation. Nevertheless his experience of Indian politics was limited and his judgment was undoubtedly too much swayed by the towering spiritual authority of Gandhi.

Through the autumn of 1939 Stafford's interest in India had grown. In September he declared in *Tribune* that 'it would be the height of cynicism to ask the Indians to play their part in defending democracy and freedom on Poland or the rest of Europe, while at the same time denying to them such freedom or democracy'[5] and he expressed open distrust of the National Government on the issue of Indian independence in the Commons debate on 26 October, attacking their 'lack of appreciation of the new circumstances which have inevitably arisen with the coming of the struggle in Europe'.[6] At the start of November, realising that the resolution of India's position in the war was as important as Russia's, he decided to add India to his trip and began to draw up his own plan for conciliation, which closely resembled that which Attlee, Bevan and Richard Crossman had discussed with Nehru and had received his tentative support at the ICG. As the view of Labour politicians on the plan was almost irrelevant at this point Cripps took his plan round a series of more influential figures, including Sir George Schuster, Lord Hailey, Wedgwood Benn and, at the suggestion of Rab Butler, the Chief of the India Office, Sir Findlater Stewart.

The plan was simple. The British Government would commit itself to summoning a Constituent Assembly within a year of the end of the war. In the absence of any better agreed upon system of representation this should be constituted on the basis of the present provincial electorates, plus 'a proportional representation from any [princely] states who would introduce sufficient democracy to enable representatives to be elected to the Constituent Assembly'. All votes in the new Assembly should require a three fifths majority but Britain would abide by its views provided it entered into a fifteen-year Treaty while transition to autonomy would be carried through. On 16 November Cripps wrote to Nehru that he thought both Halifax and Zetland, the Secretary of State for India, were broadly impressed by his plan and were moving towards the idea of a constituent assembly and treaty, but eventually Stewart expressed his outright opposition to the plan and Zetland became more non-committal.

So when Stafford and Geoffrey arrived in Karachi they were on their own and Stafford admitted to his diary that they were there 'to learn and not to teach anyone anything'.[7] They arrived on 7 December and were garlanded with flowers before being taken immediately into an unofficial press conference where questions were fired at Cripps from all sides, even though the Karachi stop was only for refuelling. After an hour they got back in their plane and proceeded to Allahabad, the first main stop on the tour, where they were to be met by Jawaharlal Nehru.

Nehru was already a personal friend and regular correspondent who had boasted to Cripps of the 1937 election results, 'we had the government apparatus and all other vested interests against us and all means, fair and otherwise, were employed to defeat us. But the enthusiasm for the Congress was so tremendous that it swept everything before it.'[8] Cripps had unsuccessfully backed Nehru in the internal dispute within Congress as to whether to take office in the new provincial legislatures without any British commitment to independence or even Dominion status. Nehru was in a good mood when Stafford visited his home at Anand Bhavan. At fifty he was the same age as Stafford, and he entertained him well. On the issue of Stafford's plan he was now more cautious than he had been at the 1938 ICG meeting, distrusting the Government's offer of Dominion status and insisting that a fifteen-year Treaty would be too long a commitment for an independent India but he was prepared to acknowledge that it was 'broadly . . . on the right lines'.[9]

Stafford and Geoffrey stayed in Allahabad for a couple of days, and were shown round by Nehru's brother-in-law Ranjit Pandit, who, like Nehru, had spent some years in a British prison. Cripps wrote 'the whole place left an impression of an enormous vitality that had been released among the people by the fact that with their own government they were responsible for their own affairs, and even the resignation of the Congress Ministry is not likely to effect (sic) this particular development'.[10] The things he noticed were often technical, matters of educational systems and agriculture and there is little of the personal impression left by India in his diary and notes, although he did recount in Allahabad,

> We went inside one of the houses – all of which are built of mud with sun-baked tile roofs, and the poverty was awful. It consisted of two rooms, the first used as a sort of kitchen, about six feet by twelve, and lit only by such light as came through the door, and the other room opening off it, about the same size, and light of its own. The entire household goods consisted of not more than a dozen utensils and a few pieces of white cloth, but the whole place was spotlessly clean. They don't seem to mind how filthy the village is, but the house must be properly kept.[11]

Two days later, on the Sunday, they set off by train for Delhi, where the meetings came thick and fast. First was G.D. Birla, the industrialist Congress supporter who felt that Congress had taken too harsh a stance against the Muslims in the provinces they had controlled since 1937 and had thereby raised the stakes. The only answer was creation of separate Muslim and Hindu states. Next came Liaquat Ali Khan, the Secretary of the Muslim League, who in effect took a similar line, arguing that the Muslims no longer felt that a European-style democracy offered enough of a guarantee for minorities, and that there were therefore only three options: partition; free sovereign states with Hindu and Muslim federations and a confederation of the two; Dominion status for each province with a central federation to which the provinces could grant what powers they wished and out of which any province could choose to opt.

That same night the two set off for Lahore, again by train. This time it was the turn of the Punjab Prime Minister, Sikander Hyat-Khan, followed by the leaders of the Akali Sikh Party and some more Muslims from Mahasabha, before returning to Delhi to see some Viceregal officials. The next day they set off for Bombay, where Cripps addressed the Civil Liberties Union at the Opera House before meeting the Governor of the Province and the leader of the Untouchables. On 15 December he went to see Jinnah at his house on Malabar Hill in Bombay. Though the meeting started badly because Jinnah feared that Cripps had been 'shepherded around the country by the Congress', Cripps soon convinced him that his mind was not yet made up and Jinnah proceeded to explain his opposition to English democracy.

From Bombay Stafford went on to Hyderabad to meet with the Nizam, whence finally he proceeded to Wardha to see Gandhi. Nehru had arranged the meeting and escorted the visitors the five miles from Wardha itself to the tiny village of Segoon where Gandhi lived in his mud hut. A first meeting was followed by another the following day when Gandhi allowed that the Cripps scheme 'would form an acceptable basis for negotiation'. Cripps wrote of Gandhi,

One cannot but be impressed with the vigour with which

Gandhi holds to his creed, and the calmness with which he is prepared for any sacrifice in order to attain it. His whole way of life, with its extreme simplicity and selflessness, is part of his creed and demonstrates his sincerity . . . I feel there is a much better chance of the solution of the problem while he is still alive and in control than there will be if and when he goes.[12]

Cripps's penultimate Indian meeting was then with the Viceroy in Calcutta, to whom he explained both his own plan and the reception he had received form the various leaders he had met. He wrote to Nehru of the meeting with Linlithgow, 'On the whole I am not at all displeased, though the rather sphinx-like nature of the Viceroy made it difficult to find out what is cooking in his mind . . . I am sure he wants sincerely to settle the matter if he can.'[13]

Whether the excursion can be considered a success is a matter of quite whose opinion one takes. If Cripps had intended to break the log-jam in Indian negotiations, he failed. Jinnah told him he would meet with Nehru, but Nehru refused to see any of the Muslim leaders until they called off their celebrations for a 'day of deliverance' from Congress provincial government. Civil disobedience recommenced in 1940, the Government declined to make any further moves towards independence and the Muslim League started to call for a separate Muslim state. If, on the other hand, Cripps was genuine in his assertion that this was no more than a fact-finding mission, then he was successful. He managed to see in a little less than three weeks nearly all the Indian leaders and to have open one to one meetings with them – something that had evaded even the Viceroy.

The one other matter of interest in Stafford's own account of the India venture is his complete indifference to anything other than the political task in hand. He relates nothing of his own personal feelings, and his 'diary' reads more like civil servant notes of meetings. Numbers are given, sizes measured, times recorded, but nothing of the person appears, so as to whether or not Cripps fulfilled any task other than the simple garnering of information it is difficult to imagine. Certainly he filled his time. The timetable for 21 December ran: arrival 10.00, breakfast at Girivilas Palace, Sarangarh 10.30, drive to Amaldiggi jungle 11.30, begin beat 12.00, tea 3.30, talk at Palace 5.00, depart for Raigarh 6.15, train to Calcutta 8.10.[14] As Stafford admitted to a Chatham House meeting on his return, 'in spite of every temptation, I did not have a single day's sightseeing, as I devoted myself wholly to seeing people or things such as transport facilities, research institutes, universities etc.'[15] The whole trip was at a break-neck speed and there is some truth in the accusation that in his later dealings with India Stafford allowed himself to be swayed too much by the spiritual authority he, like so many others, accorded Gandhi. Here was a man that Stafford actually felt in some awe of, a man of a different faith but who yet embodied a Christianity more profound than most Christians could muster. Like Cripps a lawyer by trade he had faced opprobrium too and it is difficult not to see the comparisons between the two men, although Gandhi reckoned that Stafford was lacking in humility. Although Cripps later felt that Gandhi was less than helpful in the negotiating process, there was a lot in him he admired. Exceptionally for an Englishman, Stafford removed his shoes when he met with Gandhi (and was much derided for it by Brendan Bracken and Churchill), and although the harsh asceticism of the Mahatma was not to Stafford's mind, this sense of a politician carrying spiritual authority through 'living the life' undoubtedly appealed to him.

After India came China, and although there was not the same diplomatic task for Stafford to work on, China had exercised his mind since the Japanese invasion of Manchuria in 1931 and he was determined to visit General Chiang

Kai-Shek, who had moved the Government out of the Japanese warpath to Chongqing.

This was the path least travelled of all Stafford's journeys and it involved a convoluted route by plane to Rangoon and Mandalay, and then on by car and truck down the upper reaches of the Salween River, followed by crossing the Nu Jiang river before climbing to the small market towns of Baoshan, Yongqing, Yangbi, Xiaquan, Xiangyun and finally Yao'an, where finally a soldier notified the group that Chiang had detailed his private Beechcraft plane to take them the final leg to Kunming before carrying on to Chongqing.

It was an amazing journey, crossing into China from Burma, by mistake, on a bamboo bridge, skirting the Himalayas, spending nights in tiny guest houses and being greeted along the way by a deputation from Chiang and the British Governor in Burma, the superintendent of the Curtiss-Wright aircraft factory on the Chinese border, and an armed guard of honour in Xiaguan. On arriving in Kunming, Chiang's hospitality again came to the fore, and during their five-day stay Stafford saw every factory and educational establishment imaginable while Geoffrey ensured that everybody back in Britain knew what Stafford was up to by issuing constant press releases. After a speech to a thousand students from the Yunnan University, which was reported in *The Times*, Stafford and Geoffrey carried on to Chongqing where they went immediately to see the Foreign Minister Mr Wang, followed by the British Ambassador.

On 16 January Geoffrey was taken ill and had to spend a fortnight in hospital but Stafford carried on with his round of meetings with Sun Of, one of the sons of Sun Yat-Sen, the father of the Chinese Republic, and with Chiang himself. Of the General he said:

He is a fine clean-looking man and is very impressive with his modesty and sincerity. He hardly spoke at all except to elucidate some point or to express approval of some idea. I gave him a long sketch of foreign policy of Great Britain as frankly as I could and I found that he had said to the British Ambassador very much what I had said to the cabinet as to the danger of the German pact last summer. He is obviously of the opinion that Communism is unsuitable for China at this stage and I agree with him.[16]

Stafford loved China. He believed that 'the only really great security for the world in the Far East [was] a Chinese united democratic government, eventually victorious over Japan'[17] and he got on well with both the General and his wife, not least because they respected and flattered him. The grandiloquent Cripps enjoyed this role-playing at diplomacy and it is not difficult to imagine the pained expressions of the Embassy staff when Chiang asked Stafford to work for him. Stafford liked to feel needed and he lighted on the Soviet Ambassador. 'I thought the Ambassador was an attractive young man and just occasionally he smiled and then he looked very sociable and friendly. He told me he had a telegram from Maisky about me and that he was therefore dealing with me very frankly as a friend of the USSR.'[18] Whether this was just ambassadorial flattery is impossible to tell, but it is true that the Russians were sufficiently intrigued by Stafford's trip to allow him to travel on to the province of Sinkiang on the Russian border for a meeting with officials from Moscow. In the meantime he set off for another major Chinese city, Chengdu, and was more than delighted to be asked by the Chinese authorities to draw up plans for gasoline distribution and the Haiphong railway transport, both of which, so he maintained, were put into operation.

On his return from Chengdu, and just before leaving for Urumqi via Chengdu and the 'silk road', on 4 February Stafford and the newly recovered Geoffrey received notice that when they arrived in Urumqi there would be a plane waiting across the border at Alma Ata to take them on to Moscow. Geoffrey was amused to note that on 6 February Stafford 'stepped into a German aeroplane wearing Madame [Chiang]'s suit of rompers, his fur-lined Chinese gown, felt boots, a fur cap and [their guide] Don's scarf and walking stick. My garb was a little more assorted – Madame's rompers, my own socks, stockings and shoes, the Vice-Consul's heavy overcoat, the Consul's golf jacket, and no hat at all as I proposed to buy a fur one.'[19]

So they set off for Moscow for the meeting which was at the heart of the long tour, excited and somewhat flattered. On the whole this was never a very creative emotional concoction for Stafford, and this proved no exception. The journey was slow and delayed due to bad weather and problems with customs, but eventually they arrived in Moscow, where they were met at the airport by the assistant head of the Foreign Office press department. It was a very brief visit, thirty-six hours in all, and the highlight, a meeting with Molotov at the Kremlin, was only a qualified success as a rather poor interpreter rendered little other than the general sense of what the two were saying. Nevertheless Cripps was pleased with the meeting and recorded as much, noting that Molotov said that Britain's policy towards Russia had always been hostile and the Russian reluctance to enter into trade negotiations was entirely due to the apparent British hostility. Clearly this suited Cripps's argument with the British Government and it may well be that either Molotov wanted to say what he knew Cripps wanted to hear or else he genuinely felt that this was the best way to explain away the Nazi-Soviet pact. Cripps maintained that he 'asked him about the chances of some agreement either of a trade or a political nature being arrived at between Great Britain and Russia. He said that if at any time the British Government would adopt a friendly attitude towards Russia there would be no difficulty in coming to an arrangement either on trade or political lines, but without this it would be impossible.' It is not difficult to hear in Stafford's report the strains of 'I told you so' and it is difficult to believe that 'the only thing he asked me to do was to try to make clear to people in England the real basis of Russian policy. He assured me that Russia was not at all unmindful of its friends and supporters in other countries and was most anxious to preserve their goodwill.'[20] What is also difficult to conjecture is quite why Molotov had agreed to the meeting and the Russians had gone quite so far out of their way to get him to Moscow. After all Stafford was only an independent back-bencher, with no political power base or allies. He had come on a private visit and whilst his long-established contacts in India had made it easy for him to arrange to meet nearly every leader in the sub-continent, with Russia his only direct contacts were through the Ambassador in London, Ivan Maisky, and Pollitt, who was now out of favour. Cripps clearly felt that his consistent advocacy of an Anglo-Soviet treaty had stood him in good stead, but the truth is that Molotov must have assumed that at the very least this was a way of keeping the door ajar for a possible British initiative. Whether he was disappointed that Cripps had nothing to offer is another matter.

Either way, Cripps's sojourn in Moscow was no more than that, a single day, and he was soon back on his plane, after some more snowy delays, and on the way to Sinkiang via Urumqi and so back to Chongqing where he met again with Chiang and cabled Halifax to ask whether he should return urgently to London for a debriefing. Disappointingly Butler replied to say there was no need for him to return yet and so he began to wend his weary way through Kowloon to Hong Kong and Shanghai before setting off for Tokyo. Here Cripps was met by both the British Ambassador, who was very pro-Japanese and was clearly worried that Stafford would upset the apple cart, and members of the Japanese parliament. From there the two travellers began the homeward trek, via the Philippines, Los Angeles, Washington and the *Rex* which set sail from New York on 12 April. The day before his birthday, on 23 April 1940, Stafford arrived back in London, having finished his trip via Genoa and Paris.

16

An 'all-in' Government

As usual Stafford's arrival back in London on 23 April 1940 was just in the nick of time. He had spent 145 days abroad, had covered 45,107 miles, had visited fourteen countries and seen what he called the rulers of 1,300 million of the world's population. He had also managed to stay in the news back in Britain with brief reports of him cropping up in every part of the globe.

In his absence the phoney war had taken shape. Russia's fractiousness had led her to impose military control over the three Baltic states of Latvia, Estonia and Lithuania before Stafford left but when she threatened the same against the Finns they refused to accept Soviet rule and on 30 November, the day Stafford set off for India, Finland was invaded. The Finns managed to hold the Soviet troops off whilst the League of Nations, largely at the insistence of the French, expelled Russia from its ranks. British opinion was united in condemnation of Russia, with Labour and Conservatives alike attacking the 'Soviet aggression', and Pritt's lonely defence of the Soviet action earning him his expulsion from the Labour Party. The united clamour against Moscow played well into the hands of Chamberlain, who was tempted to engage with the French in an assault on the Russians, either as a way of showing that he would deal equally assertively with dictators of whatever hue, or so as to gain access to Norwegian waters, which would have to be crossed to reach Finland. Churchill, now First Lord of the Admiralty, had tried to get just such a plan through the War Cabinet in September 1939 under the title 'Operation Catherine', but had been out-manoeuvred by the First Sea Lord, so when a plan was hatched by others to take the strategic Norwegian port of Narvik, and thereby close off the Germans' chief source of Swedish ore, Churchill pushed for a full escalation of the war by a direct attack on the iron ore traffic. This was overruled by the rest of the Cabinet who were still anxious not to lose the support of Norway and Sweden.

On 12 March Finland capitulated and the prospect of war in Scandinavia receded. In the meantime the French, first under Daladier and then under the rather more belligerent Paul Reynaud, urged a far more aggressive line against Germany and from the end of March started to demand a full engagement with the Germans, attacking the iron ore traffic, seizing Norwegian ports and bombing Russian oil sources in Baku. At a meeting of the Supreme War Council on 28 March Chamberlain berated Reynaud for warmongering and successfully proposed instead the mining of the Norwegian leads, effectively blocking German traffic. The plan was ill-conceived, however. It would take weeks to get an expeditionary force together and in the meantime the Germans were expected, as A. J. P. Taylor put it, 'to do nothing'. In fact Hitler was far ahead of the game and on 8 April the German invasion of Scandinavia began. Denmark caved in immediately and raids were made into Norway which the War Cabinet resolved to repulse. Churchill leapt into action, infuriating both the Secretary of the Military Co-ordination Committee Colonel Hastings 'Pug' Ismay and the Secretary of State for War, Oliver Stanley, by his peremptory behaviour. Nevertheless he got his way and Chamberlain allowed him greater sway in operational matters. The campaign was almost bound to fail, though. By the end of April British troops, having essayed a major assault on the Germans, were evacuating from Norway and the political storm that had long been brewing over the North Sea swung round and settled over Westminster and the first squalls broke.

So, just a week after Stafford's return to England the news broke of the ignominious British withdrawal from Norway and MPs began to question whether the Government could survive. As Parliament was approaching the Whitsun recess Attlee wisely decided to use the motion of adjournment for the recess as the excuse for a debate on the conduct of the war, thereby hoping to garner in a fair few dissident Tories if there should be a division – a matter that was still uncertain. In the event the debate was fully charged. Admiral Sir Roger Keyes, the Conservative MP for Plymouth North, sailing into port in full naval uniform and with his First World War medals gleaming with supercilious anger, launched a full frontal attack with all guns blazing against the whole Government except for Churchill. Nicolson, who had little time for Chamberlain, maintained 'Thereafter the weakness of the Margesson [Chamberlain's chief whip] system is displayed by the fact that none of the Yes-men are of any value whatsoever, whereas all the more able Conservatives have been driven into the ranks of the rebels.'[1] To prove the point Leo Amery then rallied as much moral authority as he could muster behind his concluding quotation from Cromwell's dismissal of the Long Parliament, 'You have sat too long here for any good you have been doing. Depart, I say, and let us have done with you. In the name of God, go.'[2]

The second day of the debate was as the first, except that in the morning the Labour Party had decided to challenge the adjournment. There would, therefore, be a vote, as Morrison announced in opening the debate for the Opposition on the morning of 8 May. Interestingly Bevan and Strauss had opposed going to a division in the Parliamentary Labour Party meeting, perhaps because they reckoned that Chamberlain was immovable, or, more likely, because they feared someone even worse taking the premiership. Chamberlain, rather foolishly, decided to turn the division into a personal matter of confidence and so began a final day of manoeuvring with constant lobbying of putative rebel Tories. Churchill, of course, was in a difficult position. For a start he was at least as much to blame as Chamberlain for the disastrous Norwegian campaign, yet he had to show unstinting loyalty to the Prime Minister. Others, however, were keen to let him off the hook, especially Lloyd George, who might still have been harbouring thoughts of the premiership for himself should Chamberlain fall. In spite of this he urged Churchill, 'The right Hon. Gentleman must not allow himself to be converted into an air-raid shelter to keep the splinters from hitting his colleagues' and ended his speech, 'I say solemnly that the Prime Minister should give an example of sacrifice, because there is nothing that can contribute more to victory in this war than that he should sacrifice the seals of office.'[3]

In an attempt to woo Tory support Cripps's contribution to the debate was wittier than usual. Referring to one of the loyal Tories he noted that, '[Mr Lambert] asked that the Government, substantially under the same leadership, should have certain accretions, that the Mad Hatter's Tea Party should have another session, and he fails to realise that you cannot identify the leadership of a particular government with the interests of the country'. Cripps's peroration, though, would still probably have left his colleagues feeling they had been bludgeoned to death by righteousness.

Every Hon. Member today has a duty which I believe far transcends any party loyalty; it is a duty to the people of the country as a whole. To allow personal interest or party loyalty to stand in the way of necessary changes of government is at the present time to act as a traitor to one's country. We as a House bear the ultimate responsibility to the people so long as we pose as a democracy.

If we shirk that responsibility we join the 5th column as Hitler's helpers.[4]

Cripps's attempt to win over Tories was so much wasted breath, though. The rebels were already well organised. There was a joint meeting of the Eden group and the all-party group, with Amery in the chair, and well before Churchill rose to make his loyal summing-up for the Government, they had decided to vote with Labour. When the vote was announced – a technical victory but moral defeat of 281 to 200 for Chamberlain – Harold Macmillan and the Labour MP Josiah Wedgwood had to be shouted down when they started singing 'Rule Britannia'.

It took less than two days to get rid of Chamberlain, but as with most successions to the premiership there was a deal of negotiation, false humility and pretend loyalty to be got through in the meantime. First Chamberlain sought to win back the rebels, who announced they would only take part in a new Government if Labour and Liberals joined as well. On the afternoon of 9 May Chamberlain met with Halifax, Churchill and Margesson, still intent on remaining Prime Minister. Churchill, in the meantime, had held private meetings with Beaverbrook and Brendan Bracken at which he had resolved not to go back on his previous position that he would serve under anyone, and that if asked who he favoured, would simply remain silent. When Chamberlain reached the question of whom he should recommend to the King as his successor if he went to resign, Churchill stuck to his plan. Halifax, who had been touted by many in both the Labour Party and on the Tory back benches, gave way first in the ensuing two minutes silence, acknowledging that it would be difficult for a Peer to be Prime Minister 'in such a war as this'. He had, in fact, intimated to others that he did not want the job and when Butler had seen him earlier in the day he had seen that he 'was indeed bent on self abnegation'.[5] So

Chamberlain made overtures to Labour in the shape of Attlee and Greenwood, who said they would consult their colleagues at the Labour Party Conference which was about to start in Bournemouth. The National Executive's reply, that they would serve under a *new* Prime Minister, followed hard on the heels of a special Cabinet meeting at which Kingsley Wood, who had been Chamberlain's most loyal sergeant at arms, but had lunched with Churchill and Eden the day before, told him he must go. Now that the writing was covering all four walls, the ceiling and the floor, Chamberlain went to the King to resign, telling him that Halifax did not wish to be Prime Minister. At 6 p.m. Winston Churchill kissed hands with the King and started to form his new 'all-in' administration. As Butler later put it, 'It will always be one of the ironies of history that the man who stood most exposed to blame for this defeat . . . became PM as a result of it.'[6] Some bitterness remained, at least on Halifax's part, who told Butler when he criticised him for not taking on the job, 'You know my reasons. It's no use discussing that – but the gangsters will shortly be in complete control.'[7]

In all of this Stafford was more an onlooker than a participant and though he had close connections with several of the Tories by this stage, he had backed the wrong horse in the race for the succession. Halifax had been his favoured candidate and it is not inconceivable that despite the arithmetical improbability of any coalition Prime Minister being able to get Labour to agree to Cripps taking a seat in the Cabinet, Stafford may well have been hoping for some role in a Halifax administration. On 6 May the *Daily Mail* had anonymously published his suggested new Cabinet with Halifax at the top and he had campaigned assiduously for everyone to reject an all-in Government under Chamberlain in the run-up to the Norway vote in the sure hope that this was the only way of delivering a Halifax premiership. This was hardly likely to have endeared him to Churchill. Yet he did also have contacts

with Churchill. Not only had he worked as assistant superintendent in one of Churchill's World War One munitions
factories, but his brother Freddie had been a friend of
Winston's ever since their days in the army before the war.
Freddie had kept in with Winston and soon after the Second
World War had started, when he had been told that he was too
old for active service, had got Churchill to get him a posting
in the Royal Naval Volunteer Reserve. Furthermore, Stafford
had made early overtures to the Eden and Macmillan groups
both of which backed Churchill, and Stafford maintained in
his diary in October 1939 that Churchill 'thought it would be
a good thing if I could go to Russia, and eagerly threw out the
suggestion I might go as Ambassador – which I did not
encourage, as it would be, I think, of little help'.[8] So the
prospect of a job was not entirely out of the question.

Nevertheless, in the vote of confidence debate on the new
Government, with Conservatives, Labour and Liberals now
all ranged together, Stafford's immediate concern was for how
Parliament could work without any formal opposition. It was
an issue that had concerned him ever since he had heard of
the threat of war in September 1938 on the boat back from
Jamaica. Then he put it in terms of what Labour should do:

> If one is to support the war or at least not actively oppose
> it, one must be prepared to do the best for the victory of
> one's own country . . . Although the temptation to join in
> [a coalition government] is very great indeed, as one is
> always inclined to believe that one could do some good,
> yet it is true that there must be a leadership left outside
> which can watch constantly for the right moment for the
> workers to exert their power when the war is on the
> decline . . . It would therefore seem that the best solution
> of the problem for the workers . . . is for the Labour Party
> to split as it did in the former war and for one part of it to
> do what it can to protect the workers while the war is still

being fought and the other part to be ready to step in when the workers are disillusioned by the result.'[9]

Now he was thinking of what he should do. Should he be the leader, officially or unofficially, of the Parliamentary Opposition? In late April he had rejected pacifist opposition to the war as suggested to him by Lansbury, whose death was announced as the Norway debate began, but he might still have been attracted to a role of 'devil's advocate' if it had not been for the fact that Bevan had already taken the post.

In the meantime the issue of Russia's involvement in the war had not stepped any further away from the precipice. The Germans had invaded Belgium and Holland on the morning of 10 May, and Russia might therefore suppose that the war would now start to face further West, but the question of Scandinavia remained and neither Halifax nor the Churchill Government was yet ready to entertain the idea of full diplomatic relations being resumed. Russia, moreover, was deeply sceptical about the new government, especially as both Halifax and Chamberlain remained in the Cabinet. Russia feared the Britain would make peace with Germany, especially after Hitler's armies broke through at Sedan on 14 May and started their relentless push towards Paris. Some backbenchers had been pressing Halifax's Number Two, Butler, to send a new Ambassador to Moscow, but the Labour Party clearly voted, by a large majority, at the National Executive meeting of 8 May, not to reopen negotiations with Russia. It was therefore a step forwards of a kind when on 15 May Attlee suggested in the first meeting of the War Cabinet that 'an important figure in public life' be sent to Moscow.

The next day Churchill went to Paris and returned depressed at the prospect of losing France, just as Holland fell to Hitler. Maisky, meanwhile, was busy trying to persuade Butler that informal discussions would happen as soon as possible, even going so far as to argue that Sir Maurice Peterson, who had just been recalled from Madrid, should be appointed the new Ambassador to Moscow. Butler was simultaneously trying to bring Halifax round to the view that there was something an ambassador could achieve beyond simply picking up scraps of information. On the evening of 16 May Halifax and Cripps had a long meeting, possibly the one referred to by Walter Monckton, in which Cripps tried to persuade Halifax that the Russians genuinely wanted 'to play the game in more friendly fashion' and in which he offered to go back to Moscow as a special envoy.[10] The next morning Halifax sought Butler's views. Butler, in the words of Gabriel Gorodetsky, 'enthusiastically recommended Cripps, whose strength lay in mastering and presenting a brief and in assessing a position'.[11] So Halifax raised the matter briefly with Churchill before the Cabinet meeting on the Saturday and it was agreed, though after Dalton (now Minister of Economic Warfare) had thrown 'some doubts on his suitability' on the Friday his mission was downgraded to exploring and reporting with 'no power to make a settlement on his own'.[12] The terms of reference were vague. Cripps was 'to ascertain from the Soviet Government their attitude on various questions in which the Ministry of Economic Warfare and other departments were interested and to report as to the possibility of overcoming the various difficulties which had arisen in regard to these matters'.[13] Though not Ambassador he 'would of course enjoy full liberty to explore in discussion any other question which he or the Soviet Government wished to raise'.[14] Dalton insisted that one of his department, Michael Postan, should accompany him, although in the end he was turned back at Sofia as the Russians would not allow him a visa. The Foreign Office similarly drafted in Dan Lascelles to act as a guardian, whilst Cripps himself insisted on being accompanied by Geoffrey Wilson.

On 20 May Halifax and Dalton jointly made the formal offer to Cripps, determining that although the discussions were to be primarily related to trade it was accepted that some overflow into politics was inevitable. Cripps, of course, was only interested in the politics and only accepted the task on the understanding that it was evidence of a new attitude towards Russia on behalf of the Government. Considerable doubt remained as to the exact nature of his mission, but Cripps interpreted it to Maisky as a goodwill gesture. Dalton, meanwhile, noted that the Russians were 'very touchy and troublesome' and were insisting that they wanted a proper Ambassador. 'This affair runs on for several days and I tell Butler that I am quite prepared for Cripps to be given any title or status that they like and that, now that this experiment is launched, it might well be worth while considering whether we should not leave him in Moscow as a permanent Ambassador.'[15] On 20 May Maisky was summoned to see Halifax, who notified him that Cripps was to be sent to Moscow and that he would 'enjoy full liberty to explore any other question' than trade.[16]

Halifax may have thought that having notified Maisky the position was clear. From the Russians' point of view, though, there remained the question of how Cripps's mission would be interpreted by the Germans. Inevitably they feared Cripps's arrival would be seen as a token of British intent to form at least a trade deal with Russia or at worst a treaty of mutual assistance. This might easily precipitate a pre-emptive strike by the Germans, which Stalin neither wanted nor could afford with a depleted and ill-prepared fighting machine. Furthermore, Maisky was still uncertain that Britain and the allies would win. Alienating the possible victors before the outcome was certain would be sheer folly, however much Maisky averred that Russia would not fight on Germany's side.

So, in the interests of studied neutrality the Russians did two things. As soon as they thought Cripps had set off they made public that he was on his way, thereby ensuring that the British could not back out. And at the same time they deliberately played down the mission's significance, referring to it merely as the resumption of trade negotiations without any relevance to trade with Germany. In fact Maisky had slightly jumped the gun as Cripps had been delayed by bad weather and had not yet left Britain when the press got hold of the news, but German nerves were stilled and von Schulenburg reported that there was 'no reason for apprehension concerning Cripps's mission'.[17] The next part of the Russian plan was to get Cripps appointed as the full Ambassador, so Maisky told Halifax on 26 May, still assuming that Stafford had left the country, that the Soviet Government would only deal with Cripps, or anyone else that the Cabinet chose to send if they were full Ambassador. It is not known whether the Russians had caught wind of the fact that the Cabinet had in the meantime agreed to send a full Ambassador to Russia after the Cripps mission was over, and had even agreed that it should be Peterson, but their tactics certainly put Halifax in a quandary. The decision to have an Ambassador had already been made and the public knew Cripps was going out. To refuse to make Stafford Ambassador would not only mean abandoning the Cripps mission, which would be an embarrassing public climb down, but it would also mean angering the Russians at the start of what was meant to be an attempt to improve relations. Yet to accept Stafford as Ambassador would mean that the Russians had effectively chosen the British Ambassador, a point Halifax made to Maisky. The biggest obstacle, however, was the fact that Stafford had made it pretty clear, to Churchill and to others, that he did not want to be Ambassador. It was therefore with some relief that Halifax heard from Cripps on 17 May. Cripps had spoken to Maisky and understood the new Russian requirements. He was prepared to be appointed Ambassador and indeed saw it as probably essential. The Russians were giving a vote of confidence in him personally. So he got Halifax to agree to do 'whatever was necessary'[18] to get him ambassadorial recognition and on 28 May set off for Moscow, still formally titled 'envoy'.

Why Cripps? Certainly there were other possibilities, either for the Embassy or for the trade mission. Indeed it was unusual to use a member of Parliament for an ambassadorial post at all, even in wartime. Peers were often used – there was some talk of a 'rude duke' being sent – but not MPs, and Cripps had to get special dispensation once he was appointed. Cripps's own explanation was that his left-wing credentials stood him in good stead as far as the Russians were concerned. Churchill, though, maintained that this was completely irrelevant, and that Cripps did not 'realise sufficiently that Soviet Communists hate extreme left wing politicians even more than they do Tories or Liberals'.[19] A brief discussion with Josiah Wedgwood, the Labour MP who also offered himself for the post, though, rather gives the lie to Churchill's asseverations as he told Wedgwood: 'My dear Jos, you are not *really* rich enough. It is the most expensive Embassy we have. Cripps is the one suitable left wing man we have who is rolling in money.'[20] Many of the Tories in the Government were simply too sceptical about the possibility of enticing Stalin in to the alliance to be able to make a decent fist of it. After all, most of the Foreign Office had opposed the whole idea of closer relations with Russia for at least a decade. Orme Sargent, one of the senior civil servants at the Foreign Office, noted contemptuously 'Three days ago the Yugoslav Minister asked me whether it was true that we were sending a distinguished English Communist on a mission to the Bolshevik Government.'[21] Alex Cadogan, as Permanent Under-Secretary to the FO from 1938 was more than sceptical, both of the mission and of Cripps's abilities, and it was only Butler who really saw any value in the venture, toning down the cynicism in the official briefings for the mission and arguing that Cripps was remarkably sanguine about his chances of achieving anything by way of 'swinging' the country. As he put it 'I hold that it is better to keep in touch with Russia . . . rather than ignore the Soviet and to proceed further with our circle of acquaintanceship dwindling and our enemies increasing.'[22] Whatever the issues at the Foreign Office, though, it was clear that if anyone was to go to Russia, either as Ambassador or as trade missioner, that person had to believe in the task in hand and be able to carry enough conviction to gain the confidence of the Kremlin, even if this led only to a very vague improvement in relations. For this it was necessary that the candidate should at least be broadly sympathetic to Russia and to Communism, which precluded Tories and those who had been particularly outspoken on the issue of Finland.

In truth, though, the real issue for Stalin and Molotov was not whether the Ambassador's political views meant he was a man they could do business with. What was far more significant was whether there was any business to do, and this depended on whether the Ambassador carried any clout, either within Parliament or the War Cabinet. They may not need the Ambassador immediately, especially if the pact with Germany held, but when they did need to negotiate they wanted to be sure that they would be dealing with someone whose voice would be heard back in Britain.

17

Building the Grand Alliance

Moscow in 1940 was not considered a peach job. The Embassy itself was reckoned to be dingy and the city drab and un-exciting. The previous Ambassador had left without much sadness and had little confidence that the Soviet leadership was worth dealing with.

Stafford, however, with that sense of self-confident excite-ment that was peculiar to him, set out from Poole on 28 May and arrived in Moscow on 11 June determined to make the job a success. In a sense he had to. Having set sail on the wide ocean of independent politics, and with no expectation of returning to the Labour fold, he had to prove his mettle.

The flight itself was not propitious. Stafford left Britain as a special envoy hoping that he might be made Ambassador. On the plane to Athens he was informed that *Tass* had carried Molotov's announcement that the Soviets would only let him in if he was coming as Ambassador and he was finally in-formed on 2 June that the Cabinet had agreed on 31 May, not only to his becoming Ambassador, but that he could do so without relinquishing his Parliamentary seat. One issue re-mained: how to formalise his credentials. Telegraphing them would hardly satisfy the suspicious Kremlin and besides it was impossible to telegraph the King's signature, so Stafford's first days in Moscow were spent as Ambassador in title but not in law.

In the absence of specific diplomatic tasks Stafford decided to deal first with the Embassy itself, whose dilapidation was a monument in stone and faded damask to decades of British diffidence. The drawing room was ghastly: 'The gilt and ormolu furniture is covered with a flowered silk brocade in a sort of pale beige which is most sickly, and the pink and blue flowers are pale and colourless. There is a particularly ugly screen in a brilliant light blue which swears at everything else . . . and a long plain stiff sofa with no cushions at all which would spoil any room.' His own study 'which has three full-length life-size (or much larger) portraits of royalty, an old ugly Turkish carpet and rather decayed red-silk walls and a dark ceiling and some nondescript furniture spotted about, looks too awful and I haven't yet been able to think of anything that can be done to make it liveable in.' Indeed it was 'barrack-like ugly'.[1] The Embassy's main saving grace was its location, immediately opposite the Kremlin, with the finest view in the city of its gilt domes. Stafford ruminated.

> I sat out and walked and lay on a garden seat after dinner last night smoking a cigar for an hour in the garden and it was a perfect warm soft starlight night. Searchlight beams were playing and dancing in the incredibly soft velvet of the sky, and on the other side of the embassy the Kremlin was looking its really beautiful best. There is some quality of romanticness about it, set on its hill above the river, with the most beautiful wall in the world surrounding it, that makes it a perpetual mystery and gives it at the same time a calm solidity.[2]

Cripps was not primarily there to gaze at the stars and reorder the cushions, however, and while he made an effort to make the Embassy presentable, his first concerns were not only to complete the process of presenting his credentials, but to get a grip on the running of the Embassy, a task he had not really bargained for when he first suggested himself for a trade delegation. Indeed, apart form running Goodfellows and his brief period at Queen's Ferry, this was the first time that he had staff to manage, yet already there appeared some of the traits of his administrative style that were so to characterise his later ministries. He took an immediate interest in the work of not only the senior diplomats, but of every member of the staff, both British and Russian, and tried to master French again so as to be able to converse with the junior staff.

In all Stafford was to spend eighteen months in Moscow, and though he was the most consistent of all those who took a part in the hammering out of Anglo-Soviet relations, he was to find himself constantly at the whim not only of Hitler and Stalin's plans, but also of the machinations of Westminster. To the Russians he was an ambiguous symbol of British intent; to the Germans a living embodiment of a possible Anglo-Soviet alliance. As Orme Sargent put it, Stalin could keep the Germans at least briefly at bay by 'pointing to Sir S. Cripps on the doormat, and by threatening to have him in and start talking'. Unfortunately for Cripps, that invitation might never come and the Ambassador would have to 'cultivate virtues of patience and long-suffering'.[3]

There were other constants. One was the degree of mutual mistrust that existed between Britain and Russia. On the British side this was most manifest in the Foreign Office, where Alec Cadogan and Orme Sargent consistently undermined any attempt to foster a solid relationship. The Molotov-Ribbentrop pact of non-aggression was clear evidence that Russia saw its future with Germany. Both their political systems depended on dictatorship and Britain had neither anything to offer Russia nor means of making her fear her, so any thoughts of wooing her were sheer flights of fancy. Cadogan was particularly acerbic in his condemnation of the Russians and when Eden succeeded Halifax at the Foreign Office was 'glad to find A[nthony] not "ideological" and quite alive to

[the] uselessness of expecting anything from these cynical, blood-stained murderers'.[4] This distrust, which at times reached paranoid proportions, had a lengthy and honourable pedigree, but compared with the excessively pragmatic approach Britain had adopted towards Germany, such anti-Communist dogmatism was sheer hypocrisy.

As for the Russians, their mistrust of Britain was equally long-standing and Cripps's arrival only barely covered the cracks they perceived behind the British diplomatic facade. Constant assertions by the British that they were genuinely interested in improving relations seemed implausible when every direct issue – recognition of Russian sovereignty in the Baltic states, post-war borders – was met with a blank wall. Furthermore, some of the blind arrogance of the British actively militated against developing a trusting relationship. Thus Churchill's silence after Hitler's deputy Hess landed in Britain on 12 May, the retention in the Cabinet of the appeasers Chamberlain and Halifax, the rather sudden recall of Cripps in June 1941, the débâcle over Cripps's credentials, all made Molotov and Stalin deeply suspicious. They clearly supposed that Britain, who in their eyes shared an ideology with Germany, would be happy to make peace with Hitler and right up until the German attack, as Litvinov confessed, 'all believed that the British fleet was steaming up the North Sea for joint attack with Hitler on Leningrad and Kronstadt'.[5]

The second constant with which Cripps had to contend was the determined refusal in Britain to believe that Germany would invade Russia. At first this was a simple reaction to the Nazi-Soviet pact, but over time it became an article of faith that blinded Britain to the true lie of the land. Yet when Cripps addressed the Cabinet in June 1941, just prior to the invasion, he reckoned that Russia would only be able to hold out for about four weeks, and Jack Dill only gave them six weeks at the most, so it seems bizarre that anyone would not assume that Hitler would move against a nation that was, by all accounts, unable to defend itself. Halifax later admitted: 'I never believed it would happen, and was greatly surprised. Nor yet have I succeeded in finding any explanation of it that satisfies my intellect.'[6] Even when the evidence for German offensive troop movements was overwhelming, the Cabinet resolutely held to the belief that Russia would not fight but would make whatever concessions Germany required.

The third constant was that Hitler always intended to attack Russia, not just as a means of blackmail, but so as to defeat it – and perhaps so as to vanquish the ghost of Napoleon. While he was still engaged in the drive to the West and planning the invasion of Britain, he determined that it was not enough just to keep Russia nervous and sweet. He was unnerved by Cripps's arrival and recognised that volatility such as he aimed at in the Balkans might easily push Russia into British hands, and so within eight weeks of Stafford's arrival in Moscow he briefed his senior staff that the Russian invasion was vital. 'Our action must be directed to eliminate all factors that let England hope for a change in the situation ... Russia is the factor on which Britain is relying the most ... with Russia smashed, Britain's last hope will be shattered.'[7] Hitler was wrong, of course. Churchill had no more interest in Russia than in Australia, but the strategic point was right and long before either the putative deployment of German troops to the Russian border before the Romanian coup or the actual invasion in June 1941, Hitler had, on 18 December, issued Directive 21 setting in train the plans for 'Operation Barbarossa'. For at least a year Hitler knew his intended target and recognised that he had to cover his traces. Hence the complicated series of tentative offers, maintaining trade links which were vital to the German war effort, and using every diplomatic trick in the book to ensure that Molotov made no firm deal with Cripps.

One final constant was the Russian determination to defend her borders, either through the annexation of 'soft' territories or the creation of neutral buffer states. Often misinterpreted as Soviet colonialisation, this was one of Stafford's greatest headaches as it gave the anti-Soviets in the Foreign Office an excuse for arguing that Russia was no better than Germany.

Stafford contended against all these constants with tenacity but with little subtlety. His line changed little from the day that he arrived and if anyone was to be thanked for the original concept of the Grand Alliance it was Cripps. For the whole aim of his original suggestion to Halifax was that the re-opening of the trade negotiations with Russia might both destabilise the deals with Germany and ensure Russia's eventual co-operation with the Allied war effort, either as a combatant or a trading partner. Stafford's argument was just as ideological as Churchill's of course. He believed fervently that Fascism was fundamentally inimical to Communism and while he felt 'a great deal of harm has been done to the reputation of this country by its over-enthusiastic supporters who have pictured it as proceeding at full speed along a broad and beautiful highway'[8] yet he held that Russian Communism had more in common with British democracy than with German dictatorship. He railed against 'the universal hymn of hate whenever a few Englishmen meet together against the Russians' arguing that 'it is this atmosphere which has made it impossible ever to have any reasonable agreement between a Conservative Government in Great Britain and Russia'.[9] So for Cripps the key lay in establishing war aims to which the Russians could subscribe. After meeting with the Soviets he wrote back to Britain,

It is, I think, perfectly clear that if we are to develop a closer political contact with the Union of Soviet Socialist Republics we must make up our minds about the nature of 'equilibrium' for which we are working. Presumably it must be one in which this country [Russia] plays an important part and it is on this point above all that the

243

Soviet Government will require reassuring.'[10]

The Soviet position, of course, fitted neatly with Cripps's own fervent desire to see Britain declare a radical set of war aims envisioning a new, post-Capitalist world, so when Halifax replied to Hitler's defiant speech at the Reichstag of 17 July 1940 with a simple reiteration of the desire to restore Europe's freedom, he fumed that it was 'Victorian Church-of-Englandism crying in the wilderness! No realisation that there were any problems except keeping British predominance in the world and a conviction that it must be God's purpose for the British Ruling Class to rule the world.'[11]

Sir John Colville, Churchill's private secretary, who did not subscribe to the general air of British scepticism, summarised Cripps's position in September 1940,

> The Russo-German alliance is very close, closer indeed than before since Russia is afraid of Germany and friendship is a means of defence. We must not rely on any breach between them or look for divergence of policy. This is the opinion I have held all along and it is interesting that such an ardent supporter of the extreme Left as Cripps should support it.[12]

Though Cripps's belief in the possibility of an Anglo-Soviet alliance was constant, his estimation of how it might be arrived at varied enormously, and it is in the eddying political currents and undercurrents that the strengths and weaknesses of his diplomacy float to the surface.

Broadly speaking his time as Ambassador fell into four periods: the first flush; the long period up until December 1940 with Halifax at the Foreign Office; the period under Eden which led up to the invasion; and the final period up to his return to Britain in January 1942.

The first phase was marked as much by Stafford's own

personal excitement and self-confidence as by his fairly rapid dejection. He had been accompanied on his flight to Moscow by the new French Ambassador, Labonne, who had a clear and urgent task of trying to compel the Russians to join the Allies. Labonne's only card was to suggest obliquely that if Russia did not provide some form of assistance the French might have to combine with the Germans, but now that rumours of the French collapse were widespread, this was rather an idle threat and Molotov dismissed it as too late in the day. By contrast, Cripps had a less-defined task and two possible avenues to go down: trade negotiations or political agreement. Unwisely he only made passing reference to trade issues and in his first meeting with Molotov he pushed for Russia to join in creating a Balkan bloc to deter German aggression. This immediately raised the question of Romania, where Russia had already staked a claim and was about to invade. Trying to steer into safer waters, Cripps then further undermined his own credibility by asserting that there was no chance of France surrendering to Germany and the meeting ended with Molotov largely unimpressed. While the need was 'clearly greater than ever' Cripps cabled back to Britain, 'with every hour that passes it is becoming more unlikely that [the] Soviet Government will abandon their present attitude of reluctance to acquiesce in a German hegemony in Europe.'[13]

The next task was to get in to see Stalin. This in itself would not be easy. The last foreign emissary to see him had been Ribbentrop in 1939, and all through the trade negotiations up to now the Russians had been trying to get the two leaders to negotiate without intermediaries. Cripps therefore drafted a letter from Churchill to Stalin offering concessions in the Balkans as a means of establishing that he was there to do serious business. These concessions were removed by the Cabinet and the final document that Cripps handed to Stalin on 1 July was threadbare, offering little more than general discussions of the problem of Germany's domination of

Europe. The meeting lasted nearly three hours, but Cripps came away certain that Britain had not managed to shift Russia one inch and that the implicit suggestion that Britain saw the war with Germany as merely an attempt to restore the old equilibrium was clearly a stumbling block to a Soviet vision for a new Europe.

With his first attempts at taking the rapprochement of the Soviets into a new gear frustrated Cripps was both lonely and depressed. There were plans for Isobel, Theresa and Peggy to join him, but it would take several weeks for them to get to Moscow and so he bought a companion, an Airedale which he called Joe after Stalin and which accompanied him everywhere except to the Kremlin and to dinner parties. As he wrote to his old legal friend Walter Monckton in August, 'I feel very isolated and useless here, as the difficulties of doing anything are insuperable. The semi-hostile attitude of HMG is of no use.'[14] Part of his depression stemmed from his realisation that 'we were too late to do any good in this phase and can now only stand by in the hope that in the next phase, when it comes, things may alter.'[15] The order of the day was now patience and patience was not his besetting virtue. He felt guilty at enjoying a relatively palatial existence while Britain was beginning to feel the exigencies of war, and when he heard on the BBC of his own supposedly secret talks with Stalin he furiously accused the Cabinet of leaking his cables and impugning his confidentiality. In fact it had been Stalin who had broken the confidentiality of their meeting, choosing deliberately to show the Germans that Cripps had got nowhere.

This waiting phase was to last through to Christmas 1940. The dominant issue was whether Britain was prepared to make any concessions to Russia in the Baltic. In retaliation for the appropriation of British property, Britain had confiscated Baltic gold in British banks, and was refusing to recognise Russian sovereignty. Cripps, who wrote to Monckton in

August that 'we have no influence at all except that which comes from a far-off fear of the Russians that we might one day combine with Germany against Russia'[16] continued to lobby Halifax for an out and out change of attitude towards Russia, and Cadogan noted in his diary,

> Meeting with [Halifax] on Russia. Cripps argues that we must give everything – recognition, gold, ships [-] and trust to the Russians loving us. This is simply silly. Agreed to tell him to sit tight. We will see what we can do here with Maisky. Exactly nil, I should say. Extraordinary how we go on kidding ourselves. Russian policy will change when and if they think it will suit them. And if they do think that, it won't matter whether we've kicked Maisky in the stomach. Contrariwise, we could give Maisky the garter and it wouldn't make a penn'orth of difference.[17]

Cripps was not alone in arguing for a more constructive British attitude, though. Michael Postan, now back at Dalton's Ministry for Economic Warfare, was also arguing that the Foreign Office had been too short-sighted and had effectively recognised the Baltic states without gaining any concessions in return. The Cripps position, he argued, advocating a whole scale readjustment of policy on a bipartisan basis would have been far more effective, but the Foreign Office was not prepared to listen.

Right through the summer, then, Cripps was being over-ruled by Halifax. On the one hand the outcome of the Battle of Britain was uncertain and Britain seemed an unconvincing ally. On the other the Germans moved into the Danube Basin in August without informing Molotov and Romania was forced to cede territory to Hungary and Bulgaria as a preamble to Hitler's successful October negotiations with Mussolini for an expansion into Romania and Turkey. This posed the next main diplomatic challenge for Britain who could only get Turkey to hold firm with Russian support, so Cripps was told to release to the Russians intelligence that Hitler had decided to invade not Britain but Russia. This was potentially dangerous, for right through to June 1941 the Russians interpreted British leaks of this kind as a thinly veiled attempt to entangle them in Britain's war. So Cripps took a different line, suggesting to Halifax that Britain needed to convince Russia that she 'and her allies are not seeking to impose upon Europe or upon the world a New Order, conceived in the twisted brain of some meglomaniac [sic], but they invite the cooperation of the people of every nation in the forging of a new order of civilisation better, freer and happier than any which has gone before'.[18] Britain should therefore recognize Soviet *de facto* sovereignty over all territories so far occupied by her; she should undertake to involve the Russians in all consultations with the victorious nations on post-war Europe; she should commit herself not to form any anti-Soviet alliances after the war and to provide her with all essential war supplies; all in return for a friendly attitude towards Britain and benevolent neutrality towards Turkey and Iran, possibly leading to a non-aggression treaty. The Cripps recommendations were accompanied by a private letter to Halifax in which he outlined his vision for a radical realignment of world politics. He was now more than ever convinced that what was needed was 'something really bold and imaginative' and that Britain had to reach an agreement with Russia 'on the basis of recognising a continuing friendship and a partnership in post-war reconstruction and not merely upon the basis of getting them to help us out of our awkward hole after which we might desert them and even join the enemies who now surround them'.[19] After consultation with the Cabinet a toned down letter to the Russians was drafted and delivered to Molotov's deputy Vyshinsky on 26 October.

It was too late, though, for on 7 October the Germans announced that they wanted to reopen their trade negotiations with Russia and Schulenburg came back from Berlin with a long letter which was delivered to Stalin on 17 October offering direct discussions with Hitler in Berlin on 'the historical mission of the Four Powers – the Soviet Union, Italy, Japan and Germany – to adopt a long-range policy and to direct the future development of their peoples into the right channels by delimitation of their interests on a world-wide scale'.[20] Stalin, unbeknownst to Cripps, accepted the invitation on Molotov's behalf on 21 October, a full five days before the British proposals arrived. So when Molotov set off for his meeting with Hitler on 11 November Cripps, who heard of the trip while watching a film at the US Embassy, was 'not only surprised but shocked by the news', assuming, incorrectly, that the Russians had weighed the two offers in the balance and decided to run with the Germans. According to the US Ambassador, Steinhardt, he immediately burst into a furious assault on the Russians.[21] In fact the Molotov-Hitler talks came to nothing pretty rapidly but Halifax, in an attempt to dispel any impression of Britain being dilatory or niggardly in its approach to Russia, leaked Cripps's secret proposals to the press. Yet again Cripps was angered to hear his plans broadcast on the news on the morning of 16 November, and he winged off a furious complaint to Halifax that if he was to be treated like this there was really little point in remaining in post. It was one of the few occasions when Churchill took Cripps's side, reprimanding Halifax while ensuring that Cripps was told to 'abstain from any action which might suggest impatience, suspicion or irritation'.[22]

On 12 December the British Ambassador in Washington, the Christian Scientist Lord Lothian, died after refusing medication or surgery and after some umming and awing Churchill decided to replace him, against his will, with Halifax, who in turn was replaced at the Foreign Office by Anthony Eden. So began the third phase in Stafford's period as Ambassador, which was to lead up to the June invasion. In fact Eden's appointment coincided with a marked change in Stafford's own position.

Having been thwarted at every turn he now succumbed to a sense of deep frustration and anger with the Russians and in December he began to advocate a policy of non-co-operation. Colville reported him approvingly as saying

While I do not advocate impatience or irritation I dis-agree that we should at present appear helpful or forth-coming. Having received no encouragement whatever as regards either our political or our commercial proposals, we should at all costs avoid the appearance of running after the Soviet Government (which would only be interpreted as weakness) and should await advances from them.[23]

This accorded with Eden's own feelings and when at the end of January Maisky visited Monckton followed by Eden and the Webbs only to be told off unanimously for Soviet indifference, his irritation finally got through. Almost immedi-ately Cripps was invited to see Molotov at the Kremlin. The door had at long last been opened.

Towards the end of February Eden was in Ankara with Dill and, in sheer frustration at the inactivity in which he was forced to languish, Cripps first proposed that Eden should visit Stalin, and when this was vetoed by Churchill, decided instead to visit Eden himself. In a sudden burst of energy he managed to wangle a plane out of the Soviets and he set off to Istanbul and thence by train to Ankara, arriving on Eden's final morning. Eden, however, had been up late and rose not long before lunchtime, and expressed little interest in Russia at all. When lunchtime came Cripps was left to talk to Dill, who told him that the threat of German invasion of Britain should not be underestimated, nor its success dismissed. Stafford then accompanied Eden to Istanbul via Athens, but still did not

Stafford with Theresa, 1891.

Three generations, 1891: Theresa standing left with Leonard;
Henry seated on bench with Ruth and Julia; Alfred seated
on rug with Seddon, Stafford and Freddie.

Stafford as Head of Furley's House at Winchester, 1906.

The last cigarette before leaving
for Boulogne with the Red Cross, 1914.

On holiday in Scotland with John
and Diana, 1923.

Theresa's new bright red coat, 1923.

Vegetarian lunch at Goodfellows, 1939.
Clockwise from left: Isobel, Elsie Lawrence, Purcell Weaver, Diana,
Stafford, Theresa, Stanley Roth and Geoffrey Wilson.

The Apostles of Peace

During the European War of 1914-18 Sir Stafford Cripps volunteered for active service in October, 1914, but was pronounced medically unfit. Despite this, he went to France as a Red Cross Ambulance Driver.

His experiences in the Great War taught him the futility and folly of war, and that it is always the worker who pays. He became a man of peace, and joined the Labour Party to work for the establishment of universal Peace and Socialism.

Election leaflet from the Bristol East By-Election, 1931. The Solicitor-General with George Lansbury.

In the gallery at Southport listening to the debate on their expulsion from the Labour Party, 1939. From left to right: George Strauss, Isobel, Stafford and Aneurin Bevan.

Signing the Pact of Mutual Assistance with Russia, 1941.
Molotov and Stalin are standing directly behind Stafford.

The Lord Privy Seal visits the Home Fleet, 1942.

At the Viceroy's residence in New Delhi with Lord and Lady Linlithgow, 1942.

The Cabinet Mission, 1946. From left to right:
Stafford, Pethick-Lawrence, Wavell and A.V. Alexander.

With Gandhi, 1942.

Church and State. Cyril Garbett, the Archbishop of York, with Stafford and Clement Attlee at the 1948 Labour Party Conference.

Opening the new works canteen at the Board of Trade, as Minister of Economic Affairs, with Harold Wilson, the new President of the Board of Trade, 1947.

Budget day, 1948. Leaving No. 11 Downing Street
with Isobel, John and Diana.

manage to interest him in the issue of Anglo-Soviet relations.

What he was prepared to discuss, however, was the question of Turko-Soviet relations. In his first meeting with Stalin Cripps had offered to act as go-between with Turkey over the Montreux Convention. Nothing had come of it but now that the Russians were hoping that Turkey would stand up to Germany in the Balkans there was a greater sense of urgency. So Cripps hastened back to Ankara where, with the British and Soviet Ambassadors he put together draft proposals which were submitted to the Turks before returning to Moscow. Vyshinsky, whom he met immediately on his return, was all affability and courtesy and on 10 March they discussed the Russians' draft which was being considered by the Turks. They, however, were still uncertain, and the British Cabinet, much to Cripps's indignation, refused to push them. Yet a week later they finally agreed. In similar vein the Russians signed a non-aggression pact with Yugoslavia in the small hours of 5 April – again cocking a snook at the Germans. Yet even now Eden was telling Cripps not to proceed with further offers to the Russians that involved the *de facto* recognition of Russian control of the Baltic in the absence of definite evidence that Russia had abandoned co-operation with Germany.

Meanwhile persistent rumours of a German invasion of Russia were surfacing around the world and were being peremptorily dismissed by the Foreign Office. Cripps, however, had returned from the Ankara meeting convinced that Germany and Russia would be at war by the summer, and made his first explicit report on the matter on 24 March, saying that the invasion of Britain had been abandoned and that the move against Russia would take the form of a three-pronged attack under Field Marshals von Bock, von Rundstedt and von List. Churchill later maintained that he, virtually alone, came to the conclusion that Germany was definitely intent on invading Russia and began to reassess the Russians' value to the Alliance. The evidence, however, suggests that he was still sluggish well into the Autumn. The intercepted Enigma reports, which he had sight of as Defence Secretary on 28 March gave almost conclusive evidence that Germany would attack. Yet at the 31 March Cabinet, when Soviet relations were finally reviewed, he gave no explicit guidance at all and it was not until later news from, among others, the exiled Prince Paul of Romania, confirmed it that Churchill made any attempt at involving Russia.

So on 3 April Churchill resolved to send Stalin the news in a deliberately cryptic personal message

I have sure information from a trusted agent that when the Germans thought they had got Yugoslavia in the net – that is to say, after March 20 – they began to move three out of the five Panzer divisions from Romania to Southern Poland. The moment they heard of the Serbian revolution this movement was countermanded. Your Excellency will readily appreciate the significance of these facts.[24]

The draft was sent to Cripps, together with instructions on what to talk about with Stalin. Churchill claims that Cripps did not reply until 12 April, yet on 5 April Cripps told him that delivering such an obscure message was out of the question as it would only increase the air of suspicion. Stalin did not now want to see either Eden or Churchill, specifically because he feared such an overt gesture would finally precipitate war, and besides Cripps was convinced that the Russians already knew what Churchill was telling them. Cripps suggested the telegram should go to Molotov instead, to which Churchill agreed on 7 April. When Cripps brought up further reservations Churchill ordered that the message *must* be delivered, but when his reply to Cripps went through Eden's office the Foreign Secretary toned down the instructions by adding to Churchill's 'Prime Minister still thinks message should be delivered' his own 'and I hope you will now find this possible.'[25] On 19 April, more than two weeks after the original Churchill instruction, it was delivered to Vyshinsky for Stalin.

It was around this time that Sargent first mooted that Cripps should be recalled for 'consultation and instructions', although when Butler was asked to comment he not only defended Cripps but also made Eden aware that his left-wing sympathisers would be only too pleased to see him in London and indeed felt he should be more prominently involved in British political life. The matter was put to one side, but on 20 May Eden raised it again and Stafford was advised on 2 June that he was required in London. A brief holiday had been planned by Isobel for them both in Sweden and they took advantage of this to travel to Britain.

The recall of Cripps did nothing for Soviet relations. By the beginning of May Britain had resumed its policy of aloofness largely out of fear of making a false move. The only courses open were to suggest either that Britain might conclude a peace with Germany or that she was prepared to enter a political agreement with Russia. The former might force Stalin to appease Germany, and the latter was still not countenanced by Churchill. When, therefore, Hitler's deputy Rudolf Hess parachuted into Britain on 12 May, and Churchill refused to comment, the Russians grew more nervy. Their response came soon after Cripps's arrival back in London and seems to have been orchestrated by Maisky, although he later maintained that it was Stalin's fault that the now abundantly clear German intentions were not being taken seriously. So, four days after Maisky claimed to have cabled Moscow with the unmistakable news of German offensive moves a *Tass* communiqué was issued on 14 June which must have been drafted by Maisky and dismissed reports of German moves as 'nothing but clumsy propaganda by forces interested in the extension of the war'.[26] Even at this late hour, Russia was determined to keep the ball in the German court and to give Hitler no excuse for action. So Stalin turned down requests from his navy to put the fleet on alert and it was not until 18 June that he gave orders for precautionary measures to be adopted by ground, sea and air forces. Even on 21 and 22 June the Russians refused to believe what was happening, having always assumed that there would be some kind of ultimatum before war was declared.

Cripps arrived back in London on the 12 June and met with Churchill and Eden after Cabinet that night. By now Cripps was certain that whatever ultimatum the Germans made to Russia would be so couched that Russia had no alternative but to fight. It was therefore important that Britain should tell Russia as transparently as possible that she would collaborate with her if hostilities commenced and as a direct result Eden told Maisky that Britain would send a military mission to Moscow. At the subsequent Cabinet meeting on 16 June Cripps then challenged the military by calling for a clear commitment to real collaboration with Russia in the event of war and refused to speculate on the likelihood of Russia surviving a German onslaught, only reporting that it was a widely held belief in the diplomatic circle in Moscow that the Red Army could only last about three to four weeks. Eden, who lunched at the Savoy with Jack Dill, Air Chief Marshal Charles Portal, Alexander and Cripps recorded

Both JD and P were convinced that Hitler intends to smash Russian military power now, and that he is right to do so. Stafford Cripps thinks we should do better if Soviet is not involved this year and remains a potential threat. This I do not think Hitler will permit. Russia will either have to accept crushing terms of 'collaboration' or be attacked.[27]

Early on Sunday morning, 22 June, 'Barbarossa' began and the Germans made rapid gains. Churchill was at Chequers with both Eden and Roosevelt's roving ambassador the 'gentle dreamy idealist'[28] John Winant who had been hastily flown over from Washington the previous evening. Colville recorded in his diary, 'I went a round of the bedrooms breaking the news and produced a smile of satisfaction on the faces of the PM, Eden and Winant. Winant, however, suspects it may all be a put-up job between Hitler and Stalin. (Later the PM and Cripps laughed this to scorn).'[29] Later in the morning Beaverbrook turned up as well as Stafford and Isobel, who stayed through into the evening when Churchill made his famous speech declaring his resolve 'to destroy Hitler and every vestige of the Nazi regime. From this nothing will turn us – nothing . . . We will never parley, we will never negotiate, with Hitler or any of his gang.' Churchill still maintained his opposition to Communism, but saw a greater issue now at stake and announced that 'any man or State who fights against Nazism will have our aid . . . I will say, if Hitler imagines that his attack upon Soviet Russia will cause the slightest division of aim or slackening of effort in the great democracies, who are resolved on his doom, he is greatly mistaken.'[30] It was both a clever speech and a disingenuous one, offering Russia all she had so far asked for but deliberately stopping short of referring to her as an ally.

There has been much discussion about whether or not Cripps or Beaverbrook were involved in drafting Churchill's speech. Colville maintained that while he took Isobel for walk ('she is intelligent and sensitive and obviously very observant') 'Cripps and WC prepare[d the] speech for broadcast.'[31] T. J. Leasor put it more romantically, 'Churchill, caught between the Scylla of a cautious Cripps and the Charybdis of an audacious Beaverbrook made a bold decision: to announce . . . all-out aid to the Russians.'[32] In fact nothing could be further from the truth. Cripps was not cautious, Beaverbrook was not audacious, and Churchill was scarcely in any doubt about what to do as the decision had really been made a full ten days earlier by the threesome of Cripps, Eden and Churchill. Furthermore, Churchill specifically shied away from 'all-out aid'. Beaverbrook's recollection was more accurate: 'Cripps and I sat listening to the Prime Minister's conclusions. We not only followed him but we agreed with him in all he said.'[33] If Churchill hesitated about anything it was how to appear to offer everything without actually making any commitments and how to reconcile his own distrust of Communism with the new situation. In both of these regards it is possible that Cripps was of some use to Churchill, although the fact that Churchill refused to divulge the exact contents of his speech to Eden throughout the day makes it more likely that Churchill played his cards very close to his chest. Either way Churchill's insinuation that this was one of the great determining moments in history and that he spent the day locked in a personal dilemma owes more to his own romantic temperament than to history.

On the face of it, Cripps's task was now over. As H. Hanak put it, 'the German attack on the Soviet Union had made his further stay in Moscow unnecessary. His task was completed, altough the actual metamorphosis of the Soviet Union from an hostile neutral to an ally was the consequence of German and not British action.'[34] The truth was, though, that Russia was not yet an ally at all (Churchill even forbade the playing of the *Internationale* along with the other allied national anthems at the end of BBC broadcasts) and while Stafford had been thinking of returning to Britain for some time he now resolved that there was still work to be done in driving through a real collaboration. He wrote to Monckton

I am anxious that the fullest use should be made of the new relationship with this country to strengthen the morale in the factories and mines . . . the probabilities are that if anyone is thinking at all of this side of the question they will be thinking in terms of the middle class people who have to be converted to the idea of an agreement with the awful Bolsheviki!!![35]

Stafford landed in Archangel on 26 June for the final phase of his ambassadorship. Things had changed. There was now free access to Molotov and he noted the change of atmosphere in a letter to his daughter Peggy in Tehran, 'our cars are treated just like the Kremlin cars and the yellow lights are switched on for us at the crossings.'[36] Yet there was still not the degree of trust that Cripps hoped for and when Molotov insisted in one of their two meetings on 27 June on a political agreement Cripps was rather shirty, saying 'our new relations [have] only existed since last Sunday and it [would be] better to wait till we [have] learnt to trust each other.'[37] Still, both Cripps and the head of the British military mission, Major Mason-Macfarlane (later a Labour MP), were impressed by the Russian spirit of 1812 defiance and after seeing Stalin on 8 July Cripps was able to report that 'all the Russians wanted in the way of an agreement at the moment was a pledge of mutual support without precise statements about quantity or quality and an undertaking on both sides not to conclude a separate peace.'[38]

So at 5 p.m. on 12 July, Stafford and Isobel's thirtieth wedding anniversary, Stalin, Molotov and Vyshinsky, Cripps and Mason-Macfarlane met to sign the Anglo-Soviet Agreement that finally levered the third block of the Grand Alliance into place. There were modest celebrations – champagne and chocolate – and Cripps dressed rather nattily in a 'costume of white trousers and blue coat'.[39]

By now the formalities were less important than the reality of war. Germany had made dramatic advances and there was talk that Russia would soon cave in. The Germans had reached the suburbs of Smolensk and Kiev, advancing more than 250 miles in less than two weeks and when Smolensk fell soon after the agreement was signed, Moscow was in serious danger. Nine days later the bombing of Moscow began in earnest and the Embassy, being so close to the Kremlin, became a regular target. Stafford admitted to Peggy, 'I am a bit muzzy after our third successive night raid ... I told Dunlop last night when we were sitting round in the basement gossiping, that I thought you had trained me quite well for air raids by your parties as the time the air raids stop is about the same as the time the parties used to cease.'[40]

On 29 June General Zhukov made his first request to Britain for military supplies, including 3,000 fighter aircraft, 3,000 bombers and 20,000 anti-aircraft guns. It was a futile gesture as Stalin knew Britain was unlikely to imperil its own actions in the middle East, but it was a way of telling the Americans that Russia needed help, and Roosevelt dutifully promised to increase production to assist both theatres of war. Cripps was still worried, though, and wrote to Churchill

> I think so far we have done quite well in overcoming the 20 years of distrust and suspicion ... there is I think a liability in some quarters to regard this campaign as a matter of a few days and to over-emphasize difficulties that might occur if there was a collapse here. In order to avoid these difficulties we are in danger of encouraging the collapse if we do not fully and frankly give the Russians everything possible to help and strengthen their resistance ... I would very much like you to see all those concerned and impress this point of view upon them so that there is no delay and no red-tapism stands in the way.[41]

Throughout July and August the Russians tried to get Churchill to budge on one of two issues, either the opening up of a new front or the provision of further war supplies. In the run-up to the planned first conference between Roosevelt and Churchill at Placentia Bay in Newfoundland, Roosevelt's closest adviser Harry Hopkins visited Stalin and was heavily courted by Cripps, who was now angling to be released from his ambassadorship so that he could return to London to join the War Cabinet and come to Moscow as a special emissary to enter tripartite discussions on future collaboration. He also drafted a three-page letter to Stalin from Roosevelt and Churchill which was subsequently adopted by the Placentia Bay summit and made the final commitment to a full war conference in Moscow. Yet Churchill announced that Britain's representative would be neither Cripps nor Eden but Beaverbrook. When Beaverbrook turned out to be rather keener on aid to Russia than Churchill had intended, it was suggested that he should be accompanied by Eden, but eventually Beaverbrook was sent on his own and the Americans replaced Hopkins, who was ill, with Averil Harriman. The next day Cripps was given a dramatic letter from Stalin to Churchill in which the extreme urgency of the situation was impressed upon him in almost apocalyptic language. Yet again Churchill procrastinated and a letter was dispatched to Stalin which managed to face both ways, declaring an intention to meet Stalin's demands, but reaffirming the primacy of the Middle Eastern front.

On 8 and 9 September the Germans redoubled their efforts around Leningrad and the pincer movement of Guderian and Kleist delivered Kiev into Hitler's hands on 18 September. Odessa was encircled. On 10 September the date of the Moscow conference was finally agreed and Cripps and Steinhardt notified Molotov that the delegations would be arriving on 1 October. The day before Beaverbrook left Britain the plan to maintain the Middle East front as the main battleground was reasserted. So Beaverbrook had no freedom to negotiate a second front. Yet the Americans insisted that supplies to Russia be improved and Hopkins telegraphed to

Churchill from his sickbed, 'still an amazing number of people here who do not want to help Russia and who don't seem to be able to pound into their thick heads the strategic importance of that front.'[42]

When Beaverbrook arrived in Russia he was almost ostentatiously rude to Cripps, refusing to take his advice or read a memorandum he had prepared for him, and declining even to reply to dinner invitations. In conversation with Stalin he broke protocol by asking him what he thought of 'our fellow', to which Stalin replied, at least according to Harriman, with an unenthusiastic 'Oh, he's all right'. Beaverbrook then went on to declare Cripps a bore, a view he subsequently ascribed to Stalin in his report to Cabinet.

The conference ended on 2 October, and Beaverbrook, believing that Cripps would despatch uncomplimentary reports to London, preempted him by getting his report in first, implying that he had engaged in extensive discussions with the Ambassador throughout his stay. In fact Cripps generously wrote to Eden that Beaverbrook had managed a 'brilliant success'[43] at the conference and even noted in his diary 'that is the Beaver and so I feel no resentment at all as he is what he is and his individuality has had some good points for the country though some very bad ones too'.[44]

Soon after Beaverbrook's departure Walter Citrine arrived as part of a Trade Union delegation just as decisive moves in the German offensive occurred. On 13 October Kaluga and then Kalinin fell. Moscow was now only sixty miles from the front. On the day that Citrine arrived Eden's cable telling Cripps that he had to stay at his post at least until the front stabilised also came through, and the next day Cripps and Steinhardt were summoned at noon to see Molotov who informed them that the whole Diplomatic Corps was being evacuated from Moscow to the city of Kuibyshev and that they had less than eight hours to co-ordinate their staff's departure. There was a rapid bonfire of papers on the tennis court at the Embassy and hasty preparations were made before setting off for the railway station where they began a five-day journey across the monotonous Russian landscape. The siege of Moscow began.

More than ever Cripps now felt out of the picture. The only Soviet Minister in Kuibyshev was Vyshinsky and Churchill was refusing to accept his advice, which became increasingly strident. 'If we are allies, as you have announced, surely they should not merely be told that we cannot send any troops to help them, but also should have the opportunity to discuss the matter.'[45] By the end of October Cripps was finally losing his temper with Churchill. The Moscow conference, he felt, had been conducted without his having any clear idea of what was going on. He had been deliberately kept in the dark and it was impossible for him to do his job. On 2 November he unilaterally prepared a note to Stalin in which he sought to open the strategic discussions that he had now discovered Beaverbrook had suggested. Such an open act of defiance was extraordinary, but by now Cripps was practically seeking dismissal by Churchill, 'as it would prevent Winston using my resignation against me which of course he will do if I have to resign on a difference with him'.[46]

All that prevented Cripps from sending the letter was the arrival in Kuibyshev of Monckton who was on an official trip for the Ministry of Information with Arthur Greenwood's son in tow. Monckton did not get an opportunity to talk confidentially with Stafford for a couple of days, but when he did they sat together long into the night and Monckton managed to calm his friend nad persuade him not to send the letter to Stalin. Monckton wrote, 'I have had a delightful evening with Stafford alone tonight discussing old days and ways and cases and friends – and his new book and the future of the world and oh! Eternity and all things.'[47] Frustration, exacerbated by loneliness was soon dissipated by such bonhomie and Stafford resolved to stay until Eden or Churchill released him.

Meanwhile the Russian war was still going badly. On 9 November Tikhvin fell, leaving Leningrad almost entirely surrounded and German troops between forty and eighty miles outside Moscow. A telegram from Stalin to Churchill which was delivered by Maisky on 11 November, heated Winston almost to the point of boiling whilst his Ambassador fumed that 'I came here to do a special job and not as a professional diplomatist, and it was understood that when the job was at an end I should leave. Owing to the policy of His Majesty's Government the job is now at an end and there is nothing more that I can do.'[48] Cripps's telegrams, persistently arguing for discussions between the two Governments on both real military help and post-war reconstruction, infuriated Churchill, who began to demand that he be brought to London to be rebuked, though Eden, now convinced by Cripps's advice, persuaded him that it might be better for him to go to Russia to meet with Stalin and to bring Cripps to heel. Churchill, nevertheless, was tempted to have a public show-down with Cripps and drafted a rebarbative letter ending 'You must not underrate the strength of the case I could deploy in the House of Commons and on the broadcast ... You should weigh all this before engaging in a most unequal struggle which could only injure the interests to which you are attached.'[49] In fact Eden, who was conspiring with Maisky to get Stalin to send an apologetic note to Churchill, had Cadogan draft a more moderate cable which was eventually sent to Cripps. On 16 November the Germans launched their final assault on Moscow, hoping to beat 'General Winter', and on 20 November Britain notified Russia that a new offensive had started in North Africa, which would undoubtedly draw some German forces away from the Russian front. That same day Stalin's letter of apology arrived and Churchill, Attlee and Beaverbrook drafted a reply committing Eden to a visit, although again there was no agreement as to what exactly Eden was going to be able to offer – a problem that had not been resolved by the time he set off, suffering from gastric flu and accompanied by Cadogan, on 7 December.

In the meantime the Japanese had attacked Pearl Harbour and Britain was forced to reinforce Malaya, so Eden could no longer even offer Stalin the ten RAF squadrons he had anticipated. When he arrived in Murmansk on 12 December he set off by train for Moscow, to be joined by Cripps on the way. As before, they used the journey to discuss at length what was to be mooted on either side. Cripps believed firmly that any vague British statement would be worse than useless and would simply antagonise the Russians, so drafted an alternative to Eden's original memorandum. Cadogan, who was impressed by Cripps's argument, managed to amalgamate the two documents. The next day Eden met with Stalin while Cripps took notes and fussed about the tea and cakes, which were soon followed by brandy, zakoushka and champagne. Stalin, as Cripps had foreseen, had done some preparation and, newly emboldened by the successful repulse of the German advance on Moscow, presented Eden with two draft treaties, one for wartime collaboration and the other for post-war recognition of Russia's 1941 borders. The meeting broke up without agreement and was resumed at midnight on 17 December when Stalin reiterated his demand for border recognition, against which Eden held firm. Though he avoided giving Stalin a conclusive refusal Eden later wrote, 'I had some hope at the end that I had persuaded [Stalin] of impossibility of his demand. Cripps, who was most complimentary about my handling of the talk, and I think for the first thought that there might after all be something in this rather flotsam Tory, and Alec both thought so.'[50] Yet Cripps complained 'we shall fight two separate wars and we shall suffer as a result. It is all a muddle and a tragedy of another missed opportunity.'[51]

Eden left on Christmas Eve, having scattered a couple of promises: to Stalin that he would work on the Cabinet so as to gain approval for his insistence on the 1941 borders; and to

Cripps that he could return to Britain. Cripps wrote in his diary,

> In England many people and especially the skilled pro-
> fessionals of war were almost wishing for the defeat of the
> Soviet Armies to prove the rightness of the forecasts
> which had been made of their easy defeat by Hitler. I
> have had as a result a straining anxiety to see these false
> prophets proved false and a lurking fear from time to
> time that after all perhaps they might prove not so wrong.
> Now whatever happens in the future they have been
> finally and conclusively proved to be wrong, and all the
> wishful thinking which lay behind their forecasts has been
> equally proved to be nothing but the reflection of their
> own biased views.'[52]

In January he was free to return and set off from Kuibyshev for Moscow before flying to Archangel and thence to Murmansk. On 23 January 1942 he arrived back in London.

18

Patience

Stafford's eighteen months as Ambassador, especially when taken together with his six months travelling in the Far East, provided a lacuna of introspection for a man not accustomed to such leisure. For the first time in many years he had to endure an enforced stretch of inactivity. That is not to say that he was not doing anything – on the contrary he made himself busy travelling, collecting information, arranging meetings and writing letters – but the fact remained that throughout this time he was out of action, a passive, patient figure, not an actor in the drama of the war but an attendant upon others who were. His seeming exile in foreign parts was exacerbated by the manifest level of distrust and unco-operation that existed between the Foreign Office and the Ambassador. He felt very lonely and hated 'being here quite ineffectually, while everything is going to pot'.[1]

Also for the first time in many years Stafford and Isobel were separated for long periods. There had been major changes in the family since Stafford's expulsion from the Labour Party. The two older children, John and Diana, were now grown up. John had married Ursula Davy in 1936, Toby Weaver married Marjorie Trevelyan, Charles's daughter, in 1941 and Diana had briefly married Purcell Weaver in Jamaica in 1938, although the marriage was soon annulled as it was never consummated and Diana had a nervous breakdown.

Theresa had followed her brother John to Oxford and was now living in London and Peggy had just started at the Whitehall Secretarial College, when it was evacuated to Shillingstone. Furthermore, in the general clear-out that Stafford had indulged in in 1939 Goodfellows had been sold and a smaller new house, Frith Hill in the village of Sapperton, had been bought, although the final transactions ended up being completed by Diana and Elsie Lawrence who continued to live with the family well after Stafford's death. At the same time Alfred was ill and Marion was suffering from arthritis which Beatrice Webb ascribed to 'being kept in closed-up rooms and denied physical exercise'.[2] Almost immediately after Stafford returned to Moscow to sign the pact with Russia Alfred died on 3 July having seen his son briefly during his recall. Beatrice, who heard the news over the wireless, recorded, 'In the last years of decrepitude he was something of an egotist, and poor devoted Marion had a hard time of it. But in spite of a strong strain of personal egotism, Alfred was essentially a good man.'[3] Stafford was unable to attend the funeral, and indeed by the time he returned to England the Parmoor estate had been sold to King Zog, Marion had moved to London and neither of the houses in which he had spent the best part of his life was in the family.

Nevertheless, Stafford and Isobel did manage to spend a part of his time as Ambassador together, and on 16 August 1940 Isobel, with Theresa and Peggy set sail from Liverpool on the *Duchess of Atholl*, travelling the long way via Canada, Japan and Manchuria and finally arriving in Russia on 26 September. The family ended up staying in Moscow all the way through to Stafford's recall the following summer, and because work and home were in the same building there were some noticeable effects on Stafford. Not only did Peggy, with her new shorthand and typing skills, work as her father's secretary, but Isobel and Stafford began to work together politically. This had already started back in England as

Stafford would send letters to Isobel which she then dis-
seminated to their friends, but when in Moscow Isobel was
not only, as Ambassador's wife, the focus for entertaining the
diplomatic fraternity, but an intelligent partner in the work.
After Stafford returned to Moscow in June 1941 she was to
play a key part in keeping the idea of Stafford's return to
British political life alive, arranging meetings with Walter
Monckton and with Eden, keeping the Webbs informed of
what he was up to. Indeed there was a period in late 1941
when Eden was getting more reliable information from Isobel
about Stafford's views than from the Ambassador.

Almost immediately after Stafford returned to Moscow
Isobel wrote to Monckton from Stafford's cousin Barbara
Drake's home in Sheffield Terrace:

> I am feeling more humble and more responsible than I
> have ever done in my life and wonder just if I have the
> courage to have faith. What it comes to is that these
> young people – David Astor and others, turn to you and
> me to guide them. You, because all their hopes centre on
> Stafford with you working together when he comes back
> and they believe in you. My part can only be to ask as a
> kind of Mother Confessor!!![4]

In her diary she wrote,

> This great country sits Sphinx like! Hiding its fears and
> no doubt, waiting for us to be 'worth while', as afar as
> She is concerned. Germany, they must fear, but at the
> moment it is She who can help [Russia most]. *We* do feel
> strongly that if only our home powers that be could see
> the way to being a little more pliable over *secondary* things,
> & avoid such devastatingly curious psychological errors
> at critical moments, it might help a lot! Still I do believe
> *no one* could understand the atmosphere unless they came

here, but we can pray for them to grow in imagination! 'To give or not to go that little bit beyond half-way' at the right moment. If only people could realise, that, *that* is a sign of statesmanship & greatness, not *weakness*.[5]

Both Peggy and Theresa recalled the stay in the Embassy as idyllic. Theresa's room, overlooking the Kremlin, had one of the most beautiful views in the world, and there was an Embassy *dacha* in the country which they visited most weekends. There were trips to the theatre and (in Stafford's case for the first time) the opera, and they enjoyed attending the military demonstrations in Red Square. Moreover there was a group of other diplomatic young adults with whom to form strong friendships. Isobel and Peggy also took the opportunity in February to visit Sweden and Peggy celebrated her twentieth birthday in Moscow in some style:

After an excellent buffet, during which I drank more than I have done since we came here, we danced. I don't think I sat down for a moment throughout the evening, except at about midnight when I collapsed at the table . . . Militic discarded his coat and tie and appeared in a dressing gown, which changed hands several times during the evening. He was very drunk at one time and I had to claim Bogic's protection. At about three thirty, when it was quite light, we went into the garden and Chanpeignois climbed a tree and pretended to be a nightingale.[6]

When Stafford was recalled for consultations, at first a reluctant and then an urgent evacuation of the British Embassy began. At the same time as Stafford and Isobel set off via Sweden, Theresa and Geoffrey Wilson left for Iran. So Peggy was left on her own with her mother and sister's luggage to pack up for the full evacuation that began with the women on 13 June. In fact Peggy did not leave until 22 June when she, together with the luggage, followed Theresa to Iran. Theresa and Geoffrey had intended to have moved on by now, but were still in Tehran when Peggy arrived, and so retrieved their bags before taking their leave of Peggy who had decided to stay in Tehran working as a secretary in the consular department, where she stayed until she returned to Britain to spend the last year of the war in London in the Ministry of Information working on Russian affairs. Theresa, by contrast, served in the WRNS in Gibraltar, where she met her fiancé, Robert Ricketts, whom she married in the midst of the General Election campaign in 1945, whilst John, the sole pacifist, ran a farm as a Conscientious Objector.

Thus, though Stafford's external career had taken a turn for the better in this period as Ambassador, his internal life had suffered several blows. Not only had he had to deal with the personal sense of failure that attended the expulsion in 1939, but he had effectively cleared out the broom cupboards of his life. His family home was gone, most of his children had left home, his father had died and the one child who remained at home, Diana, was something of a worry. His life was again a blank sheet and it is against this personal background that the developments in Stafford's political ideas have to be seen. For many historians have supposed that Stafford's experience of Russia disillusioned him with Communism, and that it was this disillusionment that gradually weened him off the revolutionary stances of the Socialist League.

The truth is quite different. For a start, of all the left-wingers of the thirties Stafford was always the least convinced by Russian Communism, and it is hard to find any comments of his that go anywhere near the affirmation of Soviet Communism that the Webbs, Hewlett Johnson, Victor Gollancz, D. N. Pritt or even his own son John doled out. Indeed it is remarkable that right up until 1939 he never visited Russia. Even Dalton had gone out with the New Fabian Research Bureau in the early thirties, but Stafford chose instead to visit solely in

Europe and the Americas. So though Stafford supported a semi-Communist interpretation of Socialism and worked closely with Communists, there is no evidence that he held any kind of candle for the Soviet system. His interest in Russia was simply that if war were to be waged across Europe against Fascism it would be sheer folly to alienate Soviet Russia on account of any ideological objection. If anything it was pragmatism based on a refusal to allow 'the universal hymn of hatred whenever a few Englishmen meet together against the Russians'[7] to hold political sway that informed his desire to see a Soviet-British alliance, not any belief in Communism.

The other problem with the thesis that Stafford became disillusioned with Communism is that it hinges on a single letter sent to Walter Monckton in 1941, in which he wrote, 'One thing has been proved here – so far – and that is that you cannot leap into Utopia in one bound. It's a long and painful journey whatever route you travel and it is always difficult to tell whether you are on the right road.'[8] Ostensibly this sounds like a recantation of revolutionary ideas, especially when it is backed up with Stafford's assertion that Stalin's 'methods have been very many of them excessively cruel by our standards' and his apparent unease at 'the government of secret police and spies which is the only method for a dictatorship', but in actual fact this anti-Utopian phrase of Stafford's, one which he repeated on several occasions and became something of a mantra of his during the forties, owes more to his own personal journey than to an analysis of Soviet Communism. For this period of Stafford's life saw something of a reawakening of strong religious ideals, and it is intriguing that the first call for Stafford's new political alliances lay almost exclusively with people with whom he shared a faith, Halifax and Monckton.

One other feature of his religious idealism came very much to the fore, and that was his much commented on vegetarianism. Roy Jenkins detailed the physical transformation he underwent: 'In the early and middle thirties he had been black-haired and rather chubby. He wore round spectacles with rims. It was possible to think of him as a precocious schoolboy who had turned into a clever but immature lawyer. At the age of about 48 he thinned down and assumed a more ascetic and formidable visage.'[9] Jenkins ascribed the Crippsian metamorphosis just to his system of 'conscious bodily control', but in fact there were two medical changes in Stafford's life in the late thirties.

The first was largely due to the influence of Purcell Weaver, who on finishing his solicitor's exams in early 1934 had a major emotional breakdown and sailed to Samoa for a period of recuperation. After seeing a variety of quacks and therapists he was to set sail for San Francisco, where he was to meet his brother Toby, on 8 May, but ended up getting stuck in Tahiti with a severe bout of fever. Travelling in the south of the island he met an Englishwoman who introduced him to the theories of a doctor Edmond Szekély who was practising in the island despite having been forbidden by the local authorities. Purcell went to see Szekély, who prescribed an 'oranges only' diet, and after three months Purcell started to translate his works into English. So enthralled was he that he decided to renounce the legal profession and become a therapist. So, on returning to England in November 1934 he set about recruiting potential students of the ideas of Szekély and launched the Bureau of Cosmotherapy at Lawrence Weaver House in Leatherhead. Undoubtedly Purcell tried the Szekély system out on the rest of his adopted family and Diana became the family's most ardent cosmovitalist, writing a book of 'Simple Salads' for the Bureau in 1938, in which were outlined all the basic principles of what Szekély considered to be the main principle of good health, namely a healthy diet,

Eat chiefly raw foods for health and length of life. Eat only fresh natural foods – not tinned and chemical foods. Eat simply – not more than four or five kinds of food at a

271

meal. Eat only compatible foods . . . Eat very slowly and chew every mouthful to a liquid . . . Eat no meat, fish, white flour, white sugar, common salt, tinned foods or pasteurised foods. Replace ordinary tea or coffee with herbal teas and fruit or cereal coffees. Give up smoking, which leads to all sorts of troubles. Breathe fresh air instead.[10]

Stafford stuck to all of this except for the injunction to stop smoking, and many of the family also abided by the Diana/Purcell regime, though Theresa later gave up on vegetarianism when it became 'quite simply too complicated' during the war. It is interesting that Isobel, who was less convinced by the faddishness of the regime, wrote with a dose of scepticism to Monckton that Stafford was ill during the bombing of Moscow from 'tiredness with raids, sleeping in a damp room, eating too much rich food (he says) and jumping in and out of bed to sign things when he had a violent nettle-rash'.[11]

As we have already seen, Stafford spent much of his life suffering from a variety of conditions, although the predominant ague seems to have been recurrent colitis. In 1930 he had tried the cure at Baden Baden, and when Purcell came across the ideas of Szekély he was an enthusiastic supporter. It also brought him into contact with a group of therapists such as Alexander, whose 'technique' both he and Theresa, the tallest members of the family, were trained in by the master himself and from the late thirties on all photos of Stafford show a man sitting with excellent carriage. It also brought him into contact with the Swiss doctor Maxsimilian Bircher-Benner, whose works had been available in translation in Britain since the late twenties, and who ran a clinic in Zurich along similar lines to the Szekély ideas. Both Szekély's and Bircher-Benner's work extended well beyond simple vegetarianism. Bircher-Benner's best known work, *Food Science for All*, was subtitled *A new sunlight theory of nutrition*, and focused on a semi-spiritual ethic of nutrition which asserted that 'only the whole fruit, the whole nut, the whole grain of corn or the whole plant-organ (leaf, bulb, etc.) can form a valid unit of nutrition, a nutrition-integral'[12] and, yet more improbably, enforced 'nutrition according to the Holy Grail which gives new strength, frees from suffering and corresponds to the meaning of life'.[13] Bircher-Benner's analysis of colitis was that it arose 'from a constantly operative damage to the whole organism, which is repeated daily and first of all attacks the vegetative nervous system, then the blood and finally the bowels',[14] a form of auto-intoxication which could be cured by a 'strict raw-food diet and later vegetarian diet rich in un-cooked food'.[15] Mushrooms were not allowed as they grew in the dark and from manure and the eating of cooked food was condemned as a sign of a 'degenerate' man. It was to the Bircher-Benner clinic that Stafford regularly retreated after the war for medical assistance, and there he later died.

In the meantime he had clearly read not only Bircher-Benner but Szekély as well, and there are distinct elements of Szekély's spiritual writings, as translated by Purcell Weaver, that fed through into Stafford's new thinking on political and personal issues. Interestingly, the English edition of Szekély's *Cosmos, Man and Society, a Paneubiotic Synthesis*, which Purcell translated in 1936, contained lithographs by the same Arthur Wragg who was the main illustrator for *Tribune*, and many of its ideas, using personal willpower to cure illness and surmount obstacles informed Stafford's growing disaffection not so much with Communism as with ideological rather than spiritual ways of transforming the world. As Szekély put it, in words remarkably similar to Stafford's own,

The man with this outlook will not believe that any world-conception or any religious, scientific or political movement can transform today's world-chaos into an earthly paradise tomorrow, or ignorant, hating men into angels.

He does not expect this to be accomplished by any movement or person, nor will be try any *short cuts to Utopia* [my italics], but he does know that humanity is still young.[16]

All of this tallied well with Stafford's new belief that neither dictatorship nor Party politics was the answer. 'I am more than ever convinced,' he wrote to Monckton, 'of the undesirability of dictatorship and totalitarian regimes, but also more than ever convinced that some better forms of democracy must be invented if we are to prove democracy the right form of government – not for some ruling class – but for the people as a whole.'[17] What interested him was what would happen after the war, and the job he really wanted was to be in charge of post-war reconstruction, determining Britain's war aims and giving the nation a sense of something to fight for. As he wrote with some bitterness to Walter Monckton at the beginning of his stay in Moscow, 'I realise that it doesn't in the least matter my being here for the present and for another year or so maybe, because there is now nothing that can be done in England until the revolutionary situation arises which will immediately follow this war and then I shall probably get back in plenty of time to enter a concentration camp!!'[18] Nevertheless he wrote a short paper outlining four possible post-war economic areas, in which he envisaged Britain acting as a link between the European bloc and the US, and sent it off to Churchill in August. Though Colville reported it as 'interesting' Winston wrote a letter for circulation with it round the Cabinet,

It seems to me that the ideas set forth by Sir S. Cripps upon the post-war position of the British Empire are far too airy and speculative to be useful at the present moment, when we have to win the war in order to survive. In these circumstances, unless any of my colleagues desire it, it seems hardly necessary to bring this excursion of our Ambassador to the USSR formally before Cabinet.[19]

So though Stafford might have hoped for fuller contribution to British politics, Churchill was less than keen to see him meddling.

Of course, if Party politics was no more – and it seems that Stafford asserted both to Arthur Greenwood's son in late 1941 and to Beatrice Webb in February 1942 that he had no intention of 'joining [a Party] that already exists or of creating a new one'[20] – then there had to be some other way for Stafford to re-engage with politics back in Britain. He had not originally intended to be sent to Moscow as Ambassador at all, let alone for such a lengthy period as eighteen months, and soon after his arrival he was angling for a way back.

There was talk of him for a variety of jobs. Thus, according to John Colville, when there was some discussion in December 1940 of Beaverbrook's threat of resignation, the Tory Chief Whip David Margesson suggested Cripps for the job because his 'outstanding ability was being wasted in Moscow, where little could be done . . . whereas at home Cripps would not only be a great asset as a Minister but also as a counter-weight to Bevin in the Labour Party'.[21] Indeed Colville, despite having had early misgivings about him, felt 'Cripps . . . will go far, whether Right or Left are in control. He is much the ablest man in the Labour Party.'[22] When another job cropped up, however, on Lord Lothian's death, Colville's suggestion of Cripps for the Washington Embassy was abruptly dismissed by Churchill who replied that 'He was a lunatic in a country of lunatics and it would be a pity to move him.'[23] In June 1941 *The Times* argued that he should be given a new job back in Britain simply because there was 'a pressing need for all available talent; and now nowhere more than in strengthening the quality of the Labour Party representation in the supreme councils of the nation'.[24]

The most personal channel into British politics, however, was Walter Monckton, and he and Stafford kept up a stream of correspondence, only interrupted by the unreliability of the postal service. Here Stafford openly discussed what role he might play after the war or on his return to Britain, with clear intentions of challenging for the leadership if possible. Following on from the discussions in late 1939, allies were mentioned and a draft programme was even circulated first to Halifax and thence to Cranborne and Butler. Cranborne's response was typical: 'a very curious document. There is nothing in it to which, one would have thought, anyone could take exception! On the other hand it is so shadowy as hardly to mean anything at all.'[25]

In September 1940 Monckton still felt that despite a call in the *New Statesman* for Stafford to resign, 'the people are wrong who think your own personal position – important because of the future of all of us – is suffering or will suffer because of your mission'.[26] By January 1941, though, he was beginning to

fear that too long a stay in such an unsatisfactory position might injure your prospects of leading us a little later on. The fact is that there is no satisfactory successor or alternative to Winston. I am pretty clear now that Ernie Bevin will not fill the part. Anthony [Eden] is too conventional a thinker to make a great leader, and one looks in vain among the rest for the right quality of mind and character.[27]

Certainly this was a point Stafford agreed on. In fact when he received this letter, dated 20 January, nearly three months later, he responded by firing off a telegram to ask whether he should resign immediately, an indication of both his sense of frustration with the slow pace of negotiations and of his own desire to return. By then, however, Monckton had again changed his mind and within a few days Stafford was himself writing that he felt it more important to stay in Moscow: 'If when this critical period is over it becomes clear that there is no more to be done here then I shall leave the place and go home, but if the tension continues and there is not a resolution of it then I must stay, as I should probably have to do if war broke out with Germany.'[28]

By the following summer, though, there was a clear sense that the only internal candidate to replace Churchill was Eden, but even he was weak. Stafford wrote, 'I don't think that Anthony could ever make a satisfactory PM in critical times, he's not big enough for the job. Isn't there anyone else emerging? It will have to be someone with at least a radical mind if he is to cope with the situation.'[29] A few days later he went on as if to answer his own question, 'I am almost finished with what I can usefully [do] here and I feel that very soon now I can be of more use at home . . . I have told Anthony that I do not propose to remain here all winter . . . I do not like the idea that the remedying of this is in the hands of Winston and Beaverbrook! The time is coming when something will have to be done about it!'[30]

Meanwhile, back in Britain members of the Coalition had been forced to learn how to work together and Churchill had been boxed into a position where in order to get the full co-operation of his Labour colleagues he had to acquiesce to the beginnings of a social programme to which he was not himself committed. In March 1941 William Temple, as Archbishop of York, held a major conference at Malvern on the relationship between Christianity and politics, and wrote an immensely successful book on the back of it, *Christianity and the Social Order*, which gave overt backing to the welfare state, a term he himself had first coined. Many of those who attended the conference were Stafford's natural allies, George Bell, Richard Acland and others, and it is interesting to conjecture how different the conference might have been had Stafford been able to attend.

One other significant development during 1941 back in England was the growth of the 1941 Group which had sprung out of the metaphorical loins of the writer J. B. Priestley who had done a series of postscripts after the radio news on Sunday evenings in June and July 1940. These had caught the national imagination with their homely combination of evocations of Englishness and perceptive comments on the future of British society after the war. His political comments started simply. 'Sometimes I feel that you and I – all of us ordinary people – are on one side of a high fence, and on the other side of this fence under a buzzing cloud of secretaries, are the official and important personages,' he said on 30 June. Three weeks later he was getting more explicit. The war was 'one chapter in a tremendous history, the history of a changing world, the break-down of one vast system and the building up of another and better one'. Now he was calling for Britain 'really [to] plan and build up a nobler world in which ordinary, decent folk can not only find justice and security but also beauty and delight ... We must stop thinking in terms of property and power and begin thinking in terms of community and creation.' In the usual 'Thought for the day' manner there was a great deal of criticism. The talks had been too socialistic or too political, or not patriotic enough. But there was also a deal of enthusiasm for the task of contemplating the shape of the world for which the pilots were fighting. So, at the start of 1941 Priestley initiated the 1941 Committee, though Monckton, who attended the first meeting, was not impressed either with Priestley ('vain and behaves like a prima donna'[31]) or with the Committee which was 'large and amorphous, it contains no-one of political experience and standing, and suffers more and more from the leadership of Priestley'.[32]

It is against this background that Monckton was writing to Stafford at the beginning on 1941,

I hope very much that your mind will be running on the

lines of coming back, without office at first, critical no doubt but not an opponent of the Government at present, and that you will take a little time to get in touch with the feeling of the younger people, who are undoubtedly anxious that the war should be waged as a total war and less as a part-time occupation for people who are trying to run it on peace-time conditions.[33]

So for Stafford the issues were clear. What was Britain fighting for? Just to defeat Hitler, or to build a new society? The questions arose personally for him because he assumed that having clearly made the transition to being acceptable in the eyes of Churchill and the left-leaning Tories like Monckton and Butler, perhaps he could forge a new coalition, or at least put together a creditable opposition. Its basis would have to be the overt statement of a fully radical programme for the post-war. As he said to Monckton,

I feel very much as you do about the weakness of the lack of provision as to the future. Some day some how this ghastly business will stop and then the real difficulties will start politically . . . the things we do now, the attitudes we take up, the propaganda we make, the forces we strengthen or weaken, will all of them play a part in the formation of the new world.[34]

Either way, ideological panaceas were now redundant. 'There may be many material things we can't do now to purpose the way but we can adopt a moral and intellectual attitude which will encourage the right line of development.'[35]

One question remains. Was Cripps any good as Ambassador? Certainly he lacked some of the usual Ambassadorial characteristics – patience, tact, deviousness – and he had a habit of behaving more like a politician than as a Government representative. He also overestimated the effect his

appointment would have on Russian opinion and was as un-
perceptive about Stalin as he was about many of his 1930s
colleagues. Beatrice Webb, who was herself no great judge of
personality, received news from Isobel of Stafford's impres-
sions of Stalin and claimed

> He likes Stalin, with whom he is now on intimate and
> confidential terms. From his picture, he seems a singularly
> direct and honest-minded man, with no pretentiousness,
> no sign of wishing to be a personage; not too optimistic –
> in short, a business man, completely absorbed in carrying
> out scientific humanism in his own country with the
> largest measure of health and happiness for all the people
> and getting a durable world peace.[36]

It is difficult to assess who exactly was the greater wishful
thinker in this analysis. Stafford also, of course, failed to gain
the real confidence of either Halifax or Eden, either because
he fussed too much or because the spin he gave on everything
was too clearly pointed at issues other than Russia. He never
managed to overcome Foreign Office distrust nor Churchill's
covert antipathy to his political views.

Having said all of that it was, for much of 1940 and 1941,
Stafford's constancy of purpose alone that kept alive even the
slightest possibility of the Anglo-Soviet alliance. It was Hitler
that eventually made Russia join the war, but without Cripps's
constant presence on the doorstep it is probable that Stalin
would have entertained rather longer conjecture of a swift
surrender. Furthermore, Cripps learnt how to run an organisation for the first time in Moscow and when he left it was
not his diplomatic counterparts that bade him farewell, but
his heads of section who toasted his eagerly anticipated
premiership.

Good Ambassador or poor, by the beginning of 1942
Stafford was determined to return to England, and on 4

January, as if to announce his application for a job in the Cabinet he telegrammed Monckton, 'Your man returns immediately and hopes he may meet you before long in London.'[37] In hyperbolic mode A. J. P. Taylor wrote, 'And so it came about that Sir Stafford Cripps's return from Russia was greeted with almost as much excitement and anticipation as was Napoleon's return from Elba. He marched on Parliament as triumphantly as Napoleon marched on Paris.'[38]

19

Challenging Churchill

In January 1942 Churchill's stock was low and going lower. In every theatre of war there had been major setbacks. In the Far East the Japanese romped into Hong Kong on Christmas Day, Malaya was taken, Burma attacked, India threatened. Two British ships, the *Prince of Wales* and the *Repulse*, were sunk on 10 December with the loss of 600 lives. In North Africa General Auchinleck was forced out of Cyrenaica at the end of January, while General Perceval surrendered in Singapore with 60,000 troops on 15 February – the largest ever British surrender. To add to British indignity, on 12 February three German battle cruisers, the *Scharnhorst*, the *Gneisenau* and the *Prince Eugen* managed to sail through the Straits of Dover unharmed, while across Europe and the Middle East there was stalemate. Indeed the only forces that seemed to be making any headway at all were the Red Army.

The setbacks meant that once Churchill had returned from the Arcadia conference in Washington, he had to spend January dealing as much with political manoeuvres as with military ones. The House of Commons was in a decidedly sultry and potentially volatile mood. Chips Channon recorded on 9 January, 'Seventeen MPs dined last night at the Dorchester... Anthony Eden was present, and seemed upset when every MP present told him that the Government was doomed. It was no use, they said, the PM coming back and making one of his magical speeches. This time, it would serve no purpose. The Government must be reformed, and that soon.'[1] Churchill's intention was to win the House over with a speech, although by the time he addressed the Commons in the debate on 27 January he had so irritated MPs by trying to have his speech broadcast to the nation, that his thick-with-cold and lack-lustre performance fell on bored ears and many Members deserted the Chamber before he had finished. A second speech two days later was more successful and he won the vote by 464 to 1 with two ILP Members acting as tellers for the Noes, but he still had to bolster his support by trawling the smoking room. Even Conservative friends were left asking 'Why is the PM so unpopular in the House, he, a life-long House of Commons man?'[2]

The answer lay in the perilous state of the war and a growing feeling that Churchill's central strategy was at fault. Churchill had staked everything on America who, with far superior resources, had finally joined the war after the Japanese attack on Pearl Harbour in December. Now the issue was whether Roosevelt would choose simply to fight an 'American' war and leave Europe, North Africa and the Middle East to those directly involved. This would leave Britain exposed, so it was a major relief when Roosevelt agreed at the Arcadia conference that the defeat of Germany was the key to the war and that America and Britain must therefore deploy troops in whichever theatre was most likely to deliver that defeat. By common consent this meant the Middle East and North Africa.

The problem was that this precluded either a real second front to relieve the Russians or the provision of major resources to the Red Army. Yet in the British imagination the Russian war had taken on a romantic allure that far outweighed any other considerations. If it was a choice between battles in the snow or in the sand both the British press and the factory workers were for Russia. Images of plucky Soviet troops in the besieged Leningrad, of the defeat of Napoleon in 1812, of adversity overcome against all the odds, appealed to a nation obsessed with the underdog. The political climate was balmy for anyone who could legitimately claim to speak for Russia acquiring an aura of spunky loyalty.

There was another factor that told for Cripps. For as Paul Addison has pointed out, by the start of 1942 although Churchill was still the darling of the country, embraced equally by the Left as by the Right, there was a growing admission that he was not as adept, or as interested, in the Home Front as he was in the war. The war may have led to an electoral truce between the Parties but, unlike the First World War, the majority of the armed forces were based still in Britain and the usual peacetime political issues – education, health and housing – mattered just as much as ever. There was a sense of looking for some individual, ideally from the Left, who could embody the nation's Home Front aspirations just as Churchill, who was far more popular than his Government, embodied the war effort.

There was hardly a superfluity of candidates. Attlee, Bevin, Greenwood and Morrison were all too bound into the Government to acquire any independent prestige and in opinion polls on who should succeed Churchill should anything happen to him, all came a long way behind Eden. Outside the leadership of the main parties there were figures like Richard Acland, who in 1941 set up the Forward March group, based on a speech of Churchill's and in 1942 formed the Common Wealth Party; William Temple, who became Archbishop of Canterbury in 1942 and whose *Christianity and the Social Order* was a bestseller; Priestley, another Common Wealth figure; and William Beveridge whose famous report was to appear later in the year. But these were not potential national leaders or even had Ministerial experience, which meant there was a vacancy. Only Cripps could combine the *cachet* of having been in Russia with an aura of novelty, a reputation for independence, and previous Government experience without disturbing the Party balance in the Government.

Harold Macmillan, in a letter to Beaverbrook in October 1941 laid out his understanding of the cause of the Government's political malaise and effectively wrote the job description for just such a figure. The problems were fivefold:

> 1. Our impotence to help Russia by direct military effort causes us to search our hearts again. 2. A sense of lack of grip by the Government on internal questions – labour supply, production policy etc. 3. The 'old gang' are unpopular (Halifax, Simon, Kingsley Wood, E. Brown) the 'new gang' are largely regarded as failures. (Greenwood, Attlee, Duff Cooper) . . . 4. All the symptoms are developing which marked the end of the *Asquith* coalition (a coalition of parties) and the formation of the *Lloyd George* coalition (a coalition of personalities). But in this case the second coalition must be under the same leadership. The Prime Minister's position is as high as ever. But he is thought to be let down by his loyalties. 5. The War Front and the Home Front should be divided. We want a leader for all that comes under the Home Front.[3]

So there was open talk of reconstructing the Government and it was generally perceived that simply reshuffling the cards would not suffice. Before Cripps's return there had already been some discussion of his joining the Cabinet. At the National Labour Executive meeting on 14 January even the possibility of his replacing Churchill was raised, although Harold Nicolson was 'disgusted by all this [talk]' as he saw 'Winston [as] the embodiment of the nation's will'.[4]

As soon as Cripps arrived in London on 23 January he was fully briefed by Tom Harrison and David Astor on behalf of the 1941 Committee, so he was fully aware not only of his own strength in any discussions with Churchill, but also of the competition. For the only other person who could play the Russian card and purport to take up the Home Front was Beaverbrook. In terms of the Russian issue Beaverbrook's strength lay in the much publicised success of his meeting with Stalin which he contrasted with the rather feeble attempts of the Ambassador. On the home front, however, he was weak. It was commonly accepted that any leader of the Home Front would have to command the confidence and loyalty of the Unions, yet Bevin, the voice of the workers, was heartily opposed to Beaverbrook. Moreover his approach to political alliances was rather helter-skelter and as a Churchill henchman he fell foul of Macmillan's objection that the PM was undermined by his loyalties.

By contrast Cripps's position was remarkably strong. *The Times* carried a photograph of him at Euston the day after his return and a letter from Beveridge complaining that Churchill refused to bring people into the War Cabinet except by reference to 'Party machines',[5] the *Evening Standard* proclaimed 'Watch Cripps Now' and Commander King-Hall told the Commons 'thousands of people are setting great hopes on Sir Stafford Cripps'. Not only was there tacit public criticism of Britain's failure to support Russia in her darkest hour, but he could legitimately suppose that if he were to announce that he had returned from Moscow because he had no confidence in Churchill, although there might be an attempt to vilify him as a mad left-winger, his criticism might precipitate a national crisis of confidence. Either Churchill would fall or Britain would falter.

Cripps, and those around him, who according to Dalton were led by Bevan and Strauss, made the estimation that this strength was worth a place in the War Cabinet and this is what Cripps decided to hold out for. Churchill, meantime, with the vote of confidence debate upon him, decided to make Cripps an offer – the Ministry of Supply. This was the post held by Beaverbrook, who was to go to a revamped Ministry of War

Production, but unlike Beaverbrook, Cripps was not to be in the War Cabinet, so he was being offered a down-graded job.

Dalton maintained in his diary two things that are probably untrue at this point. The first is that Cripps originally 'as good as accepted' the job and that it was only when Bevin 'worked upon him and told him what a dreadful man the Beaver was . . . that Cripps then said that he would only take it on if he was a member of the War Cabinet'. The truth is that Cripps had no need of Bevin to know that Beaverbrook was a difficult man. After all he had been systematically excluded from Beaverbrook's mission to Moscow. The only estimation to be made was whether he could succeed in twisting Churchill's arm, or whether he would be better off taking over Bevan's role as devil's advocate. In fact Beaverbrook went to see Cripps on 26 January and impressed upon him that he could write himself his own ticket, so though Cripps hesitated and there was talk of Bevin having called on him three times in as many days, it is improbable that it was Bevin's advice that swayed Cripps away from accepting this first offer.

The offer was widely known, and Cripps's rejection of it leant him a yet greater air of independence. Vera Brittain, who was bewildered by the lack of public explanation of the refusal, reckoned, 'it looks as though he [is] really going to have courage to lead the opposition and criticise the government'.[6] This publicity made Cripps fractious, demanding that the *Herald* should print a statement that the story they had run about the offer of the Ministry of Supply was untrue. The editor, Maurice Webb, told him 'If you will authorise me to publish a statement by yourself, in inverted commas, "I have not been offered the Ministry of Supply", I will do so,'[7] whereupon Cripps backed down. It is not surprising that Hugh Gaitskell, then a Dalton protégé and Private Secretary, reckoned Cripps was proving himself just as big a fool as ever in domestic politics.

The other point upon which Dalton was probably wrong is

that he gave credence to Maurice Webb's story that Cripps sent Churchill a second letter deliberately after the vote of confidence on 29 January, raising problems and then a third letter turning the offer down. Since the offer had only been made on 27 January, less than a week after Cripps's return to London, it seems more likely that Cripps was genuinely uncertain whether to accept the offer or not and any prevarication depended more on his own strength relative to that of Churchill, which was to be tested in the coming vote. In the end what must have weighed most heavily with him was not only the fact that he thought he could probably do better if he held out, but also the determination not to work with Beaverbrook or to accept a Beaverbrook cast-off.

A measure of Cripps's strength is demonstrated by the spin his refusal put Churchill into, as noted by Nicolson on 12 February, 'What has saddened me is . . . a conversation with Violet [Bonham-Carter]. She had been to see Winston yesterday and for the first time in their long friendship she had found him depressed. He was querulous about criticism, unhappy at Cripps's not consenting to take office, worried about the absence of alternative Ministers whom he could invite into the Government.'[8] Nevertheless Churchill went ahead with a minor reconstruction of the Government and on 4 February announced the appointment of Beaverbrook to the Ministry of Production, a post in which he might have been expected to make a real mark as Home Front Overlord. If Churchill had hoped that this minor reconstruction of the Government was enough, the next few days' military setbacks, with the Germans sailing through the English Channel and the loss of Singapore gave yet greater impetus to the call for an overhaul.

In response to the Beaverbrook appointment Cripps deliberately upped the ante with a couple of speeches, one at a packed meeting in the Bristol Hippodrome and the other broadcast as a postscript after the radio news, on Sunday 8 February. Beatrice Webb, who had intended to listen to the broadcast, fell asleep and managed to miss the 'first words of his appeal for greater effort to help heroic Russia' but was critical of what she did hear:

> Though he has a good voice he is not an effective broad-caster; he is dull and monotonous in tone, and conventional in wording... His postscript was more like the appeal of a Christian gentleman for 'a good cause' than the pronouncement on world policy by the future leader of an insurgent political party – which we are hoping he will turn out to be before the next general election.[9]

Beatrice was in a minority, though, for in this first broadcast and in its successor on the 21st, Cripps managed to catch the imagination of the country. It was a deliberately personal address.

> I hope that all of you who are listening in are settled comfortably by your radio, warm and well-sheltered and with a feeling of gratitude that even though some of you have been bombed out of your own home, gratitude that you still have a roof over your head, enough food to eat and the means of keeping out the cold. You've had snow and cold this winter, but not the cold of Russia, where 30 to 40 degrees below zero are no exceptional experience. You've known the tragic horrors of prolonged aerial bombardment. Many of you have lost members of your families or friends. And still more of you will have had your homes and your possessions destroyed. But you have not experienced the brutalities and the savage violence and rapine of the Nazi invaders... I want you to realise the differences between the fortunes of war as you have experienced them and as they have been suffered by millions of our Russian allies.

He appealed to a moral sense, to a greater and an equal sacrifice by all.

The Russians will tolerate nothing that decreases the war effort or the efficiencies of their fighting forces. Hoarders of food, black-marketeers and other saboteurs, who take advantage of the difficult conditions of the country, are given short shrift when they are discovered. It would be difficult for Russians to understand the tolerance which is shown to such fifth columnists in this country.

He ended with a direct challenge,

Can you do more than you're doing now to help the Common Cause? Are your hardships and sacrifices comparable to those of the Soviet citizens who are fighting your battle just as you are fighting theirs? Are you making one hundred per cent effort? The future beckons us across the bleak and agonising months of war that still lie between us and victory. Let us hasten forward, impelled by our own efforts and sacrifices, to greet that more sane and happy future.[10]

It was delivered steadily in that slightly clipped but warm-toned patrician voice that somehow reassured and his ratings improved dramatically overnight. With photos in all the papers of gallant snow-bound Russians appearing every day to back his story, he had played his strongest suit.

Churchill's troubles were increasing. His own broadcast on the 15th went badly and Nicolson feared 'a slump in public opinion which will deprive Winston of his legend ... The country is too nervous and irritable to be fobbed off with fine phrases.'[11] Indeed two days later the House of Commons was still restless according to Channon, and Churchill's own rating was low: 'The PM came into the Chamber and I saw him scowl. No cheer greeted him as he arrived. Nor as he answered questions. He seemed to have "lost the House".'[12]

Cripps also managed, perhaps inadvertently, to twist his refusal of Supply to his own advantage by making it abundantly clear to Churchill that he and Beaverbrook were not bosom pals and even suggesting he should be removed from the War Cabinet and sent to America to co-ordinate Anglo-American supplies. This held out to Churchill the possibility of making a Cripps appointment serve more than one function. He already agreed with the view expressed by Eden at lunch on 16 February that 'Cripps was no self-seeker and would try to play his part in the team',[13] but if he was to put Cripps in the War Cabinet, he had to be getting double value out of the appointment. Now it would not only give him an opportunity to sack the ineffectual Greenwood, it would also provide a balance for the robust Bevin and, equally importantly, Attlee would have to watch his back. The only obstacle, therefore, was Beaverbrook, whom Churchill could not afford to or was not prepared to sack. If, however, a row could be engineered with Beaverbrook tendering his oft-repeated resignation, the way would be open to a full Government reconstruction with Cripps as Leader of the House and Attlee as Deputy Prime Minister.

Here there are two versions of events, Beaverbrook's and Eden's. On 17 February, in a letter to Hoare, Beaverbrook laid all the blame for any opposition to Cripps's promotion at Attlee's door. 'Cripps must be given a place in the government and indeed in the War Cabinet . . . I am a Crippsite. So is the PM. We are for Cripps. We want him to lead the house,' he claimed. 'Mr Attlee has imposed his veto. Having excommunicated Cripps in the peace, he is not going to make him assistant pope in the war.'[14] Eden, however, did not ascribe any dissent to Attlee at all. Indeed he maintained that it was Beaverbrook who opposed the idea of Cripps as Leader of the House and recorded that at 4.30 p.m. on the following day

Cripps came to him 'in a high state of excitement to say that he had been with Winston for 2 hours and that he had decided to come in and help. I said, "Good, in what capacity?" Stafford: "Leader of the House. Unless you want it, that is what I should like most." '[15] An hour later there was a joint meeting with Attlee and Churchill and at ten fifteen at night in a meeting between Churchill, Eden, Beaverbrook and the Conservative Chief Whip, James Stuart, it was only Beaverbrook who was still arguing for someone other than Cripps to be Leader of the House, ideally Eden. Stuart even maintained that Cripps would be welcome as Leader to the Conservative Members because he was unwelcome to the Labour Party. If anything it was Beaverbrook's antipathy to Attlee that dictated his objection to the mooted changes, as he refused to countenance the idea of Attlee's becoming Deputy Prime Minister. Certainly there was no love lost between Attlee and Beaverbrook. Attlee, when later asked to write some obituary words after Beaverbrook's death declined, saying 'He was the only evil man I ever met. I could find nothing good to say about him.'[16] Historians have tended to accept the Beaverbrook line, however, that Attlee tried to veto Cripps, though Attlee himself later stated clearly that he 'warmly welcomed'[17] the move.

The one aspect of the meetings on the 18th that Eden omitted was the bizarre attack that Beaverbrook launched on Attlee in front of both Eden and Brendan Bracken at the end of which he stormed out while threatening to resign. Beaverbrook's biographer, A. J. P. Taylor, maintains that this showdown with Attlee was expressly engineered by Churchill in order to resolve the Cripps *versus* Beaverbrook impasse but Bevin's biographer, Alan Bullock, reckons Beaverbrook stormed out of a Cabinet meeting on the very day of the announcements of the new Cabinet in response to the battle between *Bevin* and Beaverbrook over the remit of the new Ministry of War Production – a battle that Bevin won.

Beaverbrook, Attlee and Bevin were thus all disabled as potential threats in one fell swoop and as for Cripps, well 'Cripps could be manoeuvred; Beaverbrook could not'.[18]

So Churchill finally made up his mind. On the evening of the 19th the new War Cabinet was made known. It was smaller than before – now only seven instead of nine. Beaverbrook had resigned, citing asthma, and was replaced by Oliver Lyttelton, recalled from Cairo. Greenwood and Kingsley Wood were out, as Cripps had requested, though Wood remained Chancellor. Attlee was now Deputy Prime Minister, and Cripps was Leader of the House and Lord Privy Seal. Dalton noted, 'The entry of Cripps as L.P.S. is very interesting. If he has grown out of being a bloody fool, he will be first-class, and, in any case, if things go badly for a few months, his stock, now artificially inflated, will fall heavily and he will have to bear a large part of the responsibility.'[19] Nicolson was equally double-edged: 'He may be the future PM, but he has not the shine or muscle of Winston.'[20]

Considering all the negotiations that finally delivered Cripps his seat in the War Cabinet, there was little sense of his deliberately being given a job that was suited to him – but then he had not been given a job in order to *do* anything. The reason he was appointed was simply that Churchill had no choice. The winds of national opinion blew more easily through this seven-year-old Parliament and Cripps was popular at a time when a few grains of popularity might carry the Coalition through to a military success. Even Captain Cunningham-Reid, the defendant in the one matrimonial case Cripps had ever taken on, was insinuating that Churchill should be replaced and his book *If not Churchill – Who?* was a bestseller. So Cripps's post, created out of Churchill's role as Leader of the House and Attlee's formal post as Lord Privy Seal, was deliberately amorphous and indistinct. The only aspects of it that were laid down were tedious – dealing with the arrangements for Members' refreshments, for passes, for the opening of the subway entrance to Westminster tube station – and his Parliamentary appearances were largely confined to the business of the House rather than the conduct of the war.

Taylor, typically ascribing a more Machiavellian purpose to Churchill than is fair, reckoned Cripps 'was given the limelight instead of power' and several historians have argued that he was set up to fail, put in a post ill-suited to his abilities, given enough rope to hang himself and never given the wherewithal to do a decent job. There are elements of truth in each of these accusations, but Taylor's version ascribes purpose and pattern to a series of events that owed more to the fortunes of war than to any intention to sink Cripps without trace.

Yet for all that Cripps told Eden that this was the job he wanted, it was not right for him. For a start he was still Party-less and had no political strength in the House. He could attend no Parliamentary Party meetings. The only vote he could securely muster into the lobbies was his own and his statement in his first speech as Lord Privy Seal exposed the weakness of his Janus-like position: 'I shall regard my position as Leader of the House as having for its object the inter-pretation of the views of the House to the War Cabinet and also the views of the War Cabinet to the House.'[21] This was a dangerous task. Not only did it require that Stafford should toe the Churchill line at a time when he was convinced that without a second front Churchill's management of the War was unlikely to deliver the telling blow that was so badly needed but it also meant he had to speak for a House with which he had little affinity. James Chuter Ede, later a Labour Home Secretary, then working under Rab Butler at the Board of Education, noted that Butler 'did not know how 400 Tories would like being led by Cripps. I said Cripps would be a success all the while he was speaking to a brief prepared by someone else.'[22] Butler hit the nail on the head when he pointed out that the person who would be writing Stafford's brief would be Churchill himself. And there was the rub. For Cripps without real responsibility was likely to be truculent. The choices open to him were few. To appear too loyal meant losing the backing of those who had pushed for his inclusion in the Cabinet because of his independent views on Russia and the conduct of the war. To open a public breach with the PM would be to appear disloyal. It was the time-honoured quandary of the rebel promoted out of harm's way, yet the only escape route normally available, namely hard work, was not open to him. Leader of the House in title but not in fact, he soon found that Churchill, either by force of habit or by design, still determined the majority of House business. A member of the inner counsels of Government he was soon disabused of the belief that the war was run by the War Cabinet. All that was left was the task that his successor, Eden, described perspicaciously:

> Leading the House of Commons is not something which can be rushed, even in wartime. Most Members of Parliament are prima-donnas. They like attention, which is a time-consuming form of flattery. Make them feel they are all that matters and they will purr. Let them suspect that they are not the centre of events, but only a short and unwelcome interlude in an overcrowded day, and they will exact a merciless tribute from your time. War conditions also obtruded another paradox. Though the Government was a coalition of all the parties and had therefore the support of virtually the whole House, where responsibility was spread so wide many felt that they could leave its actual discharge to others. There was always the danger that what all were supposed to do, too few could be found to do.[23]

This was not what Cripps was good at, but he made a genuine attempt. 'It may be thought that with a totalitarian

Parliament the conduct of the war might be easier for those who are in change of it. But we are fighting for something better than totalitarianism',[24] he announced in his first speech, which was watched like a hawk by many in the Chamber, especially Nye Bevan, and was commended by Tories and Labour for a 'simplicity and directness . . . to which . . . we have recently been unaccustomed'.[25] The theme of his Russia broadcast recurred, namely the need for a far stronger effort by the whole nation. If Winston could offer the nation 'blood, sweat and tears', Stafford was in the business of seizing the moral high ground even more securely. 'We are not engaged in a war effort in which we can have as our motto "Business as usual" or "Pleasure as usual" ' he declared, adding 'Personal extravagances must be eliminated, together with every other form of wastage, large or small, and all unnecessary expenditure.'[26]

Cripps was fully aware, however, of the cul-de-sac into which he had now allowed himself to be pushed and he attempted two routes out: activity and conspiracy.

In looking for a mission Cripps's immediate instinct was to look abroad and with the Japanese making serious inroads into Burma he suggested to Churchill that a personal mission by him to India might well succeed in securing Indian cooperation in the war. The issues at stake in India, were, of course, just as they had been in 1939, except that the clamour for independence was more intense and the exigencies of war necessitated a resolution of the matter so as to safeguard against Japanese invasion of India (although this was never in fact a Japanese intention) and so as to satisfy the pro-independence White House.

So, on becoming Lord Privy Seal Cripps joined a Cabinet Committee on India chaired by Attlee which included the Tory India Secretary Leo Amery, the National Liberal Lord Chancellor John Simon, and the two Civil Servants turned Independent MPs, the Lord President of the Council John

Anderson and the Secretary of State for War, James Grigg. At first there were two draft declarations, one by Amery and another by Cripps, which bore a striking resemblance to the plan he had touted around the sub-continent in 1939. Now a new draft was drawn up, largely based on the Cripps version and promising Dominion status after the war, guaranteeing India's right to leave the Commonwealth should she so wish and granting the individual provinces and princely states, such as those with Muslim legislatures, the right not to join the new State, and, by extension, to form their own State. This was tantamount to acceptance of the Muslim League principle of partition and the creation of Pakistan, and undoubtedly went further in bowing to the demands of minorities that the Congress Party could accede to, but the hope was clearly that the offer of future Dominion status would suffice in winning over Indian co-operation. The document made one other promise for the present, however: 'The task of organizing to the full the military, moral and material resources of India must be the responsibility of the Government of India with the co-operation of the peoples of India. His Majesty's Government desire and invite the immediate and effective participation of the leaders of the principal sections of the Indian people in the counsels of their country'.[27]

After some discussion between the Viceroy and the War Cabinet it was agreed that if the declaration was to be issued it needed to be subjected to some market testing in India first, which meant that someone had to visit India and do the rounds of the various political groupings. Cripps distrusted Amery and was eager to prevent him from going. He was even more keen to find himself a job and volunteered for the task, and on 9 March, less than three weeks after he joined it, the War Cabinet agreed to accept his offer. The announcement in the House caused something of a stir, not least because Churchill referred to him as 'my Rt. Hon. Friend the Lord Privy Seal'. So recent was Cripps's promotion that half the

House thought Attlee was being sent and there was an 'almost conspicuous chill' until people realised that it was Cripps that was going and 'everyone [was] delighted'.[28]

There were obvious reasons for Cripps going. Not only was he personally committed to the process of Indian independence and a friend of several of the Indian leaders, but he had visited India on just such a mission before. Cripps undoubtedly also believed that he would succeed, and even in the last days of the mission reckoned that it could be rescued from collapse. Whether this was due to a misguided belief in his own ability to persuade others, or an overly optimistic interpretation of the political situation in India or a misunderstanding as to his own room for manoeuvre, he was to be badly disappointed. From Churchill's point of view, however, the advantages to Cripps's being sent were even more obvious. It got him out of the way for at least a fortnight. It gave an impression that something was being done. It drew plaudits from the Chairman of the Senate Foreign Affairs Committee, Senator Connally, and, in the words of Amery, the choice of Cripps was wise:

> From the point of view of putting across what is essentially a Conservative policy, both as regards the future and as regards the immediate refusal to transfer control to the Executive, there is much to be said for sending out someone who has always been an extreme left-winger and in close touch with Nehru and the Congress. The immediate effect on your Muslims, as with my Tory friends here, may be alarming, but the result in the end should be both to increase the chances of success, slight as they are, and to mitigate any blame thrown upon the Government as a whole for failure.[29]

So Cripps set off for India with a promise of future Dominion status (which the British conceived of as virtual independence), with some suggestions as to how that might be brought about and with a very vague mandate as to what concessions might be made during the war towards 'Indianizing' the government of India while still under British rule. He arrived in Delhi on 22 March with his private secretary the Welshman David Owen, Frank Turnbull of the India Office and another secretary Graham Spry. Meetings were held first of all with the Viceroy's Executive Council, both as a body and then individually, and the full details of the proposed declaration were disclosed to them. Next came the Party leaders: Maulana Azad for the Congress Party, Jinnah for the Muslim League, Fazlul Haq for the Azad Muslim Party, Ambedkar for the 'Untouchables', the liberal M.R. Jayakar, and Jamsaheb of Nawanagar as Chancellor of the Chamber of Princes. He also encouraged Gandhi, whose statement on hearing of the Cripps mission that 'Sir Stafford Cripps and I are food faddists and that is the similarity between us' had intimated a less than optimistic approach to any meeting, to come down from Wardha to see him. Gandhi was scathing and though it had been agreed that only one person from each Party would meet with Cripps, he let his own view be known, 'If the Congress President [Azad] asks my advice I will say that the British proposals form a post-dated cheque' and someone later added 'on a crashing bank'.

Nevertheless, on the 29th the proposals were made public and the following evening, following day-long meetings of both the Congress and the Muslim League, Cripps made a national broadcast outlining the offer. Nehru, who had been in Allahabad preparing his daughter's wedding when the mission was announced, met and dined with Cripps in the hope of getting some further concessions out of him. Nehru, who had spent part of 1941 in prison, had played a significant part within Congress in pushing through, against Gandhi's pacifist line, a policy of co-operation with Britain to defeat Fascism so long as it was based on constitutional equality. In

Congress eyes this meant not only future independence but an immediate move towards an Indian Cabinet working with the Viceroy much as the British Cabinet worked with the King.

The main point at issue rapidly became the question of defence. For Nehru and Azad were determined that the first step in co-operation had to be the appointment of an Indian Defence Minister to whom Wavell, as Commander-in-Chief, would report. Nehru's biographer, M. J. Akbar maintains that the original idea for an Indian Defence Minister came from Churchill but was vetoed by the Viceroy before Cripps set out from England. This is extremely unlikely. Churchill would not even allow the surrender of strategic authority over the war to his own Cabinet, let alone to a Minister in India, and while Cripps's and Roosevelt's special emissary Colonel Johnson tried to hammer out a form of words that would accommodate both Wavell and Congress's objections, the Cabinet decided to recall Cripps and sent a curt telegram telling him to stick to his brief. In fact Cripps had probably not deviated all that much from the straight and narrow and it is just as probable that either Azad misinterpreted Cripps at their first meeting or that Cripps deliberately left the 'Indianising' point ambiguous in the hope that if there was broad agreement then specific issues might be negotiated by the Viceroy once he had returned to London.

Either way he had counted without the implacable opposition of Congress. Their first reply to the proposals, with cavils about the Defence Minister, the acceptance of possible partition and the inclusion in the proposed constituent assembly of non-elected princely states representatives who might decide to pull out, led to Cripps delaying his return home because he felt there was still a chance of success. But on the same day as his telegram arrived from London, Congress gave their final reply,

Unhappily, even in this grave hour of peril, the British

Government is unable to give up its wrecking policy. We are driven to the conclusion that it attaches more import-ance to holding on to its rule in India as long as it can and promoting discord and disruption here with that end in view than to an effective defence of India against the aggression and invasion that overhang it.[30]

Stafford, rather despondently telegrammed back to Churchill the grounds for the Congress decision, 'In the view of Congress there should be immediately a National [Indian] Government, and that without constitutional changes there should be "definite assurances in conventions which would indicate that the new Government would function as a free Government whose members would act as members of a Cabinet in a constitutional Government".'[31] Churchill's con-ventional reply rather betrayed his lack of interest in the final outcome so long as something appeared to have been done, 'you have done everything in human power, and your tenacity, perseverance, and resourcefulness have proved how great was the British desire to reach a settlement'.[32] Churchill's eyes were still on Roosevelt who now tried to get Cripps to try again, believing firmly that the British Government had been unwilling to grant self-government to India, but Churchill, convinced immediate self-government would be 'an act of madness' abandoning the Indians 'to anarchy or sub-jugation',[33] told Cripps to return, and on 12 April he set off home.

In the meantime his own public standing had remained high. A Mass Observation opinion poll now put him, on 34 per cent, second only to Eden (37 per cent) as a possible successor to Churchill 'if anything should happen' and well ahead of Attlee, Bevin or Morrison, all of whom languished in single figures. On returning to the House he was cheered louder than Churchill and the bees of popularity buzzed around his head. So, with the India mission over, he set about his second possible route out of the cul-de-sac, conspiracy.

The options here were as myriad as the permutations on Indian independence. He could try to return to the Labour Party and seek to replace Attlee as leader. This would require forming effective alliances not only with Dalton and Morrison, but with Bevin and Greenwood, whose sacking from the War Cabinet he was reputed to have required before he would join it. The difficulty here was obvious. Wounds had not yet been healed, and besides, Labour still only had just over one hundred Members. Labour clout alone was never going to be sufficient to oust Churchill or enforce a successor until there was an election, but Cripps's obsession was with the conduct of the war and the establishment of the post-war reconstruction, both of which were urgent. Moreover Stafford still felt appallingly bruised by the Southport experience and occasionally when the subject of rejoining the Party was brought up he would flare out, as he had done when young Anthony Greenwood asked him about his plans in Russia and 'he slammed the desk and said: "I shall never rejoin the Labour Party after the way they've treated me." '[34] He did, however, start to form a closer relationship with Dalton, who by the end of May reckoned that 'Cripps has been a good ally'[35] over requisitioning the mines and Patrick Gordon-Walker reported as early as 4 March that Isobel told him that 'Stafford Cripps grasps the need to team up with Bevin'.[36]

The second choice was to seek to lead the dissident and progressive Tories. Here Cripps had already made some headway, not only with the likes of Monckton, Butler and Eden but with the Astors and some of their entourage. Being Leader of the House gave him a perfect excuse for wooing Tories and he took advantage of it with a series of lunches and dinners. Dalton had a report of one of these, 'Cripps had been along to an evening gathering of a group of about thirty Conservatives, who led him on and persuaded him they all thought the same as he did and would like him to be their leader. He sucked all this up and, at the end of the meeting, said that they must all meet again soon. When he had left, there was much laughter at his expense.'[37] Quite how accurate this report was is difficult to assess. Dalton related it as part of his delight in the waning of the Cripps star and it accords with Cripps's poor judgment of his pre-war support, yet he did have real Tory allies and there was even talk of his becoming the leader of the Conservatives. The trouble with trying to woo either Labour or Tories, of course, was their mutual incompatibility. A speech designed as 'uncompromisingly and radically Socialist' such as his Commons address on 3 May could certainly not have endeared him to the Tories as it promised 'no more rich . . . and no more class distinctions'.[38] Yet Chuter Ede recorded a conversation with Walkden, Cripps's critical Labour neigh-bour in Bristol, in which he alleged there was 'a move to replace Churchill by Cripps in about six months. I said I did not see the Tories backing Cripps but he retorted they had always gone outside their party for a leader – Disraeli, J. Chamberlain and Churchill being instances.'[39]

In fact events militated against Cripps gaining steady sup-port in the Tory ranks. For early in May the problem of coal production became so acute that the Government had to consider both requisitioning the mines and rationing fuel. Neither of these issues was popular with Tories who were wedded to the mine owners and were violently opposed to anything that smacked of nationalisation. Furthermore, the thought of the gentry surviving winter in large country houses on a meagre coal allowance was not to be countenanced. The point had to be faced, though, and Cripps and Dalton (now at the Board of Trade) were in the front line. Churchill, who believed that a simple broadcast from him would encourage the miners to work harder, refused to let the Cabinet agree a White Paper prepared by Beveridge that recommended requisitioning, but was soon faced with resignation threats from Cripps, both out of an ideological belief in rationing as a way of ensuring that everyone bore the same degree of sacrifice, and a determination to see the war effort was not harmed by waste. Several Conservatives, however, vigorously opposed fuel rationing and Cripps's support for it was taken as a sign of his continuing left politics. Indeed the 1922 Committee was so angry that it demanded that his PPS, the Tory Gerald Palmer should resign.

So the third choice was to create a new Party or lead a body of Independents. Again, he already had some supporters for this cause. As early as February Chuter Ede heard that the sacked Liberal Secretary of State for War who became a National Independent MP in 1942, Leslie Hore-Belisha, the Liberal MP for Eye, E. Granville and the National Liberal MP for Denbighshire, Sir H. Morris-Jones were 'lining up behind Stafford Cripps for PM' though he felt that 'It does not seem possible that the 1922 Committee would support Cripps.'[40] When Cripps had returned from Moscow he had been briefed by the 1941 Committee which was now in the process of amalgamating with the Forward March Group, which was led by his old friend Richard Acland, under whose aegis John Cripps had fought the 1935 General Election for Labour in Exeter, where Acland's wife had previously stood under a Liberal banner, unopposed. It was still uncertain quite which way this grouping would go, especially because of the personal clashes between Priestley and Acland, but there was much in both of their positions that would have appealed to Cripps, especially the emphasis on Christianity as a force for moral regeneration and social reconstruction after the war. But direct contact with extra-parliamentary independents was impossible for a member of the War Cabinet and Cripps neither attended the LBC meeting in May which Acland addressed, nor did he get involved in the sensationally successful Independent campaigns at Grantham (25 March), Wallasey or Rugby (both 29 April). Yet these successes provided hard evidence that Britain was troubled by the Government's failures on both home and war fronts.

One curious point, not referred to in either Leonard Cripps's biography by his wife, nor in any of the biographies of Cripps, is the fact that Leonard also stood, as an Independent, in the Wallasey by-election. Indeed there was some controversy surrounding the event. George Reakes, a local journalist and councillor now working in the Censor's Office, had been encouraged to stand as an Independent by both the past Chair of the Wallasey Labour Party, Harry Lloyd, and several Conservatives who were intent on not having a 'carpet-bagger' foisted on them in the form of the official Government candidate. Just after presenting his nomination papers, so Reakes reported, 'a smart-looking woman arrived at my house in a flash car. When admitted, she said she had come to ask me to stand down and leave a straight fight between Pennington [the Conservative Government candidate] and the Hon. Leonard Cripps, who intended handing in his nomination papers as an Independent. In return she would get me a job with a shipping company of which her husband was a director.'[41] This was Miriam, and a few days later, when Reakes refused to step down, there was a meeting between Leonard and Reakes at which Leonard managed so to infuriate him with his patronising arrogance that he decided to try and ensure that Cripps lost his deposit. The campaign was curious. Ellen Wilkinson, now a junior minister, came to speak against both the Independent candidates. Acland spent a week campaigning for Reakes, while Kendall, the Grantham victor, canvassed for Cripps along with the famour comedian Arthur Riscoe. In the end Reakes won easily and Cripps did indeed lose his deposit. On the day that the two by-election victors were presented in the Commons there was high drama for the first to be presented, W. J. Brown, made a special point of shaking hands with Stafford before the Speaker, while as Reakes was presented between Acland and Bartlett there were chants of 'Where is Cripps's deposit?'.[42] Quite what Leonard's intention was is unclear. He was in all truth far from independent in his politics. He was an out and out Tory and even Stafford's new status was unlikely to have softened him to the thought of supporting his brother in a new independent grouping. Indeed it was Reakes who sounded more like Stafford, making 'direct appeals to the housewives and demand[ing] a toughening up of our war effort'.[43]

Yet the run of Independent successes continued throughout the year with Tom Driberg, a Beaverbrook journalist and Christian Socialist, winning Maldon with the backing of Acland and the local vicar, Jack Boggis, who resigned as Secretary of the Braintree Labour Party to run his campaign. This meant that by the end of June there was a small nucleus of four MPs, Acland, Driberg, Reakes (the Wallasey victor) and Vernon Bartlett, who backed a nine-point declaration that had been drawn up jointly by the 1941 Committee and the Forward Struggle Group. On 25 July a new Party was founded on this basis, Common Wealth, with two joint leaders, Priestley and Acland, and it began to set up a full electoral organisation that contested seats throughout the rest of the war, winning Eddisbury in April 1943, Skipton in January 1944 and Chelmsford in April 1945. Common Wealth also backed Jennie Lee's Independent candidature in Bristol Central in early 1943, and though Cripps, as a member of the War Cabinet, was scrupulous in maintaining an arm's length from any involvement, his secretary Gwen Hill told John Collins that he was 'throwing all his weight' on Jennie's side.[44]

Cripps's campaign for the leadership did not receive universal acclaim, though, and rumours of his ambitions were treated derisively by both Dalton and Bevin. Nicolson, who was a potential ally, went to hear him on his return from India and expressed disappointment, not with the content of his speech but with the manner of it,

He was very competent, very clear, very straightforward, very tactful. But he is so dry and inhuman; he lacks fire; he lacks sympathy. I do hate the way philanthropists are so cold in their affection for their fellow human beings. I do not think that Cripps will ever make a leader. He at present enjoys a legend, but it is a false legend. He is a perfect Lord Chancellor.[45]

The reason for any success that Cripps did have as a conspirator largely lay in Churchill's war problems. There was a strong sense that Churchill's days were numbered. Lord Hankey, the Paymaster-General, wrote to Hoare, now Ambassador to Spain, while Cripps was away in India, 'Absolutely the only thing that keeps the Government in office is the difficulty of finding a successor to the PM . . . Cripps is the favourite, but he is a dark horse . . . I imagine nothing decisive can happen until [he] gets back but . . . I shall not be surprised if the situation blew up at any time.'[46] On 21 June Britain suffered a major reversal in North Africa. Tobruk, with 30,000 troops, was taken by Rommel. Within a couple of days there was a motion of no confidence in the Government on the table, in the name of Sir John Wardlaw-Milne, chairman of the Select Committee on National Expenditure, to be debated on 1 July. Of itself this was a remarkable event. There had been no such wartime vote of confidence motion in living memory and when Driberg won Maldon on 25 June there was a feeling that perhaps the end was nigh. In the end the no confidence debate imploded. The various oppositional forces to Churchill all suggested different remedies and Wardlaw-Milne's set piece speech, with its suggestion that the King's brother the Duke of Gloucester should become Commander-in-Chief of the Armed Forces, attracted howls of laughter. Bevin and the Labour Party attacked the motion as stingingly as the Tories and it was lost by a measly 475 to 25 with only 30 or 40 abstaining. Even Reakes pleaded with Brown, Kendall and Acland not to vote with Wardlaw-Milne, though he only managed to persuade Acland. Yet again Churchill survived, although there was now a distinct minority who were prepared to put their criticism of the Prime Minister on record.

Cripps's own relations with Churchill had not been easy. On his way to India via Cairo in March Churchill had urged him to deal with General Auchinleck, who had refused to come back to Britain for consultation and was determined to remain on the defensive until July. Churchill recorded, 'I . . . hoped that [Cripps] might by his personal force bring about a solution on the spot. However, when he got to Cairo he only touched upon the surface of things.'[47] In fact Cripps, who arrived with General Nye, was very content with the meeting with Auchinleck and Monckton, thereby infuriating Churchill who ranted, 'I do not wonder everything was so pleasant, considering you seem to have accepted everything they said, and all we have got to accept is the probable loss of Malta and the army standing idle, while the Russians are resisting the German counter-stroke desperately, and while the enemy is reinforcing himself in Libya faster than we are.'[48]

In the censure debate Cripps, of course, had voted with the Government, but he also took the opportunity privately to draw to Churchill's attention some of his concerns. These focused entirely on the administration of the war and its political management, and his ideas owed much to his aide, David Owen, a part-time leader writer for *The Times*. He, in turn, was largely channelling ideas from his friend Basil Liddell Hart, a leading military correspondent and advocate of mobile mechanized warfare. Cripps prepared Churchill's briefing paper for the confidence debate outlining the criticisms that needed to be met in his speech. 'It is clear that the vote of censure does not in any way represent the general reaction of the country,' Cripps wrote, 'I do not think that the feeling is in any sense a personal one against the Prime Minister, but a general feeling of dissatisfaction that something is wrong and should be put right without delay.'[49] He raised six points, chief of which was his doubt 'as to whether either the Commander-in-Chief or the Army Commander have a real appreciation of the tactics and strategy of modern mechanised warfare'[50] and the complaint that 'after nearly three years of war we still find ourselves inferior in vital weapons such as tanks and anti-tank guns, and that this inferiority has been largely responsible for the debacle.'[51]

The day after the debate there was a second Cripps paper, this time demanding a General Planning Staff who would have a sole strategic role; an increased Ministry of Production; and a Scientific Planning Staff. Other requests included the sacking of the Minister of Supply, Andrew Duncan, and the appointment of Percy Hobart as the Commander of the Eighth Army.

The Labour MP Ivor Thomas was now convinced that

if Alexandria had fallen, Winston would have fallen also. As it is he will hold his position until we get another major reverse . . . This ought to be a 'people's War', but Winston has never, owing to his background and record, been able to capture the affections of the working classes as L. G. did . . . there will be a change in time, and inevitably (though possibly after a short interlude) Cripps will be PM . . . Whatever the Gallup Poll may reveal . . . A large number in both the Labour Party and the Conservative Party regard Eden as a weak figure who has got his present position only by birth, the right school, good looks and luck. The Conservatives, anxious to avoid Eden, are at present canvassing R. A. Butler as PM! . . . The bulk of the Labour Party would prefer Cripps to Attlee, and, combined with the Tory feeling I have mentioned, this will bring Cripps to the top. I repeat this conviction even though Cripps's stock in Left circles has fallen heavily, both in the House and outside, since he joined the Cabinet.[52]

So by the end of July there was a more or less open Cripps campaign going on and Simon Barrington-Ward, the new editor of *The Times,* was discussing whether to support the Cripps plan for a higher professional directorate advising the Cabinet on the conduct of the war and for Churchill to hand over the Ministry of Defence as a first step towards a full Cabinet revolt. His response was clear, although he still doubted Churchill's ability to remain. 'It is useless for Cripps to act alone,' he told Nedd Griggs. 'He would fail and be compromised and do more harm than good. Three or four members of the War Cabinet must act together. Nor is it sound to ask any Prime Minster to give up the Ministry of Defence or, even if the office is abolished, its functions. Asquith couldn't in 1916.'[53]

Throughout these months Cripps's level of concern rose in direct proportion to his sense of exclusion from the central planning of the war. He complained that he never saw Churchill except at Cabinet meetings. He objected to being kept out of the Defence Committee, and resented the continuing presence of Beaverbrook. He felt that there was a ban on any publicity for him and Barrington-Ward noted in September: 'He is more and more left out. No talk with Winston lately. Even the business of the House, of which Cripps is the Leader, is settled between the PM and the whips. Cripps has sent in a memorandum of his views on the conduct of the war and has had a negative reply. Feels he cannot go on.'[54] While others largely left the war to Churchill, concentrating instead on social reconstruction or issues of supply and labour, Stafford stuck his nose directly into strategic military issues. So when Churchill returned from the Middle East in August he found Cripps 'had developed serious doubts about the state of national morale and the effectiveness of our machinery for the central direction of the war . . . There was, he thought, an urgent need to infuse a new spirit of vigour and enthusiasm into the nation's war effort. For this purpose he proposed a series of reforms in our machinery of government.'[55] The main reform he had in mind was the creation of a War Planning Directorate which would consist of the Minister of Defence and three advisers 'of the calibre of Chiefs of Staff who would supervise the Joint Planning staffs and would be free to devote the whole of their time to military planning in its broadest sense'. This would supersede the Chiefs of Staff Committee. In each theatre of war there would be a single Commander with full power over all the naval, land and air forces. These Commanders, advised by a small joint staff, would be responsible directly to the War Planning Directorate. Churchill was wholly opposed to the plan, calling it 'a planner's dream'[56] which would be unworkable because it would split off the decisions from those who had to carry them through and he told Cripps in no uncertain terms that he was not 'prepared to invite a Brains Trust to browse about among our secrets and add to the already immense volume of committees and reports'.[57]

Meanwhile, Cripps was sanguine about his level of support, which was beginning to ebb. At the beginning of September he had a long discussion with Gordon-Walker and Geoffrey Wilson in the course of which he admitted that 'he had come in with a large but intangible and vague popular following: which had expected him to bring a new drive into the war. He still had a big following: his private Mass Observation poll showed a steady 70 per cent popularity. But the dynamic was going out of his support. People are beginning to say – if he stays in now he has sold himself.'[58] The only answer was really to find some reason over which to resign, thus precipitating a crisis. Ideally this had to be in concert with Eden, but Cripps was fully aware that this was unlikely, and he recognised the great weakness in his own position, 'He said he really had no use if in fact Churchill could win the war by his methods.'[59]

The next week he made a disastrous mistake. The debate after Prime Minister's Questions on 8 September collapsed earlier than expected and the Chamber began to empty before Churchill finished. Cripps, instead of interpreting this as a vote of confidence in the Government's position, decided to tell the House off for its lack of dedication. Dalton called it a 'priggish sermon'[60] and Nicolson wrote to his wife Vita Sackville-West that Cripps 'profited by the occasion to give the House a rather sharp talking-to and to accuse them of preferring their luncheons to their duties. This has enraged everyone.'[61] Within a couple of weeks Ede was noting, 'I think Cripps' chance of getting the succession is less than it was – I personally never thought it very great. His attack on MPs recently is very bitterly resented by all groups. The people to whom I have spoken this week have all been very critical of his attitude to the House.'[62]

From this point on the discussions about Cripps resigning steadily grew. In part this was personal. Always one to sulk rather than tantrum Cripps was a hysteric who craved attention and his reaction to the manifest anger of the House at his telling them off, mixed with a realisation that it had been a bad mistake, made him want to take the ball away. Yet there was also a political reason for threatening to resign and both Beveridge, with whom he had now formed a close relationship, and E. H. Carr, both encouraged him to go. On the one hand, if Churchill survived his resignation he would at least have a chance to form an independent platform for himself, and if, on the other, Churchill and the Cabinet fell, then Cripps would be there to pick up the pieces. So went the argument. The only difficulty was that the fall of the Government, especially now that there had not been any serious military success for more than a year and there was a new offensive afoot in Africa, could herald the collapse of British morale. And besides, there was a possibility that a resignation at such a key time would tell against Cripps in the public mind. So he went half way with a letter to Churchill on 10 September in which he complained that he was not enjoying his full confidence and that as a result he was sacrificing his whole future for a shadow.

Nicolson recorded his own and Guy Burgess's estimation of Cripps's rumoured desire to resign over the conduct of war the day after his lapse in the House,

> Guy and I agreed that Cripps's attitude was probably wholly disinterested and sincere. That he really believed that Winston was incapable of dealing with the home front and that his handling of the minor problems of production and strategy was fumbling and imprecise. We had agreed also that Cripps would find the atmosphere of Downing Street, with its late hours, casual talk, cigar smoke and endless whisky, most unpalatable. Whereas Winston never regards with affection a man of such inhuman austerity as Cripps and cannot work with people easily unless his sentiments as well as his respect is aroused. We also agreed that Cripps who in his way is a man of great innocence and narrow vision might be quite seriously unaware that his own resignation would shake Winston very severely, that around him would gather all the elements of opposition, and that in the end he would group around him an 'alternative Government' and take Winston's place. We agreed that Cripps was actually too modest a man to realise what an immensely disturbing effect his resignation would produce, and too simple a man to see how it would be exploited by evil men to their advantage. There was a hope that if Winston would show real consideration to Cripps, and give him a vital part in the direction of the war, then something might be done to avoid this disaster.[63]

The rest of September was spent in a rather sullen contest between Cripps and Churchill. On the 27th there was a massive meeting at the Albert Hall with William Temple and

Cyril Garbett, respectively Archbishops of Canterbury and York, and Cripps made himself busy with House matters, but as October approached it became more and more apparent that some kind of breach was inevitable. Brendan Bracken, one of Churchill's closest allies, expressed his concerns to the Prime Minister, 'I'm afraid of that fellow Cripps. I think he means business. If he pulls out, there'll be a hell of a row',[64] though when Churchill himself started to fret that he might be turned out of office Bracken told him to shut up and dismissed the whole Cripps affair as a storm in a teacup. Others were more abrasive on the issue. As long ago as May Bevin had been contemptuous of Cripps's threats to resign unless requisitioning the mines was carried through Cabinet, although Bevin and Cripps were both later reported as threatening resignation if Beaverbrook was brought back.

On 30 September the group of Gordon-Walker, Geoffrey Wilson, and several others met again with Cripps until 11 p.m. and it was clear that he had made his mind up to resign, though he was not yet sure over what issue. Cripps was then summoned from his bed at 2 a.m. to see Churchill and, according to Barrington-Ward, who met with Cripps later in the day, 'They had a firm and friendly talk. Cripps said he could not go on as member of a War Cabinet not fully consulted by the P.M. . . . or as Leader of the House without the full knowledge necessary for the job.'[65] In the discussions with Gordon-Walker he reckoned on Eden as the only real alternative to Churchill who was 'now bad for the war. The greatest man with the greatest character: but he makes mistakes and makes Cabinet system impossible.'[66] Still Cripps was uncertain quite how he viewed the future. One alternative was a 'real Cabinet' with Eden, Bevin and himself building 'an overriding incentive mainly by means of a guaranteed future (education, land, Beveridge cttee etc.)' before fighting a coupon election against the 'die-hard Tories' led by Churchill. At least one element of this was cloud cuckoo-land. Cripps was not a team player and any attempt to oust Churchill would have to depend on a concerted effort. Yet when Churchill had made an outrageous speech about India in the House and Cripps, Eden and Lyttelton had agreed to go and 'beard' Churchill, the others turned up early and by the time Cripps arrived they had been won round by the Prime Minister. 'I have never been able to team up with anyone',[67] Cripps moaned.

At twelve forty-five that same night he was again summoned to Downing Street where, so he told Barrington-Ward, he was 'shown into an empty drawing room! Attlee and Anthony came in looking rather sheepish. Begged him to consider effect of his resignation abroad and on the army. Asked whether he would not consider a mission to the US to organise British activities over there: alternatively whether he would dissociate himself from the War Cabinet and take on Ministry of Aircraft Production.'[68]

Finally, at noon on the 2nd Cripps and Churchill met again to discuss his resignation and Churchill began to realise that 'it was a genuine personal difficulty and not the desire for a political coup which actuated Cripps.' This was a point that had much exercised Churchill. He had confessed to Eden only the day before that he was convinced Cripps had a 'Machiavellian political plot' in mind, a point that Eden denied, whilst making every effort, with Attlee, to 'convince Stafford Cripps of the folly of causing rift in ranks at this critical moment'.[69] Bracken was also drafted in and what might at one stage have been a back door coup or a private difference of opinion soon became a public issue in which Stafford became more and more isolated by the hour. Cleverly playing to the honourable strain in Cripps's psyche Churchill told him on the 2nd, 'You are an honest man. If you had been Ll[oyd] G[eorge] you would have resigned on the issue of a second front.' The organisation of the Government for war was, he felt, from Cripps's point of view, a bad issue for resignation and it would be in the best interests of the nation if any resignation could be delayed until after Operation Torch.[70]

So the following day Cripps wrote to Churchill, 'it is clear that nothing avoidable should be done during these particularly critical days by the suggestion of disunity or of differences as to the central direction of the war, which might disturb the morale of our fighting men or increase our international difficulties,' thereby effectively postdating his letter of resignation and handing over any element of power his resignation might have.

In the meantime Cripps and Churchill maintained an outward show of unity. Indeed Churchill took Cripps, for the first time, to review the Fleet with him and the latter 'returned bubbling with pleasure and renewed confidence', so much so that people began to predict that 'we shall not hear any more about resignation for the moment'.[71] Cripps was still confident of his own position, however, as he told Beatrice Webb when he went to see her for the last time on 26 October, 'He intimated that there were only two possible Prime Ministers: Anthony Eden and himself. Eden had all the right instincts, but was an aristocratic country squire ... In short Stafford expects that *he* would succeed Churchill as prime minister.'[72]

In turn Churchill had by now decided that as soon as he had some political slack he would do without Cripps, especially as he had now put on private record that they did not have full confidence in each other. The opportunity came, as Cripps himself had guessed, the moment Churchill began to prove that he might be able to win the war his own way. On 23 October General Montgomery, in charge of the Eighth Army, and General Alexander, Churchill's replacement for the tetchy Auchinleck, started the long-awaited fight back in the desert with a heavy bombardment of Rommel's forces at El Alamein. It was a classic set piece battle in which Montgomery had the advantage of open supply routes while Rommel's route via Malta had been cut. Twelve days later, after a heavy drain on supplies and casualties, Rommel, against Hitler's orders, began to retreat. It was immediately hyped as a great British victory, made all the sweeter by the fact that the Anglo-American invasion of Morocco and Algeria, which heralded the end of solo British endeavours in the war, did not start until three days later. In fact Britain had failed to prevent Rommel's escape but Churchill ordered church bells to be rung in Britain and claimed a total victory.

On Sunday 22 November Churchill reordered the War Cabinet and appointed Cripps Minister for Aircraft Production. Morrison was to take his place in the War Cabinet, while Colonel Jay Llewellin, generally reckoned to have been a disaster at Aircraft Production, was sent to Washington. Cranborne took on Lord Privy Seal and Eden was to lead the House. Churchill later, somewhat disingenuously, maintained that although there had been differences of opinion Cripps had never threatened to replace him as Prime Minister and the decision to move him was taken solely for practical reasons: 'an exalted brooding over the work of others is only too often the lot of a Minister without departmental duties. For a man of his keen intellect, as yet untempered by administrative experience, his exalted ideals, and his skills in theoretical exposition, this form of activity held a strong though dangerous appeal. His great intellectual energy needed to be harnessed to a more practical task.'[73] Dalton, however, reckoned differently, 'He has, I think, been very skilfully played by the PM. He may, of course, be quite good at the MAP, but seldom has anyone's political stock, having been so outrageously and unjustifiably overvalued, fallen so fast and so far.'[74]

The rise and fall of Cripps, all within one year, owed much to the fortunes of war. It was not parliamentary strength that gained him his seat in the Cabinet and when the war finally looked as if it had turned Cripps had nothing to protect him. Those who live by the sword die by the sword and Cripps, who arrived on the tide of a largely undeserved wave of popular support, departed on exactly the same wave. As John Lee argued, 'popular disenchantment with the management of the war on which Cripps's appeal depended did not carry sufficient weight in the House of Commons to deprive the coalition of its parliamentary support'.[75]

There is some truth, though, in Churchill's assertion that he regretted that Cripps 'declined my original proposal that he should join the Government in the first instance as Minister of Supply.'[76] A practical job would indeed have served him better.

20

Lancasters, Wellingtons and Magnetrons

The Ministry of Aircraft Production smacks of the political sidelines, yet in late 1942 Churchill could legitimately claim that it was an essential central part of the war effort, if not of the War Cabinet. After all, not only was aircraft manufacture the largest industry in Britain, its success was also integral to winning the war. Beaverbrook's role as Minister in the dash to produce planes to fight the Battle of Britain had in 1940 been as high profile as that of Air Vice-Marshal Dowding as Commander-in-Chief of Fighter Command. Air power had rapidly assumed a predominance in the wartime imagination for the very simple reason that for at least two years the main engagement with Germany happened in the air. Not only did Britain have to defend herself in the air, but her only means of attack was by air. So the constant supply of aeroplanes was as vital to her success as the supply of guns to the trenches in the First World War.

Britain had not entered the war with this in mind. In the First World War the Air Force was plucky but irrelevant, and by the start of the Second it could still barely challenge the kudos of the established forces. Despite the fact that other wars such as the Spanish Civil War – where Germany's bombers had razed and her fighters had strafed Guernica on behalf of Franco – had shown that the air could play a decisive part in war, Britannia was still only really interested in ruling the waves. The basic tasks for which aircraft could be used were already identified – transportation, reconnaissance, strategic bombing, strafing, mid-air fighting, air-sea rescue – but dominance of the air as a military necessity was scarcely considered and few had any real conception of what a major war in the air would entail. Uncertain of the value of air power Britain had therefore invested little in aircraft before the war began, lagging well behind Soviet Russia, Japan and Germany. In the last minute dash for armament of 1938 and 1939 there was a determined effort to increase the British air arsenal but the Luftwaffe still outstripped her with 3,609 aeroplanes against the RAF's 1,911, while Russia in 1939 alone managed to build 10,000 aeroplanes and Japan completed nearly 8,000.

Germany's conduct of the war soon began to ram the message home. Using the same techniques they had pioneered at Guernica in the attack on Poland, the Luftwaffe first demolished the puny Polish air force before dive-bombing key installations and communications routes at will and finished the task off with a relentless pummelling of Warsaw until she could take no more. In the drive towards Paris the Germans again relied on heavy air cover and it was only poor weather conditions and the dispersal of the British volunteer flotilla at Dunkirk that prevented the Luftwaffe alone from scuppering the British retreat. With Britain and Germany now facing each other across the Channel it was abundantly clear both that the only weapon available to either side was the bomber, and that Hitler was much better prepared for this eventuality. At the end of August 1941, as the German bombers assaulted the South Coast airfields by day, Britain was losing more aircraft than it could possibly replace and Dowding, with only 600 fighters, was in danger of losing the Battle of Britain as much for lack of repairs and new aeroplanes as because of losses.

On 7 September Hitler changed direction and moved the bombing North, to a direct assault on London. It was a mistake. The Messerschmidt 109s or 'Stukas' which were the staple bombing aircraft of the Luftwaffe, could only reach London with about ten minutes to spare before they had to return. Their losses increased overnight and again they changed plan, commencing a night-time bombing offensive that lasted six months. Fewer German planes were now lost, fewer than 1.5 per cent of all sorties, but more importantly, accuracy was lost as well, despite the still superior German navigational technology. By dint of military necessity as well as personal decision strategic bombing of key targets became 'tactical' bombing. Yet again the message was clear, Britain could not win without winning the war in the air of whole cities. The quantity and the quality of her aircraft would determine the outcome of the war.

By the time Stafford arrived at the Ministry, then, the argument for air power had been won. Indeed the Casablanca conference at the start of 1943 agreed that there should be a round the clock air offensive against Germany with both night-time area attacks by the RAF and, when they arrived, daytime attacks by the USAF. What was still in the balance, however, was Britain's ability to win that war. In 1941 Churchill had demanded that 14,500 bombers be built by the end of 1943, yet even the target the MAP set itself (12,159) was not reached and a measly 11,583 eventually rolled off the stocks. In July 1942 the Air Minister, Archibald Sinclair, had issued a 'Clarion Call' to the MAP asking for enough medium and heavy bombers to raise Bomber Command's air strength to fifty squadrons by the end of the year. After tough negotiations and much soul searching the Ministry had agreed to promise 780 heavy bombers during the months of September to November, yet even before the ink was dry on the paper the figures were being adjusted down. There were further problems with naval aircraft and by the end of 1942 there was throughout Whitehall 'a sense of disappointment and disquiet'.[1]

There was also considerable disquiet among service personnel about the appointment of Cripps to the MAP. The New Commander-in-Chief of Bomber Command, Arthur 'Bomber' Harris, had been particularly angered soon after his own appointment early in 1942 by one of Cripps's first speeches as Lord Privy Seal. The speech was anodyne enough, but with the tactical bombing campaign under attack on both military and moral grounds, Cripps's words were heard at Bomber Command as questioning 'the policy as to the continued use of heavy bombers and the bombing of Germany' just as the PathFinder Force assault on Cologne was being planned.

It is obviously a matter which it is almost impossible to debate in public, but, if I may, I would remind the House that this policy was initiated at a time when we were fighting alone against the combined forces of Germany and Italy and it seemed then that it was the most effective way in which we, acting alone, could take the initiative against the enemy. Since that time we have had an enormous access of support from the Russian armies, who, according to the latest news, have had yet another victory over the Germans, and also from the great potential strength of the United States of America. Naturally, in such circumstances, the original policy has come under review... I can assure the House that the Government are fully aware of the other uses to which our resources could be put, and the moment they arrive at a decision that the circumstances warrant change, a change in policy will be made.[2]

Harris was probably right. Cripps's words of February 1942 were a tactical mistake. The Arcadia conference had only just agreed American involvement in the European and Middle

Eastern war on the understanding that Britain's bombing offensive would be maintained. Just in case America should decide to rededicate her effort to the war with Japan, Bomber Command had to make it abundantly clear to Washington the following day that no change was envisaged. Yet the case for a shift in emphasis was a strong one, especially after the Path-Finder Force developed more effective means of targeting, and hitting, key installations. As Robin Higham has put it, 'If the object had been to stimulate the German war economy and to encourage the Germans to fight, no better technique than the clumsy air offensive of 1940-43 could have been devised.'[3] German morale was scarcely affected, aircraft production in Germany, far from being stopped, increased and the campaigns 'vitiated forces rather than concentrating them against decisive points, they were uneconomical of force, and they strengthened the enemy will to resist and inoculated him against all later onslaughts'.[4]

By late 1944 the rights and wrongs of the saturation bombing campaign, which had been born out of pure bombing inaccuracy but had become a doctrine at Bomber Command, were openly discussed and many of those most closely associated with opposition to the policy were close to Cripps. The Bishop of Chichester, George Bell, who was a leading ecumenist and knew many of the German Christians committed to ousting Hitler, had been a correspondent of Cripps since the thirties and was the most outspoken critic of the Government, reputedly denied the seat of Canterbury on Temple's death in 1944 by Churchill after his repudiation of the 'immoral' campaign. John Collins, the RAF chaplain at Bomber Command in High Wycombe, was also a friend of Stafford who had been introduced to him by another Christian Socialist, the vicar of St Matthew's Moorfields in Bristol, Mervyn Stockwood. Collins, intimately involved in the bombing campaign, was himself deeply distressed by a letter from a friend who had taken part in the bombing of Hamburg,

It was a nightmare experience looking down on the flaming city beneath. I felt sick as I thought of the women and children down there being mutilated, burned, killed, terror-stricken in that dreadful inferno – and I was partly responsible. Why, Padre John, do the Churches not tell us we are doing an evil job? I believe that Hitler must be defeated; I am prepared to do my bit to that end. But don't let anyone tell us that what we are doing is noble. What we are doing is evil, a necessary evil perhaps, but evil all the same.[5]

Partly to answer these questions Collins invited Stafford to speak at Wycombe at the end of 1944, much to Harris's chagrin. Cripps's address was titled 'Is God My Co-Pilot?' in reference to a recent book, *God is My Co-Pilot*, by a young Evangelical pilot called Stafford, more the philosopher than the military tactician, implicitly questioned the command structure by saying that officers 'should send men on a bombing mission only if, with a clear conscience, they were convinced that such a mission was morally justified as well as justified on grounds of military strategy and tactics'[6] – or at least that was what the officers heard. Max Hastings, in his history of Bomber Command, continues, 'At question time he was accused by one or two of the officers of saying things that, if heeded, might threaten discipline and hinder the war effort . . . The chairman found an excuse to call the meeting to an abrupt end.'[7] Whether this is actually what Cripps said is open to doubt. The speech no longer exists and his own reworked version of it which appeared in a later book, *Towards Christian Democracy*, contains no such statement, although there is a reference to the primacy of conscience, affirming 'the necessity to frame our judgements, in war as in peace, upon the basis of what we most truly and honestly believe to be God's will'.[8] Collins was ill just after Cripps's talk and when he returned to work he found the whole of Bomber Command up in arms. 'Half a dozen senior officers,' he wrote, 'have been working themselves into a fury of opposition to Cripps. And their accounts of what Cripps said are now entirely unlike anything he actually said or could have said.'[9] A reply lecture was ordered by Harris, under the title 'The Ethics of Bombing', though Collins quipped that it was more appropriate to call it 'The Bombing of Ethics'.

Cripps's philosophical and ethical questioning was anathema to some, yet it is remarkable that throughout the two and a half years that he was at the MAP these were the only moments when he gave off so much as a whiff of dissension on the overall bombing strategy. For the most part his work was confined exclusively to a single task, galvanising a diverse private industry into the greatest possible efficiency and technical competence, so as to deliver into the hands of the Air Ministry enough of the right planes to win the war. If Cripps did have quibbles he kept them to himself, and indeed he may have believed that in getting the MAP to produce planes that could be accurate he might affect the strategy towards the bombing of installations rather than populations. In itself this was a complicated enough task and to date the MAP did not have a good track record. It had only just coped with the Battle of Britain, and at the end of 1942 there were major problems to be addressed.

For a start there was the problem of chronic overestimation of production capacity, which had beset the Ministry ever since Beaverbrook's days when grossly inflated targets were seen as an incentive. Stafford took the opposite view. This over-optimistic target-setting was like proffering a carrot which 'if dangled too long . . . loses its effect altogether'.[10] It inevitably led to shortages in materials as companies ordered not for what they would actually build but for what they were targeted to build. It also led to disillusionment and wasteful haste rather than steady progress. Together with the new Chief

Executive, Air Marshal Sir Wilfrid Freeman, who since June 1938 had been the Air Member for development and production and was appointed just prior to Stafford, he put together what was described as the first 'realistic programme' for the Ministry. For the first time this would make proper allowance for holidays and absenteeism, for shortages in materials and for the complications of bringing in new models. It was a dramatic first step, cutting the projections by some 13 per cent (see table below),[11] and it was greeted by both the Cabinet and the public with some disquiet.

	Old plans	New plans	Change
Heavy bombers	6,245	4,724	−1,521
Medium bombers	3,872	3,342	−530
Light bombers	526	549	+23
Fighters	12,718	11,220	−1,498
General Reconnaissance	831	1,221	+390
Naval types	3,575	2,011	−1,564
Trainers	4,632	5,080	+448
Total	32,399	28,147	−4,252

In fact even these projections were too optimistic and though 1943 saw a one third increase in production on 1942, by September the Ministry had to decide to prioritise key aircraft such as the Lancaster, Halifax, Spitfire, Tempest and Mosquito while cutting back on the Stirling, Warwick, Wellington and Sutherland programmes. In only one month of 1943 did output exceed the 'realistic programme'. In spite of this the one particular worry that Churchill himself had articulated, that 'the failure to increase the supply of bombers was . . . the greatest danger facing the war effort as a whole',[12] had been in large measure met. Heavy bombers did start to come through in far greater numbers in the early months of 1943 and by 1944 were largely matching expectations.

In part this 'realistic programme' was a managerial decision. It improved morale within the industry by giving more companies a real chance of meeting their targets. It also rationalised supplies of materials. Equally important, however, was the political effect of the programme. For December 1942 saw a major retrenchment in all non-military departments. The battle of the Atlantic had led to the War Cabinet making the production of anti-submarine vessels and weapons an urgent priority and reductions in labour and materials were enforced on all the production departments. In such a climate the MAP could not afford to continue with its reputation for wild guesses at labour requirements, and Cripps estimated that a more realistic programme would not only be more responsible but would inspire greater confidence amongst Cabinet colleagues. In fact the significance now being attributed by the War Cabinet to the drive for aircraft production is evidenced by the fact that cuts in the MAP were far fewer than in other departments and even the RAF was expected to accept a higher cut in manpower than the MAP.[13] Bevin, however, as Minister for Labour was not convinced by the MAP's Damascene conversion, and when Cripps's new realism produced a labour request for 212,000 new workers, he quibbled.

In September 1941 Churchill's demands for dramatic increases in the bomber programme had led to a MAP request for one million extra men and women for 1942, a request Bevin had rightly considered to be a suspiciously round figure. An enquiry under Lyttelton as Minister of Production and Anderson as Lord President of the Council in July 1942 had backed Bevin in the dispute and the Cabinet on 7 October had resolved that any new labour for MAP would be targeted to those companies which had a clear track record of being able to absorb new workers. A series of prioritising measures were taken to ensure that the aircraft industry retained more of its staff while the Ministry of Supply and the Civil Defence gave up 200,000 between them to enable the protection of the aircraft programmes. With Cripps's appointment and the new 'realistic programme' there was also an equivalently lower demand for labour but Cripps's 'absolute minimum' request was met with incredulity by Bevin who stated that he knew of workers being deployed to aircraft manufacturers only to sit idle for weeks while work was found for them. Cripps took this as an affront to his new 'realism' and insisted on the 212,000 although Bevin would only promise to find 115,000 in 1943, with the rest coming later. In fact the MAP received an extra 50,000 that year, partly because Bevin was determined to catch the MAP, and Cripps, on the back foot by providing more than he thought they could possibly use. Whether Cripps or Bevin's figures were more accurate is difficult to say. Certainly, for the first time since its inception, the MAP under Cripps absorbed every one of its new cohort in 1943, and it was only at the turn of 1944, when the new workers were in place, that the MAP was able to meet its obligations. Cripps's assessment that supplies of labour were essential for further increases of output was accurate and Bevin's over-provision against his promise paid secure dividends in the massive increase in production, and productivity, in early 1944.

Labour supplies were only a tiny part of the problem, however. Just as important were the problems inherent in mass producing a rapidly changing product. As M.M. Postan has pointed out the aeroplane was the most 'unsettled and unstable of all instruments of war'. Not only was it young, but it was clear that the multiplicity of tasks to which it could be turned meant that it would inevitably have to be produced in a multiplicity of formats. It was not just the difference between fighters and bombers that mattered, nor even between light and heavy bombers, but the frequency with which narrow specifications of range, equipment and load were changed. New aeroplane types had to be designed, tested and produced, old types had to be modified and time was lost in both exercises while enormous recessions in production could be brought about by even minor changes to each model. The delays were real. The Tempest was meant to be ready at the start of 1943 but did not appear until October, the Warwick was so delayed it ended up being converted into a transport and air-sea rescue craft, while the medium bomber the Bristol Buckingham was almost obsolete by the time it appeared, its job already being done faster by the Mosquito. New models took much longer, of course, than modifications of existing models, and though the MAP took steps to shorten the whole process from original inception to final mass production by skipping the prototype stage and earmarking certain manufacturers so that the tender stage could be cut, yet it was clear that if an existing model could be modified it would save time.

Thus all five of the most successful British planes, the Spitfire, Hurricane, Mosquito, Lancaster and Wellington, were successfully modified during the course of the war. Even this delayed production, though, and the Ministry had to develop a code of practice to determine what level of modification justified a halt in production. Yet it was clear that the RAF would always prefer ninety planes that were exactly to their specification to one hundred that were mostly to their specification. Every fluctuation in the war's requirements might mean a delay in production, but the battle was as much to out-invent the German and Japanese aircraft as to out-produce them.

A typical example of the dilemma arose soon after Cripps's arrival at the Ministry. Early in 1942 it had been obvious that the Stirling and the Halifax were not up to the job, and towards the end of the year the Lancaster began to exceed expectations, managing to carry an 8,000 pound load at 240 miles per hour at a height of between 22,000 and 27,000 feet, thereby climbing well above enemy anti-aircraft guns. With the Stirling only managing 14,000 feet and the Halifax little more at 18,000, and their top speeds only just reaching 200 miles per hour, it became apparent that the production programmes needed to be altered. Harris called for all the Stirling facilities to be used for the manufacture of Lancasters and the Halifaxes to be cut in favour of Lancasters as well. This was agreed by the MAP at the end of the year, but still Harris had worries which focused on whether the Stirling manufacturers, Short and Harlands, could be turned around to anything useful at all. 'The Stirling Group has now virtually collapsed,' he wrote to Sinclair at the Air Ministry,

> They make no worth while contribution to our war effort in return for their overheads. They are at half strength, and serviceability is such that in spite of the much reduced operational rate and long periods of complete idleness due to weather, I am lucky if I can raise 30 Stirlings from 3 Group for one night's work after a week of doing nothing, or 20 the night after. There should be a whole-sale sacking of the incompetents who have turned out approximately 50 per cent rogue aircraft from Short and Harlands . . . Much the same applies to the Halifax issue . . . nothing whatever ponderable is being done to make this deplorable product worthy for war or fit to meet those jeopardies which confront our gallant crews . . . Trivialities are all they are attempting at present, with the deliberate intent of postponing the main issue until we are irretrievably committed . . . Unless we can get these two vital factors of the heavy bomber programme put right, and with miraculous despatch, we are sunk.[14]

For the Ministry then there was a clear message, articulated by Cripps, 'We have throughout applied one cardinal principle – that quality is more important that mere quantity. Nothing but the best and most up to date is good enough for our magnificent airmen. Whatever the complications or draw-backs arising from the rapid introduction of improvements or changes, we must introduce these at the earliest practicable moment.'[15] Equally important, however, was dealing with the inefficiency of the industry. In the introduction of new models, should the manufacture of old models be halted immediately or should there be a period when both models should be built simultaneously? The Ministry developed the idea of 'splicing-in' new production so as to avoid bouts of idle factories.

Should more resources be spent on building new planes or on repairing and refitting damaged machines? The Russians had decided to focus all their energies on building new planes, but Britain had recognised that repairing an aircraft was far more efficient in terms of the use of materials, even if there were losses in productivity. According to Postan 'the amount of material which was used for Lancaster spares . . . and which made possible the repair and return to service of 3,816 aircraft would, if employed in the construction of new aircraft, have yielded only 622 airframes.'[16] Within the MAP there was, however, a general predisposition to focus on new planes, partly because early attempts at repairs had fallen foul of a spares shortage. So on his arrival Cripps set up a Spares Committee with the express task of redressing the spares shortage and ensuring the repairs programme. This soon developed the conviction that there was no real shortage of spares, only a shortage of the right spares in the right place, and that the answer therefore lay with the Air Ministry who were responsible for both the spares ordering and distribution systems. Either way, by the end of 1943 much of the spares problem was resolved and in November 63,600 men and women were employed on repairs, bringing 55 per cent of aircraft into use, while the 664,200 employed on new planes only brought 45 per cent of the month's delivered aircraft. Yet again, efficiency was paramount.

Some inefficiency was manifestly the fault of poor management. Whole boards were replaced on private companies, work was redirected towards companies with more experienced management and a Production Efficiency Board was set up under Sir Charles Bruce Gardner, the former head of the British Association of Air Constructors who provided both technical and managerial advice. Cripps took a very direct personal interest in these managerial issues and it was at his instigation that Joint Production Committees were introduced in each company, bringing together management and staff. It was a move he described as 'this new weapon of industrial democracy'[17] and one he saw as a major factor in the drive for ever greater efficiency.

Just as important to Cripps, though, was the exhortative approach to efficiency. He had entered the War Cabinet demanding whether Britain was doing enough to win the war and he now set about a gruelling tour of her aircraft factories, meeting with more than a hundred Joint Production Committees, chatting to staff, encouraging, exhorting, shaming, embarrassing everyone into greater production. There were great meetings of the whole MAP staff and massive addresses to whole factories. Almost invariably he went with Isobel and they proved an exceptional team. Cripps was in his element talking about technical engineering issues with management and staff alike. His scientific training and his experience of the Ministry of Munitions in the first war meant he could master technical issues quickly, but more importantly he could convey a powerful belief that this work was every bit as essential a part of the war effort as that of an ace pilot or a commanding officer since his own service in the First World War had been entirely non-combative. He also exhibited a genuine interest in everyone in the organisation. He would talk to secretaries, to doorkeepers, to cleaners, to everyone in the Ministry, as if their work was part of the total war effort.

Isobel was also now a highly skilled politician's wife. Not only was she adept at speaking to the people that mattered, often smoothing the way for Stafford, but she threw herself into the task of encouraging morale. Allan Jarvis, who worked as Stafford's secretary, recorded,

> She somehow finds time to see and talk to, sometimes at very great length, an incredibly large number of people. Always with a view to creating or sustaining their feeling that they are working as part of a common cause. Always she shows infinite patience and understanding in smoothing our relationships between the frequently highly charged and temperamental involved. It is through this extension of his influence through her activity and her very effective projection of both their personalities that Stafford has been able to exercise his power of leadership and inspiration over such a diverse range of interests . . . It is an incredible achievement and it is the partnership as such which deserves the credit.[18]

Cripps had one further area of responsibility which appealed to the technician in him and which all the service personnel saw as key to transforming the fortunes of war. For the invention of the radio valve and the steady discovery of new applications for it set a direct challenge for the secret Radio Board which Cripps now chaired. Here again was a private industry which was still young and had to adapt very rapidly not only to a vast increase in production (between 1940 and 1944 Government expenditure on radio valves rose from £25.8 million to £123.6 million), but to constant modifications at the cutting edge of scientific discovery. Suddenly the army was using radio sets like the No. 38 which would use up seven valves during its lifetime, for mobile manoeuvres. The invention of the 'cavity magnetron' valve led to the development of centrimetric radar and its application to the shortwave ASV for detecting submarines from the air, the 271 set for naval surface search, the GLMk III anti-aircraft gun layer, and, most significantly, the H_2S, which made precision bombing possible for the first time and was deployed in the PathFinder Force from the beginning of 1943.

This proliferation of military uses had, since late 1941, far outstripped the industry's capacity to make valves, let alone its ability to produce new kinds of valve. The original demand for valves in 1943 was 39.5 million, against the industry's expected full capacity of 21.5 million, and original service requests for 1944 were 90 million.

These were the same problems as those in the aircraft industry and Cripps set about a similar process. Service expectations were cut back severely, realistic targets were set and there was direct intervention where managerial inefficiency was perceived to be the source of the problem. In fact the Radio Board was even more direct in its intervention than its parent Ministry, the MAP.

A specific problem in the radio industry was the shortage not of labour but of skilled labour. Much valve production was a standard process requiring little by way of technical expertise or supervision. By contrast developments associated with the cavity magnetron valve were costly in terms of skilled labour. Cripps agreed two responses: 'crash' programmes whereby the initial batches of new projects such as the H_2S were commissioned at almost whatever the cost; and the 'feeder' programme which divided factories into those requiring specialised technical supervision and costly plant and those with minimal requirements where a bench, a stool and the raw materials sufficed, both feeding into a master factory. Both systems delivered significant results, but in terms of Stafford's own understanding of Government's role in industry, the 'feeder' programme was perhaps the most dramatic instance of wholesale government intervention in an industry to date, moving factories, determining investment patterns and strictly regulating supply.

This was planning such as peacetime economies could only dream of and wartime had never yet experienced and it shaped not only Cripps's understanding of the task of economic management, but the whole of the post-war Labour Party. Dalton was engaged in planning where industry should be located. Bevin was planning how to get workers to where the work was. Morrison was designing Britain's cities, and the whole Party was adopting, lock stock and barrel, the Beveridge Report with its plans for a welfare state. In later days, as President of the Board of Trade Cripps was to justify a planned economy on the basis of his experience of the MAP: 'We have found that by supplying all the capital necessary to make the industry completely up to date, by planning and controlling the output, by arranging the pooling of ideas and so on, we have been able to bring the industry up to a very high point of efficiency.'[19]

All of this meant that Cripps was at work not on the grand set pieces of the war, but tending to its sinews. Yet for Cripps the most important sinew of all remained the moral purpose of the nation. The drive to efficiency and the planned economy were but parts of instilling that greater sense of the common good. Just before leaving the War Cabinet he was asked by some of the students at Aberdeen University to allow his name to go forward as a candidate for Rector. The fact that the two other people who had been approached, J. B. Priestley and Louis Mountbatten, were similarly renowned for their championship of independence and moral leadership from the left, gives some indication of the way in which Cripps was still viewed, even after his demotion. In fact all three candidates tried to withdraw in favour of each other, but in the end Mountbatten (whose sister-in-law Stafford had represented against Captain Cunningham-Reid) wrote to Cripps, 'I am so very glad that you saw your way to letting me withdraw as I should have felt very badly indeed had you not allowed me to do so. The only pleasing aspect of this incident to me is that it has given me the chance of indicating in some small measure how sincerely grateful I am for all your kindness to me.'[20]

Cripps's rectorial address was broadcast in February 1943 under the title, 'Shall the spell be broken?' and was another exercise in strengthening the moral sinews. He was keen to look beyond the war, because 'much that we have built up for the purposes of war we can adapt quickly and easily to the needs of peace'[21] and he criticised the end of the previous war when 'the progressive forces [had] failed to strike while the iron was hot. The time to get agreement on post-war plans is during the war when the atmosphere of co-operation is strong.'[22] He quoted the poet Jock Curle,

> And we would hope that something should be altered
> In the cruel careless fundamental law,
> But we must beware or the moment will escape us;
> It has done so before.
> And we must see that out of the practical slaughter
> Rise no more vapoury dreams,
> But a world where the poor are fed, the tyrants humbled,
> And men know what life means.'[23]

It was the same ideal world that one of Stafford's old Socialist League colleagues, J. T. Murphy, who had returned to his old trade in the war and was working in a aircraft factory, articulated:

> The Socialist way is that of State leadership and organi-
> sation of the people as a Community of Citizens who
> have thrown all their resources – land, factories, mills,
> mines, transport, banks, property – into the common pool
> of the State; and wherein every man and woman capable
> of rendering service is at the service of the State with
> wages equitably regulated, prices stabilised and supplies
> fairly rationed, and everyone organised for war.'[24]

Private vested interest could only frustrate the war effort. It was everyone's duty to share equally in the sacrifice, so ran the Cripps wartime creed.

Of course, this moralistic style of doing politics was not universally liked. Dalton complained that Cripps was 'a complete prig' and recounted a story that when in the presence of the Prime Minister, Cripps had asked to be excused to answer the telephone and Churchill had said when he was gone, 'There, but for the grace of God, goes God.'[25] Although this has the smack of Churchill in it, the saying is attributed to so many different times and places that it is quite possibly apocryphal, but whatever the estimation of Cripps's moralising it is almost incontrovertible that he was an adept and effective Minister. Under his aegis the MAP did manage to meet the requirements of the war. It was efficient, it remained adaptable, it established better working relationships with both the Air Ministry and the aircraft industry than had ever existed under any of his predecessors, and Cripps was a perfect Minister for dealing with the technocrats both within the Ministry and the industry.

Cripps's time at the MAP was the best apprenticeship he could have had for his post-war responsibilities, for it drew on his technocratic abilities in an environment where he had to work with the private sector on a daily basis. It meant that he both recognised the problems of poor management and weak infrastructure in much of British industry, and he became the least doctrinaire of all the Labour frontbench about the mix of private and public sector. Partnership, between management and employees, between Government and industry, was the key to a secure economic future, just as it was to getting enough aeroplanes completed. Just as significantly the sustained experience of power modified Stafford's whole approach to politics, which by the end of the war had entirely lost whatever dogmatic edge it had. If he now had an ideology it was that vested interests, of whatever kind, were harmful to the greater good, and that equality of personal and communal sacrifice could only be guaranteed in a democratically planned economy – but with the proviso that there were no short cuts to Utopia.

21

Victory upon Victory

By the start of 1945 it was apparent that the war in Europe would soon be over and all eyes moved to the distant horizon of post-war Party politics. Cripps had up until this point made it clear that he was not considering joining any Party. One of the more complicated matters, however, had always remained the question of how his own constituents viewed him and therefore whether he would survive a General Election. As with most MPs he had a rather more cavalier approach to his constituency than would either be acceptable today or have been normal in peacetime. He was only occasionally in Bristol, though he took a solicitous concern, from a distance, and his most frequent contact was through attending St Matthew's Moorfields, where he often read one of the lessons, and staying with Mervyn Stockwood. He was also still, as an Independent, free from the usual round of Party meetings. Indeed when he returned from Moscow in 1942 the local Labour Party had asked permission from Transport House to attend the Bristol Hippodrome meeting which was being held in his honour. The Transport House reply was an exemplary instance of political double-speak. Party members were allowed to attend a meeting that was in honour of Stafford Cripps the retiring Ambassador to Moscow, but not one in honour of Stafford Cripps the expelled Labour MP. In 1943 the Bristol Party, via Stockwood, tried to get him to meet with a Trade Unionist,

Bill Wilkins, in the hope of getting him to rejoin. Cripps replied

> it is out of the question my going back into the Labour
> Party under the existing circumstances. If those circum-
> stances change I am always open to reconsider the
> position. A great deal may happen before an election – I
> only hope it does so as far as the Labour Party is con-
> cerned! I don't think it is the slightest use my discussing
> the situation with Wilkins or any of the others as we
> should simply reach an impasse which would merely
> make the situation more difficult. Thank you for your
> good office. I still hope a solution may eventually be
> found.[1]

By 1945, though, Cripps had been working with his Labour colleagues for three years and at the top of the Party there was an evident thawing of political ice. Dalton had more time for him, especially after Cripps had provided secure support in the 1942 rows over the requisitioning of the mines and rationing of fuel. Morrison, his original sponsor in the Party, saw him as a strong potential ally in any future leadership bid and even Bevin, though still no Cripps advocate, was prepared to collaborate with him. Attlee, who had always remained a friend, admitted 'it was a great pleasure to me to have him as a colleague.'[2]

Yet Cripps was still wary of returning to the Labour fold. He wrote to some of his constituents in Bristol that though his views were 'still those for which you elected me, I belong to no party. It was on that basis I joined this Government and while I remain in the Government I shall join no party, old or new.' Quite how much weight Cripps ascribed to that 'while I remain in the Government' it is difficult to gauge. He took a benign interest in the successes of his old Popular Front colleague, Richard Acland, and had good connections with the Common Wealth Party whose politics were, in the words of Tom Meldrun, 'to the right of Labour and to the left of the Liberals'.[3] This was, broadly speaking, where Cripps's own politics now lay although for much of his period at the MAP he had restricted his public statements to production issues and the moral state of the nation. The only overt statement he allowed himself was to question:

> How are we to pass from this National Government, this wartime coalition of parties, to a progressive active Government, which will be prepared to carry through a programme after the war that will not give us all we want, but that will give us a sufficiency to make certain that we are on the right road to progress and that will enable us to solve the problems with which we shall be faced?[4]

Common Wealth, for all its impressive by-election gains and its innovative campaigning techniques, was never going to replace the Labour Party as a prospective Government and with Stafford's one-time support from centrist Tories now largely dissipated it was evident that there were only two choices for him when the coalition should split, either to rejoin Labour or to remain an Independent and hope both to retain his seat and be offered a post in either a Churchill or an Attlee Government. As he put it to his constituents, 'When the time comes I shall do what I have throughout sought to do and that is to take the action which I believe best serves the interest of my constituents and my country.'[5]

The Labour Party, meantime, which had always had more grass-root objections to the electoral truce than the Tories, was beginning to champ at the bit. All the opinion polls were suggesting that the Party's Parliamentary strength was a long way short of its popular support and as a military victory loomed on the horizon the contours of post-war Britain began to matter more than might be achieved in a peace-time coalition. By the start of 1945 much work had already been done on major areas of putative social change and though the 1944 Education Act was a significant bipartisan achievement between Butler the Tory Minister and Chuter Ede his Labour deputy, the Labour Party was beginning to face the fact that the post-war shopping list tucked in its back pocket was not to the taste of the Conservatives.

Yet the leadership of the Party remained committed to the coalition for some time after many ordinary members had gone off to support Common Wealth. They had good reasons. For a start they feared Labour would lose the election that would necessarily follow the split. Labour now only held 164 seats against the Tories' 359 and despite the recent by-election results the overall swing during the years of the war had been more than 10 per cent *towards* the Tories. Just as Lloyd George had swept the board after the First World War it was expected that Churchill would storm back into No. 10. Attlee even made allowances for the fairly spectacular successes of anti-Government candidates in by-elections, arguing that many official candidates were of 'poor quality' and that 'a vote for a splinter candidate does not carry with it support for an alternative Government which, if in being, might well be less attractive than the present one'.[6] To end the coalition would expose all Labour's wartime reconstruction work to jeopardy.

Moreover there were personal reasons why several of the Labour front-benchers preferred to stick with the coalition, for with Churchill in No. 10 Labour did not need to face the question of who would lead a Labour Government. There had been quietly simmering discontent with Attlee ever since he had won the deputy leadership in 1931 – a discontent that was spiced with the cardamom of bitter resentment on the part of Dalton that he had lost his seat in 1931 and therefore had not been able to stand for the post himself. Morrison was equally contemptuous of Attlee and at times it felt as if it was only the ballast of Bevin that kept the captain on board. Those who most wanted a change of leader were those who first argued for an end to the coalition, and Morrison, with one eye firmly on the rest of the Party, towards the end of 1944 started to campaign for a more assertive reconstruction policy that would expose the differences between Labour and the Conservatives.

There were other reasons why Labour should seek a dissolution as soon as the war was over. There were clear signs, for those who wished to see them, that Labour would win. During the electoral truce a variety of Labour-looking candidates had been successful in opposition to Tory replacements, especially since 1943. Common Wealth had picked up seats with what Attlee called 'a programme very like our own'[7] and there had been large swings to the left throughout 1944. Indeed when Derbyshire West, a seat that had effectively been in the gift of the Duke of Devonshire's Cavendish family for years, fell vacant on the retirement of one of the Duke's brothers-in-law, the Government Chief Whip, James Stuart, another brother-in-law, moved the writ expecting an easy victory for the Duke's heir, Lord Hartington. The election, held on 17 February 1944, was contested by Charlie White, a member of the Labour Party and the son of the only non-Cavendish to have held the seat. White stood as an Independent Labour candidate and received explicit Liberal as well as the usual Common Wealth and Independent backing and took the seat with a 16 per cent swing. Lord Cavendish said, 'I understand my father [the Duke], as a result of this, foresaw a Labour victory . . . I'm not sure he didn't make a bit of money on bets on it too.'[8] By April 1945 this pattern was even more obvious. In the Chelmsford by-election, held on 26 April, the Common Wealth candidate Wing-Commander Ernest Millington took from the Tories a seat they had won in 1935 with more than 70 per cent of the vote.

Moreover Churchill was not the electoral weapon many might have thought. For a start he had never run a General

Election campaign as Leader. Tom Harrison of Mass-Observation wrote in 1944 'supremely popular as he is today, this is closely connected with the idea of Winston the war leader, Bulldog of battle etc. Ordinary people widely assume that after the war he'll rest on his magnificent laurels. If he doesn't, many say they will withdraw support, believing him no man of peace, domestic policy or human detail.'[9]

If this was true then the potential gains to Labour Party independence far outweighed the losses, as long as the war was already won, and though Bevan was one of a very small band of Labour leaders who thought Labour could and would win the election, on 7 October 1944 the National Executive took the first step towards preparing for an election by announcing that whenever it came Labour would fight it as an independent Party.

For Cripps this was an undoubted signal that he would soon have to resolve the question of his own position.

Others were also aware that two separate manifestos were taking shape in the minds of Tory and Labour Ministers and Eden reckoned 'the sense of purpose which had held so many diverse personalities together now began to weaken.'[10] On 27 September, the day the Cabinet agreed to prolong the life of Parliament by a year, Cripps expressed concern to Attlee that the Reconstruction Committee was inclining towards a 'return to normalcy' policy. The Tory line seemed to be forming around objections to State controls which Cripps saw as 'an essential fact of the permanent full employment policy'. He went on: 'The transition period should be used for adapting our wartime controls – based on shortage of manpower – to a form suitable for peace time when we contemplate the likelihood of an excess of manpower.'[11] Churchill was equally worried about the Committee and drafted a petulant letter to Attlee, 'A solid mass of 4 Socialist politicians of the highest quality and authority, three of whom are in the War Cabinet, all working together as a team, very much dominates this committee.'[12] At the same time Labour, haunted by the ghosts of 1919 when the 'homes fit for heroes' were never built and an empty war was made even more futile by the lack of social change, was pushing for a more assertive reconstruction programme.

In December there was further controversy over Churchill's handling of Greece and the fear that the British troops were keeping a corrupt monarchy in power. This was the major source of dissension at the December Labour Party Conference at which Morrison was re-elected to the National Executive after a gap, and Ellen Wilkinson, a Morrison supporter, became Chair of the Party.

This then finally pushed Cripps into making informal overtures to Attlee about rejoining the Party. Attlee's Christmas greeting was unambiguous, 'It is a real joy to me that we shall be again together in the Party in the New Year.' Cripps then proceeded with a formal application, which was considered and agreed by the National Executive's February meeting. Cripps, ever fastidiously proper, wrote to Churchill to offer his resignation if the Prime Minister felt his new non-Independent status required it. Churchill replied with barely concealed condescension 'My dear Stafford, I have always considered you a Socialist and as belonging to the Socialist representation in the Government. Your decision raises no question affecting the balance in the Government, except of course that you will henceforth count as a Socialist instead of something even worse.'[13] Cripps later told Stockwood that Churchill was genuinely saddened that he would not now be able to speak for Cripps as an Independent in the General Election.

Cripps's move came just as the temperature began to rise within the Government. First the Reconstruction Committee was split over the issue of nationalisation of the electricity generating industry, despite the fact that two thirds of the industry was already in the hands of local authorities, with Morrison and Gwilym Lloyd George in favour of the formation of a public

345

corporation, and the Tory ministers in blank opposition. In the middle of March Churchill decided to use the Conservative Party Conference to attack some of Labour's proposals for nationalisation as a system 'borrowed from foreign lands and alien minds' and stated that his Party's election platform would largely consist of the promise to remove controls and restore private enterprise. 'Controls under the pretext of war or its aftermath which are in fact designed he declared, 'to favour the accomplishment of totalitarian systems, however innocently designed, whatever guise they take, whatever liveries they wear, whatever slogans they mouth, are a fraud which should be mercilessly exposed to the British public.'[14] By April Bracken and Attlee were exchanging fairly open personal criticism. Bevin, who was not a member of the Labour National Executive and had joined the Government as a Union Leader, despite his belief that the Coalition should be maintained at least until October, decided to squash any rumours that he was thinking of sticking with Churchill even if the rest of the Labour Party peeled off, and made a much publicised speech in which he argued that Churchill was not the leader Britain needed for the peace.

Yet Churchill still hoped to keep the alliance alive, preferably through to the end of the war with Japan. When the Germans surrendered on 8 May the issue became more urgent. There were calls, especially from Beaverbrook, for an early election. Attlee, however, was in San Francisco for the inauguration of the United Nations, so it was left to Morrison and Bevin to see Churchill on 11 May to discuss the possible dates for an election and the continuance of the Coalition. Morrison put the Labour Party case for an October election, when the electoral registers would be properly updated and the Parliamentary session would end. Churchill proposed the end of the war with Japan, which Bevin, like Attlee, would have supported, but Morrison vetoed it and the meeting ended. The next day Churchill received a request from President Truman for British opposition to Marshal Tito's occupation of Venezia Giulia. Churchill wrote to Eden, 'If there is to be trouble of this kind, the support of men like Attlee, Bevin, Morrison and George Hall is indispensable to the National presentation of the case. In that event, I should on no account agree to an election in October, but simply say that we must prolong our joint tenure.'[15] Attlee returned to Britain on the 15th and had a long discussion with Churchill in which they broadly agreed that the main aim must still be the defeat of the Japanese. Churchill's impression was that Attlee 'would do his best to keep us together' and a letter was drafted offering Attlee and the Labour Party either an immediate General Election or an extension of the Coalition until Japan surrendered. The formation of the coalition had happened while Labour was in conference and Churchill's letter, with a couple of riders added by Attlee, arrived again on the eve of a Labour Party Conference, this time at Blackpool. The National Executive met to decide how to respond. Bevin and Dalton remained in favour of continuing in the Coalition, as did Attlee. Morrison, Bevan and William Whiteley the Chief Whip, were opposed and a final position was reached where the Party agreed only to remain in the Coalition until October – an option that Churchill had not offered. Attlee reckoned that the Conference had 'decided that the time had come for the Party to resume its independence'[16] and he wrote to Churchill on the 21st confirming the decision. In fact it was Churchill that made the final decision. The moment he received Attlee's letter suggesting the October date he went to the King and resigned as Prime Minister of the Coalition Government.

The Blackpool Conference had the air of a General Election rally. Morrison gave a bravura performance and was given a long ovation for his commitments to nationalising the Bank of England, fuel and power, inland transport and iron and steel. Bevin was equally robust and Dalton gave a rallying cry while younger men like Major Denis Healey, in battledress with his cuffs turned back, denounced the corrupt ruling classes of Europe.

It was also Cripps's first Conference since Southport in 1939. If he had been nervous about his reception there was no need. His light-hearted quip 'I am bound to say I much prefer the climate of Blackpool to that of Southport'[17] was greeted with prolonged applause and his whole speech went down well.

On returning from Blackpool the Labour Ministers, including Cripps, all resigned their seals of office and Churchill formed his new Caretaker Government. Interestingly Churchill tried to keep Cripps in post, although we only have this on the say of Eden who recorded that he and Cranborne were outside the Cabinet Room when Cripps came out saying, 'It might have been different if it had been Anthony who'd asked me.'[18] Whether this is true it is difficult to say. Bracken and Beaverbrook, Churchill's closest advisers, were implacable foes of Cripps and would undoubtedly have counselled against offering him a post, and Churchill himself was never on really close terms with him. Indeed Eden described the two men as 'disparate as a lion and an okapi.'[19] Yet Churchill needed ministers to keep the show on the road for the ten weeks until the election results were known, and Cripps even if he was not formally an Independent was still independent enough of spirit for Churchill perhaps to be able to play on his sense of honour and duty. As to whether Cripps really said that he might have accepted an offer from Eden, this may be no more than self-aggrandisement on the part of Eden, but there is a ring of wistful truth in the quotation and Cripps may have been harking back more to 1942 than really commenting on the future.

For Cripps's future undoubtedly now lay with Labour and just as he turned down MacDonald in 1931 so he turned down Churchill. The following Monday were all the formalities, first at the Palace, where the Labour Ministers went to take their leave of the King, and then at Downing Street, where Churchill gathered thirty or forty of the wartime ministerial team. At the Palace the Ministers trooped in rather lugubriously – Cripps was followed by Dalton and Jowitt. Dalton noted, 'Cripps, who came out very quickly and didn't even try, as I did, to make some conversation with the poor man, said, "I said, 'Oh well, I suppose your Majesty is very busy this morning so I won't take up your time' and came straight out."'[20] Dalton attributed this to Crippsian brusqueness, though in fact there was little love lost between the two men as shown by the fact that a couple of years later, when Cripps was offering to go to India with Louis Mountbatten and Mountbatten suggested that it might be better if he stayed in London and take on the India Office, the King wrote to Mountbatten, 'You certainly had a brainwave in asking Cripps to take on the India Office. I should never relish the idea of having him either on my staff or staying in my house.'[21] Dalton's own experience with the King was worse: 'He really had nothing to say, and made no personal impact on me whatever. As nearly inanimate as an animate Monarch could be!'[22]

At the Downing Street reception at 4.30 p.m., 'standing behind the Cabinet table, now draped as a buffet, [Churchill] addressed us all, with tears visibly running down his cheeks. He said we had all come together, and had stayed together as a united band of friends, in a very trying time. History would recognise this. "The light will shine on every helmet".'[23]

The election was announced for 5 July, although after some representations from Lancashire Members it was agreed that twenty-three constituencies would be allowed to vote later in order to avoid the 'factory weeks' holidays. The service votes would also be collected during this time and the results counted on 25 July. This meant an election campaign of more than five weeks with an extra three weeks of limbo.

Cripps took as full a part in the election campaign as he had in 1935. He spoke for candidates in Coventry, Birmingham, Oldham, Stockport, Carlisle, Glasgow, Dundee, Edinburgh, Wakefield, Newcastle, Halifax, Hull, Sheffield, Bristol, Bournemouth, Exeter, Plymouth, Bath and Cardiff. He covered more miles than any of his colleagues except for Attlee and it was a sign of his evident popularity in the country and his level of acceptance in the Party that the Party managers got him to do one of the Party's ten radio Party Political Broadcasts.

The theme of this, as of all his speeches of this time, was little changed from the message he had been preaching since the start of the war. At Party Conference he had been part of the moderate faction which included both Attlee and Morrison, arguing 'we must not lead the people to believe that this is some easy Utopia into which we are inviting them to step'[24] and offering Britain a challenge as tough as that of war. 'People have seen how a total effort can conquer Hitler. They will the more readily be convinced that the same total effort, the same fierce spirit, is what is needed to conquer poverty, slums and unemployment.'[25] The answer lay with planning, he declared in Widnes, because 'it is impossible under modern circumstances to provide the opportunity of full employment for our people without that sort of planning and control which has brought us such large dividends of production during two world wars.'[26] Planning won the war and it would win the peace, but only if 'the engines of economic production' were in the hands of Government. Private enterprise was to be welcomed but it could not 'of itself bring about full employment'[27] and so was flawed as an economic model.

All of this was standard Labour Party fare. What added spice, though, was an omnipresent call for a moral agenda for Britain. Indeed his Party Political Broadcast on 20 June was probably the last explicitly Christian PPB in Britain. 'Let those of us who boast the proud title of Christian follow the precepts

of our great Teacher,' he professed, 'and make ourselves the
selfless guardians of our neighbours, unconcerned with private
wealth and interests, but anxious only to place all at the service
of the community.'[28] Economic recovery was only half the
task, for 'it is not new machines or fresh political expedients
that we need so much as decent moral principles'.[29] The basis
of Labour's stand was ethical, rooted equally in Christian
Socialism as in the working class movement and it was its
inspiration 'by a spirit of comradeship and moral purpose'[30]
that recommended it.

This Cripps message played well in Britain. Morrison, the
arch-strategist, had always argued that for Labour to win a
majority she had to appeal to the middle classes as well as to
Labour's traditional supporters, and the deliberate emphasis
on sacrifice in both Cripps's and other ministerial speeches
was designed to emphasise Labour's egalitarian beliefs. The
First World War had seen the poor and the middle classes
suffer real privations whilst the wealthy had been able to
continue their lifestyles largely undisturbed. This time rationing had curtailed luxury and there was a sense in which
sacrifice had been pooled. Everyone was in it together and the
ration book was a sign of good citizenship. The 1945 Labour
manifesto, *Let us face the future*, summarised the Party's
priorities in terms that echo new Labour's re-worded aims and
values, 'there must be priorities in the use of raw materials,
food prices must be held, homes for the people must come
before mansions, necessities for all before luxuries for the
few.'[31] With this belief in sacrifice came a belief that Britain
was going to have to work hard to win the peace and that
there was to be no substitute for hard work. As Cripps put it,
'The more we can produce the higher will be our standard of
living.'[32]

The one area of major debate within the Party remained the
question of nationalisation – or socialisation. Morrison had a
clear idea of what he intended by the term. His model was

that of the London Transport Board which he had set up in the 1920s, a public corporation in public hands but kept at an arm's length. For Bevin the corporation model did not necessarily give the real benefits of industry run for the benefit of the workers, while others preferred direct State ownership and management.

Cripps was perhaps the least convinced of all the nationalisers. Common Wealth had based its whole philosophy on common ownership and many assumed that Labour's ideals could only be achieved by State ownership of the key industries in the economy. Yet in October 1944 Cripps told Acland, who was lobbying for the nationalisation of the cotton industry, 'Oh no, my dear Richard, we have learned in the war that we CAN control industry.' In other words, there was, in Cripps's mind, no need to own an industry if you could control it just as effectively when it was still in private hands. Moreover he was convinced that after the war there would be an export crisis and 'My dear Richard, you can't nationalise the cotton industry in the middle of *that*.'[33]

Even in March 1945 Cripps was arguing explicitly against both the proposals for a National Corporation for the light metal industry and a largely private industry with a few Royal Ordnance factories, as proposed, respectively, by Bevin and Duncan. Dalton recorded 'Cripps has put in a paper arguing against both of these. I say that I am struck by this most impressive presentation of the anti-Socialist case. He doesn't think this at all funny! He says, "Well you have often done the same thing yourself in the past". Bevin says, "Well you have just been taken back into the Labour Party."'[34] Whether this rebuke stung Cripps into toeing the Party line or Cripps genuinely moved towards a more collectivist approach it is difficult to say. Certainly he had been in favour of the nationalisation of the Bank of England since the 1930s, but this was scarcely controversial and when it was passed it even received Tory support. Yet at the MAP he had never proposed nationalisation, despite the fact that as one of the youngest industries in Britain it was perhaps one of the few that could have benefited most from a centralised approach. Indeed he often boasted that as Minister he had dealt with 15,000 private companies.

Even when Cripps sounded as if he was more in line with the rest of the Party his emphasis was less on the ownership of industry as on the potential efficiency savings that could be accrued by centralisation and national direction.

> We say that all industry and all great services like transport and coal and power must be so organised as to give the people as a whole the maximum that is possible. In fact the production of the country must be considered as a great public service, as in fact it is, and that we must not only see to it that we get produced those things that we want. In other words the necessities for the country and the people must take priority over luxuries and semi-luxuries. In order to achieve that end we must be prepared to see whatever method of organising our industry proves best. We have no interest in preserving or destroying private enterprise except to create efficiency in our production.[35]

The truth is, however, that though Labour entered the election with a commitment to a series of nationalisations, it had no real idea of how this would actually be achieved. Shinwell, who went to the Ministry of Fuel after the election and whose remit therefore included the nationalisation of coal, the longest debated nationalisation of them all, even complained that there was no blueprint for nationalisation for him to follow, and there were long-running disputes between Morrison and Bevin who rightly objected that the National Corporation model did not of necessity mean either a more efficient industry or a better employer.

The Election itself was a busy one for Cripps. He was driven around by Allan Jarvis his secretary, who had replaced Gwen Hill, and kept up the usual gruelling pattern of early mornings and large numbers of public meetings. It was an exciting campaign. Sybil Thorndike and Peggy Ashcroft campaigned for Labour and such was the enthusiasm of the young Tony Benn that he even canvassed No. 10. One Labour Party organiser commented, 'Not since the field-preaching of the Wesley brothers has such a surge of "revival" swept the hamlets and county towns of Southern England. Villages steeped in century-old Tory tradition bloomed with Labour posters.'[36] Isobel, meanwhile, stayed at the family home at Sapperton, where preparations were being made for Theresa's wedding to a young solicitor she had met whilst in the WRNS. Once the voting had taken place in Bristol, on 5 July, Cripps returned to Sapperton and the family gathered on the 20th to send Theresa and Bob off. It was from their honeymoon in the Italianate village Portmeirion, built in Wales by Stafford's friend Clough Williams-Ellis, that Theresa and Bob Ricketts heard the election results. Labour, against the expectations of most of the Labour leadership except Bevan, had won and won handsomely. Churchill had told the King that he thought he would win by between thirty and eighty seats but in the event Labour had won a massive 393 seats and throughout the late morning and afternoon of the 26th first Brendan Bracken, then Macmillan and a minor galaxy of Conservative Ministers lost their seats. The Liberals had lost out badly, being reduced to a mere twelve seats and losing both their leader Sinclair and Beveridge who had briefly sat for Berwick-upon-Tweed. At seven o'clock in the evening Churchill, who had heard the first results in his bath, went to the Palace to tender his resignation and recommended that the King ask Attlee to form a Government.

Meanwhile a new drama was being acted out at Transport House where the senior Party figures were beginning to gather from lunchtime onwards. The first to get there, inevitably, were the London MPs Morrison, Attlee and Bevin, who sat with the Party's relatively new General Secretary, Morgan Phillips, in Bevin's room while the other members of the National Executive listened to the results in Phillips's room. The day before the election Morrison had notified Attlee of his intention to run against him for the leadership, and when Attlee read out Churchill's resignation message and the invitation to see the King, Morrison argued that Attlee should not accept the King's invitation to form a Government. The PLP should first meet to decide on its leader. Attlee replied that there was no requirement in the Party constitution to hold such a leadership election and that besides it would be undemocratic for the person whom the Party had presented as its leader throughout its campaign not to be its leader once the country had voted. The telephone rang in the other room. It was Cripps, for Morrison. Whilst Morrison was out of the room Bevin asked Morgan Phillips, ' "If I stood against Clem, should I win?" Morgan Phillips replied, "On a split vote, I think you would." Then Bevin turned to Attlee and said, "Clem, you go to the Palace straightaway."'[37] On Morrison's return he declared that Cripps was backing him, but there was no further discussion of a PLP election and the group parted. Attlee, unbeknown to Morrison, went directly to the Palace. Indeed he was gazetted as arriving there only thirty minutes after Churchill at 7.30 p.m. Without hesitation he accepted the King's commission to form a Government before proceeding to the victory party at Central Hall at which Morrison was still actively canvassing support both for a leadership election and for himself. Morrison's campaign continued until the next afternoon when it fizzled out in a meeting of the PLP Administrative Committee, which resolved in less than thirty minutes that Attlee should continue to form a Government. On the 28th the new Parliamentary Labour Party met at the Beaver Hall, by which time Attlee had started to put together his ministerial team. Even so Morrison insisted on a vote on the leadership, which Bevin squashed by turning it into a vote of affirmation of Attlee. Lieutenant James Callaghan, newly elected MP for Cardiff South said 'I was so ignorant that I didn't understand the undertones and I didn't realise at all there had been this attempted coup against Attlee that was staged by Morrison and others. To me they were all sitting on the platform, a band of brothers united in victory.'[38]

Most Labour historians have tended to be rather contemptuous of the Morrison ploy, but a reference to the events in Mervyn Stockwood's biography makes rather more sense of both Morrison's and Cripps's actions. Cripps had intended to drive round the constituency on the day of the election results thanking people for voting. As it was pouring in Bristol he ended up sitting in Stockwood's study, listening to the results and fielding calls from colleagues around the country. Stockwood says that Cripps had told him before the election that if Labour won Churchill would not resign as Prime Minister until there was a vote of confidence in the Commons. In the meantime the Parliamentary Labour Party would have met and elected its leader, in which contest he would back Morrison. Indeed there is evidence that this was Churchill's early intention, according to Eden at least.[39] If this was also Morrison's view prior to the election his actions are rather more understandable. Moreover, the argument that Attlee had won the election so had to be the Labour leader would have held no moral force with Cripps at all. After all neither Churchill nor Lloyd George had been elected Prime Minister in wartime, nor had Chamberlain in peace. The whole basis of the British system was that the electorate decided who they wanted as their local member and those duly elected members selected who should lead them. The national campaign, such as it was, had not yet made the election a presidential contest, and Cripps felt it was only right that there should now be an election for the leadership. When Morrison rang to say 'the old man has done it. He's gone to the Palace and the King will have to send for Attlee' Cripps must have realised that it would be Attlee, not Morrison or anyone else, who would be forming the Cabinet.

Considering it was the first majority Labour Government, Attlee's first Cabinet was remarkable in both the degree of its experience and in the breadth of its churchmanship. The key posts, Foreign Secretary and Chancellor, went respectively to Bevin and Dalton, who with Attlee and Morrison, now Lord President of the Council, had between them twenty-seven years of ministerial experience. Other stalwarts who could even hark back to previous minority Labour Governments included Pethick-Lawrence, who had been Financial Secretary to the Treasury in the 1929-31 Government and was now Secretary for India and Burma, William Jowitt, now Lord Chancellor, who had been Attorney-General under MacDonald, Arthur Greenwood, the Lord Privy Seal, who had been Parliamentary Secretary in the Ministry of Health in 1924 and Tom Williams, the new Minister for Agriculture, who had been a PPS in both the 1924 and 1929–31 administrations. Christopher Addison, now Dominions Secretary and Leader of the House of Lords, had even been Minister for Reconstruction in the First World War and Minister of Health under Lloyd George.

It was also as if the years of Coalition had washed away all unrighteousness. For seated around the same table was one Minister who had stuck with MacDonald in 1931, two that had been expelled from the Party in 1939 and three ex-members of the *Tribune* board, while the front bench even included Strachey. It was hardly a proletarian Government. Dalton and Pethick-Lawrence were Etonians, Jowitt was a Malburian, Cripps a Wykehamist, Attlee a Haileyburian. Greenwood, Chuter Ede (Home Secretary) and Ellen Wilkinson (Education) were the products of grammar schools and only Morrison, Williams, Bevan (Health), and George Isaacs

(Labour), had left state school at fourteen, while Bevin had no formal education.

The other factor about the Cabinet was quite simply that Attlee did not bear grudges. Neither Morrison nor Cripps was punished for their attempt to oust him. It is attractive to think that Attlee's own long loyalty to Cripps, even in the tough years of the Popular Front, was poorly repaid by Cripps and that Attlee could easily have taken umbrage. But it was simply not part of his make-up to bear a grudge. Indeed one of his most effective tactics was to incorporate those who attacked him into the core of his team, thereby disarming all opposition – a tactic he was to use again in 1947 when Cripps tried to persuade him to stand down.

In an era where crossing the floor of the House is seen as a massive act of betrayal and when the power of Party discipline makes it difficult to conceive of a Prime Minister taking straight into his Cabinet a newly returned prodigal, it takes an act of special understanding to comprehend Cripps's appointment to the important post of President of the Board of Trade. Attlee was still wary of his tendency to light on 'sudden ideas'[40] and was probably equally aware that if he over-promoted him more loyal colleagues would baulk. As Trevor Burridge put it, 'his solution was to have Cripps serve a political apprenticeship as President of the Board of Trade and then to put him in charge of economic policy.'[41] This is not entirely true. After all, the even more errant Bevan, who was the only Labour figure with no ministerial experience at all, was given a post. The re-creation of the Cabinet after the war necessitated a restructuring of the Board of Trade and there was much work that had been started under Dalton, principally in relation to the location of industry, that Attlee was keen to see through. Moreover Attlee already valued Cripps highly, and the warmth of his acceptance back into the fold at the May 1945 Labour Party Conference had shown that he would not be going too far out on a limb by appointing him to a senior position. Cripps had played a full role in the General Election and had even been involved, while still an Independent, in discussions about the future strength of the Parties at a special Labour Party away day in 1944. Cripps had also proved himself an adept manager of a department and clearly knew how to speak to industrialists in a language they understood. He had run Britain's largest industry for more than two years and had been at the forefront of discussions about planning. All of which made him an ideal candidate for the job of President of the Board of Trade.

Furthermore on a personal level Cripps was now far freer than ever before to devote himself to his politics. Having given up his legal practice at the start of the war, having moved to a much smaller home and with all of the children except Diana now set up on their own, Stafford and Isobel were almost entirely absorbed in the public life, with Isobel both developing interests and concerns of her own and acting as an immensely supportive wife. There were some troubles with other members of the family. In particular Leonard was showing signs of premature dementia too, and he left Miriam behind while he spent half the year in South Africa. Diana had prolonged bouts of mental instability, but broadly speaking Isobel and Stafford, supported by the loyal Elsie Lawrence, were free. Whereas in the 1920s Stafford's life had been split between Goodfellows and Chancery Lane, in the 1930s he had pursued both a legal and political career at the same time as nurturing a family, and during the war he had helped the last of his children into maturity, Theresa's marriage signalled the beginning of a period of almost total dedication to the single task of government.

22

Another Industrial Revolution

Douglas Jay, then a temporary civil servant at the Board of Trade, heard that Labour had won the election seated at his desk in what is now ICI House.

> I naturally said, 'You are joking'. The first thing that flashed through my head was the pouring rain, was it going to rain forever like this in peacetime? The second was, Good Heavens! All the arrangements we had worked on for fifteen months for industrial turn-round would now be not merely grudgingly and reluctantly accepted by a Tory government but with Dalton as Chancellor and Ernie Bevin in some other senior post, virtually anything I could propose would be pushed through. That was a very exciting moment.[1]

There was excitement in the air, fuelled equally by the octane of an unexpected victory and a resolve to get as much Socialism on the books as possible. This meant the introduction of a planned economy and the institution of welfare provision. So in eighteen months over 20 per cent of the economy was taken into public ownership or was well on course for it. As promised, the Bank of England, cable and wireless, civil aviation, coal, electricity, road haulage, the canals and railways were all nationalised by the summer of

1947. Similarly the framework of the Welfare State was constructed. The National Insurance Act of 1946 instituted compulsory insurance along the lines of the Beveridge Report. Maternity, unemployment and sickness benefits, old age and widows' pensions and funeral grants were started – from the cradle to the grave. The National Health Service Act was also on the books in 1946, to be enforced in 1948. Free milk for all schoolchildren was introduced. The Poor Law was abolished. It was such stuff as Socialist dreams of a New Jerusalem had been made of for many a year, and the speed with which legislation was enacted made the milk and honey all the sweeter.

Labour apologists have tended to suggest that the new Government gave a new lease of life to the whole machinery of government, but in truth the civil service was already well used to centralist measures and the new young planners in the Treasury, people like Otto Clarke and Alec Cairncross, simply remained in wartime top gear. Certainly some of them felt liberated. With the Tory critics gone the brakes were now off. In the economic section of the Cabinet Office the Fabian politics of James Meade, along with Richard Stone and Robert Hall might have given an extra impetus to Parliamentary business, aided by the Cabinet's Socialisation of Industry Committee, but in large measure the nationalisation programme was unopposed. It was less the dynamism of Labour's ideas than an enormous majority and a quiescent Opposition that made it quite easy to get legislation rapidly through the House, even through the Lords.

The same was true for the rapid development of the welfare state. James Griffiths's National Insurance Act sailed through Parliament with only a minor squall from the left who argued for more generous provision. In August 1946 family allowances began, granting five shillings a week for every dependent child after the first as well as the whole panoply of 'insurance' cover. The NHS Act was more contentious, and had a more rebarbative champion in Bevan. Especially controversial were proposals to take over the voluntary hospitals and the insistence on salaried doctors. The BMA opposed it and the Tories voted against, but the nation backed it and when the two-year set-up period was over it finally lurched into being with a minimum of tears.

Traditionally it has been upon these two pillars of Labour's programme that the 1945-51 governments have been judged and the third strand of the new Government's task has been that most often ignored by Labour's more dewy-eyed romantics – the economic battle which fell to Stafford's Board of Trade. Yet it was in every respect as important as the nationalisation programme or the welfare provision, as indicated by the fact that Cripps's appointment came along with the first four that were announced before Attlee went to Potsdam for negotiations with Stalin and Truman – and arguably it is the one area where the Attlee Government's reputation is largely still intact. It was a battle that Britain had to win, for the very simple reason that to all intents and purposes at the end of the war Britain was bankrupt. Once she had spent her reserves in the first two years of the war she had only been able to continue her military commitment by dint of the US Lend-Lease Act which allowed her to buy US materials and products on tick. The moment the war with Japan ended the US would stop the agreement and Britain would have to start paying her way. There were vast sterling debts – more than £1 billion to India and £475 million to Palestine, Egypt and Sudan. All of this at a time when British military commitments were still very costly with troops still deployed in the Far East and mopping up still to be done all over Europe – spending vital dollars abroad and worsening the balance of payments.

Keynes brought home the dire situation in which the Government found itself in a memorandum to the Cabinet on 13 August. Britain would have to make 'very early and very drastic economies in [its] huge cash expenditure overseas' as 'an absolute condition of maintaining our solvency'. Imports would have to be rigorously controlled, exports rapidly increased. Yet even with a generous assumption that exports would increase by 50 per cent and that there would be invisible income of some £150 million, it was likely that Britain would run a cumulative deficit of £1,250 million over the three years to 1948 before the 'pipe dream' of bringing the balance of payments into equilibrium in 1949. Keynes's only prescription was the begging bowl. 'The conclusion is inescapable that there is no source from which we can raise sufficient funds to enable us to live and spend on the scale we contemplate except the United States.'[2] He summed up the task ahead in blunt terms:

> there are three essential conditions without which we have not a hope of escaping what might be described, without exaggeration, and without implying we should not eventually recover from it, a financial Dunkirk. These conditions are (a) an intense concentration on the expansion of exports, (b) drastic and immediate economies in our overseas expenditure, and substantial aid from the United Sates on terms which we can accept. They can only be fulfilled by a combination of the greatest enterprise, ruthlessness and tact.[3]

The next day, 14 August, far sooner than either Churchill or Attlee had anticipated, Japan surrendered. Attlee, appearing the following morning with Bevin and Morrison on the balcony of the Ministry of Health, warned 'It is right for a short time that we should relax and celebrate the victory. But I want to remind you that after we have had this short holiday we have to work hard to win the peace as we have won the war.'[4] He was not joking. A week later President Truman signed the end of Lend-Lease and Britain's financial problems began in earnest. The trouble was that the Cabinet refused to countenance major cuts in military expenditure overseas until far too late, by which time it was evident that the drive for exports could not be met not least because too many men were still in the forces and there was a real labour shortage. So the drain abroad continued. The Tories argued for cuts in domestic expenditure, though in large measure this was irrelevant to the balance of payments. What mattered was the pattern of domestic consumption. If Britain ate too much American corn, smoked too much American tobacco or spun too much American cotton, insolvency was assured. Keynes was deputed to negotiate a loan of $5 billion, of which he felt immensely confident.

The Americans, however, were less susceptible to the argument that Britain had borne the brunt of a war that had been fought in America's interest than Keynes had expected. Altruism cut no American ice and the negotiations took almost a full year before he and the Cabinet Secretary, Edward Bridges, finally returned with a deal granting $3.75 billion. Yet even this was hedged around with conditions that made it almost intolerable. Free convertibility of sterling was insisted on, to commence a year after the loan was ratified, and repayments, spread over fifty years, would be charged at an interest rate of 2 per cent. British commercial policy had to be liberalised and the Bretton Woods Agreement ratified. As Trevor Burridge has pointed out, 'No British Prime Minister could possibly have been enthusiastic about the terms of the American loan; equally, no Prime Minister could have rejected them.'[5] Indeed not all the Party members were in favour. Alexander, Bevan and Shinwell opposed the terms in Cabinet and it was only a 'firm coalition' of Dalton, Bevin and Cripps taking on 'the assault in successive waves and effectively back[ing] each other up'[6] that ensured the Cabinet swallowed the bitter draft. Barbara Betts (late Castle), who had been elected one of the two MPs for Blackburn and was now, along with the other Blackburn MP, John Edwards, one of Cripps's PPSs, 'managed to get ten minutes with Stafford Cripps in the tea room. "I am sorry, Stafford," [she] told him hesitantly, "but I cannot vote for the American loan – my conscience won't let me." "Then your conscience is wrong," said Stafford briskly and spent the rest of the conversation swamping me with intellectual brilliance. I had no time to answer before he hurried away.'[7] Attlee acerbically called the US loan terms 'Free trade for all the world but not for themselves', but it was ratified on 15 July 1946, with convertibility to come on 15 July 1947. Bevin wrote to Cripps,

> There does seem to be an assumption that Britain is down and out because of what she has done in this war. When the PM made his statement in the House on Lend Lease, we were met with headlines in the US calling us 'Cry Babies' . . . I cannot help feeling that Britain has got to stand up for herself . . . and the world must realise that though we have paid such a terrible price in this war we are not down and out. We shall survive.[8]

The second half of the balance of payments strategy, such as it was, now had to take all the political and economic flak and this gave Stafford's Board of Trade a vital role. The difference between the hoped-for $5 billion and the actual $3.75 billion, supplemented by a Canadian loan, had to be made up. Keynes's original strictures still had to be observed – an immediate hike in exports and a determined effort to keep imports, especially US and other dollar imports, down. Both of these tasks were difficult. For a start British industry was in no state to achieve vast increases in production. Its management, weaned on Gentleman's Relish, had little idea of how to run an efficient enterprise. Innovation and new technology still took a small eternity to trundle through from design to implementation. Finance houses took few risks in home industry. Research and Development were undervalued.

Skilled labour was in chronic short supply thanks to an educational system that had totally ignored engineering and science in the pursuit of scholastic excellence in other fields, as the Barlow report showed. When Germany was developing the polytechnics, Britain was only just introducing science courses into Oxbridge. Plant and machinery had enjoyed so little investment that many factories were still equipped with Edwardian or even Victorian machines. Productivity had scarcely entered the British vocabulary, let alone its mentality.

What was needed was an industrial revolution. What it got was nationalisation in some industries and Stafford Cripps in the rest.

In the battle of production Cripps had some formidable weaponry at his disposal. His Howitzer, however, was his own political persona. Just as in the MAP he set off round the country on a gruelling tour of factories, this time with Betts or with Edwards, encouraging, exhorting, browbeating Britain into producing more goods for export. He spoke, he lectured, he preached. Britain must work harder. Britain must, for a time, forgo luxuries. From August through to January 1946, almost without a break, he travelled the length and breadth of Britain.

No one could have done the job better. His diet, his frugality, his early hours, his cold baths and his upright posture – none of them the result of conscious puritanism – were well known and gave him the air of sacrifice. He was reckoned to live a simple life despite his great wealth. He had made the same sacrifices as everyone else. So what might have come across as pompous, self-serving cant in another politician, appeared more like honest 'tell it as it is' common sense. It was a public persona that was accentuated by his physical appearance, now more gaunt than in the 1930s, with rimless glasses that made his face less round. As Brendan Bracken, who loathed him, put it 'Cripps has a great following. The British public either like fat men or high-minded skeletons.'[9]

He was fully aware of how he looked and came across. Indeed Isobel had urged him to be cautious of appearing a kill-joy in the war and had suggested, rather improbably, that developing an interest in male voice choirs would help dispel the vague odours of sanctity that attended him. Cripps had now deliberately chosen a woman PPS to soften his image and to provide a woman's perspective on many of the production issues that so directly affected housewives, though Betts herself rather imperiously dismissed his motives, 'Typically, Stafford had decided he needed a man for the heavy administrative side and a woman to advise him on the complaints that were rolling in from women about clothes rationing and other problems caused by the shortage of raw materials.'[10]

Cripps's exhortative approach was, as often as not, expressed in explicitly Christian terms. Citing a marooned householder in a flood who had needed the help of local villagers, even those who did not know him, he proclaimed,

> In just the same way we must realise that our country is now in a jam, and whether domestically or industrially we must act as Christians, giving of ourselves to help others ... I believe most profoundly that what we are lacking today in our productive effort in this country is a Christian approach – a Christian background.

The answer, he felt, lay in giving Britain a sense of moral purpose.

> Our industrial morale is low because a merely materialistic, self-centred outlook on our work cannot give us a high morale. The stimulation of a patriotic war with its call for self-sacrifice in a wider and nobler cause has gone and nothing has as yet taken its place. Inducements of a material kind can never and will never replace the spiritual urge which transcends our own personal interests.[11]

Stafford recognised, however, that industry could not be reformed by moral injunction alone and the Board of Trade held on to all the controls it had enjoyed in the war, using them remorselessly to enforce the push for exports. Raw materials, nearly all of them imports, were only allocated in industries that could produce for export, and even within industries individual companies were favoured that could prove their export capacity. Not everyone agreed with the policy. Speaking at a dinner of the Society of Motor Manufacturers and Traders in November 1945, he was heckled when he told them that instead of producing for a protected home market, they should export at least 50 per cent of their vehicles. 'No', 'Tripe', people shouted. Cripps replied in semi-religious cadences, 'I have often wondered whether you thought Great Britain was here to support the motor industry, or the motor industry was here to support Great Britain.'[12]

Cripps continued with tight controls in the car industry. A limit was placed on the number of cars that could be sold to the home market – and even those were only sold to people with special Government certificates of need. Inevitably this put a strain on the industry. Those, companies, such as Rover, which had only really produced luxury goods for the home market before the war, were in danger of getting no steel at all unless they completely turned around their production and their overseas sales force. Some companies ended up producing vast numbers of outdated models for the foreign market which sold well enough for a few years, but as soon as the French and German car industries took off, having spent more time and money on research and development, the British car industry sailed into the doldrums – where it remained well into the 1980s.

One major success story, however, was a direct result of a Cripps intervention. The development of the Land Rover – a combination of some clapped out farm jeeps and a new Rover engine – by Maurice Wilkes, a director of engineering at Rover, was given hefty support and encouragement by the President of the Board of Trade.

> We were particularly fortunate in that Sir Stafford Cripps – and one doesn't want to bring politics into this in any way – was a very far-seeing and a brilliant chap. He was President of the Board of Trade at that time and expressed a wish to come down to the works and see what we were doing. Fortunately at that stage we had just made the first small experimental batch of those vehicles which used extensively non-rationed materials, particularly aluminium. He accepted the representations that we made to him that here was something new for the British motor industry which had a future not only for exports but for agriculture. He gave it his full support and indeed when he became Chancellor of the Exchequer he specifically exempted Land Rovers from purchase tax. So we were able to do what the Japanese and the Germans did, and what any manufacturer who wants to export successfully does, we were able to build up at least a modicum of a home market from which we could then go out into the world and export.[13]

It was not just in the car industry that controls and regulations determined the drive for exports. Potteries – long an interest of Stafford's since his Ashtead days – were required to produce only utility designs for the home market while the more ornate patterns went abroad. Thousands and thousands of plain white cups and saucers were churned out. Clothing was not only rationed, but manufacturers were forced to produce standard utility ranges for the home market which were economical on imported cotton. When Christian Dior in March 1947 introduced his 'New Look' with a swirling, feminine, eight-inches-from-the-ground skirt *Vogue* called it a 'new love affair'. Cripps saw it as an extravagant waste of dollars and tried to co-opt the British Guild of Creative Designers to back the national effort by emphasising the chic qualities of short skirts. Housewives may have been complaining at this stringency, but the redoubtable Bessie Braddock, who would have taken a fair few metres of cotton to attire, even in a short skirt, proclaimed at Labour Party Conference, 'The problem today as it affects British women is to get hold of clothes. They have not agitated for the longer skirt. Their strong feeling is that things should be left as they are. Most women today are glad to get any clothes they can get hold of, and people who worry about longer skirts might do something more useful with their time.'[14] Furniture, cutlery, pots and pans – everything that a man or woman could want, was produced to a utility design and then rationed. Even royal weddings fell foul of the controls and Princess Elizabeth was allowed 100 coupons for her wedding in November 1947, with bridesmaids getting twenty-three coupons and pages ten. Formal dress was declared optional for the event. Churchill and Lord Woolton, who shadowed Strachey as Minister for Food, might have felt the continuing controls were unnecessary and called for the Government to 'set the people free', but industrialists like Arthur Bryan reckoned the use of such controls was a success. 'If there hadn't been controls at that time, I'm quite convinced that the manufacturers of the day would have sold to the easiest market at the biggest profit.'[15]

Cripps, a technician by nature, whose main hobby for years had been carpentry, took an equally significant interest in design, for it was clear that if Britain was to sell her goods abroad she had to produce marketable products. So one of his first acts was to sponsor the 'Britain can make it' exhibition to be held at the Victoria and Albert Museum in September 1946 and in which 1,300 firms took part.

In some industries it became rapidly apparent that there were special problems that could not simply be resolved by the pattern of carrot and stick, exhortation and control that had been the staple of the MAP. The cotton industry in particular was in dire need of reform. A study in 1944 had found that automation had been introduced to 95 per cent of US looms and only 5 per cent of British ones. Two million people were still employed in it, but its production was lagging behind 1937 figures. As Dalton put it in 1944 'this industry, more than most, is in the hands of old men, prone to take short views.'[16] Stafford and Barbara went to Blackburn to ask the workers to do double shifts. A working party was set up with four employers' representatives, four Trade Unionists and four independent members with a Chairman appointed by the Board of Trade. It was to report swiftly with suggestions for reorganisation of the industry, which it did by Christmas. Its conclusions were damning, 'a substantial proportion of the machinery now in place is . . . not only old in type but beyond its efficient working life.'[17] Yet Cripps opposed nationalisation for the industry and even Dalton's idea of a statutory board was rejected in favour of a mere consultative body, the Cotton Board, which was set up in 1947. The row in the Board of Trade lost Cripps his Parliamentary Secretary, Ellis Smith, who resigned in January 1946 over the refusal to nationalise cotton. Indeed it was not until 1948 that the Government, with Harold Wilson at the Board of Trade, brought in the Cotton Spinning Re-equipment Subsidy Act, which was designed to encourage the complete technical overhaul of the industry, but only achieved a pathetically minimal uptake.

Cotton was not the only industry to have a working party. Similar groups were set up for seventeen industries, modelled on the Joint Production Committees of the MAP, bringing together Trade Unionists and employers. None of them was effective in doing any more than garnering useful information. The galvanising of British industry required either some enormous spasm of energy that would shake it out of its lethargy or else an even greater degree of national intervention and investment in infrastructure, which Britain could simply not afford.

The Board of Trade's work was also complicated by Cripps's uncertain grasp on industrial relations, exhibited most forcefully by a tactless, though honest, speech on 20 October 1946 in Bristol, when he admitted,

> From my experience there is not as yet a very large number of workers in Britain capable of taking over large enterprises. I have on many occasions tried to get representatives of the workers on all sorts of bodies and working parties. It has always been extremely difficult to get enough people qualified to do that sort of job. Until there has been more experience of the workers of the managerial side of industry, I think it would be impossible to have worker-controlled industry in Britain, even if it were on the whole desirable.[18]

The hornets were stirred, both at Transport House and in Fleet Street, though the Labour Party and the Trade Unions were themselves only cautiously interested in what was termed the 'socialisation' of industry. Morrisonian Corporations had next to no Trade Union involvement at Board level and indeed the Trade Unionists who did sit on new nationalised boards immediately resigned from the Unions so as to stress that they were not there as Trade Union representatives. The call for a better deal in industry did not yet mean a partnership with management. Some members of the Cabinet were strong supporters of an increased role in management for Trade Unions. Bevan and Shinwell sought a real change in the employer employee relationship, but for the most part the Trade Unions accepted the National Corporation model for the nationalised industries, despite the fact that 'It created public figures, often patrician capitalists or even generals, as much remote proconsular figures as were imperial representatives in Curzon's India.'[19] In this sense Cripps was ahead of his time, believing that only a real partnership could deliver the goods, whether in a private industry or a nationalised one. It was a principle he had exemplified in his own work. Every department he had run had regular team meetings, every member of staff was considered an equal member of the team and he had a reputation for speaking on equal terms to secretaries, doorkeepers, cleaning staff, at a time when strict hierarchies in industry reflected class divisions with a rigidity that paralysed innovation.

Cripps himself took great pride in the business of management. He saw it as a skilled trade, not just something to be picked up by an amateur. Barbara Betts, often quite critical of him, thought he was an excellent manager.

> I learned a lot from Stafford about the art of government. As head of one of the largest and most complex departments, he was ruthless about saving time. When I started with him he called me into his office and said, 'I am always glad to hear what you have to say, but preferably do it verbally. If you must put it down on paper you must do it on half a sheet.' ... he drove himself and others remorselessly.[20]

He was also strict with himself about not undermining his own staff. Edwin Plowden, who later worked with him at the Treasury and had also been at the MAP, said of him

> Cripps also never forgot that people needed to be led rather than directed. He once said to me, and with good reason, 'I consider myself to be one of the best draftsmen in the country, and I itch to re-write almost every paper which crosses my desk However, I refrain from doing so because if I did I should never get the best out of my officials – they would become disillusioned and say,

"Why try, he alters everything anyway." Thus unless a paper is truly bad, I content myself with comments and the odd amendment.' [21]

This managerial incisiveness made Stafford the most interventionist of all the Ministers and his personal directness meant he had little 'use for red tape and cut through civil service rigidities to get his way'.[22]

Nevertheless Cripps's comments on Trade Unionists infuriated his local Trades Council and he was called to account by his local Party, who were beginning to worry that the rebel they had stuck by through thick and thin was now proving something of a moderate.

The final weapon in the Board of Trade's arsenal was the last Act to pass under the wire before the end of the Parliamentary session of 1944-5, Dalton's Distribution of Industry Act, which was finally, after a tiny amendment, passed under the caretaker Government. As Douglas Jay noted, this was the most potent tool the Government had invented for itself, even if it had assumed that it would be implemented, reluctantly, by a Conservative Government. Cripps adopted it wholeheartedly. Its aim, to redistribute industry, was the closest thing to his pre-war obsession with the Deprived Areas, and he relished the task of planning where industry should go so that Britain would meet both its economic obligations to increase exports and its moral obligations to provide full employment. Under the Act, Industrial Development Certificates had to be issued as a prerequisite for planning permission, new towns like Stevenage were built (by his friend Clough Williams-Ellis), old industrial estates were revitalised, new ones started – all with the aim of preventing large pockets of unemployment, especially in the North East, Scotland and Wales. Regional unemployment had been the scourge of the 1930s, peaking in the North East at 38 per cent in 1932, and it was a real achievement that by 1948 it was only 3 per cent and

1.5 per cent in 1951. As Ben Pimlott has pointed out, the general pattern of lowering unemployment was more a factor of the general economy and of labour shortages than of the Act itself, but an untrammelled market approach post-war would undoubtedly have led to higher unemployment in areas outside the South East of England.

It has occasionally been insinuated that Cripps, as President of the Board of Trade, was not in the inner circle of the Attlee Government. This is far from the truth. From the very beginning he was involved in the full array of Cabinet committees through which most of the new Government's business passed. He was one of the three ministers involved in establishing the American loan. He sat on Morrison's Lord President's Committee, which oversaw the whole process of nationalisation and had control of the whole planning brief. He also managed the single most important aspect of the Government's economic policy. In alliance with Dalton he drove the agenda in most financial areas and outshone Morrison in the economic field.

Moreover, within nine months of the General Election Cripps was to take the lead in one of the Attlee Government's most determined and successful foreign policy developments. For if Cripps's public persona and wartime experience made him invaluable in the economic battle, his longstanding personal connections put him in a unique position to resolve the problem of Indian independence. And problem it still was. Ever since Keir Hardie the British left had been committed to independence, but the complications of geography and creed had remained intractable, with the rival claims of Muslim, Hindu, Sikh and Christian stymying a peaceful outcome. Even within the Muslim and Hindu political forces there was little unanimity, splitting Kashmir and making Congress an unreliable negotiating partner. Yet, as Wavell told Churchill in October 1944, 'the future of India is the problem on which the British Commonwealth and the

British reputation will stand or fall in the post-war period.'[23]

At the start of 1946 the Cabinet resolved to strain every sinew in the hope of cutting the Gordian knot. A unique proposition was put – a Cabinet Mission of three Ministers of the Crown, deputed to act with the Viceroy and to negotiate independence in the form of Dominion status, no longer post-dated, but with immediate effect.

Pethick-Lawrence, as Secretary of State for India, despite being in his seventy-fifth year, was inevitably part of the team. Like Cripps he had been a devoted advocate of independence for years, and, again like Cripps, was one of the few MPs to mention India in his election address. He had also been a colleague of Cripps's back in the 1931 Government when he had to stand in for Snowden when he was ill and Cripps had helped him on the Land Valuation Bill. He had even briefly joined the Socialist League 'out of respect for Stafford Cripps'.[24] The third member of the team, the Co-operator A. V. Alexander, First Lord of the Admiralty in three administrations (1929–32, 1940–5, 1945–6) was less obvious, although his known sympathies with Jinnah and the Muslim League might have been expected to balance out his two Congress-inclined compatriots. He nonetheless saw himself as the 'ballast'. Cripps also took with him another Labour MP, the young Woodrow Wyatt, and his personal secretary, John Blaker. Pethick-Lawrence described the team which gathered in Delhi on 24 March, 'All my colleagues are delightful and so different. Cripps the brilliant rapier-witted improviser with strong left tendencies, vegetarian teetotaller; Alexander, the Britisher, who wants Cheddar cheese and English food and is so proud of the British navy; the Viceroy, the soldier, sparing of speech, suspicious of new-fangled ideas and I imagine of all foreign ways of thought and action, straightforward, blunt, but with his own sense of humour.'[25]

It was to be a long and exhausting stay. Nominally Pethick-Lawrence was in charge of the Mission, but in practice much of the tight negotiation was led by Cripps, who sped from one group to another, vainly spinning plates. As Pethick-Lawrence put it, 'Sir Stafford Cripps is like the dove that Noah sends out from the Ark. He is constantly going out making contacts but up till now finding no solid ground.'[26]

From the outset both the Muslim League and Congress were hazy in their approach, arguing with more passion than precision for fixed positions that did not hold up to Cripps's cross-examination. Jinnah said he wanted the creation of Pakistan, but could not state quite what it would include, simply averring that it would not be subject to a Hindu hegemony. Azad, Nehru and Gandhi, all speaking for Congress, gave different slants on what they sought, falling back on the simple assertion that nothing less than full and immediate independence would suffice. Gandhi pretty much refused to deal with the long-term issues until all political prisoners were released. With no proposals forthcoming from either side, the Mission decided to draft their own, to be discussed at a conference in the foothills of the Himalayas at Simla. There should be a Union Government covering foreign affairs, defence and communications; two groups of provinces, one broadly Hindu, the other Muslim, which would deal with anything they felt could or should be treated in common; all other powers would be vested in the provinces themselves.

The first session of the conference, at the start of May, was hopeful. There was some apparent movement on the part of Jinnah, who no longer seemed to be insisting on a sovereign state of Pakistan, and though Congress stated an immediate objection to the idea of compulsory intermediate federations of provinces, Jinnah and Nehru came to a position whereby the Muslim League would accept the Union if the Congress accepted the federations. The Mission then drew up some 'suggested points for agreement' in which the idea of federations of provinces was toned down: there would be a ten year get out clause and an option not to join any grouping. This troubled Jinnah as he felt Assam would peel off from Bengal, but he did not rule out of court a suggestion by Nehru that the two of them should meet to agree an umpire to facilitate the drawing up of the new constitution under the Constituent Assembly. Cripps wrote to Nehru, 'I felt inordinately proud of my friendship with you yesterday afternoon and I do congratulate you and your colleagues upon their most statesmanlike attitude. I pray that success may come to your labours and that you two may be hailed as Saviours of India as indeed you will be if you succeed in coming to an agreement.'[27]

So far so good. The high tide soon turned, however. Jinnah refused to admit that he had agreed to independent arbitration and began to reassert the need for a separate Pakistan which would only delegate powers to a Union on three subjects if Pakistan was effectively recognised by a Muslim provincial grouping. Congress's hackles rose and though it seemed that the discussion now hinged almost entirely on semantic bluff and double bluff, the Mission decided no new advance could be made without a new initiative from their own side. So a new Mission plan was drawn up and published, after the Cabinet finally gave its approval, on 16 May. This stated that Pakistan was 'impracticable' as it would simply institute two new non-Muslim minorities of nearly 40 per cent in the North West areas and 48 per cent in the North East. The new constitution would now be drawn up by a Constituent Assembly elected by the Hindu, Muslim and Sikh MPs of the Provincial Legislative Assemblies in proportion to their populations, plus ninety-three representatives from the Indian native states (the princely states). Any province would be able to call for a reconsideration of the terms of the constitution after ten years and there would now be three groupings, not two, thereby allowing for both a Punjab, North-West Frontier Province and Sind federation and a Bengal and Assam federation – both of which would have narrow Muslim majorities. The plan, at least Cripps's fourth or fifth, was published on 16 May.

Pethick-Lawrence broadcast to the nation, Attlee notified Britain and Cripps and Alexander tried to field questions at a press conference.

Two days later Cripps fainted in the middle of a meeting and was rushed off to hospital. There is little evidence of what exactly was wrong with him. There were suggestions of Isobel coming out to take him back to Britain, but there was little sense of a medical emergency, and though it is possible that he had already contracted the cancer that was to kill him, it is far more likely that he was simply suffering from exhaustion brought on by workaholism. Of course it had always been in Stafford's nature to work hard, with early mornings and an almost aggressive belief in the power of concentration. The Protestant work ethic, dressed up in the honourable attire of Anglican duty, was an immensely powerful force throughout his life, but without Isobel to moderate it, and with the further impetus of the immense frustrations of Indian politics, it burnt a hole in Stafford's health. August to January had been rigorous. March to May had been exhausting and Cripps now remained in bed until 2 June. By then a new problem had arisen over whether the all-Indian Interim Government would only include Muslim League Muslims or would include someone such as Sheikh Abdullah of Kashmir, a Congress member.

Four days after Cripps's return the Muslim League announced its acceptance of the Mission plan 'inasmuch as the basis and the foundation of Pakistan are inherent in the Mission's plan by virtue of the compulsory groupings', and while Wavell was telling Azad that grouping was not compulsory, it seemed that a Congress agreement was on the cards as well. Indeed Jinnah was so confident that agreement was now possible that he told Cripps he would not only like to be in the Interim Government but what post he would like – Defence.

Yet Cripps was not satisfied. He realised that if Congress continued to push for a non-league Muslim in the Interim

Government, Jinnah might back out. He insisted that Jinnah be asked what his exact conditions were and threatened to resign unless his suggestion was put to the Cabinet. Pethick-Lawrence, by contrast wanted to meet the Congress demand, which Wavell and Alexander ruled out. In the end the matter was resolved by no offer being made to the Muslim League to join the Interim Government at all.

On 29 June, having spent far longer than they had originally intended, the Mission returned to Britain, believing they had secured the broad agreement of both parties and leaving the fine-tuning of the Interim Government appointments to the Viceroy. Within a fortnight Nehru had reinterpreted the Plan and Jinnah's reaction to Nehru's new exegesis was to back out as well. Wavell wrote to his friend Mountbatten, 'It looks as if after many weeks of bargaining, the Congress [are] going to run true to form and turn down yet another offer. What will happen next is uncertain, but it will certainly be difficult and unpleasant.'[28] He was right: 16 August was declared a Direct Action Day by the Muslim League. In three days 5,000 were killed and 15,000 injured in rioting in Calcutta. There was violence in East Bengal and Bihar while there was a fear that the whole administration would collapse. Wavell was at his wits' end, 'I have tried everything I know to solve the problem of handing over India to its people, and I can see no light. I have only one solution, which I call Operation Madhouse – withdrawal of the British province by province, beginning with women and children, then civilians, then the army.'[29] Nevertheless Wavell plodded on, steadily losing the respect of the Indians who felt he had reneged on the Mission plan. Equally importantly he started seriously to advocate his 'Breakdown' plan, rapidly angering Attlee with his idea of a swift withdrawal from India. Attlee called his suggestion 'an inglorious end to our long association with India. World opinion would regard it as a policy of scuttle unworthy of a great power.'[30] Wavell met with Attlee on 19 December: 'Two hours of desultory discussion resulted in no progress at all, with the PM now definitely hostile to the Breakdown Plan. They are all frightened of anything which involves Parliamentary legislation, and therefore try to make out that the Plan is either necessary or misguided. It is all very disheartening, once again they have run out.'[31]

What he did not realise was that Attlee had already been in discussions for several weeks with the person he wanted to replace Wavell, though it was not until the end of January that he was formally dismissed. Attlee made one of his inspired choices at this point. 'Dickie Mountbatten stood out a mile,' he later confessed. 'Burma showed it. The so-called experts had been wrong about Aung Sang, and Dickie had been right.'[32] At first, though, Mountbatten was reluctant to take the post on. Cripps and others were called on to put considerable pressure on him. First he suggested that Pethick-Lawrence should go out with him. Then Cripps suggested he should also go, though Mountbatten complained to the King, 'I don't want to be hamstrung by having to bring out a third version of the Cripps offer!!!'[33] He replied more tactfully to Attlee, 'The presence of a man of his prestige and experience could not fail to reduce me to a mere figurehead.'[34] Instead it was agreed that Cripps would inform those leading Indians with whom he had already good personal relations prior to the announce-ment of the appointment, that Mountbatten sought their support. On 1 January 1947 Mountbatten met with Attlee and Cripps and demanded that he should not have Whitehall ministers breathing down his neck.

> Mr Attlee consulted Sir Stafford Cripps and even after twenty-two years I can remember his next words. 'You are asking for plenipotentiary powers above His Majesty's Government. No one has ever been given such powers in this century.' There was a silence for quite a while, then he went on, 'surely you can't mean this?' 'Escape at last'

I thought as I firmly replied that I did indeed mean just that and would quite understand if as a result the appointment was withdrawn. But Cripps nodded his head and Attlee replied, 'All right, you've got the powers, and the job.'[35]

On 20 February, despite a last minute plea from Wavell to reconsider the situation, the announcement of Mountbatten's appointment was made. A debate on India was arranged for 6 March, which Cripps opened with considerable emotion.

Mountbatten was a success. Just like his predecessors his aim was independence for a united India, but it was now plain that unity and independence were mutually incompatible. So a new idea was mooted, first by Cripps and then taken up by Attlee, that a fixed date for Britain's final departure should be announced as a way of sharpening the minds of both Congress and the Muslim League on the need to come to an agreement. Mountbatten subsequently suggested that the original idea for a fixed date was his own. In fact, though, Cripps's suggestion of 31 March 1948 was first discussed at the Cabinet India Committee on 20 December, before Wavell had even been dismissed. It was also discussed at the Cabinet meeting on 31 December, when Cripps argued that the announcement should not be made too soon lest it make the creation of a united India more rather than less difficult, implying that he still felt Jinnah was prepared to forgo a separate Pakistan. It was only on 3 January that Mountbatten wrote to Attlee, 'It makes all the difference to me to know that you propose to make a statement in the House, terminating the British "Raj" on a definite and specified date; or earlier than this date, if the Indian Parties can agree a constitution and form a Government, before this.'[36]

Once he was out in India Mountbatten came up with an early plan, which he was sure would be acceptable to both Nehru and Jinnah, granting Dominion status to both Pakistan and India and allowing the North-West Frontier states to chose for themselves whether they went with India or Pakistan. His chief of staff, Pug Ismay, had got the Cabinet back in London to agree to this in principle, largely on the grounds that both Indian parties agreed. In fact when Mountbatten rather previously showed Nehru the draft agreement after dinner on 10 May – the day before it was to be made public – he complained that this was not partition but balkanisation and refused to co-operate. Mountbatten was now in a difficult position, having only just got Cabinet permission for a deal that had collapsed before he could submit it. So he took a risk and changed the offer the next day to a promise that the new India and Pakistan would be allowed to join the Commonwealth. When this new plan was conveyed to London a suggestion was made that either Cripps should visit Mountbatten to sort things out or Mountbatten should travel to London to explain his actions. Mountbatten hastily clambered aboard an aeroplane, and was soon in front of the Cabinet getting unanimous approval for his actions. Cripps wrote to congratulate him 'Magnificent. We have been thinking of you hour by hour, and what you have accomplished has exceeded even our expectations and hopes. I know you have a very tough job ahead but I hope you have now got out of the dangers of a land-locked harbour on to the High Sea where the storms will be easier to ride.'[37]

On 15 July 1947 Cripps moved the second reading of the Indian Independence Bill 'with deep emotion and humility'. It was not a long speech but it ended with a typical Cripps peroration, 'Their leaders, who have struggled and suffered for the faith that was in them through long and hard years, we salute now as fellow-workers in the cause of world peace and progress. May the sun which is now rising on their independence, never set upon their freedom and prosperity.'[38] On 15 August India and Pakistan came into being. The work that Cripps had campaigned for since the 1920s was complete. It is tempting to believe that this was down to Mountbatten, a more expert negotiator than Cripps, who had, after all, had three goes at India. The truth is, however, that Cripps had always been hampered by the British position. Under Chamberlain he had no formal remit, under Churchill he was dealing with a man who believed that Indians were 'a beastly people with a beastly religion',[39] and under Attlee, while he had a Cabinet that dearly wanted independence, the intractable problems of the paramountcy of the princely states and the partition question remained. What changed was the British attitude, not the negotiator, and the worries that existed in 1942 about the North-West Frontier states remain unresolved today. Nevertheless Indian Independence gave the Attlee Government a degree of cachet with the Americans, who had favoured Independence, especially from Britain, for many years, and the Labour Government felt suitably grateful to Mountbatten. Indeed when the Mountbattens returned to Britain and were hard up the Government put forward a Married Woman (Restraint upon Expectation) Bill to enable Edwina to access funds in a trust. The Bill was opposed by anti-Independence Tories and supported by Cripps, so Mountbatten maintained, because he had told Stafford that the only alternative was for Edwina and him to divorce and live together in sin. 'Stafford said that the Government would go to great lengths to avoid our having to take such steps; so that is always a threat to hold over them.'[40]

Cripps's interlude in India took nearly a full four months out of his period at the Board of Trade, yet on his return he immersed himself immediately in the resurgent problems of the balance of payments. His remit was broad and in one session, 1946–7, he spoke on tractor production, hedging gloves, rubber boots, artists brushes, timber, pineapples, mattresses, gelatine, cellophane, chlorine, clothing coupons, footwear, bedding, horticulture, herring barrels, loofahs and glycerine. In part this was just the nature of the brief, but the mere fact that his Hansard Index entry for the Parliamentary session covers twenty-three columns, while Dalton covered eighteen, Bevin eight and Morrison five, demonstrates the sheer volume of his Parliamentary work. In addition there were the Board of Trade initiatives, the British Industries Fair of May 1947, the development of the British Institute of Management, the Council of Industrial Design, the initial preparations for the 1951 exhibition (later annexed by Morrison).

He also took a very direct interest in the British film industry, although the intervention of both Cripps and Dalton, and later Wilson, was not entirely successful. The situation in the British film industry was almost identical to that of nearly every other British industry. As with cotton the British market was heavily dependent on American imports. So these years which saw the number of cinema attendances in Britain soar meant that the Gaumonts and other cinemas notched up an enormous balance of payments deficit with Hollywood, while extravagance and poor management of the British studios meant that production was slow. In order to tackle this directly in the spring of 1947 Dalton and Cripps began to suggest a 25 per cent *ad valorem* tax on all American film imports. J. Arthur Rank caught wind of these plans when he was on holiday in Hollywood, visiting his grandchild, and on his return to England in July remonstrated with Morrison: 'I do know something about Americans. I know they'll be bloody mad with you. Perhaps you'll save sixteen million dollars; but you'll have to spend sixty million getting back the goodwill you'll lose.'[41] In fact Dalton and Cripps had their eyes on rather larger figures of £57 million out of the £70 million imports, and at the end of July the import tax was imposed not at 25 per cent but at 75. Rank was right. The Americans were furious and an immediate embargo was placed on exports to Britain, which meant that the British cinemas all started to show the old stockpiled American films already in their cellars, for which they still had to pay. The Exchequer earned some more money, but the dollar export was scarcely affected, while the public had to put up with repeats. As Wilson later put it 'we were actually paying $50 million for the privilege of seeing *Hellzapoppin*' for the third time and *Ben Hur* for the 23rd.'[42]

The problem now was how to get the British film industry to provide enough films for the home market so that cinemas would not have to resort to repeats. According to John Davis, Arthur Rank's lieutenant at the Rank Organisation which dominated the British production industry, Cripps and Wilson took the rather direct approach of visiting Rank in October and telling him 'this is a serious problem for England and we need your help to increase your production of good British movies.'[43] Partly because Cripps and Wilson had appealed to his sense of loyalty and perhaps also out of a friendship with Cripps himself, Rank agreed to front the major production drive and committed to make forty-seven new films in the next twelve months. As with much of the over-hasty production drive of the period in other industries, much of what was produced was dross with notable exceptions such as Laurence Olivier's *Hamlet, Kind Hearts and Coronets* and *Passage to Pimlico*, all of which were completed in 1948. By the time many of these rapidly-produced British films were ready for release, however, Government policy had changed and the 75 per cent tax had been abolished out of deference to American Treasury pressure and British public opinion. This left the British film industry exposed on its commercial flank because having effectively been guaranteed a protected market they ended up competing with Hollywood on terms, only protected by a quota system – and even that was abolished after six months. Undoubtedly Rank felt betrayed by the vacillations of the Government. Stafford had spoken at a dinner in his honour in early 1947 and said that he appreciated 'very fully the difficulties of giving a free and unhampered rein to artistic genius while at the same time keeping the operations of your enterprise within the bounds of commercial sanity',[44] yet Government policy had made it almost impossible to operate within any commercial bounds at all. If this was democratic planning what would deregulation be like?

What is particularly interesting about the Board of Trade's involvement with the film industry throughout this period, though, is not only the vaguaries of the democratic planning policy but also the especially personal interest Cripps took both as President of the Board of Trade and as Chancellor. Despite his reputation for asceticism he was, if anything, rather more filmstruck than his junior colleague and formed a strong friendship with one of Rank's most flamboyant producers, Filippo Del Giudice, who was notorious for living with his Norwegian mistress Greta Gynt and for throwing wildly extravagant parties. Indeed Del Giudice was cited by Hugh Gaitskell as evidence of Stafford's appalling judgment of character, though what may have actually drawn the two men together was either a shared religious faith (Del Giudice ended up in a monastery) or Isobel's interest in some of the films he produced (which included *Blithe Spirit, In Which We Serve,* and *Brief Encounter).* Certainly Wilson, much later, in his rather catty *Memoirs,* blamed Stafford's apparent infatuation on Isobel:

> The truth was that Sir Stafford was not austere when it came to the financing of films. More accurately, Stafford was a soft touch when his wife Isobel came on to the set. She was a warm-hearted lady, a devoted supporter and indeed leader of many good causes. Amongst these was encouragement in season and out for an immigrant film producer named Del Giudice. Cripps, who was counting every penny for the welfare state ... was ready to raid the tills for Del.[45]

Certainly by now Stafford and Isobel were an effective

political team. Once the family had grown up Isobel took on much more than was normally expected of a politician's wife, taking a lead in charitable ventures and often replying to Stafford's personal and political mail, meeting up with old friends, calming relations with Bevan or with Attlee through Jennie Lee or Vi Attlee. Indeed she had also been a very active Chair of the British United Aid to China Fund, for whom she travelled in June 1946, just as Stafford returned from India, to see Chiang Kai-Shek. She was even awarded a GBE in 1946 for her Chinese work. Their small flat at 3 Whitehall Court in London meant that throughout the period at the Board of Trade, apart from during their separate travels in 1946, Isobel and Stafford saw more of each other than at any other stage in their married life and they undoubtedly felt their work was one and the same.

All of this made for the most concentrated and consistently applied period of Stafford's political career to date. There was one task, one message and one goal. It was exactly the kind of environment in which Stafford flourished, his meticulous mind attracted to integrity, clarity and consistency, and he was an indubitable success.

23

Economic Affairs

Hugh Dalton called 1947 his 'annus horrendus' and it certainly started badly, with the coldest winter since 1881, assisting if not actually precipitating a fuel crisis that not only threatened people's lives but also undermined the production drive, with factories idle and people stranded at home. Problems in the coal industry had been spotted on the horizon by Douglas Jay early in 1946 and Gaitskell had been appointed Shinwell's Parliamentary Secretary in May partly because Attlee, Dalton and Cripps all shared a feeling that the mines were in need of more careful attention than either Shinwell or Gaitskell's predecessor, Will Foster, were willing or able to give them. Yet the Ministry itself, and the Minister, were resolute that the miners would pull through. Shinwell gave constantly optimistic reports which suggested that whatever the civil service were saying about poor prospects for the industry, he knew better. The miners would work harder out of personal respect for him.

In fact, of course, the Ministry was totally absorbed at the time with the laborious process of nationalisation, and though Gaitskell was made fully aware of the impending disaster by both Jay and James Meade in the Economic Section of the Cabinet Office, he either failed to communicate the problem with sufficient urgency to his boss, or else Shinwell was too emotionally involved in the industry to see what was coming.

Peter Hennessy has noted perspicaciously the emotional hold the mines held over Labour: 'Coal never lost its symbolic, almost romantic, place in the Labour movement as the industry where the excesses of capitalism had left blood in the seams.'[1] But such romanticism served the Party ill. The industry needed a kick up the pants, especially if growing consumption was to be met out of increased production rather than stockpiles. Instead Labour patted itself on the back as the National Coal Board signs were hammered into place on 1 January. Yet in December coal stocks were being eaten into far faster than the Ministry had anticipated, with 607,000 tons a week disappearing, against the forecast of 514,000.

Cripps was less sentimental than most about the mines and though it was not part of his brief he was drafted in to resolve the problems of over-consumption and under-production in the new year. On 13 January he announced the 'Cripps plan'. It was a similar trick to that employed at the MAP with the 'realistic programme'. For it gave the appearance of no nonsense honesty and sought to sell tough cutbacks to the country on the basis that 'at least we're telling you it as it really is'. Power stations were to be given absolute priority for coal, industry would have to accept half their previous quota and only those supplying essential goods would receive any additional supplies. It was a harsh East wind that put paid to the Cripps plan, carrying with it first sleet, then a blizzard, with hard, hard frost and bitter cold. There were fifteen foot snowdrifts. London suffered a whole week of 16° Fahrenheit of frost. A third of Britain's sheep froze to death. With towns and villages cut off for days it was impossible to get fuel supplies through, and to keep out the cold ever more coal was thrown on the fire. The plan had been fatally flawed. Cripps had taken Shinwell's statistics at face value and even with a balmier winter it is likely that the crisis would not have deepened. As it was this was the coldest February for three centuries, and Cripps must have been reminded more of

Moscow than of Britain. Anger with Shinwell mounted in the Cabinet and on 6 February he was forced by Attlee, at the insistence of Cripps and Dalton, into being entirely frank about the problems. New announcements were made. There would be domestic power cuts, parts of the country would have no electricity for industry and some power stations would be closed. The results were disastrous. Factories closed. Nearly 800,000 people were laid off. And by mid-February 2.25 million were unemployed. It was not until the weather improved that unemployment figures began to creep back down.

The effect on Cripps was marked. For a start he was furious with Shinwell, although he should perhaps have been warned by Attlee that the figures upon which he was basing his plan were entirely false. He demanded Shinwell's resignation, though Attlee refused to move him until the autumn. Even now Shinwell could not help passing the buck and he blamed the weather, the Ministry of Transport, the fact that there had been no blueprint for nationalisation when he took over. Cripps would have agreed with Lord Swinton that the crisis was due 'not to an act of God, but the inactivity of Emmanuel'.[2] What particularly angered Cripps was the fact that he unnecessarily had to squander political capital carefully built up. When he said something people believed him, but with the apparent failure of the Cripps plan this was no longer so certain.

It also affected production, for not only were factories closed down due to the crisis, but whole production schedules were thrown into disarray. Exports dropped by 25 per cent and though Hilary Marquand, the Secretary for Overseas Trade, had reported at the start of the month that the 1946 target of £750 million had been exceeded by £150 million, there was a real fear that this setback would drastically affect the 1947 balance of payments. A proper supply of fuel was essential to maintaining a high level of production and Shinwell had failed to deliver, just as the National Coal Board came into existence. Inevitably the result would be an undermining of the export drive, of the nationalisation programme and of Cripps's own standing.

A few days later, on 10 March, Cripps had an opportunity to restore his reputation for fiscal rectitude. Morrison was ill and the first Economic Survey, which Cripps had himself conceived of and drafted, had to be presented to the House. Cripps deputised for Morrison and spoke impressively for six minutes short of two hours. It was Cripps's first outing on the economic front but it was impressive and restored his reputation overnight. The problems, as he exposed them, were much as they had been since 1945: too much expenditure on imports, too little progress in exports. If inflation was to be kept low, a wages policy was essential and if there were to be imports they should be from soft currency areas. It was no longer just a matter of short-term answers, but a long-term approach was vital. The Government wanted now to be more proactive. Full-time planning units were being set up in every Government department and they would be co-ordinated by a small central planning board, while the arrangements for 'ensuring the co-operation of industry in the planning organisation'[3] was being reviewed. In a phrase reminiscent of his 1930s distinction between Fascist planning and a Socialist programme, he again saw

an essential difference between totalitarian and democratic planning. The former subordinates all individual desires and preferences to the demands of the state. For this purpose, it uses various methods of compulsion upon the individual which deprive him of the freedom of choice. Such methods may be necessary even in a democratic country during the extreme emergency of a great war. Thus the British people gave their wartime Government the power to direct labour. But, in normal times, the people of a democratic country will not give up their freedom of choice to their Government. A democratic Government must therefore conduct its economic planning in a manner which preserves the maximum possible freedom of choice to the individual citizen.[4]

This meant that any effective economic planning had to rely upon the individual co-operation of both sides of industry.

Democratic planning . . . is something towards which we must feel our way with care and we must not be driven along the path upon which some would apparently have us travel of compulsion and direction, or into the jungle of chaotic failure which luxuriated in the aimless and unplanned laissez-faire atmosphere of the period between the wars.[5]

In nearly every regard this speech was identical to anything any one of his senior colleagues could have said. Nor was it markedly different from anything he had himself been arguing since 1945. Still there is the stress on a mixed economy, avoiding, as far as possible, compulsory planning mechanisms. Yet there was a new emphasis. For Cripps, earlier than most, had discerned that the Government still had major economic problems. The production battle had not yet been won, but the emotional ties of the war were weakening month by month. Controls, especially rationing, upon which the balance of payments strategy depended so heavily, would have to go eventually unless the Government was to fritter away all its electoral support.

What was essential, then, was the mastery of the economic front with more than just exhortations to greater effort so that 'History will recall these months through which we are now passing, as a great opportunity, boldly seized and courageously undertaken by the whole British people.'[6] The trouble was, though this was not yet admitted publicly, the structure for dealing effectively with the economy simply did not exist. The new central planning staff was a step forward, but the economic brief still lay with the lackadaisical Lord President's Committee. Equally feeble was its supplementary body, the Ministerial Economic Planning Committee, which had been a first attempt to force the pace and which brought together Cripps, Dalton, Morrison and Isaacs. At its first meeting Cripps had pointed out that 'the Government had not yet formulated a plan for the employment of the national resources and could not hope to do so for several months to come'[7] and his increasing frustration began to show. Morrison's illness further highlighted the Government's failure to deal with the problem, while Attlee almost paraded his economic disinterest. The answer, so Cripps began to believe and espouse, lay in creating a separate Ministry which would have direct responsibility for the whole planning of the economy. The new central planning board should report to a new economic overlord who would drive through the 'National Economic Plan'.

Events soon gave evidence to back up Cripps's worries, which were shared by the Chancellor. Dalton had warned the Cabinet as early as October 1946 that 'we are using up the United States and Canadian loans, and our other prospective external financial resources for 1947 and 1948, much too fast. This results from . . . the rise in American prices and from the heavy and continuing drain due to military and political expenditure outside this country.'[8] Again the direct problem was dollars – the indirect problem, the balance of payments. Yet few steps had been taken to rectify the position and a mixture of the fuel crisis and a continuing rise in US prices had exacerbated things. Dollars were now happily being spent on foodstuffs, on raw materials and on the overseas commitment at a shocking rate. In the first six months of the year $315 million were spent every month. In the three weeks from 20 July first $106 million, then $126 million, and finally $127 million were spent. At this rate the US loan would not last beyond November at the outside and might well be exhausted by September, leaving Britain with only her pound and gold reserves to stave off the creditors. Meanwhile convertibility of the pound, as agreed in the US loan, came into force on 15 July, precipitating an even greater flood of dollars. Foolishly, the Treasury had advised Dalton that any possible run on the pound could be absorbed, despite the fact that export targets had not been met and it was almost inevitable that as soon as countries that held sterling could do so they were likely to exchange it for dollars in order to buy the American goods for which they had been waiting. Convertibility, at first slowly and then rapidly, accelerated the flow of dollars out of the country and on 30 July an emergency meeting of the five senior ministers was held to prepare for the next day's Cabinet meeting. Dalton proposed a series of cutbacks, in imports, in foreign commitments, in the armed forces. Bevin, who had dined over well, was opposed. Morrison stormed out, angered by Bevin's 'drunken monologue'[9] and the next day Dalton, Bevan and Cripps told Attlee they would resign unless Dalton's measures were adopted.

Dalton complained that Attlee showed 'no power of gripping and guiding the talk'[10] and it is clear that Attlee had much to answer for in the whole crisis. Bevin's position was clear. He refused to countenance any diminution in the armed forces and dallied far too long in getting men back into civvy street out of a belief that any military cutbacks would signal to the world that Britain was no longer a world power. This cost the balance of payments dearly both in terms of the dollars spent abroad to keep the armed forces in service and in terms of the labour that was not available for productive work in Britain. Attlee, who was always closer to Bevin than to any other of his senior ministers, never managed to face the problem, and

Dalton, Morrison and Cripps were thrown together as allies, determined to face the reality that something had to give.

Give it did. Dalton's measures, in part, were agreed and in a special two-day debate on the State of the Nation on 6–7 August the Government announced new austerities to try and slow the drain down. The miners were to work an extra half an hour a day, food imports from hard currency areas were to be slashed by £12 million a month and the petrol ration was to be cut by a third. Still there were only minor cuts in the overseas budget, which in 1947 cost the nation a ludicrous £200 million. Still the drain continued – $150 million in August. So on 17 August Dalton decided to persuade his colleagues of the need to suspend convertibility. Cripps came to see him in the early afternoon, already 'firmly in favour' of suspension, though also threatening to resign 'unless the Cabinet will face the consequences, in ration cuts etc., of our latest move'.[11] The two of them went on to see Bevin, who succumbed, and that evening the proposal was agreed by the Cabinet. The next day Wilfrid Eady flew to Washington, to tell the Americans, and the announcement was made on the evening of the 19th, to take effect the following day. Four days later more cuts were announced, suspending foreign travel, abolishing the basic petrol ration, restricting public dinners and cutting the meat ration.

In the meantime the Americans had begun to realise that their own economic future relied on a healthy European market, and Dalton in the middle of June noted that the new US Secretary of State, General George Marshall, 'gives the impression of wanting to do something big'.[12] This 'something big' was to be Labour's life-support system through to 1950 – Marshall Aid, or to give it its proper title, the 'European Recovery Programme', whereby some $17 billion were disbursed across Europe to be set against identified strategic economic targets. Britain alone received $2.7 billion, a billion more than Germany.

It was a development that Cripps seized on in his winding up of the debate on the first day of the debate on the new measures. 'A great many small and economically separate nations cannot deal individually with this situation,' he announced. 'None of us is large enough in ourselves to command the necessary resources. That is why the suggestion put forward by Mr Marshall for an integration of European economy is to be welcomed, so that Europe as a whole can tackle the problem of the unbalance of trade and productivity.'[13] As in his speech in Morrison's stead he plugged the need for a fuller economic programme. 'We must not allow ourselves to be blinded to long-term developments by the intensity of the short-term difficulties ... We must, therefore, face long-term measures for adjusting the European economy and our economy, if we are ever to free Europe and our own country from a continuing dependence upon the generosity of the Western hemisphere.'[14] The reality was that Britain now had to operate in a world which had changed from a sellers' to a buyers' market. Expanding British markets was becoming all the more difficult , so 'the cutting down of imports can, and must, in the emergency make some contribution to easing the present situation, but we must not try to solve our difficulties by a permanent lowering standard of living of the people of this country, which, of course, such a cut implies.'[15]

Cripps ended his speech in style. Dalton indeed recorded, 'I have never heard him better. He showed great vigour and energy and restored to our own ranks a much greater sense of confidence.'[16] Cripps declaimed,

The time for the realisation of our aims and hopes has been set back by the inescapable economic facts of world development. We can offer no immediate prospect of relief. The struggle of production, the battle of the balance of payments, is as tough a proposition as any this country has ever faced, and there is no easy way out. Production, and production alone, can find us relief in our immediate situation. It is no part of the British character to resign ourselves to such difficulties or to fail to take the measures, however hard, to overcome them. It has been truly said that by our faith we can move mountains. It is by our faith in ourselves, in our country, in the free democratic traditions for which the people of this country have for centuries fought and battled, and for which they must fight again as willingly on the economic front as upon the oceans, on the land and in the air, it is by our faith in the deep spiritual values that we acknowledge in our Christian faith, that we shall be enabled and inspired to move the present mountains of our difficulties, and so emerge into that new and fertile plain of prosperity which we shall travel in happiness only as the result of our own efforts and our own vision.[17]

Yet again the Cripps persona came to the fore. Personal sacrifice, eternal verities, hard work, up-front honesty, patriotism, faith – herein lay Britain's future, and Cripps, more than any other on the front bench, had the heady mixture coursing through his veins.

The convertibility crisis, and Cripps's reception in the debate of 7-8 August, redoubled his concern about the failure to right the economic ship. Now he blamed both Attlee and Morrison, two of his oldest allies, and there was renewed talk of replacing the Prime Minister. The only person – perhaps apart from himself, though he never mentioned this – who could really front the economic battle was Bevin and he should either do so as economic overlord or as PM – or as both. It was an idea put by Dalton to Bevin on the way back from the Durham Miners' Gala on 26 July and again by Cripps when he and Dalton went to see the Foreign Secretary on the day of the convertibility decision. Bevin's reply, 'What's Clem ever done to me?' might have dissuaded Cripps from going further.

It did not. On 5 September he took the matter up again, suggesting that Morrison, Dalton and himself, should 'go together to Attlee and tell him he ought to resign in favour of Bevin. Attlee would then have to agree, and, at a Party meeting, Morrison could move and I [Dalton] could second Bevin, and that would settle it.'[18] This was an odd choice. Morrison was well known to hate Bevin, while Bevin had already stated his loyalty to Attlee. Moreover Cripps had supported Morrison in 1945, so why the change? For a start Morrison was unwell, having had a heart attack earlier in the year, and both Cripps and Dalton blamed the overall failure to tackle the economy in a programmatic manner on him. Dalton maintained that Attlee and Cripps agreed with him that Morrison, 'cannot handle these planning problems . . . He eats out of the hand of his twittering little bird-watcher (Max Nicholson), and . . . reads out briefs in Cabinet without really understanding them.'[19]

Nevertheless Cripps went to see Morrison, who replied that while he would be delighted to see the Prime Minister replaced he 'thought he himself had better qualifications than Bevin'.[20] Morrison sounded Dalton out, who was similarly reluctant to put his head above the parapet. Both of them had already got into trouble in July when they had been implicated in an attempted coup by George Brown and Gordon-Walker. So Morrison decided to sit and wait. Cripps now tried a new ploy, this time telling Dalton that he would go and see Attlee himself and persuade him to stand down.

If Attlee took this reasonably well, and said that the suggestion was so important that he must consult with his colleagues, Cripps would be willing to wait . . . for a few days. If Attlee was 'tempery' and brushed it aside, Cripps would say that he [Cripps] must resign. If he resigned – in addition to the usual exchange of letters, in which he would speak, in general terms, of the need for 'a major reconstruction of the government' – he would hold a Press Conference, or hold a meeting, and say that he thought Bevin should be Prime Minister. This would start a commotion in the country, in the Press and in the Party. A Party meeting would probably have to be summoned at once. There was a danger that Bevin wouldn't stand, unless he felt sure of winning. On the other hand, he might be greatly encouraged to stand by a good Press. If Morrison won at the Party meeting, Cripps doubted whether he would be able to form a Government... If Attlee was maintained as Leader at the Party meeting, the Government would stagger on for a few months longer and then collapse.[21]

This was vintage Cripps. Gross over-confidence mixed with a mildly hysterical tendency to use the resignation weapon at the slightest provocation. It was brave, ambitious, foolhardy, arrogant, ill-considered – all the things he had been throughout the thirties and in 1942. Another Prime Minister would probably have sacked him on the spot. Attlee decided to promote him instead. Here there are at least two versions of the story. In Attlee's version when Cripps had finished speaking he rang up Bevin and said, 'Stafford's here: he says you want to change your job,' to which Bevin replied that he did not want to move from the Foreign Office. Because Cripps's argument had been that the need for a change was because only Bevin could tackle the economic front, Attlee then suggested that it would be better if Cripps took over a new role to do precisely that, effectively taking a large chunk of Morrison's job. In the other version Attlee's question to Bevin was different, 'Ernie, Stafford's here. He says you want my job.' When Bevin replied that he did not, Attlee agreed, 'Thought not.' In a third version there was no dramatic phone call and Attlee sent William Whiteley, the Chief Whip, to sound out the Foreign Secretary.

This last version was that of Patrick Gordon-Walker, once a member of the 1942 Cripps succession plot, and now, having won a by-election at Smethwick, Morrison's PPS. It was expressed in a letter to Morrison later in September, by which time the appointment of Cripps to his new post was already known. In his diary, however, Gordon-Walker maintained that in order to protect his own back Morrison drafted letters condemning the plan which were placed with his secretary in case the Cripps challenge went badly wrong. Gordon-Walker then told Morrison to tell the Chief Whip of what Cripps planned, because he thought 'it ought to get to the PM',[22] while he was to discuss it with the Chair of the Parliamentary Labour Party, Maurice Webb.

Whichever version is true – and the idea of Attlee getting Whiteley to see Bevin seems as unlikely as the phone call – the incident poignantly displayed the childishness of Cripps and the magnanimity and political astuteness of Attlee. One can just imagine the proudly bold Cripps telling his erstwhile ally Attlee that he had to go, without having a single soldier prepared to back him up – and the effortless Attlee, who undoubtedly already knew of the moves afoot (not least because the *Daily Mail* had run the story attributing it to a source close to Isobel), neatly killing two birds with one stone: the man who would be kingmaker appointed to solve the problem he had himself identified; the one man who was prepared to put himself on the line given the task of making austerity attractive. As Kenneth Harris points out, the plot made no difference to Attlee's relations with the plotters. He never mentioned it in his autobiography or in his letters and 'He was as fond of Cripps as ever, and was no more distrustful of Dalton and Morrison than he had ever been.'[23]

Still Attlee had to explain the move to Morrison, now on holiday. 'I propose, therefore,' he wrote, 'to make a Minister for Economic Affairs, whose job would be to coordinate our economic efforts at home and abroad and to see to the carrying out of the economic plan under the general direction of [the new Economic Committee]. I propose that Cripps should fill this post.'[24] There were other changes. The Committee on Economic Planning and the Lord President's Committee were to be amalgamated into the Economic Policy Committee which would consist of the Big Five plus Addison and was to be run by Cripps's old colleague from the MAP, Edwin Plowden, the Government's Chief Planning Officer. Harold Wilson, who had replaced Hilary Marquand as Overseas Trade Secretary, was appointed President of the Board of Trade, at thirty-one the youngest member of the Cabinet since Lord Henry Petty in 1806. This, one of Attlee's bolder appointments, was thanks to Cripps who, according to Gordon-Walker, citing a conversation with Maurice, had 'proposed that Harold Wilson should be at the B of T which would make it a subordinate department under C'.[25]

The appointment of a younger minister was deliberate, and though Morrison had also urged Wilson on Attlee, it was Cripps's opinion, so Attlee later owned, that 'fortified' him.[26] Cripps made other requests, which soon necessitated a fairly major Cabinet reshuffle and took several weeks, during which Cripps remained at the Board of Trade. Both he and Dalton, as well as Whiteley, insisted that Shinwell must now finally go. Gaitskell, the young Cripps/Dalton nominee, was bumped up the ladder, though not into the Cabinet. John Wilmot, once Dalton's PPS and since 1945 the Minister of Supply, was replaced, again at Cripps's request, by George Strauss, his old Popular Front compatriot. When the reshuffle was finally announced, on 8 October, it was evident that Cripps had not only a new job, but a new empire, covering Supply, labour, fuel and power. As Gaitskell put it, 'Cripps wants to run the whole thing with HW, GS and myself as his lieutenants.'[27] It was a pattern that was noted by Robert Hall at the Economic Section of the Cabinet Office: 'Cripps has now got three young men whom he seems to trust – in the Board of Trade, Supply and Fuel and Power.' He acknowledged too that the Cripps ascendancy was assured, 'It won't be for lack of power if Cripps fails – he has all the key posts.'[28]

Though the reshuffle took time, partly thanks to key figures being on holiday, there was immediately much to do. On the day that Cripps had fronted Attlee his Export Programme had gone through the Cabinet, surprisingly without too much fuss. Now there was the Import Programme, with cuts in foodstuffs, to get through both the Cabinet and the House of Commons. There was a meeting of the Big Five at Chequers where Cripps's strategy for halving the dollar gap by the end of 1948 was agreed before being put to the Cabinet the following day. Strachey, backed up by Bevan, vociferously opposed any food cuts, but the programme was agreed and presented to the Commons on the 23rd. This was the most drastic of all the speeches Cripps had to give as it would mean a real drop in the standard of living. Yet the *New Statesman* greeted the new Minister for Economic Affairs, 'The Cripps speech brought home, much more clearly than had been said before, the extreme gravity of Great Britain's international position. It also gave the impression that the problem is at last being courageously and realistically handled.'[29]

Meanwhile Cripps and Dalton had started discussions about the supplementary Budget that Dalton was going to give in November as part of the attempt to plaster over the gaping hole in the nation's economic affairs. Dalton described them as 'useful' although others were aware that there were tensions between them which might easily flare up at some later point. Burke Trend recalled that 'Dalton was wary of Cripps. Cripps seemed to want to plan the economy without any concern about the domestic policy for which Dalton cared.'[30] Harold Nicolson went further, recording a conversation with Amery in which he had argued that there would soon be a conflict between the two, 'The former will wish to tell the public the harsh truth; the latter will wish to soap them over with half-lies. It is extraordinary how much respect Cripps arouses. He is really the leading figure in the country today!'[31]

As events turned out there was little time for any conflict to arise. Cripps's import programme was likely to put some inflationary pressure on the economy so he and Dalton worked together on a deflationary supplementary Budget which was to be given on 12 November. Dalton, who had declared himself 'a bit below my optimum' and had indeed suffered from mild depression and a desire to resign for several months, lunched with his PPS Douglas Jay before going to the Lords, where the Commons were still meeting due to the wartime bombing of the Commons Chamber. It was not a long Budget, though it was easily his most controversial, increasing taxes as a deliberate measure to try and bring a halt to inflation. He expected to raise an extra £48 million by the end of the financial year and £208 million in a full year. It was, as Ben Pimlott has made clear, a ground-breaking Budget, primarily because it was the first time that the Budget had been used to determine the economy.

On his way into the Chamber, however, Dalton loitered for a few minutes and got into conversation with a journalist from one of the London evening papers, the *Star*. The journalist was well known to Dalton, one of his two or three best friends in the Parliamentary lobby, and when he was asked what he had in store Dalton told him, 'in a single sentence, what the principal points would be – no more on tobacco; a penny on beer; something on dogs and pools but not on horses; increase in Purchase Tax, but only on articles now taxable; Profits Tax doubled'.[32] The journalist, recognising a scoop when he saw one, immediately dashed it off to the paper while Dalton went into the Chamber to start his speech. The details appeared, as a stop press item, several minutes before Dalton actually announced them. The following day, when Dalton was made aware of what had happened, he tendered his resignation at a meeting with Morrison, Cripps and the Chief Whip. Attlee turned it down. Dalton again met with Attlee later in the day and repeated his offer. Attlee, so Dalton recorded, 'replied that he felt he must [accept it] but I was moved to see that he was much more deeply moved than I was at this moment. He said he hated – hated – he repeated the word several times – hated to lose me.'[33] Finally Attlee accepted the inevitable and allowed Dalton to resign, instantly replacing him with the only possible alternative, Cripps.

The press had been suggesting for several weeks that there were splits between Cripps and Dalton. The *Observer*, who now welcomed the new appointment, reckoned that 'Sir Stafford . . . was insistent that drastic measures were necessary, and there can be little doubt that he found Mr Dalton's proposals inadequate. It can be taken for granted that the next Budget will make the present one look like a jollification.'[34] In similar vein the *Manchester Guardian* maintained that 'Mr Dalton would always yield to the call of popularity. Sir Stafford Cripps will always listen to the call of conscience.'[35] Dalton, however, dismissed this as

> all quite baseless. He and I had had serious differences in the past, before the war, as was publicly known. But over the last twelve exceedingly difficult months, no two members of the Government had seen more closely eye to eye on all questions than Cripps and myself. I had wanted him to be Minister of Economic Affairs and had told the Prime Minister so, before the appointment was made. Since it was made, there had been no friction between us; we had worked in the closest harmony.[36]

Ben Pimlott's view of the Budget crisis is not complimentary to Cripps. Broadly speaking he reckons that Dalton's accident was just an excuse for his dismissal, and that he was the courageous Chancellor who pushed through the first Budget that would actually switch from using control mechanisms to macro mechanism to restrict the economy. Yet Dalton's expression of indebtedness to Cripps was genuine, and it is certainly true that without Cripps's egging him on to be honest about the economic situation it would have been more difficult to win the battles in the Cabinet, let alone in the Commons. It was the combination of the two that made the November Budget possible, and it was Cripps's measures, moved only days earlier, that made the Budget measures vital. Dalton was hardly the only tough politician prepared to make difficult decisions. Moreover Cripps had made it clear himself in the Economic Survey debate and in the August speech that the whole way in which the economy was presented to the House, the way economic factors were to be used and played, was to change. No longer would it be tight physical controls – totalitarian planning – but the Budget, manipulating the economy by more distant strings – democratic planning – that would be the Government's way of working. The Government's main instrument was to be demand management through the annual budget rather than any coherent planning of resources.

One final change levied against Cripps at this point was made by Gaitskell, still a Dalton protégé. 'Cripps showed no remorse and I could not help feeling that he had now satisfied one more ambition by becoming Chancellor.'[37] The truth is that Cripps showed no remorse because he never showed remorse. When he felt guilty, his acknowledgement of guilt was to act it out in yet further hard work and more early mornings. Dalton was by now his firmest ally and whilst Cripps might have fought for Dalton's remaining as Chancellor, and Dalton might have managed to survive, the truth was that in straitened circumstances the Government needed an unimpeachable Chancellor. Dalton had lost his edge during the year. He was weary. Cripps may have made the correct assumption that the best way to ensure the National Economic Plan was to take the opportunity of combining the post of

Chancellor with that of Minister for Economic Affairs. Just as Churchill remained silent over the question of who should succeed Chamberlain, so for Cripps now silence was the surest way to Downing Street – either No. 10 or No. 11.

24

The First Modern Chancellor

Fortune, Providence, hazard or Stafford's own political manoeuvring placed him in November 1947 in the most powerful
position of any British Chancellor bar Pitt or Gladstone, and
even before he moved into No. 11 Downing Street he set about
requisitioning and deploying the resources he reckoned he
needed to do the job he knew needed to be done. Morrison
had failed as the economic overlord because he had no real
grasp of economics or understanding of the private sector.
Dalton had been converted to the task of economic regeneration too late, and when he successively identified the sharks of
the dollar gap and inflation in the economic ocean he neither
had the Cabinet support nor the personal clout to be able to
carry through the necessary measures. Cripps had identified
the problems at least as early as the start of 1947 when he
put together the Economic Survey and he knew that if he was
not to flail in the same waters as Dalton he needed strong
collegiate support.

The September negotiations, designed to create a team for
Cripps as Minister of Economic Affairs, bore the ripest of
fruits with Cripps now as Chancellor.

The team was in two parts. On the one hand there were
the Ministers, many of whom had been appointed
specifically at Cripps's request to work in tandem with him,
amongst whom were the pick of Labour's new intake. Cripps

has often been accused of being a poor team player and an appalling judge of character, but in the period between the challenge to Attlee and Christmas 1947 he created certainly the most economically competent and perhaps the most talented team of individuals the Party has ever produced. Harold Wilson, the rather dry and ultimately devious economist, had been appointed President of the Board of Trade at the same time as Cripps had taken the Economic Affairs portfolio and was to follow extremely closely in his footsteps for the next two years. Hugh Gaitskell, another youngster, was now promoted to Minister for Fuel and Power. Gaitskell had originally been a Dalton protégé, but Cripps had spotted him as early as August 1945 when he approached him about the possibility of a job in the Government. Gaitskell had actually been an absentee candidate in the election having suffered a minor heart attack, and he was excessively honest in saying that he still needed time to recover. In fact, they had met years earlier when Gaitskell had won the Winchester essay competition sponsored by Cripps. Another Wykehamist (and an exact contemporary of Richard Crossman) also joined the team, as Economic Secretary, Douglas Jay, who had won a by-election in 1946 after spending the war as a civil servant first in the Ministry of Supply and then the Board of Trade and the first year of Attlee's premiership as his personal assistant. The new Paymaster-General, also in the Treasury team, was another young economist, Hilary Marquand, who completed a set of young Parliamentary recruits with genuine under-standing of economics.

Also part of the Cripps team from the outset were the older statesmen Strauss and Strachey, whose roles at Supply and Food were vital to the core economic project and who were now officially reporting to him in his capacity as Minister for Economic Affairs. Both of these were, of course, longstanding colleagues from the thirties and had suffered similar public ostracism in the run-up to the war but were now fully rehabilitated.

Within weeks of his appointment, Cripps had not only recruited this brood. He had also formed this disparate group into a team held together almost entirely by a common sense of loyalty to Cripps. Dalton had brought many of the team into the political world, but it was now Stafford who reaped where his predecessor had sown. Cripps suggested that the group should meet regularly for a meal, and for the next two years every second Thursday saw the same team of Ministers dine, debate and argue the toss together. Gaitskell was so taken with the group that he resolved in December 'we must now try and bring Evan [Durbin] into the inner Cripps circle. If we can do this I shall really begin to feel quite happy about the Government.'[1]

This team was the backbone of the Cripps era. It had intellectual muscle, it understood economics, and it could, for the most part, get its way in Cabinet. It acted as an informal caucus, rehearsing ideas and issues well before they were placed before the Cabinet or the public, and though it was pleasantly free from the cabal-like atmosphere of other groupings, it both grounded Stafford in a younger generation of Labour politicians and gave him the backing for the first time of a fraternity who were genuinely intellectual, in a way he was not. It was also sufficiently diverse within the Labour Party spectrum to enable the rapid dissemination of ideas throughout the Party.

Cripps himself bore great authority. As Robert Hall, the Head of the Economic Secretariat of the Cabinet Office, attested, 'Stafford was by far the strongest and most respected man in the Cabinet'[2] and by now, according to Jay 'the reputations of Attlee and Cripps were the Government's greatest assets'.[3] He also had the great advantage of a long relationship with the single most recalcitrant member of the Cabinet, Bevan, who would often rant and rave against his colleagues, and could only be silenced by the two men in Cabinet he genuinely respected, Cripps and Attlee. Bevan's intense personal admiration for Cripps was a vital part of the cement of the Labour Cabinet through to 1950 and, arguably, it was only when Cripps resigned that Bevan's flights of political fancy became untetherable. Cripps was aware of the effect he had on Bevan and was adept at keeping his old friend in line. He used Isobel, Jennie Lee, officials, or even, on one occasion, Nye's mother in Tredegar, to break unpalatable news to him and although Bevan's ministry fell well outside the economic brief, Cripps soon brought him into the group's discussions, perhaps aware that the spending capacity of the newborn National Health Service was likely to prove one of the most uncontainable elements of any future Budget.

By April 1948 Gaitskell was thoroughly impressed by the new Chancellor:

> At our dinner with the Chancellor last night Bevan was also present and appears to have joined the group. I must say that Stafford is showing much more political acumen than I expected. He is obviously anxious to have Bevan as an ally. And the group is now fairly powerful consisting as it does, apart from the Chancellor and myself, of the Ministers of Health, Supply, Food, the Economic Secretary, Paymaster-general and President of the Board of Trade. I could not help feeling that Stafford was surveying his future Cabinet. It would be surprising if he did not himself expect to be Prime Minister one day. But these things depend more on accident of old age and health than anything else.[4]

The Cripps team was not limited to Parliamentary colleagues, however. One of the first appointments Cripps had engineered, back in the March 1947 discussions of the national economic strategy, was that of Edwin Plowden, his one-time

MAP Chief Executive, as the new Director of Planning in charge of CEPS (the Central Economic Planning Staff). Plowden was an able industrialist and a natural colleague for Cripps, sharing his religious understanding as well as his analysis of the weaknesses of the British economy. Moreover they respected one another. Plowden said quite simply of Cripps, 'He was a wonderful man to work for, and I had a great affection for him'[5] while Hall acknowledged Plowden's pleasure at Cripps's promotion because he was the only member of the Cabinet he respected, having found that 'neither Attlee nor Morrison as "economic overlord" gave any lead to their colleagues'.[6] The feeling was mutual and sustained, despite occasional bouts of sullen depression on the part of Plowden when he felt that the rest of Cabinet was unprepared to take his advice or take tough decisions.

The rest of the official team which provided the machinery of the Cripps era was just as strong as the ministerial one. The Australian Robert Hall, who took over the Economic Secretariat in September from the ailing and dispirited Meade was a Socialist Rhodes Scholar who had been a Second World War civil servant at the Ministry of Supply at the same time as Jay and his 'long sustained and harmonious partnership' with Plowden was the foundation stone upon which the official team was built. Other figures such as Otto Clarke and Leslie Rowan at the Overseas department, Wilfrid Eady on incomes policy, Dennis Rickett, Alan Hitchman and Austin Robinson on the CEPS staff, as well as first Burke Trend and then William Armstrong who ran Cripps's private office, all shared a strong intellectual pedigree and a common conception of the main problems facing the British economy.

It was with this team that Stafford enjoyed something to him unique, for according to Hall 'he commanded almost uncritical respect among senior civil servants, which is very unusual in my experience. He was a wonderful man to work for especially if he respected you.'[7] A large part of the reason he enjoyed this particular rapport was the simple fact that he was able to get his policies through Cabinet. It was a lawyer's skill, the ability to pick up a brief, master it and convince others of an argument that had been drafted by someone else. As Plowden put it, 'It is easy to see the value to the Treasury of having its case argued in the Cabinet and Parliament by a man of Cripps's intellect and ability. In this was, he was the perfect minister. He was also a great communicator. He would regularly address hundreds of Treasury officials in mass meetings at Caxton Hall to explain what he was trying to do and to build up their confidence.'[8] Hall saw it rather more prosaically, 'once he was convinced he made much more of one's arguments than one could oneself and he was almost over-loyal to his subordinates, not only would he take their faults on himself but he tended to think more of them because he was defending them.'[9] Gaitskell was not quite so sure, especially when he later became Cripps's deputy at the Treasury, 'One of the illusions about him which I have discovered really is an illusion is that in bargaining either with his colleagues or with outsiders he is particularly tough . . . I find myself in the rather surprising position of having to stiffen him up.'[10]

Cripps's memory also became legendary among senior officials. Plowden indeed reckoned it to be like that of Macaulay, and cited an extract from Cripps's own journal to prove the point,

> The Express train reached Holyhead about seven in the evening. We sailed as soon as we got on board. The breeze was fresh and adverse and the sea rough. The sun set in glory and then the starlight was like the starlight of the Trades. I put on my great-coat and sat on the deck during the whole voyage. As I could not read, I used an excellent substitute for reading. I went through Paradise Lost in my head. I could still repeat half of it, and that the

best half. I really never enjoyed it so much.[11]

Quite whether Stafford could have recalled whole passages of Milton verbatim is difficult to know. In a computerless age human memory was a far more valuable commodity than today and it was not only Baden-Powell with his Kim's Game that would have taught young boys the skills of memory. And Milton would have been suitable material for Wykehamist rote learning. Yet it seems odd that Cripps should be so open as to let Plowden see his journal. What is equally remarkable, however, is the fact that Plowden recorded Stafford's account without a hint of sarcasm. Even the usually cynical Gaitskell was impressed by Stafford's 'most amazingly keen intelligence' as demonstrated by his performance in a Cabinet meeting where Cripps had summarised a particularly complicated issue: 'Cripps without the slightest difficulty gave the most lucid and detailed account of the problem, which he began by saying, "The minister of Fuel of course knows much more about this than I do". I sat there just gaping with admiration. I whispered to Strachey what an amazing performance it was, and he said, "That's what he does when he gets up at four in the morning."'[12]

One final aspect of Stafford's working style that made him both respected and revered within the civil service was his practice of 'morning prayers', so nicknamed because of the equally devout personal faith of the two protagonists, Cripps and Plowden. Cripps had begun the system of early morning meetings at the Board of Trade, but it was only as Chancellor that it bore its most prolific fruit. The idea was simple, a daily twenty-minute early morning meeting of the ministerial and official team, informal in style, with a variable agenda, enabling everyone to update each other before the day began. Originally Cripps had demanded a 9.00 a.m. start, but civil service objections, based on the fact that normal working hours in the Ministry were from 10.00 a.m. till late, meant that they did not start until 9.30, and 10.00 on Mondays. Even so the hour was considered early, but the fact that Cripps would have been at work already for two or three hours, together with his passion for punctuality, meant everyone did their best to get there on time. 'To be one minute late for a meeting was pardonable, five minutes was not. Senior civil servants were sometimes to be seen running down Great George Street to avoid the sarcastic greeting that often met latecomers.'[13]

These were not the only meetings Cripps brought in. For the first time weekend meetings of the ministerial and official team were held in the run-up to the Budget, suitably, Jay felt, at a rest home for nervous wrecks. There were new committees set up, for Overseas Negotiations, for the Investment Programme, the Import Programme and for Raw Materials, each of which was delegated to a member of the team, every member of which, Cripps averred, was equally important. Cripps insisted on knowing of any staff illnesses or bereavements in the Department and he sent literally thousands of hand-written notes, memoranda and letters to individual members of the Treasury staff, all in the red ink that he now adopted.

In the whole of Cripps's professional life the first two years of his Chancellorship were probably the most enjoyable of all. He was working with able colleagues and administrators. He was part of a team that shared the same aspirations. He was working at full stretch and he had a clear purpose – the development and successful implementation of what he termed the National Economic Plan.

Almost as soon as the preliminaries of becoming Chancellor were complete (Isobel and Stafford, unlike some other Chancellors, including his successor Gaitskell, decided to live in No. 11), Cripps set about the task of fleshing out exactly what this Plan would consist of, and preparing for his first Budget.

In the two years up until 1947 the answer to Britain's

economic problems had seemed to lie with that cover-all term 'democratic planning'. As Stafford had argued since March 1947 more than a simple plan for increased production was now needed, and the advice he had been giving Dalton he now began to take for himself. The plain and simple issue at stake was exactly the same now as it had been for the last two years – the dollar gap. As Gaitskell reminded him,'The essential thing to keep firmly in mind in face of the cataract of advice and propaganda pouring in upon us is that the only major economic problem is the dollar gap. Employment is high, production is high, the overall balance of payments is not bad, there is inflationary pressure, but no runaway infla- tion. If it were not for this dollar gap we should have little to worry about.'[14]

The problem, then, was simple. The solution was not. For a start the mild inflationary pressure already evident in the economy – partly the result of Dalton's policy of 'cheap money' – could easily exacerbate the dollar gap if British prices took off, making British goods even less competitive in dollar markets. The full panoply of economic tools had to be deployed to ensure that inflation was kept down. Yet excessive management of the economy might well lead to deflation and precipitate a slump which would affect both employment and the overall balance of payments including non-dollar markets. Moreover any inflation in the US would immediately tell on the dollar gap as certain raw materials – especially food, tobacco and cotton – were largely bought from the US, in dollars. Britain was then excessively vulnerable to economic factors outside its own borders. Yet to date there was no real tradition of demand management of the economy, nor of the use of the Budget or any fiscal measures either to ensure low inflation or to maintain high levels of employment. Cripps's Economic Survey of 1947 had paved the way, and Dalton's supplementary Budget of November 1947 had made an attempt at disinflationary measures, but it was not until

Cripps's first Budget of April 1948 that the clear bringing together of economic and financial strategies in the National Economic Plan was established. It was this, in Plowden's view, that made him 'the first of the modern chancellors'.[15]

Cripps made it abundantly clear,

> Government expenditure and revenue ought not to be considered in isolation from their effects upon the general economic prospects of the country, nor can any survey of the economic situation of the country be complete without a knowledge of the Government's Budget proposals. The combination under a single Minister of the co-ordination of our external and internal economy with the control of Government expenditure and revenue was an important change in our planning machinery. The new task of the Chancellor of the Exchequer is not merely to balance the Budget: it is a much wider one – to match our resources against our needs so that the main features of our economy may be worked out for the benefit of the community as a whole. This means that the Budget must be complementary to, and indeed, in some sense a part of the National Economic Plan.[16]

If anything he was understating his case. From now on the Budget would be the single most important element of the Government's Economic Plan because to all intents and purposes the Chancellor for once had the full control of the whole economic field. Not just revenue and expenditure, but imports, exports, investment, wages policy, supply – all these now fell in the Chancellor's domain.

Alec Cairncross alleged that Cripps was no innovator as Chancellor and that the extent of his innovation lay in his work at the Board of Trade. This thesis is based primarily on the belief that Dalton had already set the tone before Cripps with a deflationary Supplementary Budget in November. The

417

truth is, however, that Dalton's two other Budgets were any-thing but deflationary, and the real innovation lay not only in the acknowledgment that the Budget could be a major weapon in the battle against inflation, but that the integration of economic and financial strategies was the only way of resol-ving the real problem – the dollar gap. Each of the steps towards this integrated approach was instigated by Cripps: the 1947 Economic Survey, the first of its kind, the expenditure cuts in November 1947, the preluding of the Budget announce-ments with the 1948 Economic Survey, the wage freeze policy – even the Budget surplus which Dalton had predicted in November only became a deflationary tool in the hands of Cripps.

The first building block in Cripps's deflationary policy, inevitably, had to be wage restraint, either voluntary or com-pulsory, and within weeks of assuming the Chancellorship he was trying to get the Trade Unions to adopt a voluntary code in return for a matching dividend restraint code to be agreed by the Federation of British Industry. The wages policy proved more difficult to get through Cabinet than it did the Trade Unions, with both Bevin and Isaacs attacking Cripps's Cabinet paper in February 1948 because it stipulated not just a general Government statement on wages, but a 'special tribunal to review all wage claims'.[17] In fact the policy had originally been mooted at a weekend of the Cripps group attended by Marquand, Gaitskell, Strauss and Cripps, but when the paper was sent back by Cabinet for further revision, it was only amended to remove the compulsory element before being agreed several weeks later at a meeting when Bevin was absent and Isaacs was more quiescent. So Cripps approached the TUC and spoke at a special executive conference in Margate, even handing out detailed financial statistics to all the delegates before asking them to agree an informal policy instigating a wage freeze. Despite his one time poor relationship with the Trade Unions he managed to secure the support of Arthur Deakin of the Transport Workers, Tom Williamson of the General and Municipal Workers and his old Popular Front colleague Will Lawther of the NUM, and a wage freeze lasted through from April 1948 until the autumn of 1950.

By the time of his first Budget then, Stafford already had one part of the disinflationary equation in his Gladstone bag. He also had the vast majority of the other economic levers to hand. Ministries that had previously fought their corner assiduously against Treasury interference now accepted the need for a concerted economic policy. As Hall rejoiced in March 1948, 'there has been a revolution in Government policy since Stafford Cripps has been the undisputed master in the field and on the whole Plowden has been his prophet... All the old barriers are coming down between Treasury and other policy and there is very little of a rearguard action.'[18]

Stafford's Budget was courageous, at least in Hall's eyes: 'It is the first time anyone has ever tried to make a Budget designed to affect the whole situation and it is all rather frightening.'[19] Its disinflationary approach was venturesome both economically and politically. For if demand was restricted too much a slump such as that after the First World War was a real possibility. The course taken, refusing to use any price mechanisms such as interest rates, meant that rationing and price controls would have to remain while food subsidies were cut, thereby putting up the price of food. This was clearly not likely to win votes and the Tory attack throughout the Cripps Chancellorship was particularly aimed at this evident 'austerity'. As John Colville put it, Cripps was 'suspected of believing that the hair shirts which he chose for his own wardrobe should be manufactured and distributed to the whole community'.[20] There was even a ditty that went the rounds,

It was gay in the days of Maid Marian
E'er we'd heard of the word proletarian,
But our land's in eclipse
In the grip of old Cripps
That teetotal totalitarian.[21]

Cripps's footing, however, was sure. The economic risk of
free fall deflation and slump was minimised by the fact that
his £118 million savings and increased taxation were matched
by £108 million of tax concessions. As for the political risks,
Cripps met them head on. He laid the problem fairly and
squarely before the country, 'We shall have to devote this
opportunity not to an early improvement of our standard of
living, but to a strengthening of our physical resources.'[22] He
went on, 'Sufficient purchasing power must be withheld by
taxation and by voluntary saving, to offset the purchasing
power created by public expenditure and capital investment.'[23]
The aim of the Budget was twofold, 'to obtain . . . a real and
substantial surplus, which more than provides for all Government expenditure, capital and current, and leaves over a
balance, to be used to counter the inflationary pressure, and
second so to adjust taxation as to encourage production, by
providing a better incentive to producers'.[24]

His delivery of the speech was measured and straight, with
none of the relaxed joshing that had characterised Dalton.
There were few gestures, physical or oratorical, and there was
only one joke, when he referred to the removal of Excise Duty
on soda water. Clearly sensitive to the charge that a teetotaller
was suspending taxation on soft drinks, he pointed out that he
did not drink the stuff and 'we think that very little soda water
is drunk neat in this country today. I hope that nobody as a
result of this will accuse me of encouraging inflationary
tendencies.'[25] The plainness of the speech matched the
exactness he expected of the nation and if anything it was
only the fact that Cripps himself was known to live a simple

life that made his message of 'strength through sacrifice' at all palatable. This was the truth, undisguised, made plain for all to see, without a hint of Party advantage. When there was wild talk in the press a couple of weeks later Cripps successfully calmed jittery nerves with another straight speech.

The 1948 Budget could only be regarded as a success. Churchill, a former Chancellor who nonetheless understood as little about economics as Attlee, complimented Cripps with more than the usual pleasantries, as 'the overlord of our economic life' for his 'comprehensive, lucid statement', although he objected to the disinflationary measures which he felt could lead to 'too much money chasing too few goods'.[26] The Budget did exactly what it was intended to do. Inflation was kept low, the first warning shots were fired in the Cabinet battle over Government welfare expenditure, and the economic climate was set for increased production. The dollar gap was addressed and Britain entered a dynamic period of production growth while keeping its personal spending in check.

Cripps's other innovation, the 'once-for-all levy' based on individuals' investment income was also popular with the Labour Party, as it allowed room for major tax concessions for the majority while maintaining high taxation as a counter-inflationary strategy and enabling high levels of expenditure on welfare reform. 'Some,' as Cripps put it, 'particularly those with considerable invested capital are being asked to bear greater burdens of the special effort of this year; others, particularly those to whom we look for our production and who rely upon moderate incomes, will benefit by very substantial reliefs on their taxation. This is both fair, and in accordance with our economic needs'[27] – and, he might have added, is the only politically motivated aspect of this Budget.

Thus was set the tone for the Cripps era. The basic rate of income tax remained at nine shillings in the pound (45p). Physical controls in the form of rationing and food subsidies remained the order of the day with limits on bread, meat (thirteen ounces a week) cheese (one and a half ounces) butter and margarine (six ounces), milk (two pints) and eggs (one per person). As Stafford put it in the *Economist* Britain's consumption needs came 'last in the list of priorities. First [were] exports; second capital investment in industry; and last the needs, comforts and amenities of the family.'[28] It was a period of remarkable economic success – rapid growth, well in excess of expectations, full employment, low interest rates and a finally buoyant balance of payments position.

Cripps's task, as countless Conservative assaults on his record made clear, was made all the easier because of a single speech given on 6 June 1947 at Harvard by the US Secretary of State, George Marshall, in which he made his historic offer of US financial support for European economic recovery. By the time Cripps was Chancellor he and Bevin had already spent two months on the process of setting up the Committee for European Economic Co-operation (CEEC) and trying to agree a European plan which would attract American funding in the form of the European Recovery Programme, or Marshall Aid. There were major problems which conflicted with Bevin's and Attlee's clear intention that Britain should lose none of her world leader nation status as the Americans were insisting that financial support was contingent on the thirteen states who were eligible framing a single plan for economic recovery rather than individual national plans. This was effectively throwing Britain's economic future in with the rest of Europe rather than retaining an independent role, thereby raising the great leviathan of 'sovereignty' from its slumbers. Yet Cripps was clear that without Marshall Aid Britain could stand little chance of survival. In June 1948 his Cabinet paper on the economic consequences of receiving no ERP aid was brutally clear 'we should be faced with an abrupt transition from a partially suppressed inflation to something not unlike a slump'[29] and two days later Marshall Aid was agreed. The temptation, of course, with such largesse coming into the British coffers (in all some $2.7 billion) was to spend it, and Stafford spent much of his remaining time as Chancellor ensuring that both the Cabinet and the country realised that Marshall Aid was not an indefinite flow of free cash. It would be exhausted in 1951 and Britain had to remain fiscally responsible, trying as far as possible to harness all the Marshall dollars to long-term investment that would deliver for future prosperity.

By the time of Stafford's second Budget in April 1949 these same concerns were expressing themselves all the more strongly, and Stafford replied in the same vein. By now Government expenditure was beginning to spiral, especially in those areas where Labour was most protective, the Social Services – its pride and joy. In 1947-8 the NHS had cost £143 million. Now Cripps was anticipating £260 million for the following year. The only answer was to be clear that 'such expenditure must be paid for out of the current income of the community, by taxation. If we do not do this unflinchingly, we shall face inflation. Inflation is not an evil that once checked, disappears; the threat remains and we must be on our guard against it.'[30] So Cripps used the Budget to make his general comments about Government expenditure restraint of 1948 relate directly to the NHS. In a phrase that raised Bevan's hackles, he enunciated this fiscal prudence: 'We must . . . moderate the speed of our advance in the extended application of the existing Social Services to our progressive ability to pay for them by an increase in our national income.'[31]

Here Stafford's footing was less sure. Bevan, who argued that a ceiling on the NHS would emasculate Labour's most important claim to international fame, was a tough opponent and though Stafford's sympathies lay with the burgeoning NHS he was convinced that there had to be a cap on expenditure unless inflation was to destroy the significant advances that had been made in the battle of the dollar gap. The balance of payments was indeed, at least in total, including all the non-dollar areas, now in the black, but the dollar drain remained a problem which would always be vulnerable to prices in both the US and Britain. The Budget surplus could not be seen as a slush fund for Bevan. Hall saw this as a crucial test for both the Labour Party and the nation and noted that during the Budget speech 'the Government benches disliked the very plain statements that we had to pay for our social services, while the Opposition applauded. If they are unwilling to pay . . . then we cannot get out for we will neither meet our dollar gap until we have to because the gold has gone, nor check inflation.'[32] Gaitskell, who had been one of the major advocates of this 'austere' budget in which everyone had anticipated pre-election tax cuts, himself disapproved of the hefty cuts in food subsidies which he felt should have been restricted to meat so that Peron's fascist Argentina could be blamed. Bevan just thought the cuts were 'out of character'.[33] Yet Stafford got his way partly because his colleagues in Cabinet had been so profoundly shocked by the convertibility crisis that they were prepared to accept almost any lead Stafford gave them, even if it meant a degree of unpopularity. Labour's poor showing in the May local elections subsequently showed that the Budget was hardly populist, but by now many of the once doctrinaire had been straitened by the experience of government and Stafford's line of what was best for Britain held.

There was one other possible way out of the dollar impasse – devaluation – and in the early months of 1949 rumours of a major exchange rate change began to surface. Devaluations by their very nature are more uncomfortable for the politicians than they are for economists. As David Marquand, Hilary's son, put it, 'To the economist, devaluation is nothing more dramatic than a device to be resorted to, coolly and without emotion, when prices in one country are out of line with prices in another.'[34] For a politician, by contrast, it can feel more like a public castration. Not only does the perpetrator have to pretend, if asked, that he is not going to devalue, right up to the last minute, but once the deed is done he has to face the obloquy of Opposition Members arguing both that he has deceived the public and that national honour has been lost by cheapening the national currency.

Inevitably enough, it was the economists who first suggested devaluation in 1949, when Hall approached Cripps at least as early as the day of the Budget. Both he and Plowden were now convinced of the need to devalue, as was Wilson's economist at the Board of Trade, Alec Cairncross. The matter had already been raised publicly, by both the Swedish Government who wanted it discussed by the OEEC in November 1948 and the US Treasury Secretary John Snyder. Indeed on 6 April 1949 the IMF agreed to ask its Managing Director to begin an inquiry into European exchange rates. The argument for devaluation was simple. The US recession, which began in late 1948 had exacerbated the UK economic problems more than any other nation in Europe. The problem was the dollar drain both from Britain and the rest of the sterling area (most notably India). In truth the dollar was too cheap, and dollar imports therefore too cheap as well. Devaluation of the pound was properly a revaluation of the dollar. As Alec Cairncross put it, the UK was

in danger of running out of dollars as a result of settling its deficit in 'hard' currencies and at the same time of running up equal or larger inconvertible balances in 'soft' currencies through the sale of 'unrequited' exports. It was necessary to make the soft currencies harder and the hard currencies softer; there could be no more effective way of doing this than by making hard currencies dearer in terms of soft currencies. This in turn could best be brought about by devaluing sterling against the dollar and inducing other countries to devalue their currencies simultaneously.[35]

At the outset nearly all the ministerial team were opposed to devaluation. Cripps simply viewed it as immoral because 'other countries held their reserves in sterling'.[36] So he refused to countenance the proposals that both Hall and Plowden now started to advocate. In June, however, he warned the Cabinet that the drain on dollars was again a major problem, that within a year the reserves would be exhausted and that sterling might collapse. Stopgap proposals were agreed, with a 25 per cent cut in all dollar expenditure and the suspension of fresh dollar commitments until September. Inevitably this antagonised the Americans who began to urge devaluation of the pound by the beginning of July, while the Southern Rhodesian Finance Minister argued at the Commonwealth Finance Ministers Conference in London that a devaluation was the only way to rectify the fact that UK and sterling area exports were simply too expensive with a rate of $4.03 to the pound.

This public talk of devaluation put pressure on the Chancellor to make a public statement of the Government's intentions, which he did in Rome in May, stating unequivocally that he had no intention of devaluing. Unfortunately, partly because it was the truth and partly because he wanted it to remain the truth, he was too convincing in his rejection of devaluation. Neither the Treasury nor the Bank of England, both of which were largely still opposed themselves, ever engaged sufficiently with the possible devaluation before it actually happened, so were not properly prepared for it. The opposition of Edward Bridges, the Head of the Treasury, was so intense that even when it was agreed he code-named it 'Caliban'. Gaitskell reported at the end of June, 'The Chancellor is obviously torn. Plowden has for long favoured devaluation; other parties in the Treasury favour deflation, but they all seem to want to cling to multilateralism and convertibility as our aim. Douglas [Jay] is opposed to this and has a continual struggle inside the Treasury for Stafford's soul.'[37]

Meanwhile, others in the Cabinet began to support the idea, although at the Economic Policy Committee meeting on 28 June Herbert Morrison was a sole devaluer. Cripps now suggested that there were only three ways forward – severe deflation, devaluation or improved competitive power achieved through higher productivity – and stated that 'I do not think this is the right time to carry [devaluation] out, whatever the ultimate decision may be.'[38] At the 1 July Cabinet meeting Morrison restated his case while Cripps argued for cutting food subsidies again, which both Dalton and Bevin rather dishonestly opposed on the grounds that such budgetary issues were not relevant to the dollar gap. Cripps, who had been up most of the night in Paris, caved in swiftly, telling Dalton that 'You see I don't support it' and effectively blaming his officials.[39] By mid-July, though, the two key figures in Stafford's economic support group, Gaitskell and Jay, were both in favour of a rapid devaluation, Jay having changed his mind walking on Hampstead Heath and Gaitskell at his home on the same day, Saturday 17 July. The timing was important, for in the meantime Cripps had become ill again and had planned a long summer stay at the Bircher-Benner clinic in Zurich, which was to start on 18 July. The rush of extra EPC meetings in early July had been primarily aimed at getting the issues resolved before Cripps went away for his recuperation. Attlee then announced on the Monday after the Gaitskell and Jay conversions that the Chancellor would be deputised for in his absence by Gaitskell, Jay and Wilson. The following day Jay and Gaitskell met and agreed their new position in favour of devaluation. This meant the initiative was now securely in the hands of two now ardent pro-devaluers, who managed to get broad agreement in favour of devaluation out of the Cripps group of Ministers who met on the 21st without Wilson and set about lobbying Dalton, Bevin and Attlee just as reserves dipped below £400 million. Wilson, so the others felt, changed his mind three times in eight days on the matter although his broad agreement was finally secured. According to Plowden, on 25 July a group of Gaitskell, Jay, Wilson and Attlee agreed that devaluation was now inevitable, a position that was backed up by a letter from Bridges, Hall, Eady and himself which urged additional anti-inflationary measures to accompany devaluation. The Cabinet meeting four days later agreed devaluation 'in principle'.

The issue now was not whether but when. Here there were two problems. The first was that it was unanimously agreed that the announcement could only be made by Cripps – who neither yet knew of the decision, nor agreed with it. Cripps was to be away for at least a month, and would then require briefing and time to prepare for an announcement. This would then take the decisions very close to the September meetings in Washington when Cripps was to see Snyder and meet with the IMF. The choice was then either to go forward without Cripps, which was unimaginable, or to wait until after the Washington talks, which would mean a devaluation in mid-September, far later than either Jay or Gaitskell wanted.

In the meantime the decision had to be announced to Cripps. Wilson told the Cabinet that as he was holidaying on the Continent he would be happy to convey a message to the Chancellor in person, though Attlee, perhaps seeing this as a ploy, decided that a personal letter from him should be carried by Wilson instead. This Wilson did, having warned Isobel in advance that he was coming and there was a highly secretive handing over of the letter in a Zurich suburb, before an initial response, again conveyed by Wilson, was drafted by Stafford in which he told Attlee that he was still unconvinced by the arguments, though at this stage he only quibbled about the timetable for the announcement which he was prepared to discuss on his return.

This discussion was scheduled for Thursday 18 August. Gaitskell, now the main protagonist in favour of devaluation, prepared two papers for the Chancellor explaining his support for an early devaluation on 28 August and presented them to him at Chequers when they met the day after Cripps's arrival. Again Gaitskell was to be disappointed. 'The Chancellor looked very thin and it was a thoroughly bad omen when in my presence he handed to Bridges all the papers Bridges had given him and said, "I am not going to do any work for a week. I must go home and sleep."'[40] Without reading either document Cripps made it clear that while he was prepared to devalue he was opposed to an early date and Attlee decided to curtail discussion. On 29 August at the first of two meetings of the Cabinet devaluation was agreed, to be announced after the Washington talks, at a rate to be set by Cripps and Bevin who two days later set sail on the RMS *Mauretania*, accompanied by Plowden, Roger Makin and Bevin's wife.

By all accounts it was a strange voyage. Both Cripps and Bevin were ill men, Bevin resorting to amyl nitrate for a heart condition and Cripps still recuperating. Bevin was a late riser and rarely appeared on deck before 5 p.m. Cripps, as usual, was up well before dawn and spent most of the day taking the air before retiring at 5 p.m. In fact they did not manage to meet for the first four days of the journey and Plowden and Makin had to hold separate briefings for them. It was also a rough crossing and the swimming pool was emptied. Yet Cripps insisted that the captain refill it so that he could take a regular dip, even though the swell was so high that it threatened to tip him out on to the side.

The *Mauretania* docked in New York on 6 September where Cripps and Bevin were met by Bridges who had flown over. The final decision now had to be taken – the new rate. Gaitskell in his memorandum to Cripps had suggested a variable rate of between $2.60 and $2.80 and at the Cabinet meeting on 29 August Cripps had stated that it should be no less than $3.00 and Bevin that it should be $3.20. In the event Cripps and Plowden had to go to Bevin's room to meet with him in his pyjamas to get a final decision. Cripps suggested that they should consult the Americans, a point fiercely contested by Plowden, who suggested $2.80. Bevin asked what effect it would have on the price of bread and when Plowden calmed his political concerns, the figure of $2.80 was agreed.

The subsequent meetings with Snyder were more successful than either Bevin or Cripps had anticipated. Snyder had always shown a degree of hostility towards the British up until now, but the decision to devalue and to warn the Americans in advance played well with the Treasury Secretary and a broad measure of agreement was established. Britain was allowed to use ERP dollars to buy Canadian wheat, US tariffs were to be simplified and relaxed and the Americans would consider further help with the run-down of sterling reserves. In return Britain would take part in the European Payments Union and would assist in the liberalisation of trade while gradually drawing down the sterling balances and they were studying incentives for increasing exports to the US under a new commercial treaty with the USA.

Back in London the Cabinet met secretly on Saturday 17 September, the ministers arriving through the back door, and agreed the new rate. The following evening Cripps announced the devaluation on the radio. The original draft for the devaluation announcement had started with both the announcement of the devaluation itself and an apology. Cripps changed the speech, though, arguing that Bevin had always taught him never to apologise and that if he announced the new rate at the start of the broadcast nobody would listen to the rest of the economic arguments for the devaluation. Cairncross reckoned that this, with his attempt to oust Attlee, was one of only two real mistakes he made and that he should have accepted both Plowden and Hall's advice to apologise first. Plowden said that Clem Leslie reckoned this 'redraft... was to damage [his] reputation, as people thought he was trying to brazen it out, something the public thought was unlike him.'[41]

Leah Manning certainly felt aggrieved and poured out all her accumulated bile on the matter:

> He was sanctimonious. He always seemed to do the obviously wrong thing, such as voting against sanctions at the time of the Abyssinian crisis. He was prepared to tell the expedient lie. Now one can forgive Harold Wilson, or Jim Callaghan, or George Brown – they are politicians and never set up a 'holier than thou' attitude. But when Cripps publicly denied that he had devaluation in mind, and then devalued within a few days, I felt that that was unforgivable behaviour in one who professed complete probity in public life.[42]

Cripps himself felt he had to explain himself and in the Mansion House speech in October he said, 'Our action had been discussed, debated and indeed almost expected, throughout the world . . . though the actual date and the degree of change in the sterling exchange rate may have taken people by surprise – no one can suggest that it was a matter suddenly sprung upon an unsuspecting world.'[43]

Should Cripps have resigned? Edmund Dell in his book *The Chancellors* states baldly that he should have done, though his argument is less with Cripps's going back on his public disavowal of devaluation intentions than because he reckons he simply was not a strong enough Chancellor in restraining the spending urges of his colleagues. As we have seen, Leah Manning certainly felt he should have resigned and the Opposition made political hay of his evident personal discomfort. Much of this was readily dismissed Party political point scoring, but there was one confrontation that hurt. For Stafford had deliberately warned Churchill on the afternoon of devaluation , in confidence, as leader of the Opposition, of what his broadcast would make clear. Churchill, not unusually, so Jay relates, got all romantic about their wartime comradeship and

Stafford felt warmed by the encounter with his old boss who even congratulated him on his wise decision. When devaluation was debated in the Commons, however, Churchill went for the jugular and accused Stafford of having lied to the public. It was the same accusation as another MP, Godfrey Nicholson, had levied at him, and it stung. When Nicholson refused to retract his accusation on the grounds that he had meant 'political' not 'personal' dishonesty, Stafford had haughtily replied 'I do not recognise the distinction.'[44] This time, far more hurt, Stafford took umbrage and a year later refused to accept an honorary degree from Bristol University because it was to be presented by Churchill.

A large part of Stafford's pain, of course, was not just spiritual pride, but a real perception that there was truth in Churchill's argument. After all Dalton had resigned over a trifle whereas he had even continued telling the public there would be no devaluation after he had notified the Americans. The least he could do was insist that there should be a rapid General Election to gain a mandate for his continuing in post. The truth is, of course, that the Government could not have afforded even an honourable resignation from Cripps. In the economic difficulties which then still faced the nation the living embodiment of rectitude, probity and responsibility, which Cripps was, was vital to the enduring level of Government support. Cripps might well have been prepared to resign. After all his health was not good. But Attlee would never have accepted his resignation, and well into 1950 his colleagues were urging him to remain in post. As Plowden put it 'Hugh Gaitskell and I had to emphasise repeatedly to him how much the nation needed him in order to keep up his spirits and to stop him from resigning.'[45]

Moreover the task of devaluation was not a simple one act play and there was work to be done in making devaluation work to Britain's best advantage. For as the letter from Bridges and Plowden in July had pointed out, it would not of itself right the nation's economy and would have to be accompanied by a new package of measures designed to prevent inflation by cutting Government expenditure. As Hall argued in his diary, a 'stiff dose of disinflation was called for if the opportunities opened up by devaluation were not to be lost; and the fact that the budget surplus looked like being £160 million less than was expected in April while small savers were drawing down their deposits by c. £40 million p.a. pointed to necessary cuts of £200 million to restore pressure of demand to level planned. £100 million more cuts would free resources.'[46] On 12 October Cripps met with Bridges, Plowden and Hall to agree a figure for cuts below which he would have to tender his resignation, agreeing, according to Hall, on £200 million. This Cripps put to the EPC, stating as his opening gambit that he would resign unless economies of at least £300 million were made. This figure was in fact slightly reduced, by £20 million, to the target that Bridges had fixed on, though even this figure attracted the resignation threats of Bevan, Alexander and Bevin. Nevertheless cuts were eventually agreed, split between Government expenditure and investment and including a £35 million cut in the house building programme, although Hall and Cairncross both reckoned that these were never real cuts and it was impossible to test in the end whether they were properly implemented. Certainly Plowden thought that 'the financial measures that accompanied [devaluation] were by no means as wide-ranging as they should have been'.[47] At the same time Cripps managed to get a new agreement with the TUC instituting a yet tighter wage policy, so that the effect of devaluation on prices was almost minimal. Plowden reckoned the whole devaluation a success.

Although devaluation was delayed for too long, leading to an excessive loss to the reserves . . . its results were satisfactory in terms of both the short and the longer term, both from the point of view of Britain and the world as a whole ... The rate of $2.80 to the pound was subsequently maintained for 18 years and this period of almost two decades witnessed unprecedented exchange rate stability, economic growth and employment levels throughout the world.[48]

All of this pointed to a conviction that Stafford was right not to resign. If he had gone Attlee would have been hard pressed to find another Chancellor who could have seen anything like the necessary economies through Cabinet. Stafford had to finish the job and even though the economies were probably never fully implemented, yet Stafford's role as the linchpin in the Cabinet and the repository of the nation's economic trust, while wounded was not fatally harmed.

Not everyone, of course, was as keen on Cripps as either Plowden or Attlee. Indeed Cripps had, for the first time in his political career, difficulties with his constituency Party in 1948. As with most national political figures of the day he was not a particularly frequent attender of the constituency and though the local Party had stuck by him through his wilderness years, now that he had become the fiscally responsible, or in some eyes, right-wing, Chancellor, there were doubts about whether he should still represent the constituency at the next election. It was Mervyn Stockwood, now a local councillor in Bristol, who warned him of the threats to deselect him in April, to which Isobel replied on Stafford's behalf in a particularly emotional and confused letter.

There is only one way to approach this and that is by digging down into the deepest roots of humility, as far as one can understand it. I only wish they could be as loyal to him as he is to them, but how can one expect them to be in the lives they have to lead? I feel I could burst into tears. They need a shepherd and it is a reflection on us if we fail to meet the challenge. The personal hurt just does not matter if we mean anything by a Christian profession.[49]

These days it seems almost inconceivable that an MP would not regularly attend his local Party meeting, but the threats continued that if he did not justify himself to the local Party and attend the selection meeting he would almost certainly be deselected. Stafford's own response was typically robust, as he relayed to Stockwood the day after the meeting of 28 September, which he attended unexpectedly. 'I took the opportunity of saying that I knew the gossip that was going about. I said I was not prepared to accept the candidature unless all this sort of thing stopped immediately.'[50] Needless to say he was reselected unopposed.

Stafford also came in for criticism, however, from some of his erstwhile colleagues from the 1930s. While Strauss, Bevan and Strachey were now part of the Government, Pritt, who had been expelled from the Labour Party in the war for his support for Russia over Finland, was now openly critical of him, and some of his extra-parliamentary colleagues from the Popular Front were equally uncertain of the 'austere' Chancellor. The most perspicacious of all these was Victor Gollancz, who had by now undergone not exactly a conversion, but a renewal of a Christian faith. Late in 1949 he launched several outspoken attacks on the Government's economic policy, specifically citing Stafford. It was not the usual complaint, however. If anything Gollancz was the genuine ascetic.

You go fatally wrong when you regard material conditions as the most important thing in life: and your error is increased when you talk of high standards of living in the terms in which it is appropriate for men to talk about their religion . . . curiously enough I find this odd philosophy most insistently expressed by, I think, the only member of the Government who constantly proclaims his Christianity, I mean my friend Sir Stafford Cripps. Sir Stafford will speak with the utmost eloquence about the necessity of self-sacrifice on the part of each one of us and about the great and high conflict to which we are called. But when it comes to it, why are we to sacrifice ourselves? In order that we may have more to eat and more clothes to wear later on. And what is the high struggle? Precisely the struggle to win back our standard of living.[51]

Gollancz was just as perplexed, however, by the 'disastrous schizophrenia' of Stafford's position with regard to the 'private enterprise sector'.

In the *same speech* business men are begged to cut costs to increase production etc. etc. in the public interest – ie they are talked to as public servants: and *in that same speech* these same men, in their aspect as 'profit makers' . . . are sneered at and talked about as if they were criminals. It just won't do. All profit making may be wrong, and indeed, as you know, I think it is wrong – I think so far more uncompromisingly than Stafford Cripps ever did or will: but the private enterprise sector cannot possibly continue unless at any rate some profits are made: and to blackguard men whom you are appealing to in fact as public servants, merely because . . . they must make profits as the very condition of their existence – this is contemptible.[52]

It was a fair comment, though perhaps aimed at the wrong target. Labour had proclaimed the common purpose as opposed to private interests ever since the war, and yet its economic policy relied on the private sector succeeding in

winning new markets, increasing productivity and competi-
tiveness. Nationalisation had been asserted as a morally
superior system. Co-operation in the national interest was the
ethical bedrock of Socialism. This meant that despite Labour's
dependence on the private sector it had never really
articulated a coherent understanding of the role of competition
in the economy. Stafford, both at the Board of Trade and in
the Treasury, was inevitably involved in trying to establish
creative partnerships with the private sector, but the language
of Socialism still did not value competition. In part Cripps
was a hostage to the collectivist drive of the Labour Party, but
his own experience, as a director of Eno's, as a manager of the
South Bucks Standard, and even at the MAP should have placed
him in a unique position among all the Labour frontbenchers,
to articulate that belief in a mixed economy which necessitated
just as strong an understanding of competition as of co-
operation.

The Cripps response to Gollancz in fact came from Isobel,
again taking up the cudgels on Stafford's behalf and completely avoiding the issue. She wrote on 19 December 1949,
'Why are you so bitter against Stafford? There is sadness in
this for people who in their ways seem out for the same kind
of things. Bitterness corrodes the spirit. Could we meet one
day – you & I – & talk quietly – unless you would rather not.'[53]
Gollancz's reply admitted that he had

> from time to time, felt some irritation. This has arisen
> because Stafford is one of the very few people in the
> Government who really care about ethical religion, and
> one of the only two who constantly and publicly (and
> very rightly) declare that they care about it. Now when I
> say that the Government's policy has been materialistic
> and anti-internationalist, that is another way of saying
> that, in my view, it has been anti-Christian: and accord-
> ingly I have found it difficult on occasion not to feel

irritation when the man most symbolically associated with what I feel to be an anti-Christian policy has publicly proclaimed Christian ethics. This doesn't mean for a single second (if I may be excused for even suggesting such a thing) that I doubt Stafford's complete sincerity: it has simply seemed to me a case of the partial blindness that descends on even the best men when they are absorbed in the daily necessities of politics.[54]

It was those daily necessities of politics that brought Stafford to the most uncertain moment of his mature career when he had to implement a policy he had opposed for months and said he was not contemplating. His response was to seek an election as soon as possible in the belief that a Labour victory would justify both his actions and his remaining as Chancellor.

25

A Final Budget

Cripps had been urging an early General Election since just after his 1949 Budget. Indeed on the very day of the Budget Gaitskell noted in his diary that most of the Cripps group were in favour of an autumn election, even though this would mean losing the proposed Parliament Bill and the Steel [Nationalisation] Bill. In the July run-up to devaluation Cripps even hoped there would be an election before the autumn, though the fact that this would mean a campaign in the middle of the Summer holiday – when he would be in Zurich – meant that the rest of the Cabinet argued him down. In August Gaitskell's 'political strategy' memorandum to senior Party figures was still envisaging the possibility of going to full term, though he felt that any 'convenient lull' in the economic storm should be taken advantage of and that the PM should not 'pin [us] down to next June'.[1] By the end of the year, though, Cripps was insisting, with the usual threats of resignation, that the Election must be before April. His grounds were straightforward, though to any modern Chancellor they might seem extraordinary. For his major concern was that his policies as Chancellor should have a direct mandate from the people. A more strategic politician might have wanted to use a Budget to foster electoral good will. For Stafford this was downright immoral, for the Budget had to be in the national interest before any Party considerations could be taken. Attlee told

Jay 'he's no judge of politics'[2] but had little choice but to cave in as Stafford was simply not willing to give another Budget before the Election was called. The agreed date was 23 February and Attlee went to the Palace to seek a dissolution on 10 January.

Most Labour politicians expected to win, despite the fact that the opinion polls had not looked good for some time and the 1949 local elections had seen large Labour losses. Gaitskell reported a party on new Year's Eve given by the Crippses to the Production Ministers and their wives 'which was, alas, far from gay' as 'there was no drink except sherry and apple juice. The meal was pretty foul and conversation, not surprisingly, drab and common place . . . It was . . . the atmosphere of austerity and prudery which affected everybody. Lady Cripps was the originator of most of this, as at our Group dinners with Stafford things are much more lively.'[3] Much of the conversation hinged on Labour's prospects, with everyone writing on a piece of paper what they expected to be the result. Jay, the most pessimistic, went for a Tory majority of thirty, Gaitskell for a Labour one of thirty. Bevan retorted that with such a small majority he would 'rather not be in power at all'.[4]

Cripps had an exciting campaign, with as full a diary as ever. There were many more insults flying around than usual, however, with Stafford taking as much of the flak as anyone. After he had called Churchill a guttersnipe at a constituency meeting in Bristol, Brendan Bracken rejoined, 'Let me just say that the snipe is a far better bird than that new and queerest of birds – the vegetarian vulture.'[5] Stafford also attacked the 'Radio Doctor' Charlie Hill to great acclaim and advised Attlee not to allow Morrison to give the final election broadcast, reserving it to himself lest he contemplate another plot.[6]

In the event Labour did win and even increased its vote by more than a million, while falling back less than 2 per cent. The redrawing of constituencies (including Stafford's) and the tendency for the Labour vote to stack up in strongholds, however, meant that it was a very narrow win – a majority of only five. In many ways this was the worst of all possible worlds for Stafford, who was by now far from well. Not only did a tiny majority mean that there would be plenty of late night attendances in store, but the pressure to maintain unity within the Parliamentary Party was all the more acute, at a time when Stafford was fully aware that there would be tough Budget decisions to be taken. Stafford had already let it be known that 'he thought the Party could not continue to be run in the new Parliament by the old men at present at the top'[7] and had perhaps considered retiring. He even told Plowden 'Edwin, I'm trapped. I intended to go after the election, but with a majority of six [either Cripps's figure or Plowden's memory was wrong] I can't possibly do so now.'[8] In case Attlee had been thinking of letting Cripps go, Dalton made it equally clear to him that 'Cripps was absolutely irreplaceable as Chancellor. No one else could do it, until, in due course, one came down the line to the "young economists".'[9] Yet Cripps was horrendously over-stretched, especially for a man whose health was evidently not secure. Dalton continued, 'Cripps had much too much to do – old Treasury + new Planning + constant travelling abroad. I thought he should have a Minister of State, who could relieve him of some of this. Without it, the system would break down, and Cripps with it . . . I thought Gaitskell was the man for the job.'[10]

Attlee agreed and when the election was over Gaitskell was duly appointed as Stafford's Minister of State for Economic Affairs, immediately taking over from the Chancellor a whole range of duties, including all the negotiations over the European Payments Union and the US discussions over financing rearmament. Gaitskell's relations with senior figures at the Treasury were already good, and with his friend Jay now the Minister for Pensions a new working team was seamlessly established. Stafford trusted Gaitskell and was happy from the beginning to alternate with him almost as a Deputy

Chancellor, although after a while it made more sense for the two to have separate responsibilities.

Almost immediately there was the problem of the April Budget, which raised issues that had been dormant since the previous autumn, but which were essential to the maintenance of the Budget surplus. For despite Stafford's assertions in the 1949 Budget that increases in Social Services expenditure would have to be met out of growth, the NHS had continued to grow inexorably. A supplementary allocation had to be agreed in March and now Plowden, Jay and Gaitskell were clamouring for a tight restriction of NHS spending. Cripps had not stood still in the intervening year. Indeed there had been sharp differences between him and Bevan in Cabinet when he had proposed first prescription charges on 20 October and then dental and ophthalmic charges as a way of redressing the balance. With the new Budget to be considered both Plowden and Gaitskell were convinced that delay could no longer be brooked. 'I begged Stafford to insist on two things,' recorded Gaitskell. 'First, Treasury control should be established as effectively as it is over Government expenditure and secondly there should be a definite limit placed on the total National Health Service expenditure. I would have liked this to have been below next year's estimates, so that we should be quietly committed up to the hilt to finding the rest of the money . . . by making charges.'[11] Thus, after forty-eight energetic hours of hectoring by Gaitskell, Cripps approached the 13 March Cabinet meeting resolved to secure a tough ceiling on NHS costs. The debate was eventually resolved by Attlee who proposed that the Commons debate on the supplementary allocation the following day should be introduced by Cripps, who would make a general statement introducing the concept of the ceiling, while Bevan would limit himself to defending the inevitable allegations of waste. So the moment passed.

On 3 April, however, there was to be a further round of

talks, in anticipation of the Budget. The day before the meeting Cripps wrote to Attlee,

> The discussion tomorrow may lead Bevan to resigning . . . I agree no cuts if there are *certain* means to stop supplementaries . . . It will anyhow take time to work out the best way of making charges. So I would agree to *powers* being taken now but no fresh charges till it's clear the ceiling is being exceeded. This means we would have to decide *before the end of the session* whether charges are needed. It would bring great pressure on those responsible for the Service to make economies quickly. I'm sorry to inflict all this on you, but I want to avoid an awkward political situation arising just now. I couldn't agree to nothing being done; this is the least I can agree to.[12]

This was a clever tactic, especially when it was accompanied by Attlee's suggestion that there should be a new Cabinet committee, which he would chair, to oversee NHS spending on a monthly basis. Both Cripps and Bevan could safely say that they had won. There would be greater control and the in principle decision to charge had been made, but charges had not yet been enforced on a Minister who would resign. This was left for Gaitskell to force through a year later.

It also left Cripps free to make the position clear in the Budget two weeks later.

> It is clear that it is not possible in existing circumstances to permit any overall increase in expenditure on the Health Services. Any expansion in one part of the Service must in future be met by economies or, if necessary, by contraction in others . . . It is not proposed to impose any charge immediately in connection with prescriptions, since it is hoped that a more easily administered method of economising in this branch of expenditure can be

introduced shortly. The power to charge will, of course, remain so that it can be used later if needed.[13]

As for the rest of Stafford's 1950 Budget the themes were almost identical to his two previous ones. The Budget surplus was not to be seen as 'the declared profits of a company' or a 'fund available for distribution by way of remission of taxation'. Inflation had to be seen off through a mixture of disinflationary high overall taxation and wage restraint and 'democratic planning' was the only way of achieving 'a Happy Country in which there is equality of opportunity, and not too great a disparity of personal incomes, and in which every man and woman can feel that they are welcomed and have a full part to play and are invited to take their share in the democratic control of their country's economy'.[14] There was no attempt to reduce the overall burden of taxation although income tax rates were cut and petrol duty was increased to compensate. So a third surplus, this time £700 million, was anticipated, some 7 per cent of GNP. Again it was not a particularly popular policy in the Cabinet or on the Labour benches, but Stafford maintained that the main aim of economic policy was 'to manage demand and offset cyclical fluctuations in the economy through fiscal policy without producing inflation or unemployment'.[15] Bevan, still upset about the threat to charge for NHS services, stopped going to the Cripps group dinners in June after Gaitskell and he regularly fell out over the matter.

Meanwhile Stafford was increasingly out of action through illness. Ever since the summer of 1949 he had been complaining of insomnia and Attlee noticed a tetchiness and readiness 'to resign over anything'.[16] Gaitskell soon had to deputise for him at a wide range of events, not just those that fell to his agreed remit. Thus in March he took the press conference on the Economic Survey, and in October he even gave the Mansion House speech, the first time that it had not been given by the Chancellor. By late May Gaitskell was noting 'he certainly regards himself as almost an invalid, and Edwin Plowden mentioned to me the other day that he thought he was rather a hypochondriac'.[17] Yet Stafford was torn between a desire for a long holiday, possibly even a year off, and a deep-seated refusal to slow down, however much Burke Trend and Jay tried to get him to do so. As Trend put it, 'The fact is that the things of this world mean nothing to him.'[18] Yet Stafford did tell both Gaitskell and Plowden in May 'that he was going to resign at the end of the summer session' and even wrote a letter of resignation to Attlee. Gaitskell argued hard both with him and with Isobel that he could not take a year long holiday as the Government had a majority now of only three, and that he was physically much better as a result of not having to work so hard and having had a Whitsun holiday. Gaitskell's motives may not have been exactly pure in this, for while Stafford remained and delegated to him he was effectively building up his claim to the succession. The sooner Stafford went the less likely it was that he should inherit the Chancellorship. Nevertheless Stafford agreed to plough on, on the understanding that he would be allowed a proper holiday in the summer, with no guarantee of returning from it. Indeed he still even suggested that if the equally ailing Bevin should go he would move to the Foreign Office.

This level of activity might well have been all right if the economy had continued as it was in early 1950 when the main benefits of the devaluation were beginning to be felt. As Kenneth Morgan put it

Britain's economy showed all the symptoms of steady growth without overheating. It was amongst the most thriving periods economically that the country as a whole had experienced since the late Victorian era. Cripps himself with a strict regime of budgetary management, and with high government taxation to make up the difference between public expenditure and the goods available for private consumption, had created the basis for a new affluence.'[19]

By the end of June, however, there was a new problem to be faced, with a renewed round of Cabinet battles and international negotiations. For on 25 June the 38th parallel dividing North and South Korea was crossed by Soviet-backed North Korean troops and the Korean War began. Immediately the Americans clamoured first for withdrawal and then for the rearmament of the West. They wanted to know, by 5 August, 'the nature and extent of the increased effort both as regards increases in forces and increases in military production which His Majesty's Government as a North Atlantic Treaty Power are willing and able to undertake'. Inevitably, as Cripps had to point out to his colleagues, even though the US were offering some financial assistance for this rearmament, there would be new pressures on the Budget. Either there would have to be further taxation, or cuts in expenditure or in investment. Needless to say Bevan could see where this was leading and tried to head off the almost inevitable assault on NHS funding that a new military commitment was bound to entail, but was defeated in Cabinet.

The Korean War may, as Gaitskell noted, have 'helped persuade him . . . that he could not just fade out at the present', but the Cabinet meeting of at which the supplementary military requirements were agreed was almost Cripps's last act as Chancellor. Yet he set off for his long summer 'holiday' (planned to last from August to November) still reserving the right not to come back at all if he did not think he was well enough. Gaitskell noted, 'for my part I am pretty certain he will come back, and may come back earlier, especially if the international situation gets worse. Meanwhile I have been left in charge and in order to impress outsiders and officials, at his suggestion, have moved into his enormous room.'[20]

Stafford and Isobel then immured themselves for most of August and September in almost total seclusion in Sapperton before making another journey to Zurich, where they arrived at the Bircher-Benner Clinic on 10 October. This was to be a brief stay on the way to Lake Garda for a fortnight's holiday, but some X-rays were taken which showed that Stafford's health was now extremely unlikely to improve sufficiently for him ever to return to work. So he took his doctor's advice and on 4 October he wrote to Attlee to tell him that he would have to take at least a year out and that he was offering his resignation. Meanwhile he and Isobel continued with their holiday, though Stafford spent most of his time in his hotel room at Lake Garda. They returned to Britain on the 16th, when the papers reported he had been suffering from 'colitis' despite the fact that he had been diagnosed as having both spondylitis and cancer.

The next morning he met Attlee for an hour and they finally agreed the inevitable. Two days later he set off for Bristol where he announced his resignation, as Chancellor and as an MP, to his constituency Party. As usual he stayed at the Moorfields vicarage the night before the announcement and told Stockwood his plans, pledging him to secrecy. A reporter, who had caught wind of the story, actually broke into the vicarage and hid behind a sofa in the hope of a scoop, but Stafford discovered him 'and led him to the front door in withering silence'. That night he told Stockwood, 'Be sure to call me early in the morning. I want my last engagement in Bristol to be at the Communion Table.'[21] The next morning he took the train up to London and formally tendered his resignation before clearing his desk at the Treasury.

In many ways, even if Stafford had been healthy his resignation would have come sooner rather than later. He had felt devaluation had undermined his credibility. His honour had been questioned. And just as importantly the Cripps group of Ministers was no longer united. Wilson had backed Bevan against Cripps in the debate over post-devaluation economies, and the devaluation vacillations of the President of the Board of Trade had angered both Jay and Gaitskell. Bevan himself was no longer attending the dinners, and there was a sense in which devaluation had proved a sharp shock for all those who believed in Stafford's ability to provide direction to Labour's economic thinking, not least because he had almost been forced into the decision by his junior ministers. Stafford remained not because he wanted to but because Plowden, Gaitskell, Jay, Hall, Attlee, Dalton, all persuaded him that Labour needed him. It was little surprise that when he finally managed to break free he also resigned from Parliament.

The timing of Stafford's holiday and resignation meant that the last time he spoke in Parliament was in July, and his only return to the Commons during the summer was to vote in the censure debate on the nationalisation of Iron and Steel, on 19 September. Curiously Gaitskell recalled this as being in November, despite the fact that Stafford had already taken the Chiltern Hundreds by then and the writ for the by-election had been served. What is probably accurate, however, is Gaitskell's recollection of Stafford's appearance: 'he looked thin but quite rosy-cheeked . . . later I heard he had some kind of attack and 24 hours later in the Lobby he looked pretty ill.'[22]

So Stafford's Parliamentary career ended. The papers were almost rhapsodic in their praise for him, even those which had been most critical of his 'austerities'. By contrast Stafford was hurt that when he handed in his seals of office on the Friday, the King was perfunctory in the extreme and barely even acknowledged his presence. Whether this was deliberate rudeness or inadvertent shyness to a man whose early public views on the monarchy had been less than flattering, what is particularly notable is quite how distressed Stafford was by the occasion despite having been brusque himself when he handed in his seals in 1945.

There were spontaneously warm farewells though. Gollancz wrote to Stafford,

if, decades or even perhaps hundreds of years hence, it is understood in this country that political and economic policies are valuable only insofar as they are expressions of moral and religious principle, you will have done more than any man of our time, if I may say so, to give that understanding. I do not know whether you are spiritually as well as physically tired. If so, believe me – *experto crede* – that it passes completely and leaves only a deeper faith and a greater inner wealth.[23]

26

The Laws of God, the Laws of Man

When Stafford resigned, despite the fact that the prognosis for his spondylitis was not good, the public statements about his illness were toned down. He had 'colitis' or an 'intestinal complaint' or he was suffering from 'exhaustion', and there was much talk of his returning to 'public work' after a year's rest. Almost certainly what he meant by 'public work' was some kind of religious work, for ever since his mother had hoped that he would be 'trained to be [an] undogmatic and unsectarian Christian' he had been a man of deep religious convictions. In his early life he had expressed this through the diocesan synod and the Church Assembly, through his devotion to the cause of the World Alliance and his regular attendance at Filkins parish church. Yet the World Alliance's mixed reception and the failure of the Churches to rally Christians across Europe so as to prevent war had undermined his faith in the institution and hierarchy of the Church and its lily-livered lethargy was just as much a target for his derision in the thirties as the Labour leadership. So though he remained a communicant throughout the 1930s his involvement in the Church was limited to his local parish church. Yet even here he faced controversy. For the Anglo-Catholic vicar, Mr Austin, out of disapproval of Stafford's views on the monarchy, refused to allow him to read the lesson at Communion as he had done since moving to Goodfellows, and the family had to decamp to the tiny Norman church at the other end of the village in Broughton Poggs, where the vicar's sermons were rather more to Stafford's Christian Socialist taste.

The war reawakened Stafford's religious sensibility and the long period of loneliness in Moscow stirred up deep currents of moral conviction in him. So when William Temple assumed the throne of Canterbury they formed a ready alliance. Temple's appointment while Stafford was Lord Privy Seal was heralded by the press as yet another victory for the Labour Party as Temple had briefly joined the Party as a young vicar, but it now brought Stafford and Temple together so frequently that Chips Channon complained after they, together with Cyril Garbett the Archbishop of York, addressed a mass meeting at the Albert Hall: 'The old Archbishop [Randall Davidson], heaven knows, was foolish and wicked enough, but the new obese one is positively dangerous. He now openly preaches Socialism, from a platform which he shares with Cripps – Is England mad, and doomed?'[1]

Temple's time at Canterbury was short-lived as he died in October 1944, but he was the single most important influence on the post-war Cripps. Coming from the same public school background as Stafford and holding to the same ethic of a fair society in which all could prosper and the State provided for the vulnerable, he was a natural colleague whose loss Stafford mourned at some length. The fact that he was replaced by the dull as ditchwater Geoffrey Fisher (Churchill was not going to appoint two Socialist Archbishops in a row, so George Bell was overlooked) also spurred Stafford on to act as the national apologist for Parliamentary Christian Socialism and by the end of the war religion was as important to him as politics, and prior to rejoining the Labour Party it was with left-leaning Christians like Walter Monckton rather than Socialists that he felt most at home.

Stafford and Isobel now worshipped at the little church of St Kenelm's at Sapperton, where again the vicar, Arthur Ruck, was rather more to Stafford's liking than the vicar at Oakridge Lynch, the parish in which Frith Hill actually sat. Stafford had re-established links with George Bell, the Bishop of Chichester, an old friend from World Alliance days, and was a regular guest at Stockwood's vicarage in Bristol. Together with Bell, Stockwood and John Collins (the RAF chaplain who had got him to speak at Bomber Command) he began to form something of a small Christian Socialist cell, while from late 1944 through to retirement he was the most called for of all Christian speakers. He preached in Westminster Abbey and St Paul's, at the General Assembly of the Church of Scotland, at the Church Assembly, at the Parish Church in Chatham, at Great St Mary's in Cambridge, at St Mary's Redcliffe, and at Gloucester Cathedral. Even his talks to the Marriage Guidance Council, to the Federal Bar Association in Washington, to Save the Children and to the Lancashire and Cheshire Trades Council were imbued with overt Christian references and when he went into print, with first *Towards Christian Democracy (1945)*, then *Democracy Alive* (1946) and later *God in our Work (1949)*, each text was explicitly Christian Socialist. So pervasive was Cripps's faith in all his doings that when John Freeman was writing his obituary for the *New Statesman* he maintained that all his 'life and ways stemmed from his religious faith'.

But what kind of Christian was Cripps?

Theologically he was a conservative. He believed in a personal God with whom the Christian could and should form a direct personal relationship in prayer. As Freeman put it

In the twentieth century intimacy with the Unseen is apt to mark a man, not as a witch, but at least as an uncomfortable companion. Yet this intimacy is the accurate description of [Stafford's] faith. He was a simple devout, unsectarian Christian who, with a somewhat inconsequent disregard for the profundities of theological concept, regarded his God as a personal friend.[2]

In many ways he was then a perfect example of a twentieth-century Anglican, less interested in the minutiae of theological dispute than in the expression of a seven-days-a-week faith. He felt that the Church had failed in its task of moral leadership and he took all the words for his political lexicon from the language of religion. Sacrifice, duty, honour, these were important to him both as spiritual and political terms and he argued long and hard that Christianity could not be confined to a small area termed spirituality, but was a matter that affected the whole of life.

In this, of course, Stafford was not alone. Isobel in particular had a strong faith which had not only brought her into print in the 1920s with a book of biblical quotations and prayers for each day of the month, but had been the driving force behind the several charitable groups she got involved with during and after the war. Peggy was also a devout Christian and a member of the PCC for St John's, St John's Wood where she lived in Felix Topolski's garage flat by Hampstead Heath. She was involved in the youth department of the World Council of Churches and with Attlee's daughter, who had been a missionary in South Africa, she was on the Executive Committee of an organisation called Racial Unity. Her religious fervour was every bit as potent as that of her parents. Indeed Anthony Montague Brown tells the story of a visit by the Cripps family to Paris when he was at the Embassy and had to entertain them in the Embassy's Throne Room as all the dining rooms were being refurbished. As there was a fierce storm that night and there was a power cut they had to eat by candle light. Although he and Stafford had worked together in the war Brown was nevertheless embarrassed to sit in the vast room consuming a splendid entrecote with one of the Embassy's finest bottles of claret while the Chancellor and his family drank Evian and munched on some carrots. He was even more perplexed, however, when a sudden gust of wind in the storm snuffed the candle and they were plunged into darkness. Out of the gloom it was Peggy's voice that asked, 'What is your hobby?' When Brown stated that he had none, Peggy replied, still out of the dark, 'Mine is Christianity.'[3] Brown was generous enough to suggest that he may not have been able to judge whether this was a joke or not, but the story goes to show the overwhelming earnestness that could at times overtake the family, yet with little of the disputatious judgmentalism so often associated with up-front Christianity.

As for churchmanship it has been stated that Stafford was an Anglo-Catholic, and certainly his closest clerical friends Stockwood and Collins were both High Church and Stafford seems to have chosen churches where Communion was the main Sunday service, a sacramental trait he shared with Monckton but which was unusual in his day. Yet Stafford's speeches and writings barely mention sacramental theology and remain resolutely middle ground, while if he did show any ecclesiastical partisanship it was in favour of those who saw a direct link between faith and modern politics. Ever since the days of the Christian Social Union this would have put him in the High Church camp of Gore and Westcott, while his old alliance with George Lansbury would have brought him into contact with Nonconformists like Donald Soper. The truth is, however, that Stafford's interest was not in whether clergy should wear vestments or whether North End celebration should be replaced by the priest facing the congregation. His creed was deeply individualist, appealing to a personal moral code which would equip the nation to match its words with deeds. He often cited John Ruskin, the nineteenth-century artist and Christian Socialist, with his injunction, 'If you don't want a thing don't ask for it. If you do not wish for [God's] Kingdom don't pray for it. But if you do you must do more than pray for it; you must work for it.'[4] Even Church doggerel, if it preached this connection of word and deed, was fine poetry for Stafford:

> Grant us the will to fashion as we feel,
> Grant us the strength to labour as we know,
> Grant us the purpose, ribbed and edged with steel,
> To strike the blow.

> Knowledge we ask not – knowledge thou hast lent,
> But Lord, the will – there lies our bitter need,
> Give us to build above the deep intent
> The Deed – the Deed.

This concern for the uniting of thought and action comes close to the work of the Quaker Socialist philosopher John MacMurray, although in Stafford's own written work none of his contemporary Christian Socialists, nor even Temple, Burge or Lansbury, is cited. The one person who is given credit is F. D. Roosevelt, whose five 'desires of the American people' (equality of opportunity for youth and others; jobs for those who can work; security for those who need it; the ending of privilege for the few; the preservation of civil liberties) formed the core of Cripps's first Christian book, *Towards Christian Democracy*, itself a re-working and expansion of the speech he gave at the William Temple Albert Hall meeting in 1942. Its argument is a restatement, written against the background of the closing months of the war, of the need to make Christianity a living force for what he termed 'social salvation'. Starting with an attack on the idea that faith should be concerned solely with the spiritual world he argues that the Church should be seen 'as the active protagonist of the Kingdom of Heaven, or the rule of God, here on earth, as the pioneer of social salvation, more concerned with creating the greatest sum of human good and happiness here and now, than with encouraging individual merit as a means to personal salvation hereafter.'[5]

All Christians, then 'must insist on the Church instantly under-taking its task of social salvation, as the means of perfecting the rule of God on earth,' and though 'it is not the function of the Church, as an organised body, to enter the lists of the political parties'[6] yet they should be directly engaged in the real world because 'religion should be very much of an every-day affair, and should form the background against which we set all our daily actions' rather than be seen as 'An isolated and particular side of life, as something which we primarily associate with Sunday, with a number of attendances, compul-sory or voluntary, in Church or Chapel, and as the concerns of a body of teachers set apart from the general community by their ordination.'[7]

Allied with this understanding of the role of the Church goes a very particular estimation of the duty of Christians. In what might be a personal apologia he argues:

> Courage and fearlessness of consequences are taught as outstanding Christian virtues, and in this moral leader-ship they must reach their highest level. Leadership does not consist in seeking to interpret and then to follow the wishes of the majority, but rather in the attempt to lead and direct popular thought along the channels of truly Christian action.[8]

Moreover because Christianity 'either means everything or nothing'[9] the level of personal sacrifice that is called for from both individuals and the nation is intense. 'All of us are pre-pared to give, to our last ounce, to win this war, but how many of us will be prepared to make as great a sacrifice to win the peace for Christ?'[10] Winning the peace, the 'victory over war, poverty and disease',[11] is then an explicitly moral task as Britain is not suffering 'from any lack of technical progress but from a complete lack of the moral control of our material achievements'.[12]

It has to be said that *Towards Christian Democracy* is not an important book. It has neither the intellectual rigour of the works of Dalton, of Jay or of Temple or Tawney, nor enough edge to make it exciting polemic. Yet as a historical phenomenon it is fascinating, both in terms of the national inclination to accept the collectivist thrust of the 1945 Government and in terms of Stafford's attempt to integrate the language of Christianity and politics. What is misleading, however, is its title, for though there are occasional sentences that would sit easily in a Christian Democrat tract ('there is a power existing on Earth that is far greater than any material power, that of the spirit'[13]) there is little that takes him away from the Christian Socialism of the day. Thus there is an explicit discussion of the question of private and public ownership in which he comes down in favour of collectivism while arguing that the profit motive itself is not evil:

> However we may organise that production, whether on the basis of private or public enterprise, it must still remain a community service, its object being the service given, not the personal gain or advantage of the individual ... There is nothing inherently wrong or unchristian in the ownership of private property; it is only when the nature of that ownership is such as to enable the arbitrary act of one individual to affect adversely the life and standards of another, that there is a danger and a problem which calls for our attention as Christians.[14]

In fact in his support for nationalisation the only proviso he makes is 'that the democracy controlling the State's actions must be imbued with the Christian spirit'.[15] The role of the Christian politician, then, was overtly to return the State to its Christian heritage, although Stafford never used the triumphalist language of some later Christian politicians and indeed had a thoroughly ecumenical interest not only in other Churches but in other religions as well.

Stafford's faith was heartfelt, but there is some evidence that the reinvigoration of his faith in 1944 and 1945 was no accident. For there was a concerted effort on the part of Bell, Stockwood and Collins to get Stafford more directly involved in the life of the Church. 'I was with the Cripps on Friday evening,' Collins wrote to Bell on 19 March 1945. 'He was not at all well; over tired, I think. My opinion that he is swinging more towards the Church was again confirmed; but he recognises that the C of E is near the precipice. And I fear that he may be tempted to swing back again in a reverse direction.'[16] Collins's aim was at first to get Cripps, the Minister for Aircraft Production, to meet RAF chaplains and to discuss social affairs from a Christian perspective. When Bell and Stockwood caught wind of the idea it soon grew into a plan for a new group, to be called the Church Reform Group, echoing the concerns of Temple's Life and Liberty Movement. There was an initial plan for a meeting on 13–14 April 1945 at which the group was to be inaugurated with Stafford, Isobel and Peggy all forming part of the core, along with Bell, Stockwood, Collins, Richard Acland and Guy Mayfield, another RAF chaplain. As it turned out Stafford and Isobel were not able to attend this meeting, though Peggy did take part. A few days later, despite the fact that he had not yet really contributed to the discussions, Bell wrote to Stafford 'we all depend very much on you, and I hope you do understand what an immense encouragement it is that we have your leadership to rely on'[17] and Stafford in turn agreed to a post-election meeting with a proper agenda.

Despite this fragmented start the group did now start to meet occasionally and a common agenda was drawn up, although by July Collins was 'a little worried ... by the fact that there seem to be two distinct aims in various people's minds. The one is concerned with finding ways and means of relating our religion to the practical affairs of modern life, in particular factory life, political and economic issues etc. The other is more interested in practical reforms within the C of E.'[18] Collins and Bell wanted to start with the second part, Stafford with the first. But this was not the only difference of opinion. Acland, having lost his seat in the election, was still in fighting mood, and insisted that there should be a test of membership, namely that each member should be required 'to let it be publicly known to regard the private ownership of the great productive resources as evil'.[19] This alarmed the moderates in the group, including Stafford, and it was first amended to 'that it must be known of each member of the group that he regards the system of Big Business and Mono- poly Capitalism . . . as evil'.[20] Even so Stafford wanted it changed to something vaguer to do with the profit motive such as the position he had adopted in *Towards Christian Democracy*. There was also a suggestion that the group was rather too dominated by men. Stockwood, though he later supported the ordination of women, took a rather aggressively patronising attitude on this. 'I suppose we must have a hag or two – I know a couple of dames in Bristol. But perhaps you have a few wenches up your sleeve. Moreover, Isobel may know of a bumpkin on her compost heap.'[21]

By the end of 1945 the group was still plagued by differences of opinion as to whether to deal with exclusively Anglican matters relating to ecclesiastical reform or to focus on the same issues as Temple's Malvern Conference of 1941 – industry, welfare, education. Furthermore, Stafford himself was now busy with his new post at the Board of Trade, and clearly had less time than he had expected for the group. Despite Stafford's evident difficulty in getting to attend any meetings Bell still felt that '*Cripps is vital*' and Collins drafted a memorandum for the group which called for 'virile Christian cells not only in the Churches, but also in the homes of the people and in factories, public houses, clubs etc.' which would 'enable the Gospel and the power of the Holy Spirit to permeate all facets of life, social, economic and political, whether local or national'.[22] In many ways it was a Crippsian creed. 'It is not enough for the Church to proclaim ideals; it must take an active part in political and social affairs,' it averred, while arguing that 'the Church should not identify itself with any particular political party. But it should openly and in every way possible, condemn any policy of whatever Party, which is against Christian conscience.'[23]

By Christmas the difficulties of getting the group to apply itself to practical issues and of Cripps's failure to attend became worse and an exchange of letters between Bell and Cripps suggesting an end of year meeting in Bristol with Stockwood, Collins, Acland and Cripps ended with Stafford writing on Christmas Day, 'It does not seem that we shall make a headway unless some few can really go away and think and pray and get down to the very root of things. These learned meetings will get us nowhere.'[24] By the spring the group had imploded.

Not to be deterred, Collins now launched a new initiative which came to fruition with a major meeting at Oxford Town Hall a year later on 5 December 1946 at which Gollancz and Bell as well as Acland and Barbara Ward spoke. This led to the formation of Christian Action, a body devoted to almost exactly the same ideals and principles as the Church Reform Group, but with a more coherent and active cross-party committee chaired by A. D. Lindsay of Balliol, with Lady Pakenham and Quintin Hogg as Vice-Presidents. Subsequently Halifax and Cripps became patrons along with Lord Perth for the Liberals and Stafford was active in using his legal knowledge to have the group registered as a charity.

Christian Action was by no means Stafford's only involvement with Collins and with Stockwood. Not only did Stafford actively lobby for Collins's appointment as a Canon at St Paul's Cathedral, but Isobel even wrote a letter about living with visionary men to his wife Diana to persuade her to let

John take the job and move into London. Moreover when in February 1948 Frank Pakenham, now in the Lords, drafted Collins in to organise a meeting at the Albert Hall to rally Christians in favour of Churchill's idea of a Western European Union, Cripps gave him an office and a secretary at No. 11. Every day from 6.20 a.m. to 7.20 a.m. Collins and Cripps discussed the plans while ambling together round St James's Park and Stafford was the main speaker at the eventual meeting when he proclaimed the words that are inscribed on his memorial bust in St Paul's, 'If man neglects the things of the spirit and puts aside the full armour of God, he will seal the doom of future generations.' When Cripps went to Rome in May 1949 as Chancellor he also met with Vatican officials and discussed the possibility of Anglican-Roman Catholic co-operation in the cause of a united Europe. On his return to England he suggested to Collins that he should meet Dr Gedda, the head of Catholic Action, behind Fisher's back. In fact Fisher caught wind of the meeting and managed to put a stop to it, but Stafford's relations with the Vatican remained cordial and he even sent the Pope a copy of his 1950 lecture, 'The Spiritual Crisis'.

In similar vein when Stockwood was appointed to the British Council of Churches, whose meetings were held in London, Stafford and Isobel gave him a room at No. 11, and Stafford would often walk with him round St James's Park in the early morning.

One of the intriguing factors about all these Christian contacts is that though Stafford had a reputation for asceticism, the Christians he associated with were far from puritanical. Both Collins and Stockwood enjoyed their drink and Stockwood admitted that when he stayed with the Crippses at Sapperton he used to nip off to a local hostelry for 'couponless steak and kidney pie'.[25] He rather lamented the fact that though the dinner plates at No. 11 were silver the food was largely confined to scraped carrots, and he often preferred to walk through to the Attlees' flat, which connected with the Crippses', for a more substantial meal. But Stafford was no puritan either. Even though he drank orangeade instead of the usual alcoholic tipple when delivering his Budgets, he was not an ideological teetotaller, and indeed Edwin Plowden maintained that until his stomach deteriorated he enjoyed an occasional glass of wine. He was also a very heavy smoker in a period when puritans like Donald Soper condemned smoking just as forcefully as drinking. On sexual matters he would undoubtedly have shared the assumption that sex outside marriage was wrong, but like his aunt he was a supporter of family planning. Indeed he was up-front about the issue:

> In matters relating to sex we have tended in the past to be over-prude. We have been afraid of invading our own privacy and uncertain as to our real ideas. We have been half-ashamed of our own divinely created animal instincts and so we have tried to hide them or slur them over. At the same time when we have seen the inevitable results of our own fear of sexual knowledge we have tended sometimes to be over-tolerant of and even to idealise these results . . . In this way we have made a most difficult and dangerous environment in which our young people have grown up. We have hidden the sins but at the same time widely and often attractively publicised their results.[26]

Though this might seem puritanical in the late 1990s, in 1946 it was liberal thinking. Even Stafford's diet was a concession to his ill health and the charge of Puritan, which was just as often levelled against Isobel, whom Channon described as 'his gloomy consort – voluminous and grey',[27] was unfair.

One final accusation that is often aimed against Christian politicians is the misuse of religion for party advantage, and this was no different with Cripps. One of the last things that

Stafford did for John Collins before his retirement was to preach at St Paul's for Christian Action. This was to have been the second in a series of lectures, and had been planned some time in advance, but the timing was unfortunate, for Stafford took to the pulpit on 8 January 1950, only days before the General Election campaign was announced, and many Conservatives complained that it was a misuse of the Church as a campaigning medium. Brendan Bracken whined,

> Stafford Cripps opened the government's campaign during the week-end. On Sunday he preached in St Paul's Cathedral and staked out a claim that he was a man set apart and peculiar to God. On Monday he held a vast press conference in which he claimed that everything was good in John Bull's Garden. He conveniently forgot to make any reference to Marshall Aid, without which a lot of factories would have to close down for lack of raw materials. Uriah Heep would have envied Cripps's capacity for disingenuousness.[28]

In fact the St Paul's sermon was remarkably uncontroversial and, if anything, rather dull. As usual he condemned 'uncontrolled materialism' which 'rising in a crescendo of power, must crash in self-destruction'[29] and he argued that

> we should get back to the standards which Christ set out for us by His example and by His teachings in our public as well as in our private life. Those standards are not easy to maintain and yet the whole future of humanity depends, I believe, upon our being able to make them the common factor throughout our whole national and international life.[30]

But the aim of Stafford's speech was not, as Bracken thought, to garner electoral support. Indeed he had made it clear on countless occasions that the Church should not enter the Party political lists and he had close Christian friends who did not share his Party allegiance. Nevertheless Stafford's whole political life had been built on the belief that politics without faith was missing the point. It both informed his own understanding of his vocation as an act of public service and it meant that he had a duty to proclaim his gospel of 'social salvation'. A cynic and a foe like Bracken could call him a Uriah Heep, but a friend and an eternal optimist like Gollancz was happy to say 'I have never had the slightest doubt that Stafford was one of the best men – and one of the few real socialists – of our time, and that he will rank with Schweitzer as one of the two great Christians-in-action that the last half century has produced.'[31]

Clinic

When Stafford resigned he was very ill and Isobel and he made directly for the Bircher Benner Clinic in Zurich, where his spondylitis was first treated and his doctor, Dagmar Lichte, insisted on his lying entirely immobilised on his back in a vast plaster cast for at least six months. By early December it had been agreed that a spell of 'sun treatment' at a TB clinic in Lausanne under the care of Dr Auguste Rollier and Professor Pierre Decker would be more appropriate and plans were made for his transfer. So Isobel and Stafford spent Christmas with Peggy in the hospital at Zurich. In the New Year, though, Stafford was still not well enough to go to Lausanne until March when he was given radiotherapy.

By May he was back in Zurich and though there were occasional visits including a three week stay by Stafford's stepmother Marion, it was only family, Stockwood and Ivor Watkins, the Bishop of Malmsbury, whom Isobel allowed to see him. Yet there was some recovery and Isobel wrote to George Bell,

> His spirit is strong and since we got back here 6 weeks ago good things have happened. He is free from pain and is sitting almost half up, by the head of his bed being raised. He loves lying out on his balcony where he can get a view of the Lake and mountains after being so many

months flat on his back. We have felt all the prayers to be an active healing power and this place is different from any other place I know. Apart from their efficiency and being in touch with all the latest scientific developments they work on 'man' as a 'whole person' and there is a deeply spiritual atmosphere around one.[1]

The recuperation continued through the summer and by the end of August photos were released of an emaciated Stafford leaning heavily on a stick. In October Isobel and Stafford decided that it was safe for him to return to England where they stayed with John and his wife before returning to Frith Hill where Stafford managed to vote in the General Election which saw Churchill return to power and his friend Monckton, now a Bristol MP, appointed as Minister for Labour. Gaitskell was one of Stafford's visitors during this brief period of remission and he recorded,

I found him in bed because he had suffered what Isobel called a slight set-back in his recovery. They thought that this was the result of just doing too much. Certainly he looked to me much better than the photographs taken when he arrived here from Switzerland six weeks ago. He was fatter, or not so devastatingly thin, and had put on weight. We talked for quite a time mostly about politics and the economic situation, and he seemed interested and quite lively, though by the end I think he was tired. He has certainly had a most appalling experience. He has suffered from three grave illnesses at the same time: TB abscess in the spine; tumours in the stomach and a wasting bone disease. All these are said to have cleared up but left him appallingly weak. The Doctors in Lausanne, Isobel told me, gave him up for lost. But at Zurich they never gave up and somehow or other pulled him through. One gets no clear idea of how this happened, and I rather imagine that they both look on it as a kind of miracle. They are to go back to Switzerland in January for a check-up at Zurich and then stay out there, or in Italy, until the warm weather comes here when they will return. He reads quite a lot but not very serious stuff.[2]

In fact Stafford's reading list during the whole of his time as an invalid was limited to children's literature as he asked Isobel to read *Winnie the Pooh, Dr Doolittle* and *The Secret Garden* to him, while he spent endless hours crocheting.

The remission, however, did not last and Isobel hurried him back to Zurich on 4 January 1952. Theresa, who by now had two children and was expecting a third, remembers seeing him off on the first leg at the small airfield close to both Sapperton and Stafford's childhood summer home of Longfords:

then one grey morning we drove with our two elder children, then aged four and five and a half, to Aston Down to say good-bye, when, accompanied by my mother, he was flown back to Switzerland in an air ambulance. The RAF Officers were very kind and gave the children chocolate biscuits when the plane had gone, but I can still see it taking off down that grey runway, getting smaller and smaller in the distance. We did not see my father again.[3]

By the middle of April Stafford's grasp on life was becoming ever more tenuous. He was also now suffering from leukaemia although the British newspapers reported only 'a rare and dangerous disease'. On 18 April Isobel was so worried that she called John out to be with her and he spent the weekend at the Clinic before returning to London for work. On Saturday the 19th Stafford kept drifting in and out of consciousness before going into a coma on the 20th. By now it was clear that Stafford was going to die and Isobel summoned both Peggy and Freddie. The next day he rallied in the early afternoon, but by the time Freddie arrived in the evening he had lapsed back into the coma. As Freddie saw,

> from the medical point of view, nothing further could be done. I left Isobel in Stafford's room, and went out by myself to dine at a restaurant. I ate a steak and drank a bottle of Burgundy and a brandy and smoked a cigar. All my thoughts were centred on Stafford. As I sat in the restaurant, I reflected how unjust it seemed that such a really saintly character as my brother, who had done so much good in the world, should have to suffer long years of austerity and many months of pain before dying comparatively young, while I, who had all my life sought out the fleshpots, had suffered hardly at all, and was even able to enjoy a good meal while he was dying.[4]

At 11.00 p.m. on 21 April, only a couple of days before his birthday and less than a week after the birth of his latest grandchild, Stafford died, with Isobel, alone, by his side.

The next morning Peggy arrived and was greeted at the station by Isobel.

> It was not until we were halfway out of the station that she told me that my father had passed away during the night . . . It was not until evening that I went to see my father. I had not wanted to go until I could wash and quieten down. As it was I felt little emotion as the spirit was so obviously elsewhere. What was there was peaceful and inanimate, like ivory delicately carved but it had no relationship whatever to reality. From that moment I realised how much I felt the reality of the spirit as something outside this spiritual world. I said a prayer for peace

and of thanks and knew that Daddy was at last resting in the best of hands. We collected flowers from the woods and garden.[5]

Two days later the cremation was held at the cavernous granite mausoleum in Zurich, by which time John had flown back out and most of the family were together. Peggy was impressed that 'despite the fact that this was in Switzerland . . . there were flowers from many places including the British Labour Party and the Swiss Labour Party, from the Indian Legation, and of course all our Swiss friends and family.'[6] That same day the family returned to England and the following morning gathered in Sapperton for the burial of the ashes which was done by Stockwood. There were the usual memorial services, at Bristol Cathedral and at Westminster Abbey, and the tributes poured in.

Isobel, after forty-one years of marriage and two years of unstinting dedication to Stafford, found her first refuge in the family, especially her new grandchild, and in the support of Elsie Lawrence who stayed in her service. It did not take long, however, for her to take up some of the 'public work' that Stafford might have devoted himself to. She travelled to India the following year with Bevan, she founded the Star Centre for the Disabled in Cheltenham and she campaigned against the death penalty. She also took an active interest in her daughter Peggy's marriage to the young radical Ghanaian lawyer and activist Joe Appiah. Peggy had met Joe before Stafford's death when she was Secretary of Racial Unity and had been to the West African Students Union headquarters on the Chelsea Embankment, of which he was President. Because they feared that he would not approve of a 'mixed marriage' they did not tell him of the relationship before his death and though Joe attended the memorial service at Westminster Abbey with the family, they waited for a year before announcing their engagement. When Peggy's children grew up Isobel arranged their education back in Britain, and when Joe was in prison she was happy to visit him and campaigned for Amnesty International's support for his case.

Isobel lived for twenty-seven years after Stafford's death, first at Frith Hill and then at a smaller house in nearby Minchinhampton and like his mother she took to spiritualism during these later years and often tried to contact him, attending seances run by friends who were mediums and reporting 'again and again . . . that my (Peggy's) father was doing all he could to help from the other side'.[7] Isobel had always been rather mawkish. Her one publication *God is Love* had consisted of daily readings and prayers in a very pietistic tradition, and in the phrases she selected for her printed condolence cards there is a hint of a sentimentality that belied Stafford's toughness: 'This is the comfort of friends, that though they may be said to die, yet their friendship and society are in the best sense ever present because immortal.'

Legacies

When Stafford died the noted pianist Myra Hess, who had run a much-publicised series of free concerts during the war, wrote an intriguing letter to *The Times*, as if to correct an impression that had been left by the obituary notices. 'Throughout the war years', she wrote,

> Sir Stafford and Lady Cripps would drive up to my house in Hampstead, when an hour or two could be spared from his overwhelming responsibilities, for the refreshment and relaxation of listening to music . . . I have such vivid memories of these evenings, especially in winter when Stafford would kneel on the hearth saying "nobody can lay a log fire" and proceed to build one that would last for the rest of the night.[1]

What is fascinating is not so much the picture of the work-aholic Minister taking a long evening out to lounge around listening to music, nor the list of Stafford's favourite composers (a conventional list of Mozart, Schubert and Beethoven) but the fact that Hess felt the need to correct an impression of a cold but honourable impervious puritan. Hess, like Isobel, like Gollancz, like Lansbury and ultimately like Attlee, felt the need to stand up for Stafford, to defend him. It was a theme throughout his life. There was a part of him that made others feel he was alone pitched against a hostile world and that the honourable thing was to stand by him. The sickly over-protected motherless baby lived on in the Socialist outsider, the exiled Ambassador, the ignored Lord Privy Seal, the Chancellor who told it as it was.

It was a facet of his character that was nowhere more evident than in his relations with people of a different class from his own. There is a illuminating photograph of him speaking to Lord Linlithgow in 1942 at the Viceroy's Residence in New Delhi. He is slightly bent, wearing a crumpled casual linen jacket and tie and evidently requesting something from the Viceroy. Lady Linlithgow is watching, parasol in hand, her face a picture, looking down at Stafford with as much hauteur as a Viceroy's wife could show to a left-wing politician. Her attitude is understandable. To her Stafford was a dangerous radical who had no respect for monarchy. What is more interesting is that Stafford's whole demeanour is one of defer-ence, despite the fact that he was the Lord Privy Seal at this point. He clearly felt that although he was the son of a Peer he was no aristocrat but just a successful member of the pro-fessional classes. For all his 'classless society' bombast he knew his place just as surely as he knew the pecking order at Winchester, and social differences unsettled him. Indeed it was in part this sense of social unease that affected his relations with much of the Labour movement, for he equally afforded deference to working class figures like Lansbury, Bevan and Pollitt as to aristocrats like Acland or Trevelyan. Michael Foot interpreted his fondness for working-class politicians as an act of snobbery but Stafford's perceptions were more complicated and for all his apparent charm and evident self-confidence there was in him a subtle craving for attention, a vulnerability that made people want to protect him. It was a tenderness, though, that was rarely on public view and was only intuited by those who knew him well. In part it was what others mistook for a martyr's complex, but it was also what bound

Attlee to him and made it impossible for Bevan finally to confront the Cabinet while Stafford was still alive.

When he died this same need to correct the public impression lived on. All three biographies written before his death reek of the misunderstood Cripps being defended by his loyal supporters, and even Colin Cooke's portrait in 1957 succumbed to the hagiographic urge. But a politician and a statesman cannot be judged on such subjective evidence and I must be more brutal in dealing with Cripps's legacy. For Parmoor, having been a convent for several years, now only has one nun left and is to become an old people's home. Goodfellows is only partly still standing. Christian Action closed in 1996. *Tribune* has become an atheistic and vindictive tabloid. The nationalisations of Civil Aviation, Gas, Electricity have all been overturned. And out of the twelve elections since Stafford died Labour has won only five times and governed for no more than eleven out of forty-five years, while Stafford's name has become synonymous, for those who remember it, with 'austerity' and the only memorials to him are a Jacob Epstein bust in St Paul's and a block of council flats in Islington.

So how should we judge him? Edmund Dell reckons he was not austere enough; Corelli Barnett that he was the only technocratically competent minister in a feeble team; Roy Jenkins that he was a brilliant workaholic; Alec Cairncross that he was the best and most honourable but unimaginative Chancellor Britain could have had; Edwin Plowden that he was the first modern Chancellor. In the terms of the 1945–50 Governments, and in terms of the electorate of the day, his was an almost unblemished Ministerial career. The pursuit of production targets, the determination to increase efficiency, harness innovation, improve management, target depressed areas, abolish regional unemployment, invest in infrastructure, prioritise production for export at the expense of personal luxuries – all as part of 'democratic planning' – worked. The seeds of Britain's economic recovery in the fifties were sown under Cripps at both the Board of Trade and the Treasury. Throughout his Chancellorship Britain enjoyed full employment across the country, there was a Budget surplus in every year, inflation was kept low even after devaluation, wages and dividends were restrained and Britain managed to pay for both its military commitments and the most ambitious of welfare programmes which effectively abolished the poverty that had beset returning veterans after the First World War. Britain was healthier, better housed and more securely employed than she had ever been and as Alec Cairncross said, 'It must be very doubtful whether any set of government policies could have done more . . . the one thing it had to plan, and it did plan – the balance of payments – was effectively planned.'[2] There were mistakes. He never properly resolved the impending financial crisis in the NHS. He failed to stand up to Bevin's absurdly inflated and costly international pretensions. His opposition to the independent nuclear deterrent, solely on the grounds of cost, was far too muted. His approach to Britain's role in Europe was short-sighted and his refusal to give the French and Germans advance notice of the devaluation led to unnecessary bad blood. His asseverations against devaluation were too frequent and too insistent. Yet he was one of the best administrative ministers Britain has ever had.

Stafford was not just a minister, however, and it is tempting to think of Stafford the politician as something of a failure. After all, an astute politician does not get himself exiled from the mainstream immediately before a major war, nor insist on an election immediately after a devaluation to test the popularity of the Government's economic policies. Yet this is to judge Stafford by today's terms. For most of today's political class (myself included) are hard and fast party loyalists and we have grown used to little political fluidity. Loyalty to party is *the* badge of integrity and the media judge a party by its ability to maintain unanimity of opinion. We believe in the immutability of political parties, but in the half century to 1945 this was patently untrue. Not only had the Labour Party been born and split (twice), but the Liberals had died and split and come together again and there had been twenty years of Coalition Governments. Churchill had ratted and re-ratted. Bevan had belonged to three Parties, and the bevy of Independent MPs included old school friends like D. N. Pritt and A. P. Herbert. So Stafford's belief that party mattered less than programme or than principle – a belief he shared with his father – was the product of experience as well as a moral intuition that what Burge called the 'art of constructive statesmanship' was above Party politics. As the 1990s come to a close, in an era when politicians are immensely distrusted and the whole fabric of democracy has fallen into disrepute, this appeal to a higher law than party loyalty is vital. For unless we can find a better way of running government (less confrontational in manner, more open in debate) it seems likely that politics will become so anodyne as to be meaningless and confidence in democracy will dissipate as elections become a straightforward battle between two competing tribes. That Labour and the Conservatives met in the 1997 election on similar political ground is no bad thing. Government by consent is an essential element of any democratic society. But that whole areas of serious political consideration should become the sole preserve of the populist viewpoint that will appease the tabloids must be worrying. Without honourable dissent democracy is hegemony and the intrusive lights of the media are in severe danger of scorching non-conformism from the political landscape. Moreover *Tribune* was right to commend Cripps for his refusal to meddle with the economy for Party advantage. In the end not only is it better economics, but it also makes better electoral sense to run the economy sagely in the interests of the whole nation. For electorates have long memories when it comes to major economic failures and the long-term advantage will always lie with the sound financiers rather than the electoral gimmickeers.

It would be wrong, however, to suggest that Stafford had no guile and was incapable of the darker arts. He may have been particularly inept at plotting but he was entirely aware of how to use his own persona for political ends and it was no accident that his lifestyle became so well known. (The *Picture Post* even carried details of how he did the washing up.) He deliberately used his reputation for frugal living in order to encourage what he saw as the sacrifices the nation had to make in order to win the war and the peace and he took pride in *Tribune*'s comment that

> his integrity and fundamental decency of purpose were ... more powerful electoral assets than many realised. No Government in history has ever so steadfastly declined to tinker with the economic system in order to make party capital. No Government has ever held out less glimmering hopes or told the truth more bluntly. It was largely because people felt that, in economic matters, the Government *was* Cripps that they felt it could be trusted.[3]

He even admitted to Eden, who thought that Cripps would not survive in a less stringent and austere political age, that he underestimated his versatility. This is not to suggest that Stafford adopted his austere lifestyle out of political craft. Most of his personal regime was related to his dietary needs and a faddish dedication to Cosmovitalism, but he realised that if anyone could sell sacrifice to the nation it would have to be somebody who had manifestly made sacrifices of their own. It was his duty, if he was calling on others to work 'one hundred per cent' to do so himself. So he worked early hours and long days and wore himself into his early grave. He realised that politics is not solely, or even mainly, about legislation and he elevated exhortation and leadership by example to a political art. In this sense he was simply the right man at the right moment. Britain needed to tighten her belt so as to close the dollar drain and make herself solvent again. Stafford was the embodiment of that policy who made it possible for Labour to win an election with such a record of stringency. Occasionally the leaven was lightened. Stafford made sure the 1948 London Olympics were a success, he laid the foundations for the Festival of Britain and opened the Edinburgh Festival and the Tate Gallery. Indeed he loaned a painting by Augustus John and a bronze by Jacob Epstein to the Tate. But although he was no ascetic these were small public instances of a more catholic personality that almost reinforced the convenient image of a sedulous honest broker.

Stafford was not, however, above Party knockabout and both his election in Bristol in 1935 and his role in the 1945 and 1950 election campaigns were fraught with accusations and counter-accusations. He rarely showed anger in public, but he was no slouch when it came to political invective, often successfully attacking the most popular of national figures, Churchill and the 'Radio Doctor'. Furthermore, although he could at times be prosaic in the extreme he was an expert Commons performer who could lighten the moment with humour, as in his 1939 assault on the Criminal Justice Bill: 'No doubt the Colonel Blimps will continue to tell us that they became what they are owing to the good doses of corporal punishment which they received at Eton or some other suitable seminary; and as they are what they are we shall be more than ever impressed with the *evil* results of corporal punishment.'[4]

One other thing stands in Stafford's favour. For despite the apparent dogmatism of his thirties posturing, as a minister Stafford was the least ideological of all his Labour colleagues. Having worked in and with private industry he believed neither in the private nor the public sector, but in a partnership between the two. For him nationalisation was not an ideological article of faith, but a tool, in some industries, for ensuring that private interests did not undermine the common good. If it could be proved that nationalisation would improve efficiency through economies of scale or through greater national direction, then Stafford was in favour. If not, he was opposed. A genuinely mixed social economy, with no dogmatic preference but a rational judgment was his aim. It was this common sense approach of British Socialism that so endeared the Labour Party to Reinhold Niebuhr, the American pastor who visited Stafford just before the war and was a regular correspondent. As he put it 'the British are sane rather than intellectual . . . they apply their intelligence directly to the situations in which they stand and are thus able to gauge and apprehend the imponderables of politics in a way which no consistent political theory is able to do.'[5] For Stafford, as for the modern Labour Party, this was the greatest of compliments and it is a source of regret that such pragmatism did not prevail longer before the Party started on its modernising course under Tony Blair.

In international diplomacy Stafford's record, though not impeccable, remains impressive. For although the adulation he received on his return from Moscow was undeserved and it was Hitler not Cripps that brought Russia into the war, yet without Stafford's dogged persistence Stalin might have chosen to appease Hitler rather than fight and Churchill might never have treated Russia as an ally. He was no diplomat, but his advocacy of the Grand Alliance a full ten years before Churchill laid claim to it for his own, did eventually bear fruit in the combination against Fascism.

In India Stafford's attempts were less successful. Too wedded to Congress, too much in awe of Gandhi, too friendly with Nehru, he never had the deftness of touch to get concessions out of the Indians or proper authority out of London. So an unhappy, botched compromise that fatally split Kashmir and made Pakistan almost ungovernable, came about unplanned, and even if Stafford felt Indian independence was a major achievement, the only real success lay in the fact that Indian goodwill was not entirely frittered away.

On European integration again judgment depends on your own stance. Stafford, like Churchill, believed that Britain was quintessentially different from the rest of Europe. There should be a European Union, perhaps even a United States of Europe, but Britain should stand alone, a go-between in mid ocean between America and Europe. In very large measure this was because Stafford's loyalties lay not with Europe but with the Commonwealth and he had an exaggerated expectation that even divested of her Empire Britain would remain a 'world power'. This fallacy led him to do much of the leg-work for the Organization for European Economic Co-operation and the Marshall Plan, but then refuse to co-operate in the Schuman plan for iron and steel, thus beginning the sidelining of Britain in Europe and setting the pattern for Labour's anti-European stance that lasted well into the 1990s.

Biographers are often asked whether they like their subject and I confess that I am still uncertain. There is much to admire: his independence of spirit, his receptive intelligence, his powerful memory, his belief in moral principle, his resilience and political courage, his management style and his hard work. Yet it is difficult not to have that respect clouded by the words of those who found him unemotional, rigid, arrogant, cold and impenetrable. So many of his speeches reek of such self-confidence that it is hard not to resent him, and the faint whiff of self-righteousness that attended him long after the shenanigans of the 1930s, does irritate. It was, after all, a strangely arrogant man who could tell Dalton that he could not return for the second half of a National Executive meeting because 'It's cost me £120 to be here this morning and I might just as well have sent my typist.'[6] Beatrice Webb saw this arrogance as his greatest failing, writing to Laski, 'I think he is an enigma. He is a great lawyer and a good man. But he is ignorant about political social and economic institutions. *And he does not know he is ignorant.* That is his great defect.'[7] So it is tempting to see in Stafford Cripps a prig, a moralist, a Pharisee. His daughter Peggy unwittingly wrote:

All through my life I have had to fight pride and ego-centricity . . . There are many people in the world who do all the right things, seem kind and generous, or even give away all they have and slave for others. Yet they maintain at their centre a hard core of pride in themselves and seem to have little genuine and spontaneous feeling. At the other extreme are those prodigals who are fundamentally generous and yet are completely immoral. Sometimes I feel that the latter may be nearer to God.[8]

There is truth in this. Virtue is not attractive and Cripps would have been an easier and a more attractive person if he had been a little more obviously flawed. Yet he was not as strong emotionally or physically as his work schedule and his outward appearance might suggest. Illness, whether real or hypochondriac, plagued him from his very early days and the ability to overcome tiredness and debility by sheer determination was phenomenal. And most of those who worked with him were happy to take the rough with the smooth. J. T. Murphy wrote a fairly balanced appreciation of him during the war:

A very able chairman, as one would expect a lawyer to be. I found him to be a very likeable person, though a trifle conscious of his old school tie. As an orator he loses power by reading his brief. He is not a political theorist: he has certain moral principles and Socialist ideals. For the rest, he is essentially an opportunist learning from experience and frequently burning his fingers.[9]

The major disappointment about Cripps, though, is that although he was a prudent and intelligent adminstrator he had too little concern for ideas to have a lasting effect on the Labour movement. He should have spent his exile in Moscow writing a major innovative work of political thought. He could, for instance, have written the tome that still has not been written reconciling Socialism with competition and the market, articulating the philosophy behind the partnership between private and public sectors he espoused. And if he had been in a stronger position when he rejoined the Party he might have been more courageous in opposing the automatic assumption that everything should be nationalised, or at least sought a more coherent way of nationalising industries so as to retain their competitive edge rather than simply create unelected and unaccountable monopolies that were doomed to fail. But he was never an intellectual. Systems, not ideas, excited him and his intelligence was often wasted in great feats of pedantry or of memory rather than passionate curiosity.

The only area to which he was prepared to devote intellectual energy was the synthesis of his unsectarian Christianity and politics. Even here, as Reinhold Niebuhr noted, he was no philosopher. 'Cripps was baffled by my theology,' he admitted, despite the fact that they agreed so wholeheartedly on politics. Theology, though, was never the point. What mattered was how to translate Sunday's religion into the world of work, of industry, of politics. The immediate identification of Christianity with Socialism frightened him, but the insistence that the principles of Christianity could be rendered into political action was central to his understanding of what it was to be a politician. This made Cripps an idealist, but unlike many Christian Socialists either his upbringing or his experience of exclusion from the Labour Party taught him that purity without power was impotence. It was only in exercising power that idealism made sense. Neither the backbenches nor the

Opposition benches held any attraction for him, and he was resolute and unabashed in both his personal ambition and his determination to win elections. On the eve of war Stafford made the calculation that dogma or any 'short-cut to Utopia' must be a mistake. This did not mean he cut his ideological cloth to the prevailing psephological wind, but that compromise and partnership, the tactics of realpolitik, consciously became essential parts of his political style. It meant that throughout his diplomatic and ministerial career he tried to combine idealism with power, defying the cynical cry that power must of its nature corrupt.

In this he was an incipient Labour moderniser, proclaiming that politics is a moral endeavour in which values and principles are ultimately more important than ideological niceties or over-arching blueprints for Utopia. Such idealism matched with an ambition to secure power attracted showers of cynical abuse from the likes of Churchill ('There but for the grace of God, goes God') and Bracken ('our white Gandhi'), but Stafford's secure belief was that unsectarian, undogmatic faith was still the richest seam in British politics. The challenge was to tie 'our daily action to our faith' in the sure and certain knowledge that the future of civilisation would be guaranteed 'not by our material ingenuity but by our moral strength'. Even in the more churchgoing era of the 1940s such an overtly religious political vision was courageous but the charge he gave the boys at Monkton Combe School in May 1948 was the same vocation he had always sought to follow:

> I am not suggesting that you should devote yourselves to a sort of goody-goody pie-in-the-sky-by-and-by existence, not in the least. I hope you will get right down into the political, social and economic struggle, mixing with people of all classes and kinds – the bad as well as the good – and there in the storm and uncertainty and fear that today permeates the world set yourselves to become

part of the hand of God which stretches out to bring peace and patience and high standards of truth and justice to all peoples, for only these can solve the world's troubles.[10]

Across twenty political years Stafford suffered more than his share of slings and arrows. His Anglican non-conformity gave him courage. His scientific training lent him great forensic skills. His Edwardian sense of duty pushed him into his early grave. And it was a passionate belief that time was God's most precious gift that made him hate the idle life. Small wonder he always loved to quote the words Tennyson put into the mouth of Ulysses:

> Yet all experience is an arch wherethro'
> Gleams that untravell'd world, whose margin fades
> For ever and for ever when I move.
> How dull it is to pause, to make an end,
> To rust unburnish'd, not to shine in use![11]

Nor is it a surprise that Stafford's death inspired in his American co-religionist friend Neibuhr one simple thought. 'It is one of the strangest aspects of political life that so many public men fall far below their own insight and consciousness of what is the right and wise thing to do on the assumption that their fellow men are not equal to appreciating what is good and true.'[12] For Cripps ever valued probity above popularity – which was both his strength and his weakness.

Notes

Abbreviations

AEM, Anthony Eden, *The Memoirs*, 3 Vols (Cassell, 1960–5)

BLPES, British Library of Political and Economic Science

BWD, Norman and Jeanne MacKenzie, *The Diary of Beatrice Webb*, 4 Vols. (Virago, 1984)

CCSC, Colin Cooke, *The Life of Richard Stafford Cripps* (Hodder & Stoughton, 1957)

EESC, Eric Estorick, *Stafford Cripps* (Heinemann, 1949)

GNWR, Patrick Gordon-Walker Papers, Churchill College, Cambridge

HDPD, Ben Pimlott (ed.), *The Political Diary of Hugh Dalton 1918–40, 1945–60* (Cape, 1986)

HDWD, Ben Pimlott (ed.), *The Second World War Diary of Hugh Dalton 1940–45* (Cape, 1986)

HGD, Philip Williams (ed.), *The Diary of Hugh Gaitskell 1945–56* (Cape, 1983)

LPACR, Labour Party Annual Conference Report

PRO, Public Record Office (see Bibliography)

RHD, Alec Cairncross (ed.), *The Robert Hall Diaries 1947–53*, (Unwin Hyman, 1989)

WCSWW, Winston Churchill, *The Second World War*, 6 Vols (Cassell, 1948–54)

As Stafford Cripps's private papers have not yet been amalgamated or fully catalogued, I have generally given references for printed sources such as Eric Estorick's biography rather than the primary material upon which he drew and which will eventually be placed in Nuffield College, Oxford.

Chapter 1 Mothers and Aunts

1   BWD, Vol. 2, p. 27.
2   Beatrice Webb, MS diary 6 November 1884, cited in *My Apprenticeship* (Penguin edn, 1971), p. 205.

3   Stephen Hobhouse, *Margaret Hobhouse and Her Family* (Stanhope, 1934), pp. 120–1.

4   Barbara Caine, *Destined to be Wives, the Sisters of Beatrice Webb* (Clarendon, 1986), p. 22.

5   Beatrice Webb, *My Apprenticeship* (Longmans, 1926) p. 12.

6   Alfred Cripps, *Memoir of Theresa Cripps* (privately printed, 1893), p. 18.

7   Stephen Hobhouse, *Margaret Hobhouse and Her Family*, p. 19.

8   Lawrencina Potter's journal 27 June 1858, Passfield papers.

9   Theresa Potter to Beatrice Potter 1873, Passfield papers II I (1) 106.

10   Beatrice Webb, unpublished diary, 2 June 1905, Passfield papers.

11   Georgie Potter to Beatrice Potter, 11 September, Passfield papers MS 4 f. 92.

12   Mary Potter to Beatrice Potter, no date, Beatrice Webb unpublished diaries, Passfield papers MS 4 f. 88.

13   BWD, Vol. 2, p. 27.

14   Beatrice Webb, unpublished diary 22 May 1893, Passfield papers.

15   Stephen Hobhouse, *Margaret Hobhouse and Her Family*, pp. 120–1.

16   Alfred Cripps, *Memoir of Theresa Cripps*, p. 70.

17   Beatrice Webb, cited in Cripps's memoir, cited in EESC, p. 17.

18   BWD, Vol. 2, pp. 27–8.

19   Barbara Caine, *Destined to be Wives, the Sisters of Beatrice Webb*, p. 60.

20   Colonel the Hon. Freddie Cripps, *Life's a Gamble* (Odhams Press, 1957), p. 17.

21   Ibid., p. 17.

22   Theresa Cripps's valedictory letter to her husband, cited in EESC, p. 21.

23   Cited in Stephen Hobhouse, *Margaret Hobhouse and Her Family*, p. 131.

24   Freddie Cripps, *Life's a Gamble*, p. 17.

25   Cited in EESC, p. 17.

26   Alfred Cripps memoir, cited in EESC, p. 20.

27   Cited in Stephen Hobhouse, *Margaret Hobhouse and Her Family*, p. 131.

28   Kate Courtney's journal cited ibid., p. 130.

29   BWD, Vol. 2, p. 27.

30   Ibid., p. 29.

31   Cited in Stephen Hobhouse, *Margaret Hobhouse and Her Family*, p. 131.

32   Cited in EESC, pp. 20–1.

33   Ibid., p. 21.

Chapter 2 'Dad'

1   Alfred Cripps's diary, 4 June 1890.

2   Cited in EESC, p. 31.

3   Margaret Hobhouse to Georgina Meinertzhagen, 2 June 1893, cited in Stephen Hobhouse, *Margaret Hobhouse and Her Family* (Stanhope, 1934), p. 132.

4   Alfred Cripps's letter to Stafford Cripps, 12 June 1893, cited in EESC, p. 30.

5   Alfred Cripps's letter to Stafford Cripps, 14 September 1899, cited in EESC, p. 36.

6   Alfred Cripps, *A Retrospect, looking back over a life of more than 80 years* (Heinemann, 1936), p. 8.

7   Miriam Cripps, *Family Story* (privately published, 1953), p. 44.

8   Barbara Caine, *Destined to be Wives* (Clarendon, 1986), p. 135.

9   Ruth Egerton, cited in EESC, p. 33.

10   Ibid.

11   Ibid.

12   Miriam Cripps, *Leonard Cripps* (privately published, 1960), p. 9.

13   Mary Playne to Lallie Holt, no date, Holt papers 920 Dur 11/8/25.

14   EESC, p. 31.

15   Kate Courtney's journal, Passfield papers.

16   Freddie Cripps, *Life's a Gamble* (Odhams, 1957), p. 16.

17   EESC, pp. 31-2.

18   BWD, Vol. 2, p. 61.

19   Ibid., p. 131

20   Freddie Cripps, *Life's a Gamble*, p. 42.

21   EESC, p. 32.

22   Ibid.

23   Stafford Cripps to Alfred Cripps, 1897, cited in EESC, p. 34.

24   EESC, pp. 32-3.

25   Freddie Cripps, *Life's a Gamble*, p. 24.

26   Miriam Cripps, *Leonard Cripps,* p. 10.

27   Freddie Cripps, *Life's a Gamble*, p. 23.

28   Mary Marshall to Stafford Cripps 15 September 1899, cited in EESC, p. 37.

29   Freddie Cripps, *Life's a Gamble*, p. 29.

30   Stafford Cripps to Alfred Cripps 1897, cited in EESC p. 34.

31   Freddie Cripps, *Life's a Gamble*, p. 43.

32   Ibid.

33   Charles Dickens, *Dombey and Son*, ch. 8.

Chapter 3 Winchester Notions

1   Cyril Connolly, *Enemies of Promise* (Routledge, 1938), p. 325.

2   Cited in James Sabben-Clare, *Winchester College After 600 Years, 1382-1982* (Paul Cave, 1981), p. 48.

3   Ibid., p. 143.

4   Ibid., p. 150.

5   Cited in J. d'E. Firth, *Winchester* (Blackie & Son, 1936), p. 145.

6   Seddon Cripps, *Winchester College Notions* (P. & G. Wells, 1901), p. 140.

7   Alfred Cripps, *A Retrospect, looking back over a life of more than 80 years* (Heinemann, 1936), p. 21.

8   D. N. Pritt, *The Autobiography* (Lawrence and Wishart, 1965), Vol. 1, p. 7.

9   Cited in James Sabben-Clare, *Winchester College After 600 Years,* p. 10.

10   Ibid., p. 82.

11   J. d'E. Firth, *Winchester*, p. 109.

12   Hubert Burge to Alfred Cripps, April 1907, cited in Freddie Cripps, *Life's a Gamble* (Odhams Press, 1957), p. 44.

13   Hubert Burge, *Discourses and Letters* (Chatto & Windus, 1930), p.19.

14   Lord Charnwood in Hubert Burge, *Discourses and Letters*, p. 42.

15   Ibid., p. 44.

16   Hubert Burge, *Addresses* (Medici Society, 1926), p. 49.

17   Lord Charnwood in Hubert Burge, *Discourses and Letters,* p. 51.

18   Hubert Burge, *Addresses*, p. 32.

19   Ibid., p. 37.

20   Freddie Cripps, *Life's a Gamble*, p. 32.

21   W.B. Croft to Alfred Cripps, cited in EESC, p. 39.

22   Hubert Burge to Alfred Cripps, cited in EESC, p. 39.

23   Richard Crossman, *The Charm of Politics* (Hamish Hamilton, 1958), pp 116–7.

24   J. d'E. Firth, *Winchester*, p. 89.

25   EESC, pp. 43–4.

Chapter 4 The Jewel of an Advocate

1   BWD, Vol. II, p.62.

2   Alfred Cripps, *A Retrospect, looking back over a life of more than 80 years* (Heinemann, 1936), pp. 6, 16–7.

3   Ibid., p. 50.

4   Ibid., p. 49.

5   Beatrice Webb, MS diary 6 November 1884, cited in *My Apprenticeship* (Penguin edn, 1971) p. 205

6   BWD, Vol. 2, p. 62.

7   Alfred Cripps, *A Retrospect*, p. 51.

8   Ibid., p. 62.

9   BWD, Vol. 2, p.63.

10   Cited in G.P. Gooch, *Life of Lord Courtney* (Macmillan, 1920), pp. 438–9.

11   Ibid., p. 299.

12   *South Bucks Free Press*, 7 January 1910.

13   Henry Hobhouse cited in Stephen Hobhouse, *Margaret Hobhouse and Her Family* (Stanhope, 1934), p. 127.

14   Georgina Meinertzhagen to Leonard Courtney, cited ibid., p. 89.

15   Ibid., p. 127.

16   Cited in Chris Bryant, *Possible Dreams* (Hodder & Stoughton, 1996), p. 102.

Chapter 5 Marriage and Munitions

1   *South Bucks Free Press*, 21 January 1910.

2   Ibid.

3   *South Bucks Free Press*, 28 January 1910.

4   Harold Swithinbank to Alfred Cripps, 19 January 1911, cited in EESC, p. 42.

5   Alfred Cripps, *A Retrospect, looking back over 80 years*, p. 104.

6   *Hansard*, 11 July 1939, col. 2175–6.
7   BWD, Vol. 4, 19 September 1934, p. 340.

Chapter 6 Essex Court and Goodfellows

1   EESC, p. 44.
2   EESC, p. 81.
3   Lawrence Weaver, *Small Country Houses of Today* (Country Life, 1922), Vol. 1, p. 39.
4   Peggy Appiah, 'The attic of my mind', *Something About the Author, Autobiography series*, Vol. 19, p. 53.
5   BWD, Vol. 4, 19 September 1934, p. 340.
6   Clough Williams-Ellis, *Lawrence Weaver* (G. Bles, 1933), p. 75.
7   Ibid., p. 40.
8   Herbert Morrison, *An Autobiography* (Odhams, 1960), p. 115.
9   EESC, p. 56.

Chapter 7 A Public Life

1   Alfred Cripps, *A Retrospect, looking back over a life of more than 80 years* (Heinemann, 1936), p. 110.
2   Ibid., p. 112.
3   BWD, Vol. 3, 14 July 1920, pp. 345–6.
4   Cited in Peter d'Arcy Jones, *The Christian Socialist Revival, 1877–1914* (Princeton University Press, 1968), p. 188.
5   *Goodwill*, Vol. 2, 1916–17, p. 280.
6   EESC, p. 64.
7   *Goodwill*, Vol. 4, p. 235.
8   Alfred Cripps, *A Retrospect*, p. 193.
9   BWD, Vol. 3, 15 January 1924, p. 436.
10 *Goodwill*, Vol. V, No. 12, June 1923, p. 260.
11 CCSC, p. 93.
12 EESC, p. 77.
13 CCSC, p. 103.
14 EESC, p. 77.
15 Ibid., pp. 77–8.
16 Herbert Morrison, *An Autobiography* (Odhams, 1960), p. 115.
17 EESC, p. 79
18 Leah Manning, *A Life for Education* (Victor Gollancz, 1970), p. 78.
19 Ibid., p. 80.
20 Cited in Froom Tyler, *Cripps* (Harrap, 1942), p. 17.
21 BWD, Vol. 4, 19 January 1931, p. 235.
22 D. N. Pritt, *The Autobiography* (Lawrence and Wishart, 1965), Vol. 2, pp. 27, 28.
23 EESC, pp. 88–9.

Chapter 8 A Slap-up Socialistic Policy

1   Cited in Fenner Brockway, *Bermondsey Story: The Life of Alfred Salter* (Stephen Humphrey, 1995), p. 175.
2   Clement Attlee, *As It Happened* (Heinemann, 1954), p. 76.
3   Cited in EESC, p. 91.
4   Ibid., p. 92.
5   Clement Attlee, *As It Happened*, p. 76.
6   Ibid., p. 75.
7   Ibid., p. 76.
8   Michael Foot, *Aneurin Bevan, 1897–1945* (Paladin, 1975), p. 167.
9   HDPD, Saturday 8 October 1932, p. 169.
10 Beatrice Webb, unpublished diary, 4 October 1932, BLPES.
11 BWD, Vol. 4, 7 March 1932, pp. 282–3.
12 Stafford Cripps to R. J. Furley, 31 October 1931, cited in EESC, p. 104.
13 Beatrice Webb to Stafford Cripps, 1931, cited in EESC, p. 117.
14 George Lansbury to Stafford Cripps, 17 July 1932, cited in EESC, pp. 118–9.
15 Cited in Ben Pimlott, *Labour and the Left in the 1930s* (CUP, 1977), p. 41.
16 Beatrice Webb to Alfred Cripps, 20 October 1931, cited in EESC, p. 102.
17 R. H. Tawney, *The Choice before the Labour Party* (Socialist League, 1933), p. 2.
18 Ibid., p. 1.
19 Ibid., p. 6.

Chapter 9 Loyal Grousers

1   Froom Tyler, *Cripps* (Harrap, 1942), p. 18.
2   EESC, p. 103.
3   HDPD, Monday 11 January 1932, p. 166.
4   Hugh Dalton, *The Fateful Years, 1931–45* (Muller, 1957), p. 41.
5   Ibid., pp. 148–9.
6   Ben Pimlott, *Hugh Dalton* (Harper Collins, 1995), p. 229.
7   Stafford Cripps to Alfred Cripps 12 September 1931, cited in EESC, p. 96.
8   LPACR, cited in EESC, p. 101.
9   Beatrice Webb to Alfred Cripps, 20 October 1931, cited in EESC, p. 102.
10 Oswald Mosley, *My Life* (Nelson, 1968), p. 180.
11 HDPD, Saturday 8 October 1932, p. 168.
12 Jennie Lee, *Tomorrow is a New Day* (Cresset Press, 1939), p. 182.
13 Frank Wise, 'Why we remain loyal to Labour', *New Clarion*, Vol. 1, No. 10, 13 August 1932, p. 225.
14 Cited in Ben Pimlott, *Labour and the Left in the 1930s* (CUP, 1977), p. 45.
15 Ibid., p. 46.
16 Ibid., p. 48.
17 Ibid., p. 49.

18   Ibid.
19   Harold Laski to G.D.H. Cole, 10 October 1932, Cole Papers, SSIP folder.
20   Ben Pimlott, *Labour and the Left in the 1930s*, p. 51
21   Ibid., p. 50
22   Ibid.
23   Stafford Cripps, *Can Socialism come by Constitutional Means?* (Socialist League, 1933), p. 2.
24   Ibid., p. 5.
25   Ibid., p. 13.
26   Stafford Cripps, 'We must not accept office as a Minority Party', *New Clarion*, Vol. 1, No. 10, 13 August 1932, p. 217.
27   Cited in Ben Pimlott, *Labour and the Left in the 1930s*, p. 52.
28   Cited in EESC, p. 122.
29   HDPD, Saturday 8 October 1932, p. 169.
30   Michael Foot, *Aneurin Bevan*, Vol. 1, p. 157.
31   Ben Pimlott, *Labour and the Left in the 1930s*, p. 52
32   *New Clarion*, Vol. 1, No. 4, 2 July 1932.
33   Cited in EESC, p. 124.
34   AEM, Vol. 1, p. 52.
35   HDPD, Friday 19 January 1934, pp. 181–2.
36   Michael Foot, *Aneurin Bevan*, Vol.1, p. 158.
37   D. N. Pritt, *The Autobiography* (Lawrence & Wishart, 1965), Vol. 1, p. 98–9.
38   Michael Foot, *Aneurin Bevan*, Vol. 1, p. 157.
39   Cited in Fenner Brockway, *Inside the Left, 30 years of Platform, Press, Prison and Parliament* (George Allen & Unwin, 1942), p. 246.
40   Isobel Cripps to George Lansbury, 10 January 1934, Lansbury papers, 15, ff. 72–3.

Chapter 10 Prophesying War

1   Charles Trevelyan, *Mass Resistance to War* (Socialist League, 1933), p. 1.
2   Ibid., p. 2.
3   Stafford Cripps, 'Your weapon against war', *New Clarion*, Vol. 2, No. 42, 25 March 1933, p. 302.
4   Ibid., p. 309.
5   Stafford Cripps, *Socialist Leaguer*, October/November 1934.
6   Stafford Cripps, *Fascism: The Socialist Answer* (Socialist League, 1935)
7   Stafford Cripps, *'National' Fascism in Britain* (Socialist League, no date), p. 8.
8   Cited in Ben Pimlott, *Labour and the Left in the 1930s* (CUP, 1974), p. 53.
9   Ibid., p. 54.
10   Stafford Cripps, *Fight Now Against War* (Socialist League, 1935), p. 3.
11   Ibid., p. 1.
12   Ibid., p. 3.
13   Stafford Cripps to Alfred Cripps, 20 September 1935, cited in EESC, p. 141.
14   Ibid.

15   LPACR, 1935, p. 171.
16   LPACR, 1935, p. 173.
17   Cited in Francis Williams, *Ernest Bevin* (Hutchinson, 1952), p. 196.
18   Beatrice Webb, unpublished diary, 1 October 1935, Passfield papers.
19   LPACR, 1935.
20   Ibid.
21   Ibid.
22   BWD, Vol. 4, 28 September 1935, p. 358.
23   Ibid.

Chapter 11 Uniting the Left

1   John Paton, *Left Turn* (Secker & Warburg, 1936), pp. 401–3.
2   *New Statesman and Nation*, 13 April 1940, p. 486.
3   Ben Pimlott, *Labour and the Left in the 1930s* (CUP, 1974), p. 95.
4   Barbara Castle, *Fighting all the Way* (Macmillan, 1993), p. 67.
5   Michael Foot, *Aneurin Bevan* (Paladin, 1975), Vol. 1, p. 246.
6   J. T. Murphy, *New Horizons* (John Lane, 1940), p. 312.
7   Palme Dutt, *Daily Worker*, 10 November 1934.
8   Willie Gallacher, *Daily Worker*, 21 November 1934.
9   *Daily Worker*, 26 October 1935.
10   *Manchester Guardian*, 30 November 1935.
11   Fenner Brockway, *Inside the Left, 30 years of Platform, Press, Prison and Parliament* (George Allen & Unwin, 1942), p. 264.
12   Ben Pimlott, *Labour and the Left in the 1930s*, p. 79.
13   Fenner Brockway, *Inside the Left*, p. 264.
14   Harry Pollitt in Communist Party PB minutes 13 November 1936.
15   Fenner Brockway, *Inside the Left*, p. 265.
16   Stafford Cripps, *Socialist*, March 1936.
17   Kevin Morgan, *Harry Pollitt* (MUP, 1993), p. 91.
18   Cited ibid., p. 92.
19   Jennie Lee, *Tomorrow is a New Day* (Cresset Press, 1939), p. 219.
20   Ibid.
21   Stafford Cripps, *Tribune*, No. 6, 5 February 1937.
22   *Manchester Guardian*, 16 November 1936.
23   Cited in EESC, p. 153.
24   'Clear Call for Unity', *Tribune*, No. 4, 22 January 1937.
25   Stafford Cripps, *Tribune*, No. 6, 5 February 1937.
26   Harold Laski, *Tribune*, No. 6, 5 February 1937.
27   Sidney Webb to Alfred Cripps, cited in EESC, p. 155.
28   Kingsley Martin, *Harold Laski* (Cape, 1969), p. 100.
29   Clement Attlee to Harold Laski, 22 February 1937, cited in Pimlott, *Labour and the Left in the 1930s*, p. 103.
30   Aneurin Bevan ('MP'), *Tribune*, 26 February 1937.
31   Cited in EESC, p. 159.

32   Fenner Brockway, *Inside the Left,* p. 265.
33   Ibid., p. 269.
34   Fenner Brockway, *Editor,* p. 268.
35   *News Chronicle,* 17 May 1937.
36   Stafford Cripps, *Tribune,* 21 May 1937.
37   Stafford Cripps, *Tribune,* 2 July 1937, p. 9.
38   Stafford Cripps, speech at Oldham 18 July 1937, Cripps papers, 478.
39   Stafford Cripps, speech at Norwich 6 September 1937, Cripps papers, 473.
40   Stafford Cripps, speech at Garston, 21 September 1937, Cripps papers, 471.
41   Stafford Cripps, speech at Bournemouth 5 October 1937, Cripps papers, 474.
42   Stafford Cripps, speech at Birmingham 10 October 1937, Cripps papers.
43   Fenner Brockway, *Inside the Left,* p. 269.
44   Stafford Cripps, speech at Middlesborough and Stockton, no date, Cripps papers, 472.
45   Stafford Cripps, speech at Middlesborough and Stockton, no date, Cripps papers, 472.

Chapter 12 Opposing Appeasement

1   Barbara Castle, *Fighting all the Way* (Macmillan, 1993), p. 86.
2   William Mellor, *Tribune,* 14 January 1938, p. 8.
3   LPACR, 1936, p. 247.
4   Stafford Cripps, *Tribune,* 15 October 1937, p. 1.
5   Clement Attlee to Tom Attlee, 30 November 1937, Tom Attlee papers, cited in Kenneth Harris, *Attlee,* p. 149.
6   LPACR, 1937, p. 201.
7   Michael Foot, *Aneurin Bevan* (Paladin, 1975), Vol. 1, p. 273.
8   Harold Nicolson, *Diaries and Letters 1930–64,* Condensed Edition (Flamingo, 1996), p. 120.
9   Stafford Cripps, *Tribune,* 25 February 1938, p. 1.
10   Stafford Cripps, *Tribune,* 4 March 1938, p. 1.
11   Eleanor Rathbone, *Manchester Guardian,* 2 September 1936.
12   Stafford Cripps, *Tribune* No. 1, 1 January 1937.
13   Stafford Cripps, *Tribune,* 22 April 1938, p. 6.
14   Stafford Cripps, *Tribune,* 14 April 1938, p. 5.
15   Ibid.
16   Cited in A. J. Davies, *To Build a New Jerusalem* (Michael Joseph, 1992), p. 127.
17   Michael Foot, *Aneurin Bevan,* Vol. 1, p. 280.
18   Cited in Ruth Edwards, *Victor Gollancz* (Victor Gollancz, 1987), p. 241.
19   Cited in Michael Foot, *Aneurin Bevan,* Vol. 1, p. 280.
20   David Lloyd George, *Manchester Guardian,* 2 November 1931.
21   Paul Addison, *The Road to 1945* (Pimlico, 1994), p. 39.
22   Stafford Cripps to Michael Foot, 25 July 1938, cited in Mervyn Jones, *Michael Foot* (Victor Gollancz, 1994), pp. 62–3.

23 *Hansard*, 14 March 1938, Vol. 333, col. 95.
24 Harold Nicolson, *Diaries and Letters 1930-64* (Condensed Edition), p. 138.
25 Robert Rhodes James (ed.), *Chips, The Diaries of Sir Henry Channon* (Phoenix, 1996), p. 171.
26 *Tribune*, 23 September 1938, p. 1.
27 Stafford Cripps, *Tribune*, 7 October 1938.
28 Stafford Cripps, *Hansard*, 5 October 1938.
29 Stafford Cripps, *Manchester Guardian*, 9 September 1938.
30 Patrick Gordon-Walker, *Political Diaries 1932-71* (Historians' Press, 1991), 20 October 1938, p. 87.
31 Albert Church, cited in Mervyn Jones, *A Radical Life* (Hutchinson, 1991), p. 110.
32 Stafford Cripps, *Tribune*, 2 December 1938.
33 Stafford Cripps, speech at Motherwell, no date, Cripps papers, 486.
34 Ibid.
35 Stafford Cripps, *Tribune*, 6 January 1939, p.1.
36 Cripps Memorandum, *Tribune*, 20 January 1939.
37 D. N. Pritt, *From Left to Right* (Lawrence & Wishart, 1965), p. 103.
38 D. N. Pritt, *The Autobiography*, Vol. 1, p. 98.
39 Stafford Cripps, *Tribune*, 20 January 1939, p. 20.
40 D. N. Pritt, *The Autobiography*, Vol. 1, p. 104.
41 Stafford Cripps, speech at Queens Hall, 26 January 1939, Cripps papers, 483.
42 Stafford Cripps, no date, Cripps papers, 484.
43 Stafford Cripps, *Tribune*, 10 February 1939, p. 1.
44 *Tribune*, 27 January 1939, p. 7.
45 Michael Foot, *Aneurin Bevan* (Paladin, 1975), Vol. 1, p. 289.
46 Richard Crossman, *New Statesman and Nation*, 28 January 1939.
47 *Hansard* 16 February 1939, Vol. 343, col. 2031.
48 *Tribune*, 17 March 1939.
49 John Maynard Keynes to Stafford Cripps, 9 February 1939, cited in EESC, p. 166.
50 Cited in EESC, p. 166.
51 Cited in Michael Foot, *Aneurin Bevan*, Vol. 1, p. 290.
52 BWD, Vol. 4, 21 January 1939, p. 427.
53 Clement Attlee, *Daily Herald*, 22 February 1939.
54 Clement Attlee to Tom Attlee, 23 February 1939, cited in Kenneth Harris, *Attlee* (Weidenfeld & Nicolson, 1982), p. 159.
55 Cited in Froom Tyler, *Cripps: a Portrait and a Prospect* (Harrap, 1942), p. 39.
56 Cited in EESC, p. 167.
57 Ben Pimlott, *Labour and the Left in the 1930s*, p. 179.
58 Cited in Michael Foot, *Aneurin Bevan*, Vol. 1, p. 291.
59 Aneurin Bevan, *Tribune*, 26 May 1939.
60 Cited in Michael Foot, *Aneurin Bevan*, Vol. 1, p. 291.
61 LPACR 1939, p. 227.

62   George Brown, *In My Way* (Book Club, 1971) p. 39.
63   Ibid., p. 40
64   Ibid.
65   LPACR 1939, p. 235.
66   George Brown, *In My Way*, pp. 40–1
67   Ellen Wilkinson, *Sunday Referee*, 4 June 1939.

Chapter 13 Why?

1   Herbert Morrison, *An Autobiography* (Odhams, 1960), p. 271.
2   Cited in Raymond Postgate, *Life of George Lansbury* (Longmans, 1951), p. 285.
3   Ibid., p. 285.
4   BWD, Vol. 4, 7 March 1932, pp. 282–3.
5   Peggy Appiah, 'The attic of my mind', *Something About the Author, Autobiography series*, Vol. 19, p. 58.
6   Herbert Morrison, An *Autobiography*, p. 115.
7   Ibid., p. 159.
8   Revelation 3:15–16 RSV.
9   HDPD, Monday 22 January 1934, p. 182.
10   D. N. Pritt, *The Autobiography* (Lawrence & Wishart, 1965), Vol. 1, p. 98.
11   Cited in *Tribune*, 11 June 1937, p. 8.
12   Stafford Cripps to Hewlett Johnson, 31 January 1935, cited in Robert Hughes, *The Red Dean* (Churchman, 1987), p. 88.
13   Cited in John S. Peart Binns, *Blunt* (Mountain Press, no date), p. 178.
14   Ibid., p. 179.
15   Barbara Castle, *Fighting All the Way* (Macmillan, 1993), p. 80.

Chapter 14 Applying for Active Service

1   Cited in Michael Foot, *Aneurin Bevan* (Paladin, 1982), p. 311.
2   EESC, p. 186.
3   Cited in Michael Foot, *Aneurin Bevan*, p. 311.
4   EESC p. 171.
5   EESC, p. 175.
6   A. J. P. Taylor, *English History 1914–45* (OUP, 1992), p. 448.
7   EESC, p. 175.
8   Cited in Feiling, *Chamberlain*, p. 403
9   Winston Churchill to Stafford Cripps, 8 July 1939, cited in EESC, p. 176.
10   BWD, Vol. 4, 9 July 1939, pp. 436–7.
11   Cited in EESC, p. 178.
12   Jennie Lee, *This Great Journey* (MacGibbon & Kee, 1963), p. 185
13   Stafford Cripps and Aneurin Bevan, 'Our Duty', *Tribune*, 8 September 1939, p. 1.
14   Ibid.
15   *Hansard*, 12 October 1939, col. 585.

16 *Hansard,* 12 October 1939, col. 584.
17 Stafford Cripps to Beatrice Webb, 23 June 1939, cited in Paul Addison, *The Road to 1945* (Pimlico, 1994), p. 193.
18 H. Montgomery Hyde, *Walter Monckton* (Sinclair-Stevenson, 1991), pp. 2–3.
19 EESC, p. 180–1.
20 EESC, p. 182–3.
21 *Hansard,* EESC, p. 184.
22 EESC, p. 189.
23 H. Montgomery Hyde, *Walter Monckton,* pp. 2–3.
24 EESC, p. 189–90

Chapter 15 The World Over

1   Francis Bacon, 'Of Travel', *Essays,* 18 (Everyman, 1992).
2   Winston Churchill, BBC broadcast, 29 January 1935.
3   Hugh Tinker, 'The India Conciliation Group 1931–50', *Journal of Commonwealth and Comparative Politics,* November 1976, p. 231.
4   Stafford Cripps to Nehru, 11 October 1939, *A Bunch of Old Letters* (Asia publishing house, 1958), p. 261.
5   *Tribune,* 29 September 1939, 'India and the war' p. 5.
6   *Hansard,* 26 October 1939.
7   Stafford Cripps, diary 7 December 1939.
8   Nehru to Stafford Cripps, cited in M.J. Akbar, *Nehru, The Making of India* (Viking, 1988), p. 269
9   Stafford Cripps, diary 10 December 1939.
10 Cited in EESC, p. 196.
11 Cited in EESC, pp. 196–7.
12 Stafford Cripps, diary 20 December 1939.
13 Stafford Cripps to Nehru, 24 December 1939, Jawaharlal Nehru Collection, Nehru Memorial Library, New Delhi.
14 PRO CAB 127/60.
15 PRO CAB 127/61.
16 ESSC, p. 214.
17 PRO CAB 127/61.
18 EESC, p. 214.
19 Geoffrey Wilson, diary 6 February, cited in EESC, p. 218.
20 Stafford Cripps cited in EESC, p. 223.

Chapter 16 An 'all-in' Government

1   Harold Nicolson, *Diaries and Letters 1930–64* (Flamingo, 1996), p. 181.
2   *Hansard,* 7 May 1940, cols. 1140–50.
3   *Hansard,* 8 May 1940, cols. 1277–85.
4   Ibid., cols. 1289–98.
5   R. A. Butler, *The Art of the Possible* (Penguin, 1973), p. 85.

6   Ibid., p. 84.
7   R. A. Butler, unpublished diary, 14 May 1940, Butler papers, G13.
8   Stafford Cripps, diary, 4 October 1939.
9   Stafford Cripps, diary 28 September 1938.
10   Halifax, unpublished diary, 17 May 1940.
11   Gabriel Gorodetsky, *Stafford Cripps's Mission to Moscow* (CUP, 1984), p. 31.
12   HDWD, 17 May 1940, p. 10.
13   PRO FO 371/24840 N5499 WM127 (40).
14   PRO FO 371/24847 N5648.
15   HDWD, 27 May 1940, p. 25
16   PRO CAB 65/7 132(40)38, 21 May 1940.
17   Cited in Gabriel Gorodetsky, *Stafford Cripps's Mission to Moscow*, p. 35.
18   Stafford Cripps, diary, 27 May 1940.
19   WCSWW, Vol. 2, p. 118.
20   Note by Wedgwood's daughter Helen on a letter from Cripps, 27 February 1942, Wedgwood papers.
21   Orme Sargent, 7 May 1940, PRO FO, Political, 371/24840 N 5499.
22   R. A. Butler, 23 May 1940, PRO FO 371/24847 N 5660.

Chapter 17 Building the Grand Alliance

1   Stafford Cripps, diary, 13-16 June 1940.
2   Ibid., 25 August 1940.
3   Cited in Gabriel Gorodetsky, *Stafford Cripps's Mission to Moscow* (CUP, 1984), p. 51.
4   D. Dilks (ed.), *The Diaries of Sir Alexander Cadogan* (London, 1971), p. 347.
5   Davies papers. Library of Congress, Box 11.
6   Halifax to Geoffrey Dawson, *The Times* Archives, 3 July 1941.
7   W. Warlimont, *Inside Hitler's Headquarters 1939-45* (London, 1964), pp. 113–4.
8   Stafford Cripps to Walter Monckton, 2 September 1940, Monckton papers 3, ff. 75–7.
9   Ibid.
10   PRO FO 371 24844 N5937/30/38.
11   Stafford Cripps, diary, 23 July 1940.
12   John Colville, *The Fringes of Power: Downing Street Diaries 1939–55* (Hodder & Stoughton, 1985), p. 238.
13   PRO FO 371/24844 N5808/30/38.
14   Stafford Cripps to Walter Monckton, 31 August 1940, Monckton papers 3, ff. 71–2.
15   Stafford Cripps, diary, 2, 3 6 or 10 July 1940.
16   Stafford Cripps to Walter Monckton, 31 August 1940, Monckton papers 3, ff. 71–2.
17   D. Dilks, (ed.), *The Diaries of Sir Alexander Cadogan*, p. 321.
18   Stafford Cripps, copy of letter to Halifax, 3 December 1940, Monckton papers, 3, ff. 205–11.

19   Stafford Cripps to Halifax, 10 October 1940, PRO FO 800/322.

20   Cited in Gabriel Gorodetsky, *Stafford Cripps's Mission to Moscow*, p. 80.

21   *Foreign Relations of the United States, Diplomatic Papers, 1940*, Vol. 1, General 1959, p. 573.

22   PRO FO 371 29484 N7354/40/38.

23   John Colville, *The Fringes of Power*, p. 307.

24   WCSWW, Vol. 3, pp. 320–1.

25   PRO FO 371 29479 N1510/78/38 11 April 1941.

26   Gabriel Gorodetsky, *Stafford Cripps's Mission to Moscow*, p. 156.

27   AEM, Vol. 1, p. 269.

28   John Colville, *The Fringes of Power*, p. 773.

29   Ibid., p. 405.

30   Winston Churchill, broadcast 22 June 1941, National Sound Archive.

31   John Colville, *The Fringes of Power*, p. 405

32   Thomas James Leasor, *War at the Top, based on the experiences of General Sir Leslie Hollis* (Michael Joseph, 1959), p. 155.

33   Beaverbrook papers D90.

34   H. Harnak, 'Sir Stafford Cripps as British Ambassador in Moscow May 1940–June 1941', *English Historical Review*, Vol. 94 No. 370, January 1979, p. 70.

35   Stafford Cripps to Walter Monckton, 14 July 1941, Monckton Papers 5, f. 221.

36.   Peggy Appiah, 'The attic of my mind', *Something About the Author, Autobiography series*, Vol. 19, p. 66.

37   PRO FO 371 29466 N3231/3/38.

38   ·'™ ·'·l. 1, p. 271.

39   H. C. Cassidy, *Moscow Dateline 1941–43* (London, 1943), p. 52.

40   Cited in Peggy Appiah, 'The attic of the mind', p. 66.

41   PRO PREM 3/395/16.

42   Hopkins papers, box 136, 29 September 1941.

43   FO 954/24, 2 October 1941.

44   Stafford Cripps, diary, 4 October 1941.

45   PRO of 371 29471 N6583/3/38.

46   Stafford Cripps, diary, 5 November 1941.

47   Cited in F. W. F. Smith, *Walter Monckton – the Life of Viscount Monckton of Brenchley* (Weidenfeld and Nicolson, 1969), p. 192.

48   Stafford Cripps, diary, 15 November 1941.

49   PRO CAB 65/23 114(41)1,2, 17 November 1941.

50   AEM, Vol. 1, p. 296.

51   Stafford Cripps, diary, 19 December 1941.

52   Stafford Cripps, diary, 22 December 1941.

Chapter 18 Patience

1   Stafford Cripps to Walter Monckton, 2 September 1940, Monckton papers 3, ff. 75–7.
2   BWD, Vol. 4, 30 June 1938, p. 415.
3   Ibid., 3 July 1941, p. 471
4   Isobel Cripps to Walter Monckton, 25 June 1941, Monckton Papers, 5, ff. 118–9.
5   Isobel Cripps, diary, 1 February 1941.
6   Peggy Appiah, 'The attic of my mind', *Something About the Author, Autobiography series*, Vol. 19, pp. 64–5.
7   Stafford Cripps to Walter Monckton, 2 September 1940, Monckton papers 3, ff. 75–7.
8   Ibid.
9   Roy Jenkins, *Nine Men of Power* (Hamish Hamilton, 1974), p. 93.
10 Diana Cripps, *Simple Salads* (Bureau of Cosmotherapy, 1938), pp. 20–1.
11 Isobel Cripps to Walter Monckton, 23 August 1941, Monckton Papers 6, f. 32.
12 Maxsimilian Bircher-Benner, *Food Science for All and a New Sunlight Theory of Nutrition*, trans. Arnold Eiloart (C. W. Daniel, 1929), p. 97.
13 Ibid., p. 96.
14 Maxsimilian Bircher-Benner, *The Prevention of Incurable Diseases*, trans. E. F. Meyer (John Miles, 1938), p. 22.
15 Ibid., p. 65.
16 Edmond Szekély, *Man, Art and World-Conception*, trans. Purcell Weaver (C. W. Daniel, 1947), pp. 50–1.
17 Stafford Cripps to Walter Monckton, 2 September 1940, Monckton papers 3, ff. 75–7.
18 Stafford Cripps to Walter Monckton, 25 November 1940, Monckton papers 3, ff. 115–8.
19 John Colville, *The Fringes of Power: Downing Street Diaries 1939–55* (Hodder & Stoughton, 1985), p. 215.
20 BWD, Vol. 4, 22 February 1942, p. 479.
21 John Colville, *The Fringes of Power*, p. 306.
22 Ibid., p. 307.
23 Ibid., p. 309.
24 *The Times*, 13 June 1941.
25 Bobbety Cranbourne to Walter Monckton, 16 February 1941, Monckton papers, 4, ff. 87–9.
26 Walter Monckton to Stafford Cripps, 17 September 1940, Monckton papers, 3, f. 110.
27 Walter Monckton to Stafford Cripps, 21 January 1941, Monckton papers, 4, f. 5.
28 Stafford Cripps to Walter Monckton, 17 April 1941, Monckton papers, 4, f. 202.

29 Stafford Cripps to Walter Monckton, 27 May 1941, Monckton papers, 5, f. 48.
30 Stafford Cripps to Walter Monckton, 28 August 1941, Monckton papers, 6, f. 45.
31 Walter Monckton to Stafford Cripps, 21 January 1941, Monckton papers, 4, f. 5.
32 Ibid.
33 Ibid.
34 Stafford Cripps to Walter Monckton, 25 November 1940, Monckton papers 3, ff. 115–18.
35 Ibid.
36 BWD, Vol. 4, 30 July 1941, p. 472.
37 Stafford Cripps to Walter Monckton, telegram, 4 January 1942, Monckton papers, 9, f. 4.
38 A. J. P. Taylor, *Beaverbrook* (Hamish Hamilton, 1972), p. 507.

Chapter 19 Challenging Churchill

1   Robert Rhodes James (ed.), *The Diaries of Sir Henry Channon* (Phoenix, 1993), 9 January 1942, p. 316.
2   Ibid., 27 January 1942, p. 319
3   A.J.P. Taylor, *Beaverbrook* (Hamish Hamilton, 1972), pp. 494-5.
4   Harold Nicolson, *Diaries and Letters 1930–64* (Collins, 1967), Vol. 2, p. 205.
5   *The Times*, 26 January 1942.
6   Vera Brittain, *Wartime Chronicle* (Victor Gollancz, 1989), 5 February 1942, p. 126.
7   HDWD, 4 February 1942, p. 360.
8   Harold Nicolson, *Diaries and Letters 1930–64*, Condensed Edition (Flamingo, 1996), p. 224.
9   BWD, Vol. 4, 9 February 1942, p.478.
10 Stafford Cripps, broadcast 8 February 1942, National Sound Archive.
11 Harold Nicolson, *Diaries and Letters 1930–64*, Condensed Edition, p. 225.
12 Robert Rhodes James (ed.), *The Diaries of Sir Henry Channon*, 9 January 1942, p. 322.
13 AEM, Vol. 2, p. 321.
14 Cited in A. J. P. Taylor, *Beaverbrook*, p. 513.
15 AEM, Vol. 2, p. 321.
16 Kenneth Harris, *Attlee* (Weidenfeld and Nicolson, 1995), p. 194.
17 Clement Attlee, *As It Happened* (Heinemann, 1954), p. 125.
18 A. J. P. Taylor, *Beaverbrook*, p. 515.
19 HDWD, p. 373.
20 Harold Nicolson, *Diaries and Letters 1930–64*, Vol. 2, p. 214.
21 *Hansard*, 25 February 1942, col. 312.
22 Keith Jefferys (ed.), *Labour and the Wartime Coalition: from the diary of James Chuter Ede* (Historians Press, 1987), p. 52.

23   AEM, Vol. 2, p. 352.

24   *Hansard,* 25 February 1942, col. 313.

25   Austin Hopkinson, *Hansard,* 25 February 1942, col. 321-2.

26   *Hansard,* 25 February 1942, col. 314.

27   Nicholas Mansergh (ed.), *Constitutional Relations between Britain and India. The Transfer of Power 1942-47, Vol. I: The Cripps Mission* (HMSO, 1970), Document 456.

28   Harold Nicolson, *Diaries and Letters 1930–64,* Condensed Edition, p. 226.

29   Nicholas Mansergh (ed.), *Constitutional Relations between Britain and India. The Transfer of Power 1942-47, Vol. I: The Cripps Mission,* Document 304, Amery to Linlithgow, 10 March 1942.

30   Cited in EESC, p. 314.

31   WCSWW, Vol. 4, p. 191.

32   Ibid., 11 April 1942, p. 192.

33   Ibid., p. 194.

34   Cited in Gabriel Gorodetsky, *Stafford Cripps's Mission to Moscow* (CUP, 1984) p. 265.

35   HDWD, 31 May 1942, p. 450.

36   Patrick Gordon-Walker, *Political Diaries 1932–71* (Historians Press, 1991), 4 March 1942, p. 108

37   HDWD, 24 August 1942, p. 480.

38   Harold Nicolson, *Diaries and Letters 1930–64,* Vol. 2, p. 225.

39   Keith Jefferys (ed.), *Labour and the Wartime Coalition,* Saturday May 2 1942, pp. 71–2.

40   Ibid., p. 50.

41   George Reakes, *Man of the Mersey* (Christopher Henderson, 1956), pp. 75–6.

42   Ibid., p. 80.

43   Ibid., p.75.

44   Gwen Hill to John Collins, 8 February 1943, Collins papers, 3288, f. 72.

45   Harold Nicolson, *Diaries and Letters 1930–64,* Condensed Edition, p. 229.

46   Lord Hankey to Hoare, March 12 1942, Hankey Papers, HNKY 4/34.

47   WCSWW, Vol. 4, p. 263.

48   Ibid., p. 264.

49   Ibid, p. 354.

50   Ibid., p. 355.

51   Ibid.

52   Ivor Thomas to Tom Jones, 14 August 1942, Viscount Astor Papers, Box 43 file 823.

53   Barrington-Ward, diary 31 July 1942, cited in Donald MacLachlan, *In the Chair; Barrington-Ward of the Times* (Weidenfeld & Nicolson, 1971), p. 199.

54   Barrington-Ward, diary, 11 September 1942, cited ibid., p. 200.

55   WCSWW, Vol. 4, p. 497–8.

56   Ibid., p. 498.

57   Ibid., p. 499.

58   Patrick Gordon-Walker, *Political Diaries 1932-71,* 3 September 1942, p. 110

59   Ibid., pp. 111–12.
60   HDWD, 8 September 1942, p. 490.
61   Harold Nicolson to Vita Sackville-West, 9 September 1942, *Diaries and Letters 1930–64*, Condensed Edition, p. 234.
62   Keith Jefferys (ed.), *Labour and the Wartime Coalition*, Sunday 20 September, p. 97.
63   Harold Nicolson, *Diaries and Letters 1930–64*, Condensed Edition, p. 234.
64   Cited in Charles Lysaght, *Brendan Bracken* (Allen Lane, 1979), p. 223.
65   Cited in Donald MacLachlan, *In the Chair; Barrington-Ward of the Times*, p. 200.
66   Patrick Gordon-Walker, *Political Diaries 1932–71*, 1 October 1942, pp. 113.
67   Ibid., p. 116.
68   Barrington-Ward, diary, 2 October 1942, cited in Donald MacLachlan, *In the Chair; Barrington-Ward of the Times*, p. 201.
69   AEM, Vol. 2, p. 342.
70   Barrington-Ward, diary, 2 October 1942, cited in Donald MacLachlan, *In the Chair; Barrington-Ward of the Times*, p. 201.
71   Harold Nicolson, *Diaries and Letters 1930-64*, Vol. 2, p. 250.
72   Beatrice Webb, unpublished diary, 26 October 1942, Passfield papers.
73   WCSWW, Vol. 4, p. 503.
74   HDWD, 21–2 November 1942, p. 522.
75   J.M. Lee, *The Churchill Coalition 1940-5*, (Batsford, 1980), p. 42
76   WCSWW, Vol. 4, p. 503.

Chapter 20 Lancasters, Wellingtons and Magnetrons

1   M. M. Postan, *British War Production* (Longmans, 1952), p. 305.
2   *Hansard*, 25 February 1942.
3   Robin Higham, *Air Power: A Concise History* (St Martin's Press, 1972), p. 130
4   Ibid., p. 132
5   Cited in Diana Collins, *Partners in Protest* (Victor Gollancz, 1992), p. 135.
6   Max Hastings, *Bomber Command* (Joseph, 1979), p. 250.
7   Ibid.
8   Stafford Cripps, *Towards Christian Democracy* (George Allen & Unwin, 1945), p. 89.
9   Cited in Diana Collins, *Partners in Protest*, p. 136.
10   Cited in M.M. Postan, *British War Production*, p. 306.
11   Ibid., p. 308.
12   Ibid., p. 305.
13   Ibid., p. 304.
14   Cited in Dudley Saward, *'Bomber' Harris* (Buchan & Enright, 1984), p. 190.
15   Cited in M.M. Postan, *British War Production*, p. 323.
16   Ibid., p. 318.
17   Cited in EESC, p. 322.
18   Ibid., p. 323.

19   Stafford Cripps, *Democracy Alive* (Sidgwick & Jackson, 1946), pp. 28–9.
20   Louis Mountbatten to Stafford Cripps, 24 October 1942, PRO CAB 127/86.
21   Stafford Cripps rectorial address to the University of Aberdeen, 6 February 1943, published in *Democracy Alive*, p. 12.
22   Ibid., p. 10.
23   Jock Curle, cited in Stafford Cripps, *Democracy Alive*, p. 3.
24   J.T. Murphy, *Victory Production!* (Bodley Head, John Lane, 1942), p. 11.
25   HDWD, Monday 24 May 1943, p. 595.

Chapter 21 Victory upon Victory

1   Cited in Mervyn Stockwood, *Chanctonbury Ring* (Hodder & Stoughton, 1982), p. 64.
2   Clement Attlee, *As It Happened* (Heinemann, 1954), p. 125.
3   Austin Mitchell (ed.), *Election '45* (Fabian Society, 1995).
4   Cited in EESC, p. 324.
5   Cited in EESC, p. 324.
6   Clement Attlee to Ernest Bevin, 1 March 1944, Attlee papers, University College, box 7.
7   Clement Attlee, *As It Happened*, p. 144.
8   Austin Mitchell, (ed.), *Election '45*, p. 16.
9   Mass-Observation file report No. 2084, 8 February 1944.
10   AEM, Vol. 2, p. 539.
11   Cited in Kenneth Harris, *Attlee*, p. 235.
12   PRO PREM 4/88/1 20 November 1944.
13   Cited in Roy Jenkins, *Nine Men of Power* (Hamish Hamilton, 1974), p. 98.
14   Winston Churchill, *Victory: War Speeches by the Right Hon. Winston S. Churchill* (Cassell, 1946), p. 80.
15   Churchill to Eden, 12 May 1945, PRO PREM 4/65/4.
16   Clement Attlee, *As it Happened*, p. 135.
17   Austin Mitchell, (ed.), *Election '45*, p. 20.
18   AEM, Vol. 2, p. 539.
19   AEM, Vol. 2, p. 539.
20   HDWD, 28 May 1945, p. 865.
21   George VI to Mountbatten, 8 January 1947, Broadlands archives D92.
22   HDWD, 28 May 1945, p. 865.
23   Ibid.
24   LPACR, 1945, p. 95.
25   Stafford Cripps, *Democracy Alive* (Sidgwick & Jackson, 1946), p. 24.
26   Ibid., p. 19.
27   Ibid., p. 20.
28   Ibid., p. 21.
29   Ibid., p. 22.
30   Ibid., p. 23.

31 *Let us Face the Future* (Labour Party, 1945), p. 7.
32 Stafford Cripps, *Democracy Alive*, p. 21.
33 Richard Acland diary, 12 October 1944, cited by Addison p. 262.
34 HDWD, 7 March 1945, p. 841.
35 Cited in Eric Estorick, p. 327.
36 *Labour Organiser,* August 1945, p. 11.
37 Alan Bullock, *Ernest Bevin* (Heinemann, 1960), Vol. 2, pp. 392–3.
38 Austin Mitchell, (ed.), *Election '45*, p. 104.
39 AEM, Vol. 2, p. 549.
40 *Clement Attlee: The Granada Historical Records Interview* (Panther Books, 1967), p. 43.
41 Trevor Burridge, *Clement Attlee, a Political Biography* (Cape, 1985), p.190.

Chapter 22 Another Industrial Revolution

1   Douglas Jay in Austin Mitchell, (ed.), *Election '45* (Fabian Society, 1995), p. 94.
2   PRO PREM 8/35, C P (45)112.
3   Ibid.
4   Kenneth Harris, *Attlee* (Weidenfeld & Nicolson, 1982), p. 269.
5   Trevor Burridge, *Clement Attlee, a Political Biography* (Cape, 1985), p. 205.
6   Hugh Dalton, *High Tide and After* (Muller, 1962), p. 79.
7   Barbara Castle, *Fighting all the Way* (Macmillan, 1993), pp. 139–40.
8   PRO FO 800/512/US/42/25.
9   Brendan Bracken to W.S. Robinson, 1947, cited in Charles Lysaght, *Brendan Bracken* (Allen Lane, 1979), p. 280.
10 Barbara Castle, *Fighting all the Way*, p. 136.
11 Stafford Cripps, *God in Our Work* (Thomas Nelson, 1949), pp. 2, 5.
12 William Plowden, *The Motor Car and Politics* (Bodley Head, 1971), p. 312.
13 Cited in Paul Addison, *Now the War is Over* (Pimlico, 1995), pp. 190–1.
14 Cited in Michael Sissons and P. French, *The Age of Austerity* (Hodder & Stoughton, 1963), p. 130
15 Cited in Paul Addison, *Now the War is Over*, p. 192.
16 PRO CAB 87/9, R(44)152, 2 September 1944.
17 *Cotton Industry Working Party Report* (HMSO, 1947).
18 Cited in EESC, pp. 347–8.
19 Kenneth Morgan, *The People's Peace* (OUP, 1992), p. 36.
20 Barbara Castle, *Fighting all the Way*, p. 136.
21 Edwin Plowden, *An Industrialist in the Treasury* (Deutsch, 1989), p. 21.
22 Barbara Castle, *Fighting all the Way*, p. 136.
23 Cited in R.J. Moore, *Escape from Empire* (OUP, 1983), p. 18.
24 Vera Brittain, *Pethick-Lawrence, a Portrait* (George Allen & Unwin, 1963), p. 107.
25 Ibid., p. 154.
26 Ibid., p. 155.

27 Stafford Cripps to Jawaharlal Nehru, 10 May 1946, cited in Sarvepalli Gopal, *Jawaharlal Nehru, a Biography*, (Cape, 1975), Vol. 1, p. 318.
28 Wavell to Mountbatten, 15 June 1946, Broadlands E186.
29 Cited in Ronald Lewin, *The Chief Field Marshall Lord Wavell* (London, 1980), p. 238.
30 PRO CAB 128/6 CM(46)104.
31 Penderel Moon, (ed.) *The Viceroy's Journal* (OUP, 1973), p. 397.
32 Cited in Kenneth Harris, *Attlee*, p. 373.
33 Mountbatten to King George VI, 4 January 1947, cited in *King George VI*, p. 711.
34 Mountbatten to Clement Attlee, 3 January 1947, *Transfer of Power* Vol. IX, p. 451.
35 Cited in Kenneth Harris, *Attlee*, p. 378.
36 Ibid., p. 377.
37 Stafford Cripps to Mountbatten, 6 June 1947, Broadlands E46.
38 *Hansard*, 15 July 1947, cols 227, 231-2.
39 Amery diary, 9 September 1942.
40 Mountbatten to Walter Monckton, 18 January 1948, Monckton papers 31, f. 85
41 Alan Wood, *Mr Rank: A Study of J. Arthur Rank and British Films* (Hodder & Stoughton, 1952), p. 225.
42 Ben Pimlott, *Harold Wilson* (HarperCollins, 1992), p. 118.
43 Michael Wakelin, *J. Arthur Rank, The Man Behind the Gong*, (Lion, 1996), p. 91.
44 *Kinematograph Weekly*, 23 January 1947, p. 3.
45 Harold Wilson, *Memoirs: The Making of a Prime Minister* (Weidenfeld and Nicolson, 1986), p. 104.

Chapter 23 Economic Affairs

1 Peter Hennessy, *Never Again – 1945–51* (Cape, 1992), p. 102.
2 Emmanuel Shinwell, *Conflict Without Malice* (Odhams, 1955), p. 184.
3 Stafford Cripps, *Hansard*, 10 March 1947, col. 970.
4 *Economic Survey for 1947*, para. 8.
5 *Hansard*, 10 March 1947, col. 997–8.
6 Ibid., cols. 998–9.
7 PRO CAB 134/503 MEP(46)1ST, 21 January 1946.
8 PRO CAB 134/503 MEP(46)10, 23 October 1946.
9 HDPD, 30 July 1947, p. 405.
10 Ibid.
11 HDPD, 17 August 1947, p. 409.
12 HDPD, 13 June 1947, p. 394.
13 *Hansard*, 7 August 1947, col. 1757–8.
14 *Hansard*, 7 August 1947, col. 1756–7.
15 Ibid., col. 1758.
16 *HDPD*, August 8 1947, p. 407.
17 *Hansard*, 7 August 1947, col. 1766.

18 Hugh Dalton, *High Tide and After* (Muller, 1962), p. 241.
19 HDPD, Mid-September 1947, p. 413.
20 Patrick Gordon-Walker, *Political Diaries 1932–71* (Historians Press, 1991), 8 September 1947, p. 167.
21 Hugh Dalton, *High Tide and After*, pp. 244–5.
22 Patrick Gordon-Walker, *Political Diaries*, 8 September 1947, p. 167.
23 Kenneth Harris, *Attlee*, p. 350.
24 Clement Attlee to Herbert Morrison, 19 September 1947, Attlee papers 60, ff. 144–7.
25 Patrick Gordon-Walker to Herbert Morrison, 23 September 1947, GNWR 1/6.
26 *Sunday Times*, 9 September 1964.
27 HGD, p. 36.
28 RHD, 30 September 1947 and 7 October 1947, pp. 8 and 10.
29 *New Statesman and Nation*, 1 November 1947.
30 Cited in Ben Pimlott, *Hugh Dalton* (Harper Collins, 1995), p. 518.
31 Harold Nicolson, *Diaries and Letters, 1945–62* (Collins, 1968), 8 October 1947, p. 111.
32 *Report of the Select Committee on the Budget Disclosures* (HMSO, 1947), p. v.
33 Hugh Dalton, *High Tide and After*, p. 277.
34 *Observer*, 16 November 1947.
35 *Manchester Guardian*, 15 November 1947.
36 Hugh Dalton, *High Tide and After*, p. 281.
37 HGD, p. 46.

Chapter 24 The First Modern Chancellor

1 HGD, p. 47.
2 RHD, 29 April 1952, p. 222.
3 Douglas Jay, *Change and Fortune* (Hutchinson, 1980), p. 181.
4 HGD, pp. 62–3.
5 Edwin Plowden, *An Industrialist in the Treasury* (Deutsch, 1989), p. 21.
6 Ibid., p. 13.
7 RHD, 29 April 1952 , p. 222.
8 Edwin Plowden, *An Industrialist in the Treasury*, pp. 20–1.
9 RHD, p. 222.
10 HGD, p. 187.
11 Edwin Plowden, *An Industrialist in the Treasury*, p. 20.
12 HGD, p. 55–7.
13 Edwin Plowden, *An Industrialist in the Treasury*, p. 20.
14 Attlee papers, 87, ff. 67–94.
15 Edwin Plowden, *An Industrialist in the Treasury*, p. 19.
16 *Hansard*, 6 April 1948, col. 37.
17 HGD, p. 58.
18 RHD, March 1948, p. 19.

19   RHD, 8 March 1948 p. 21.
20   John Colville, *Footprints in Time* (Collins, 1976), p. 210.
21   Ibid.
22   *Hansard,* 6 April 1948, col. 42.
23   Ibid., col. 47.
24   Ibid., col. 49.
25   Ibid., col. 62.
26   Ibid., col. 110.
27   Ibid., col. 78.
28   *Economist,* 22 January 1949.
29   PRO CP(48)61.
30   *Hansard,* 6 April 1949, col. 2077.
31   Ibid., col. 2084.
32   RHD, p. 55.
33   HGD, 11 April 1949.
34   David Marquand, 'Sir Stafford Cripps', *The Age of Austerity, 1945–51*, eds Michael Sissons and Philip French (OUP, 1986), p. 173.
35   Alec Cairncross and Barry Eschengreen, *Sterling in Decline – the Devaluations of 1931, 1947, and 1967* (Blackwell, 1983), p. 140.
36   Edwin Plowden, *An Industrialist in the Treasury*, p. 53.
37   HGD, p. 116.
38   Edmund Dell, *The Chancellors* (HarperCollins, 1996), p. 117.
39   Hugh Dalton Political Diary, 1 July 1949, p. 452.
40   HGD, pp. 136–7.
41   Edwin Plowden, *An Industrialist in the Treasury*, p. 65.
42   Leah Manning, *A Life for Education* (Victor Gollancz, 1970), p. 81.
43   Alec Cairncross and Barry Eschengreen, *Sterling in Decline – the Devaluations of 1931, 1947, and 1967*, p. 141.
44   Douglas Jay, *Change and Fortune*, p. 180.
45   Edwin Plowden, *An Industrialist in the Treasury*, p. 105.
46   RHD, p. 90.
47   Edwin Plowden, *An Industrialist in the Treasury*, p. 70.
48   Ibid., pp 69-70, 78, 79.
49   Cited in Mervyn Stockwood, *Chanctonbury Ring* (Hodder & Stoughton, 1982), p. 72.
50   Stafford Cripps to Mervyn Stockwood, 29 September 1948, cited ibid.
51   Cited in Ruth Edwards, *Victor Gollancz* (Victor Gollancz, 1987), p. 507.
52   Ibid., p. 514.
53   Ibid., p. 515.
54   Ibid., p. 518.

Chapter 25 A Final Budget

1   HGD, p. 154.
2   Douglas Jay, *Change and Fortune* (Hutchinson, 1980), p. 193.

3   HGD, p. 162.
4   Ibid.
5   Cited in Charles Lysaght, *Brendan Bracken* (Allen Lane, 1979), p. 281.
6   Kenneth Harris, *Attlee* (Weidenfeld and Nicolson, 1985), p. 445.
7   HGD, p. 104.
8   Edwin Plowden, *An Industrialist in the Treasury* (Deutsch, 1989), p. 105.
9   HDPD, 27 January 1950, p. 466.
10 Ibid.
11 HGD, 21 March 1950, p. 174.
12 Stafford Cripps to Clement Attlee, 2 April 1950, Attlee papers 100, ff. 2–4.
13 *Hansard*, 18 April 1950, col. 59–60.
14 Ibid., col. 39
15 PRO PREM 8/1186: CP(50)35, Budget Policy, Chancellor of the Exchequer, 15 March 1950.
16 Clement Attlee interview 1960, cited in Kenneth Harris, *Attlee*, p. 438.
17 HGD, p. 187.
18 Cited in Douglas Jay, *Change and Fortune*, p. 178.
19 Kenneth Morgan, *The People's Peace* (OUP, 1992), p. 74.
20 HGD, p. 192.
21 Mervyn Stockwood, *Chanctonbury Ring* (Hodder & Stoughton, 1982), p. 73.
22 HGD, p. 209.
23 Cited in Ruth Edwards, *Victor Gollancz* (Victor Gollancz, 1987), p. 507.

Chapter 26 The Laws of God, the Laws of Man

1   Robert Rhodes James, (ed.), *Chips, The Diaries of Sir Henry Channon* (Phoenix, 1996), 27 September 1942, p. 337.
2   John Freeman, 'Stafford Cripps', *New Statesman*, 26 April 1952, p. 487.
3   Anthony Montague Brown, *Long Sunset* (Cassell, 1995), p. 101.
4   Cited by Stafford Cripps, *God in our Work* (Thomas Nelson, 1949), p. 25.
5   Stafford Cripps, *Towards Christian Democracy* (George Allen & Unwin, 1945), p. 7.
6   Ibid., p. 9.
7   Ibid., p. 40.
8   Ibid., p. 10.
9   Ibid., p. 16.
10 Ibid., p. 20.
11 Ibid., p. 61.
12 Ibid., p. 31.
13 Ibid., p. 7.
14 Ibid., pp. 60, 64.
15 Ibid., p. 56.
16 John Collins to George Bell, 19 March 1945, Bell papers, 206, f. 79.
17 George Bell to Stafford Cripps, 18 April 1945, Bell papers 206, f. 117.
18 John Collins to Stafford Cripps, 25 July 1945, Collins papers, 3288, f. 232.

19 Diana Collins, *Partners in Protest* (Victor Gollancz, 1992), p. 143.
20 Ibid.
21 Ibid.
22 Ibid.
23 Ibid.
24 Stafford Cripps to George Bell, 25 December 1945, Bell papers, 206, f. 153.
25 Mervyn Stockwood, *Chanctonbury Ring* (Hodder & Stoughton, 1982), p. 71.
26 Stafford Cripps, *Democracy Alive* (Sidgwick and Jackson, 1946), pp. 100–1.
27 Robert Rhodes James, (ed.), *Chips, The Diaries of Sir Henry Channon*, 27 September 1945, p. 439.
28 Brendan Bracken to Max Beaverbrook, 10 January 1950, cited in Charles Lysaght, *Brendan Bracken* (Allen Lane, 1979), p. 281.
29 Stafford Cripps, *The Spiritual Crisis*, (Mowbray, 1950), p. 9.
30 Ibid., p. 16.
31 Cited in Ruth Edwards, *Victor Gollancz*, (Victor Gollancz, 1987), pp. 538–9.

Chapter 27 Clinic

1 Isobel Cripps to George Bell, 23 June 1951, Bell papers, 206, f. 185.
2 HGD, p. 309.
3 Personal interview with Theresa Ricketts.
4 Freddie Cripps, *Life's a Gamble* (Odhams, 1958), pp. 52–3.
5 Peggy Appiah, 'The attic of my mind', *Something About the Author, Autobiography series*, Vol. 19, p. 79.
6 Ibid.
7 Ibid., p. 77.

Chapter 28 Legacies

1 *The Times*, 12 May 1952.
2 Alec Cairncross, *Years of Recovery* (Methuen, 1985), p. 500.
3 *Tribune*, 3 November 1950.
4 *Hansard*, Vol. 342, col. 710.
5 Cited in R. W. Fox, *Reinhold Neibuhr*, Pantheon 1955, p. 150.
6 HDPD, p. 185.
7 Norman and Jeanne MacKenzie, *The Letters of Beatrice and Sidney Webb* (Virago, 1986), Vol. 2, 13 July 1942, p. 460.
8 Peggy Appiah, 'The attic of my mind', *Something About the Author, Autobiography series*, Vol. 19, p. 71
9 J. T. Murphy, *New Horizons* (John Lane, 1941), pp. 311–2.
10 Cited in Stafford Cripps, *God in our Work* (Nelson, 1949), p. 56.
11 Ibid., p. 61
12 Reinhold Neibuhr, May 17 1952, *Remembering Reinhold Neibuhr*, ed. Ursula Neibuhr, HarperSan Francisco, 1991, p. 304.

Bibliography

1. Unpublished Sources

a. Cripps's Papers

Unfortunately Stafford Cripps's papers have yet to be brought together in one place, though this should happen in the next ten years. The papers that Eric Estorick used to complete his biography were united with those held by Sir Maurice Shock while he was considering writing a biography and will eventually join the Nuffield College, Oxford, collection which at the moment is a patchy collection of speeches and press cuttings. They include diaries for the periods in India, Moscow and Jamaica and some private letters. The private papers from his ministerial career are at the Public Record Office under CAB 127/57-153 and the papers of the Ministry of Munitions (MUN), the Prime Minister's office (PREM), the Foreign Office (FO), the Ministry of Aircraft Production (AVIA), the Board of Trade (BT) and the Treasury (T) have been consulted.

b. Other Private and Institutional Papers

Clement Attlee papers, Bodleian Library, Oxford
George Bell papers, Lambeth Palace Library
Ernest Bevin papers, Churchill College, Cambridge
Walter Citrine diary in Lord Citrine papers, BLPES
G. D. H. Cole papers, Nuffield College, Oxford
India Conciliation Group papers, Friends House
John Collins papers, Lambeth Palace Library
Hugh Dalton diary and papers, BLPES
James Chuter Ede papers, British Library
Patrick Gordon-Walker papers, Churchill College, Cambridge
George Lansbury papers, BLPES
James Meade diary in Meade papers, BLPES
Walter Monckton papers, Bodleian Library, Oxford
Herbert Morrison papers, Nuffield College, Oxford
Mountbatten papers, Broadlands archive

509

Harold Nicolson diary, Balliol College, Oxford
Lord Pethick-Lawrence papers, King's College, Cambridge
Passfield papers, BLPES

c. Periodicals

The Times, Manchester Guardian, Evening Standard, Observer, Daily Mail, Picture Post, Tribune, New Statesman, Goodwill, South Bucks Standard, South Bucks Free Press, Kinematograph Weekly.

2. Published Works

a. Published works by Stafford Cripps

Britain and Austria Addresses (Anglo-Austrian Democratic Society, no date)
Parliamentary Institutions and the Transition to Socialism (Socialist League, 1933)
Can Socialism come by Constitutional Means? (Socialist League, 1933)
Why this Socialism? (Gollancz, 1934)
The Choice for Britain (Socialist League, 1934)
'National' Fascism in Britain (Socialist League, 1935)
Fight Now Against War (Socialist League, 1935)
The Struggle for Peace (Gollancz, 1936)
Empire (India League, 1938)
The Speech to Unseat the National Government (Petition Campaign, 1939)
Democracy up-to-date (George Allen & Unwin, 1939)
India - The Lord Privy Seals's Mission (Parliamentary Papers Session 41/2 Vol 8, 1942)
Shall the spell be broken? (Hodder & Stoughton, 1943)
Democracy up-to-date, revised edn (George Allen & Unwin, 1944)
Towards Christian Democracy, (George Allen & Unwin, 1945)
Democracy Alive (Sidgwick & Jackson, 1946)
The Survival of Christianity, (World's Evangelical Alliance, 1948)
The Church and the World Economic Crisis (ICF breakfast address, 1948)
God in our Work (Nelson, 1949)
The Spiritual Crisis (Mowbray, 1950)

b. Published Biography, Diaries, Letters and Memoirs

Addison, Christopher, *Four and a half years* (2 Vols), (Hutchinson, 1934).
– *Politics from within, 1911–18* (2 Vols), (Herbert Jenkins, 1924).
Amery, Leopold, *My Political Life*, (Hutchinson, 1953).
Attlee, Clement R, *As It Happened*, (Heinemann, 1954).
Barnett, Henrietta, *Life of Canon Barnett* (2 Vols), (John Murray, 1918).
Bassett, Arthur Tilney, *Life of John Edward Ellis MP*, (Macmillan, 1914).

Bibliography

Beveridge, William, *Power and Influence*, (Hodder & Stoughton, 1953).

Blunden, Margaret, *The Countess of Warwick*, (Cassell, 1967).

Bondfield, Margaret, *A Life's Work* (Hutchinson, 1948).

Brittain, Vera, *Pethwick-Lawrence, A portrait*, (Allen & Unwin, 1964).

– *Wartime Chronicle, Diary 1939–1945*, (Gollancz , 1989).

Brivati, Brian, *Hugh Gaitskell*, (Richard Cohen, 1996).

Brockway, Fenner, *Inside the Left*, (Allen & Unwin, 1942).

Brown, George, *In My Way*, (Book Club, 1971).

Brown, Anthony Montague, *Long Sunset*, (Cassell, 1995).

Bruce Lockhart, *Robert, Comes the Reckoning*, (Putnam, 1947).

Bullock, Alan, *The Life and Times of Ernest Bevin* (2 Vols), (Heinemann, 1960–7).

Butler, Ewan, *Mason-Mac, the Life of Lieutenant-General Sir Noel Mason MacFarlane*, (Macmillan, 1972).

Butler. R. A., *The Art of the Possible*, (Hamilton, 1971).

Caine, Barbara, *Destined to be Wives, the Sisters of Beatrice Webb*, (Clarendon, 1986).

Cairncross, Alec (ed.), *The Robert Hall Diaries, 1947–53*, (Unwin Hyman, 1989).

Carpenter, L. P. , *G. D. H. Cole, an intellectual biography*, (CUP, 1973).

Castle, Barbara, *Fighting All the Way*, (Macmillan, 1993).

Churchill, Winston, *Step by Step 1936–39* (Butterworth, 1939).

– *The Second World War,* (6 Vols) (Cassell, 1959).

Citrine, Walter, *In Russia Now*, (Gollancz, 1942).

Cocket, Richard (ed.), *My Dear Max, the letters of Brendan Bracken to Lord Beaverbrook 1925–58*, (Historians Press, 1990).

Cole, Margaret, *The Life of G. D. H. Cole*, (Macmillan, 1971).

Collins, Diana, *Partners in Protest, Life with Canon Collins*, (Victor Gollancz , 1992).

Colville, John, *The Fringes of Power: Downing Street Diaries, 1939–1955*, (Hodder & Stoughton, 1985).

– *Footprints in Time*, (Collins, 1976).

Cooke, Colin Arthur, *The Life of Richard Stafford Cripps*, (Hodder & Stoughton, 1957).

Cooper, Duff, *Old Men Forget*, (Rupert Hart-Davis, 1953).

Cripps, Charles Alfred, *A Retrospect, looking back over a life of more than 80 years*, (Heinemann, 1936).

Cripps, Frederick H., *Life's a Gamble, An Autobiography*, (Odhams Press, 1957).

Cripps, Miriam, *Family Story*, (privately published, 1953).

– *Leonard Cripps*, (privately published, 1960).

Crosland, Susan, *Tony Crosland*, (Jonathan Cape, 1982).

Cross, C., *Philip Snowden*, (Barrie & Rockcliff, 1966).

Dalton, Hugh, *The Fateful Years, 1931–45*, (Muller, 1957).

– *The Political Diary 1918–40, 1945–60*, ed. Ben Pimlott, (Jonathan Cape, 1986).

– *The Second World War Diary*, ed. Ben Pimlott, (Jonathan Cape, 1980).

Darke, Sidney, *The People's Archbishop*, (James Clarke, 1942).

De-la-Noy, Michael, *Mervyn Stockwood – A Lonely Life*, (Cassell, 1996).

De'Ath, W., *Barbara Castle: a Portrait from Life*, (Clifton Books, 1970).

Dilks, D. (ed.), *The Diaries of Sir Alexander Cadogan 1938–4*, (Cassell, 1971).

Donoughue, B. & Jones, G. W., *Herbert Morrison: Portrait of a Politician*, (Weidenfeld & Nicolson, 1973).

Duncan, *Life and Letters of Herbert Spencer*, (Methuen, 1908).

Dunglass, Alec, *The Way the Wind Blows*, (Collins, 1976).

Eden, Robert Anthony, *The Memoirs* (3 Vols), (Cassell, 1960–5).

Edwards, Ruth, *Victor Gollancz, A Biography*, (Gollancz, 1987).

Estorick, Eric, *Sir Stafford Cripps*, (Heinemann, 1949).

Foot, Michael, *Aneurin Bevan* (2 Vols), (Paladin, 1975).

Gilbert, Martin, *Winston Churchill*, (Heinemann, 1991).

Gooch, L. P., *Life of Lord Courtney*, (Macmillan, 1920).

Gopal, S., *Jawaharlal Nehru – a biography*, (Cape, 1975).

Hamilton, Margaret, *Remembering my Good Friends*, (Cape, 1944).

– *Arthur Henderson*, (Heinemann, 1938).

Harris, Kenneth, *Attlee*, (Weidenfeld & Nicolson, 1982).

Herbert, Alan Patrick, *Independent Member*, (Methuen, 1950).

Hobhouse, Stephen, *Margaret Hobhouse and Her Family*, (Stanhope Press, 1934).

– *Forty years and an Epilogue, An Autobiography 1881–1951*, (James Clarke & Co., 1951).

Howard, Anthony, *RAB, the Life of R. A. Butler*, (Cape, 1987).

Hyde, H. Montgomery, *Walter Monckton*, (Sinclair-Stevenson, 1991).

Ismay, Hastings, *The Memoirs of General the Lord Ismay*, (Heinemann, 1960).

Jay, Douglas, *Change and Fortune*, (Hutchinson, 1980).

Jenkins, Roy, *Nine Men of Power*, (Hamish Hamilton, 1974).

Lee, Janet (Jennie), *Tomorrow is a New Day*, (Cresset Press, 1939).

– *This Great Country*, (MacGibben & Kee, 1963).

Lee-Milne, James, *Ancestral Voices and Prophesying Peace*, (John Murray, 1995).

Lewin, Ronald, *The Chief Field Marshal Lord Wavell*, (1980).

Lysaght, C., *Brendan Bracken*, (Allen Lane, 1979).

Lyttelton, Oliver, *The Memoirs of Lord Chandos*, (Bodley Head, 1962).

MacDonald, Malcolm, *Titans and Others*, (Collins, 1972).

MacKenzie, Norman and Jeanne (eds), *The Letters of Sidney and Beatrice Webb* (3 Vols), (Virago, 1978).

– *The Diary of Beatrice Webb* (4 Vols), (Virago and BLPES, 1982–6).

MacLachlan, Donald, *In the Chair: Barrington-Ward of The Times*, (Weidenfeld & Nicolson, 1971).

Macmillan, Harold, *Winds of Change 1914–39*, (Macmillan, 1966).

– *Tides of Fortune 1945–55*, (Macmillan, 1969).

– *High Tide and After*, (Macmillan, 1962).

– *The Blast of War 1939–45*, (Macmillan, 1967).

Macnab, Geoffrey, *J. Arthus Rank and the British Film Industry*, (Routledge, 1993).

Mahon, Jack, *Harry Pollitt, a Biography*, (1976).

Maisky, Ivan, *Memoirs of a Soviet Ambassador* (trans. Andrew Rothstein), (Hutchinson, 1967).

Manning, Leah, *A Life for Education*, (Gollancz, 1970).

Martin, Kingsley, *Editor*, (Penguin, 1969).

Bibliography

Meinertzhagen, Georgina, *From Ploughshare to Parliament*, (John Murray, 1908).

Mikardo, Ian, *Back-bencher*, (Weidenfeld & Nicolson, 1988).

Minney, R. J., *The Private Papers of Hore-Belisha*, (Collins, 1960).

– *Viscount Addison, Leader of the Lords*, (Odhams, 1958).

Moon, Pendel, *The Viceroy's Journal*, (OUP, 1973).

Morgan, Kevin, *Harry Pollitt*, (Manchester University Press, 1993).

Morgan, Janet (ed.), *Backbench diaries of Richard Crossman*, (Cape, 1981).

Morrison, Herbert, *An Autobiography*, (Odhams, 1960).

Mosley, Oswald, *My Life*, (Nelson, 1968).

Murphy, J. T., *New Horizons*, (John Lane, 1940).

Nicolson, Harold, *Diaries and Letters, 1930–1964* (3 Vols Edition), (Collins, 1966–8).

– *Diaries and Letters, 1930–1964* (Condensed Edition), (Flamingo, 1996).

Orwell, Sonia and Angus, Ian (eds), *The Collected Essays, Journalism and Letters of George Orwell, My Country Right or Left*, Vol. 2, (Harmondsworth, 1970).

Parker, John, *Father of the House: 50 Years in Politics*, (Routledge & Kegan Paul, 1982).

Pearce, Robert (ed.), *Patrick Gordon-Walker, Political Diaries 1932–71*, (Historians' Press, 1991).

Pethwick-Lawrence, *Fate Has Been Kind*, (Hutchinson, 1943).

Pimlott, Ben, *Hugh Dalton*, (HarperCollins, 1995).

– *Harold Wilson*, (HarperCollins, 1992).

Plowden, Edwin, *An Industrialist in the Treasury*, (Deutsch, 1989).

Pollitt, Harvey, *Serving My Time*, (Lawrence & Wishart, 1950).

Pound, Reginald, *A. P. Herbert*, (Joseph, 1976).

Pritt, Dennis Nowell, *The Autobiography* (3 Vols), (Lawrence & Wishart, 1965).

Ramsay, Sir William, *Memorials of his Life and Work*, (Macmillan, 1918).

Reakes, George, *Man of Mersey*, (Christopher Johnson, 1956).

Rhodes James, Robert (ed.), *Chips, the diaries of Sir Henry Channon*, (Phoenix, 1996).

Robbins, Lord, *Autobiography of an Economist*, (Macmillan, 1971).

Sampson, Anthony, *Macmillan: a study in ambiguity*, (Penguin, Allen Lane, 1967).

Shinwell, Emmanuel, *I've lived through it all*, (Gollancz, 1973).

Simon, John Allsebrook, *Retrospect*, (Hutchinson, 1952).

Smith, F. E., *The Life of Viscount Monckton of Brenchley*, (Weidenfeld & Nicolson, 1969).

Smith, F. E., *Halifax*, (Hamish Hamilton, 1965).

Spencer, Herbert, *Autobiography* (2 Vols), (Williams and Northgate, 1904).

Stocks, Mary, *Eleanor Rathbone*, (Gollancz, 1949).

Stockwood, Mervyn, *Chanctonbury Ring*, (Hodder & Stoughton, 1982).

Strauss, Patricia, *Cripps – Advocate and Rebel*, (Gollancz, 1943).

– *Bevin & Co.*, (Putnam's, 1941).

Taylor, A. J. P., *Beaverbrook*, (Hamish Hamilton, 1972).

Thomas, Hugh, *John Strachey*, (Eyre Methuen, 1973).

Turnour, Edward, *Orders of the Day*, (Cassell, 1953).

Tyler, Froom, *Cripps, a portrait and a prospect*, (Harrap, 1942).
Vernon, Betty, *Ellen Wilkinson 1891–1947*, (Croom Helm, 1982).
Wakelin, Michael, *J. Arthur Rank, The Man Behind the Gong*, (Lion, 1996).
Webb, Beatrice, *My Apprenticeship*, (Penguin, 1971).
– *Our Partnership*, (Longmans, 1948).
Wheeler-Bennett, J. W., *John Anderson*, (Macmillan, 1962).
Wilkinson, Ellen, *Peeps at Politicians*, (Philip Allen, 1930).
Williams, Francis, *A P.M. Remembers*, (Heinemann, 1961).
Williams, Philip, *Hugh Gaitskell, The Diary 1945–56*, (Cape, 1983).
Williams-Ellis, Clough, *Lawrence Weaver*, (G. Bles, 1933).
Wilson, Duncan, *Leonard Woolf, a political biography*, (Hogarth, 1978).
Woolton, Lord, *Memoirs*, (Cassell, 1959).
Young, K. (ed.), *The Diaries of Sir Robert Bruce Lockhart* (2 Vols), (Macmillan, 1980).
Ziegler, Philip, *Mountbatten. The Official Biography*, (Collins, 1985).

c. *Other Sources*

Addison, Christopher, *Religion and Politics – The Social Services lecture*, (Epworth, 1931).
– *The problems of the Food Supply – Problems of a Socialist Government Series No. 9*, (Socialist League, 1935).
Addison, Paul, *The Road to 1945* (Rev. Edn), (Pimlico, 1994).
– *Now the War is Over* (Rev. Edn), (Pimlico, 1995).
Attlee, Clement R., *Local Government and Socialism – Problems of a Socialist Government Series No. 7*, (Socialist League, 1935).
Barnett, Corelli, *The Lost Victory*, (Macmillan, 1995).
– *The Audit of War*, (Macmillan, 1986).
Barnett, Samuel, *New Series*, (Longman, 1915).
– *Practicable Socialism*, (Longmans, 1894).
Bevan, Aneurin, *What We Saw in Russia*, (Labour & V. Woolf, 1931).
Bircher-Benner, Maxsimilian, *Food Science for All and a New Sunlight Theory of Nutrition* (trans. Eiloart), (C. W. Daniel, 1928).
– *The Prevention of Incurable Diseases* (trans. E. F. Meyer), (John Miles, 1938).
Brailsford, Noel, *India in Chains*, (Socialist League, no date).
Branca, Patricia, *Silent Sisterhood, Middle Class Women in the Victorian Home*, (Croom Helm, 1975).
Burge, Hubert Murray, *Discourses and Letters*, (Chatto & Windus, 1930).
Cairncross, Alec, *Years of Recovery*, (Methuen, 1985).
Cairncross, Alec & Exchengreen, Barry, *Sterling in Decline – the Devaluations of 1931, 1949 and 1967*, (Blackwell, 1983).
Cairncross, Alec and Watts, Nita, *The Economic Section, 1939–61*, (Roiutledge, 1989).
Calder, Angus and Sheridan, Dorothy (eds), *Speak for Yourself. A Mass Observation Anthology* (Cape, 1984).

Bibliography

Clay, Harold, *Trade Unionism – Capitalism in Crisis Series No. 5*, (Socialist League, no date).

– *Workers' Control – Problems of a Socialist Government Series No. 8*, (Socialist League, 1935).

Cline, C. A., *Recruits to Labour: the British Labour Party 1914–31*, (University of Syracuse, 1963).

Cole, G. D. H., & Mitchison, G. R., *The Need for a Socialist Programme – Socialist Programme Series No. 1*, (Socialist League, 1933).

Cole, G. D. H., *The People's Front*, (Gollancz, 1937).

– *The Working Class Movement and the Transition to Socialism – Capitalism in Crisis Series No. 4*, (Socialist League, 1934).

– *When the Fighting Stops*, (National Peace Council, 1943).

– *A History of the Labour Party since 1914*, (Routledge, 1948).

– *The Development of Socialism in the Last 50 Years*, (Athlone, 1952).

– *A History of Socialist Thought – Vol. 5, Socialism and Fascism 1931–39*, (Macmillan, 1960).

Coupland, Reginald, *The Cripps Mission*, (OUP, 1942).

Cripps, Charles Alfred, *A proposal for equal representation*, (Gilbert & Rivington, 1884).

– *The Foundation Oration, 'Do well and right and let the world sink'*, (UCL, 1915).

– *A treatise on the Principles of the law of compensation in reference to the Lands Clauses Consolidation Acts*, (H. Sweet, 1881).

Cripps, Diana, *Simple Salads*, (Bureau of Cosmotherapy, 1938).

Cripps, Henry William, *A practical treatise on the laws relating to the Church and the clergy*, (S. Sweet, 1845).

Cripps, Isobel, *God is Love*, (Religious Tract Society, 1832).

Cripps, John (ed.), *The Countryman Anthology*, (Arthur Barker, 1962).

Cripps, Seddon, *Winchester College Notions, by Three Beetleites*, (P. G. Wells, 1901).

Cunningham Reid, Alec, *Besides Churchill – Who?*, (W. H. Allen, 1942).

Dell, Edmund, *The Chancellors* (HarperCollins, 1996).

Fenn, Louis, *What of the Professional Classes? – Capitalism in Crisis Series No. 7*, (Socialist League, no date).

Gorodetsky, Gabriel, *Stafford Cripps's Mission to Moscow 1940–42*, (CUP, 1984).

Greene B. & Gollancz V., *God of a hundred names, prayers of many people*, (Gollancz, 1962).

Harrison, Agatha and Bailey, Gerald, *National Peace Council on India 1939–42*, (National Peace Council, 1942).

Hennessy, Peter, *Never Again: Britain 1945–51*, (Cape, 1992).

Higham, Robin, *Air Power – A Concise History*, (St Martin's Press, 1972).

Horrabin, Frank, *The Break with Imperialism – Problems of a Socialist Government Series No. 4*, (Socialist League, no date).

– *The Class Struggle – Capitalism in Crisis Series No. 8*, (Socialist League, 1935).

– *Socialism in Pictures and figures*, (Socialist League, 1933).

Horrabin, Winifred, *Is Woman's Place in the home?*, (Socialist League, no date).

Jefferys, Kevin, *The Churchill Coalition and Wartime Politics 1940–45*, (MUP, 1991).

515

Jefferys, Kevin (ed.), *Labour and the Wartime Coalition: from the Diary of James Chuter Ede* (Historians' Press, 1987).

Laski, Harold, *The Labour Party and the Constitution – Socialist Programme Series No. 2* (Socialist League, no date).

– *The Roosevelt Experiment – Capitalism in Crisis Series No. 1*, (Socialist League, 1935).

Lee, John M., *The Churchill Coalition 1940–45*, (Batsford, 1980).

Lohia, Rammanohar, *The Mystery of Sir Stafford Cripps.*

Mansergh, Nicholas (ed.), *Constitutional Relations Between Britain and India. The Transfer of Power*, (12 Vols), (HMSO, 1970–83).

Mellor, William, *The meaning of Industrial Freedom*, (Allen & Unwin, 1918).

Mellor, William, *The Co-op Movement and the Fight for Socialism – Capitalism in Crisis Series No. 6*, (Socialist League, 1935).

– *The Claim of the Unemployed – Problems of a Socialist Government Series No. 5*, (Socialist League, 1933).

– *Direct Action*, (New Era Series 8, 1920).

Mitchison, Naomi, *The Moral Basis of Politics*, (Constable, 1938).

Moore, V. Elizabeth, *We go to China with Lady Cripps*, (P.J. Press, 1948).

Moore, Robin James, *Churchill, Cripps and India*, (Clarendon, 1979).

Morgan, Kenneth, *Labour in Power, 1945–51*, (Clarendon, 1984).

– *The People's Peace*, (OUP, 1992).

Murphy, J. T., *Victory Production!*, (John Lane, 1942).

Nehru, Jawaharlal, *India, What next? The Congress Reply*, (Congress Party, 1846).

Pollitt, Harry, *Selected Speeches and Articles* (2 Vols), (Lawrence & Wishart, 1953).

Postan, M. M., *Design and Development of Weapons*, (Longmans, 1964).

– *British War Production*, (Longmans, 1953).

Priestley, J. B., *Postscripts*, (Heinemann, 1940).

Pritt, Dennis Nowell, *Choose Your future*, (Lawrence & Wishart, 1941).

– *The USSR – our ally*, (Muller, 1941).

– *Must the War spread?*, (Penguin, 1940).

– *Light on Moscow*, (Penguin, 1940 edn).

– *The Labour Government 1945–51*, (Lawrence & Wishart, 1963).

Sabben-Clare, James, *Winchester College After 600 Years*, (Paul Cave, 1981).

Salter, Arthur, *Personality in Politics*, (Faber, 1947).

Sissons, Morrison, and French P. (eds), *The Age of Austerity*, (Hodder & Stoughton, 1963).

Subrahmanyam, M., *Why Cripps Failed*, (1942).

Szekély, Edmond, *Man, Art and World-Conception* (trans. Purcell Weaver), (C. W. Daniel, 1947).

– *The Sermon on the Mount – an Essene Interpretation* (trans. Purcell Weaver), (Bureau of Cosmotherapy, 1948).

– *Cosmos, Man and Society, a Paneubiotic Synthesis* (trans. Purcell Weaver), (C. W. Daniel, 1936).

Tawney, Richard Henry, *The Choice before the Labour Party*, (Socialist League, 1933).

Thompson, Edward, *Enlist India for Freedom*, (Gollancz, 1940).

Bibliography

Travers, Morris William, *William Ramsay and UCL*, (privately published, 1952).
Trevelyan, Charles, *Challenge to Capitalism*, (Socialist League, 1932).
– *From Liberalism to Labour*, (George Allen & Unwin, 1921).
– *The Union of Democratic Control, its history and policy*, (UDC, 1919).
– *The Challenge to Capitalism – Problems of a Socialist Government Series No. 1*, (Socialist League, 1935).
– *Mass Resistance to War – Capitalism in Crisis Series No. 2*, (Socialist League, 1934).
Wise, Frank, *The Control of Finance and the Financiers – Problems of a Socialist Government No. 3*, (Socialist League, 1935).
Woolf, Leonard, *Downhill all the way*, (Hogarth, 1967).
– *The journey, not the arrival matters*, (Hogarth, 1969).

Index

Index

370, 407, 451, 466, 475, 478–9;
friend of Freddie Cripps 50, 231;
recommends Leonard Cripps for
CBE 52; and rebel Tories 164,
166, 196, 200; and SC 168–9,
274–5, 337, 482; on Russia 232,
242–3, 249–51, 260; supports
Operation Catherine 226;
becomes Prime Minister 229,
303; correspondence with
Stalin 245, 252–3, 259, 261–2;
broadcasts on Russia 254–6;
forbids Internationale 256;
Placentia Bay Conference 259;
unpopularity in 1942 282–6,
290–3, 301, 307–8; offers SC
Supply 287–8; supports strategic
priority of Middle East 282–3;
Cabinet reshuffle 293–4;
working style 295; and mines
303–4; rejects General Planning
staff 308–11; moves SC to MAP
317–19; tries to maintain coalition
342–5, 347; air power 326–7;
election leader 343–4, 354–6;
calls general election 347–9; in
Opposition 421, 431–2; dispute
with SC 312–16; First Lord of
Admiralty 204, 266; India 212,
219, 297–301, 384
Cirencester origins of SC 37, 62
Citrine, Walter (Baron) 99, 110, 112,
124, 260
Clarke, Le Gros 156
Clarke, Otto 361, 412
Clay, Harold 106
Clynes, John Robert 87, 128
Cole, G. D. H. 92–3, 96, 102–7,
131, 135, 156, 175
Cole, Margaret 102
Colefax, Sir H. A. 60
Collins, Diana 460
Collins, Canon John 306, 323–4,
452, 458–61, 463
Colville, Sir John 244, 250, 255,
274–5, 419–20
Committee for European Economic
Cooperation 422
Common Wealth Party 284, 306,
340–3, 352

Communist Party 111, 129, 153–4,
199, 202 and ch. 11 pass.
Congress Party 211–13, 215–17,
297–301, 376–83
Connally, Senator 298
Connolly, Cyril 23
Convertibility Crisis (1947) 394–6,
398
Cooke, Colin Arthur 76, 473
Cooper, Alfred Duff (1st Viscount
Norwich) 164, 285
COPEC (Conference on Politics,
Economics and Citizenship) 73,
75
Copenhagen Conference 74
Cosmovitalism 271–4, 476
Cotton industry 352, 370–1, 385
Council for an International Christian
Conference 71
Courtney, Kate (née Potter) 2, 4–7,
9–10, 15–16, 43, 45, 69–70, 91
Courtney, Leonard (1st Baron
Courtney of Penwith) 9, 40, 42–4
Cranborne, Viscount R. A. J.
('Bobbetty' Gascoyne-Cecil, 5th
Marquess of Salisbury) 152, 276,
317, 348
Cripps, A. H. Seddon (2nd Baron
Parmoor, brother) 1, 14, 17, 25,
47, 52
Cripps, Anthony (nephew) 51
Cripps, Blanche (née Potter, aunt) 2,
4–5
Cripps, Charles Alfred (1st Baron
Parmoor of Frieth, father) 28, 73,
80, 93, 122, 124, 195, 202; birth
and parents 37–9; Winchester
25, 39; family and legal career
37, 39, 47, 50, 60; Parliamentary
career 15, 30, 41, 47; buys
Parmoor 39; marriage 5;
Theresa's death 9, 12; relies on
sisters-in-law 14; attitudes on
education 14–15; relationship with
children 15, 21, 36; stands for
Parliament (1895) 15, 40, (1906)
30, 41, (1910) 41; member of
Reform Club 39; and Unionists
15, 30, 40; ennobled 42; and
Henry Hobhouse 44–5; and

521

Index

Index

Index

St Bartholomew's Hospital 37
St John the Evangelist, Frieth 8
St Jude's, Whitechapel 7–8
St Kenelm's, Sapperton 451
St Matthew's, Moorfields 323, 339
St Paul's Cathedral 463
St Petersburg 51
Stalin, Joseph 146, 236–7, 240–1, 245–6, 249, 251–4, 257, 259–63, 280, 286, 362, 478
Standish House 4
Stanley, Oliver Frederick 101, 152, 197, 201, 204–5, 226
Steinhardt, Laurence 249
Stewart, Sir Findlater 214–15
Stirling 326, 329–30
Stockwood, Mervyn (Bishop) 323, 345, 356; friendship with Bell and Collins 454, 458–62; SC visits vicarage 339–40, 447, 452; advises SC 434–5; burial of SC's ashes 469
Stone, Richard 361
Strachey, Giles Lytton 100
Strachey, Evelyn John St Loe 100–1, 155–7, 160–1, 178, 357, 370, 409–11, 414, 435
Strauss, George R. Socialist League 133, 143–4; *Tribune* 161; Popular Front 174–5, 177; readmitted to Labour Party 194–5; in Second World War 227, 286; Ministry of Supply 409–11, 418, 435
Stuart, James (Viscount Stuart of Findhorn) 292, 343
Sun Of 220
Sun Yat-sen 220
Sutherland 326
Swinford, George 65
Swinton, 1st Earl of (Philip Cunliffe-Lister) 391
Swithinbank, Commander Harold William 49–50, 66
Székély, Edmond 271–4

Talbot, Bishop Edward Stuart 74
Tangku Truce 121
Tass 238, 253
Tate Gallery 477

Tawney, Richard Henry 96–7, 135, 175–6, 457
Taylor, A. J. P. 198, 226, 281, 292, 294
Tempest aircraft 326, 329
Temple, Archbishop William 69, 158, 455, 457–8; and World Alliance 71; COPEC 75; Archbishop of York 189; Malvern Conference 277; *Christianity and the Social Order* 277, 284; Albert Hall meeting 313–14, 451; death 323
Temple, Archbishop Frederick 69
Tennyson, Alfred Lord 483
The Times 43, 153, 220, 275, 286, 308, 310
Thomas, Jimmie H. 88
Thomas, Ivor 309
Thorndike, Dame Sybil 354
Tito, Marshal 347
Tobruk 307
Toynbee Hall 91
Trades Disputes and Trade Union (Amendment) Bill 91–2
Trend, Burke (Lord) 403, 412, 445
Trevelyan, Sir Charles 136, 195, 472; Socialist League 100, 106, 108; on war 117–18, 151; Popular Front 174, 177, 265
Trevelyan, Marjorie 265
Tribune 138, 142, 145, 150, 154, 159–62, 168, 173, 178, 184, 190, 198, 202, 214, 273, 357, 473, 475–6
Truman, President Harry 347, 362–3
TUC 110, 150, 418, 433
Turnbull, Frank 299
Tyler, Froom 98

Udal, Duggie 25
Union of Democratic Control 73
Unionists 15, 30, 40, 41, 43–4
United States of America 127; Lend-Lease 362–4; loan 1947
United Front 160, 167; initial discussions 134–7; launch 138; policy 138–9; and Spanish Civil War 142–3; becomes Unity campaign 143–6, 148–9, 169, 186
University College, London 31–2, 49

533